THE BEAUTIFUL SPY

THE LIFE AND CRIMES OF VERA ERIKSEN

DAVID TREMAIN

The History Press

To my wife,
Evelyn

First published 2019

The History Press
The Mill, Brimscombe Port
Stroud, Gloucestershire, GL5 2QG
www.thehistorypress.co.uk

© David Tremain, 2019

The right of David Tremain to be identified as the Author
of this work has been asserted in accordance with the
Copyright, Designs and Patents Act 1988.

British Library Cataloguing in Publication Data.
A catalogue record for this book is available from the British Library.

ISBN 978 0 7509 8895 7

Typesetting and origination by The History Press
Printed and bound in Great Britain by TJ International Ltd

CONTENTS

ACKNOWLEDGEMENTS

All files in the National Archives are © Crown Copyright and are reproduced with permission under the terms of the Open Government Licence. Quotes from *Hansard* contain Parliamentary information licensed under the Open Parliament Licence v3.0.

Every attempt has been made to seek and obtain permission for copyright material used in this book. In certain cases this has not been possible. However, if we have inadvertently used copyright material without permission/ acknowledgements we apologise and we will make the necessary correction at the first opportunity.

The author and publisher would like to thank the following for permission to use copyright material in this book:

Arcade Publishing: Reprinted from *Zigzag: The Incredible Wartime Exploits of Double Agent Eddie Chapman* by Nicholas Booth, by permission of Arcade Publishing, an imprint of Skyhorse Publishing, Inc.; © Ben Macintyre, 2007, *Agent Zigzag*, Bloomsbury Publishing Plc; Century, for extracts from *Deadly Illusions* by John Costello & Oleg Tsarev; Dover Publications for extracts from *The Dictionary of Espionage. Spyspeak into English* by Joseph Goulden; Henry Hemming for permission to quote emails between him and the author; The History Press, for an extract from *The Spy Beside the Sea* by Adrian Searle; Giles Milton, for an extract from *Russian Roulette*; Taylor & Francis, for permission to quote from *KGB Lexicon* by Vasiliy Mitrokhin; Nigel West, for extracts from *Mortal Crimes* (Enigma Books), *The Crown Jewels* (Harper Collins), and *Spycraft Secrets: An Espionage A-Z* (The History Press), as well as emails between him and the author; Wiley-Blackwell, for permission to quote from Anthony Masters' *The Man Who Was M* © Anthony Masters, 1984: All rights reserved.

AUTHOR'S NOTE

Unless otherwise specified in the Notes, all quotes and extracts have been taken from files in the National Archives at Kew (TNA). When quoting from these files some minor formatting changes have occasionally been made to ensure the text flows better, and accents added to French and German words where they were missed out in the original text because the typewriters of the time lacked those keys; otherwise, no changes have been made to the original punctuation or spelling. In these files many MI5 documents use the term 'German S.S'. In this context it is generally meant as a generic name for the German Secret Service rather than *Schutzstaffel*, the Nazi Party's intelligence service. Likewise, the terms 'MI6' and 'SIS' are used interchangeably to mean the overseas branch of the British Intelligence Service. The symbol @ is used throughout to indicate the word alias, as in Theodor MALY @ Paul HARDT.

ABBREVIATIONS AND TERMINOLOGY

Abbreviations

ADDB	Assistant Deputy Director B Branch (MI5)
ADNI	Assistant Director Naval Intelligence
AFS	Auxiliary Fire Service
ARO	Aliens Registration Office
ARP	Air Raid Precaution
B1b	Espionage, Special Sources section (MI5)
B2	Counter-espionage (MI5)
B4a	Section involved with suspected cases of espionage by individuals living in the UK (MI5)
B4b	Espionage, Country Section (MI5)
B5b	Counter subversion (MI5)
BAOR	British Army of the Rhine (post-war)
BdS	Befeldshaber der Sicherungsstreitkräfte der Nord See (**BdS.d.N**) or der Ostee (**BdS.d.O.**) – Commander of the security forces of the North Sea (**BdS.d.N**) or Baltic Sea (**BdS.d.O.**) (Germany)
BUF	British Union of Fascists
CAC	Canadian Armoured Corps
CAN	Controller, Northern Area (SIS), post-war
CASC	Combined Arms Staff Course
CCG (BE)	Control Commission Germany (British Element)
Cheka	Vecheka (All-Russian Extraordinary Committee to Combat Counter-Revolution and Sabotage), December 1917–February 1922
CID	Criminal Investigation Department
CSDIC (WEA)	Combined Services Detailed Interrogation Centre (Western European Area) (also known as the 'London Cage' *q.v.* **MI19**)

CSWBL	Central Security War Black List
CX	Reports prepared by MI6 (SIS)
D4b	Port intelligence (MI5)
DPP	Director of Public Prosecutions
DSVP	Director Small Vessels Pool (Royal Navy)
F2c	Responsible for Russian intelligence (MI5)
FAK	Frontaufklärungskommando (Front reconnaissance [spy] command)
FAT	Frontaufklärungstrupp (Front reconnaissance [spy] troop)
FIC	Fellow of the Royal Institute of Chemistry (now Royal Society of Chemistry)
FSB	Federal'naya Sluzhba Bezopasnosti (Federal Security Service) (Russia), 1995 to present
FSP	Field Security Police
FSS	Field Security Section, Intelligence Corps
GAF	German Air Force (Luftwaffe)
GFP	German Feldpolizei
GIS	German Intelligence Service
GPO	General Post Office
GPU	State Political Directorate (USSR), February 1922–July 1923
GSI	General Staff Intelligence
HO	Home Office
HOSI	Home Office Suspect Index
HOW	Home Office Warrant
IB	Intelligence Branch
Inter-Services Research Bureau	Cover name for Special Operations Executive (SOE)
IOM	Isle of Man
IRB	Cover name for Special Operations Executive (SOE)
ISK	Intelligence Service Knox/Intelligence SectionKnox/Illicit Services Knox
ISOS	Intelligence Service Oliver Strachey/Illicit Services Oliver Strachey
KGB	Komitet Gosudarstvennoi Bezopasnosti (Committee for State Security) (USSR), 1954-1991
LMS	London, Midland & Scottish Railway
LRCP	Licentiate Member of the Royal College of Practitioners
MI5	British Security Service

MI6	British Secret Intelligence Service *q.v.* **SIS**
MI1a	Part of the Directorate of Military Intelligence in the First World War responsible for distribution of reports and intelligence records; remobilised in 1939 to interrogate enemy prisoners
MI14	A branch of Military Intelligence specialising in intelligence about Germany
MI19	Directorate of Military Intelligence (War Office): branch responsible for obtaining information from prisoners of war (*q.v.* Combined Services Detailed Interrogation Centre (**CSDIC**))
MK	Meldekopf (Advanced message centre)
MPD	Metropolitan Police District
MRCS	Member of the Royal College of Surgeons
NASA	National Aeronautics & Space Administration
NCO	Non-Commissioned Officer
NID	Naval Intelligence Division (Royal Navy)
NKVD	Narodnyy Kommissariat Vnutrennikh del (National Commissariat for Internal Affairs), (Soviet Union) July 1934–April 1943
NSDAP	Nationalsozialistische Deutsche Arbeiterpartie (National Socialist German Workers' Party – Nazi Party)
OC	Officer Commanding
OGPU	Joint State Political Directorate (USSR) July 1923– July 1934
Okhrana	Tsarist secret police
OKW	Oberkommando der Wehrmacht - Supreme Command of the Armed Forces (Germany)
OSA	Official Secrets Act
OSS	Office of Strategic Services (wartime US equivalent of SOE)
OTU	Operational Training Unit (RAF)
P&PO	Permit & Passport Office
PAIR	OSS code name for deciphered German intelligence messages *q.v.* **ISOS**
POW or **PW**	Prisoner of war
PRU	Photographic Reconnaissance Unit
RAF	Royal Air Force
RAFVR	Royal Air Force Volunteer Reserve

RCMP	Royal Canadian Mounted Police
RFC	Royal Flying Corps
RN	Royal Navy
RNAS	Royal Naval Air Service
RNVR	Royal Navy Volunteer Reserve
ROF	Royal Ordnance Factory
RSLO	Regional Security Liaison Officer (MI5)
SCO	Security Control Officer (MI5)
SD	Sicherheitsdienst (SS intelligence service)
SIME	Security Intelligence Middle East
SIS	British Secret Intelligence Service *q.v.* **MI6**
SO (I)	Staff Officer Intelligence (RN)
SOE	Special Operations Executive
SOS	School of Oriental Studies; now SOAS (School of Oriental & African Studies, University of London
SS	Schutzstaffel (Security Service of the Nazi Party); also German Secret Service
SVR	Sluzhba Vneshney Razvedki (Foreign Intelligence Service) (Russia), December 1991 to present
VB3	MI6 counter-espionage section that dealt with France, Corsica, Andorra and the Benelux countries (Belgium, the Netherlands, Luxembourg)
W/T	Wireless Telegraphy
WIR	Worker's International Relief (Comintern organisation)
WRC-1	War Room Registry (MI5). **WRC** was the Assessments Section; **WRC1** dealt with officers and agents of the old Abwehr I and III
WRNS	Women's Royal Naval Service
X-2	Counter-espionage branch of OSS

Abwehr Abbreviations

Abt	Abteilung (Abwehr branch)	
AO	Auslandorganisation; also Abwehrofficizier (Abwehr)	
Ast	Abwehrstelle (Abwehr station)	
Branch I	Espionage	
	G	False documents, secret inks
	H	Heer (Army)
	I	Communications
	L	Luft (Air)

M	Marine (Navy)
Wi	Wirtschaft (Economics)
Branch II	Sabotage
Branch III	Counter-espionage
Ic	Third general staff officer (Abwehr) c.f. **AO**
KO	Kriegsorganisation (War Organisation), Abwehr in allied and neutral countries

Terminology

Accommodation address   'A location where an agent can receive mail, even though he does not reside there or have any visible connection with anyone who does.'[*]

Cut-out   1. 'The go-between, or link, between separate components of an intelligence organization – for instance, the person who maintains contact with a clandestine agent on behalf of the handler controlling him.'[*] 2. 'An intermediary designed to eliminate the risk of direct contact between two members of an espionage ring is known as a cut-out.'[‡]

Double agent   1. 'A person who goes to work for one secret service and then changes his allegiance to a rival.'[*] 2. 'When a spy consciously betrays his (or her) controller and collaborates with an adversary to deceive the original employer, that person has become a double agent.'[‡]

Establishing bona fides   'The use of recognition signals that enables agents unknown to one another to meet and establish contact.'[*]

Illegal   1. 'An intelligence agent who operates in a target country without the benefit of official status.'[*] 2. 'Agents operating outside the protection of diplomatic immunity are generally known as illegals, although the term is usually employed in connection with Directorate S of the KGB's First Chief Directorate.'[‡]

Kriegsorganization (KO)   War Organisation; Abwehr in allied and neutral countries e.g. Switzerland, Spain, Portugal.

Nansen passport   Named after Fridtjof Nansen the Norwegian explorer, a Nansen passport was an internationally recognised travel document first issued by the League of Nations in 1922. It was issued to 800,000 Russians who had become stateless after their citizenship had been revoked by Lenin.

Rezident 1. 'An intelligence officer who is appointed to head a residency by decree of the central apparatus.'(Soviet Union/Russia)[†]; 2. 'The senior intelligence officer in a Soviet or Russian rezidentura is known as the resident, and is the equivalent of a chief of a CIA station, or a British SIS station commander…'[‡]

Sleeper agent 'An agent put into a circumstance or situation where his sole job is to wait until it becomes possible to actively gather intelligence, regardless of the length of time required.'[*]

Talent-spotter 1. 'A deep-cover agent responsible for spotting persons who are suitable recruits for intelligence work.'[*] 2. 'An agent who identifies and recommends a potential candidate for recruitment is known as a talent spotter.'[‡]

Triple agent 1. 'A triple agent pretends to be a double agent for one side, while he or she is truly a double agent for the other side.' 2. 'A double agent is said to have become a triple agent in two circumstances: either an agent is despatched originally with the purpose of becoming a double agent for an adversary, yet retaining the original loyalty; or a double agent finds a means of alerting their original employer to the fact that they are now operating under the enemy's control.'[‡]

Walk-in 1. 'A person who volunteers their services to an espionage agency' [usually off the street], or, 'an agent who works for three intelligence services but is usually truly loyal to only one of them.' 2. 'An intelligence source who makes direct contact with a diplomatic mission to deliver a pitch is known as a walk-in.'[‡]

Sources

[*] Goulden, Joseph, *The Dictionary of Espionage: Spyspeak into English* (Mineola, NY: Dover Publications, 2012). Reproduced with permission of the publisher.
[†] Mitrokhin, Vasiliy (ed), *KGB Lexicon: The Soviet Intelligence Officer's Handbook* (London; Portland: Frank Cass, 2002), p.120. Reproduced with permission of the publisher.
[‡] West, Nigel, *Spycraft Secrets: An Espionage A-Z* (Stroud: History Press, 2016). Reproduced with permission of the publisher.

INTRODUCTION

Who is Silvia? what is she,[1]

Often described as 'The most beautiful spy', Vera Eriksen could almost rival First World War spy Mata Hari and the various 'Bond girls' who followed her. Indeed, she is perhaps the archetypal 'femme fatale' of the Second World War spy, but her story is perhaps less well-known than perhaps it should be. Like most spies, nothing about her background is clear-cut, or straightforward. Many of the facts surrounding her life are contradictory; some are speculation, or simply fantasy; the rest have been expunged from her official MI5 files; and few can be verified absolutely, making it difficult to discern which are true and which are not, and who is telling the truth. Indeed MI5 often referred to her as 'a confirmed liar'. To paraphrase Shakespeare in *Two Gentlemen of Verona*), 'Who is Vera, what is she?' Or more correctly, 'Who *was* she?' She is perhaps best summed up by Winston Churchill's oft-quoted remark about Russia, '… a riddle, wrapped in a mystery, inside an enigma.'

In many ways, in spite of her involvement in espionage she also comes across as a somewhat tragic figure who was yearning for a lost love. When she set out on her spying mission in September 1940 her husband had just been killed, albeit accidentally by one of her fellow conspirators. Yet was he the love of her life or someone else? Her story is one shrouded in mystery and intrigue, and clouded by the mists of time. Even her fate at the hands of British Intelligence is contentious. Had they employed her against the Russians after the war? If so, for how long, and under what name? This seems implausible since, as we shall see later on, in captivity she became disillusioned and vowed to 'get out of the racket'. Another theory is that after the war she disappeared to the Isle of

Wight, remarried, and became a grandmother. All of this is conjecture, with no hard evidence to prove it. Yet another theory states that she died in Lancashire in 1978 having worked for MI6 after the war.

The young, attractive, Garbo-esque woman shown in photographs taken for her MI5 file the day after she was captured conjure up a number of adjectives to describe her: *hauteur*; aloof; nonchalant; *ennui*; wistful. One author goes so far as to say, 'she oozes the sexuality that seems to have been a notable feature of her life up to the 1940s and transcends the tiredness and anxiety all too obvious in those images.'[2] Nikolaus Ritter, the Abwehr officer, also known as 'Dr Rantzau', who was to play an important part in her career as a spy, summed up her attractiveness to men in his memoirs *Deckname Dr. Rantzau* written in 1972, saying that she was 'one of our most remarkable and beautiful female agents. There was hardly a man who was not entranced by her.'[3] Part of that entrancement was undoubtedly due to the aura of mystique that surrounded her. She was Slavic, had good looks, and was mysterious; in its day that was enough to get men's pulses racing. However, Ritter's affection for Vera was not reciprocated; she disliked him, for reasons we shall discover later. Remarkable, she may have been, but how successful was she as a spy?

A German film made about her in 2013, starring German actress Valerie Niehaus, had Vera portrayed as a prostitute blackmailed into spying for the Germans. While Vera was undoubtedly blackmailed, there is no evidence available to suggest that, unlike Mata Hari, she was promiscuous or ever indulged in the world's oldest profession. If anything, she was exploited by the various men with whom she came into contact. And the circumstances surrounding her recruitment into the world's second oldest profession are much more fascinating. Had the film been made during the first half of the twentieth century, Ingrid Bergman would have been the obvious choice for the lead role, or perhaps even Garbo herself.

Trying to make sense of Vera's story sometimes became a challenge, but hopefully, as we wend our way through it, all will start to become somewhat clearer. It is by no means a *fait accompli*, but is it ever possible to know the whole truth in a spy case? Hopefully, as time goes on more information will be released that will settle once and for all what the truth is. In the meantime, this is my account of her story as far as it is known.

David Tremain
Ottawa, 2019

1

A MYSTERY UNFOLDS

Our main protagonist Vera Eriksen (sometimes spelled Erikson or Erichsen) should not be confused with My Erichsson (real name Josephine Fillipine Emilie Erichsson), whose case will be examined later, and who also plays an integral part in Vera's story. Three people who are inextricably linked to Vera's life are Hilmar Dierks and Nikolaus Ritter, both operating under a variety of aliases for the Abwehr, and who also appear in accounts of other spies employed by them during the Second World War; the third is the Duchesse de Château-Thierry, a faded member of the European aristocracy.

Vera was born Vera Schalburg (sometimes spelled Shalburg, Schalbourg or von Schalburg), in Barnaul, Altai, Siberia, near the Chinese border on 23 November 1912, although another source claims it to be 10 December.[1] The discrepancy in the date might be explained by the use of either the Gregorian or Julian calendar, except this being the case, the date should have been 6 December, there being thirteen days difference between the two of them. During an interview with MI5 on 1 October 1945 Hilmar Dierks' brother Gerhard, who had been *Leiter* in Meldekopf Leer (Grenzgangerorganization) of the Abwehr,[2] claimed that she had been born in Kieff (Kiev) on 10 December 1912 and was the adopted daughter of August Schalburg and his wife née Staritzky (to be correct it should be Staritzkaya), but there is no indication of who her natural parents might have been, or even if she was illegitimate, as has been suggested. In a document in her MI5 file entitled 'Summary of Information Obtained from Vera Eriksen' (no date),[3] Vera also claimed this to be the case. The report states that:

> Her origin is something of a mystery, and her parentage doubtful. It is evident that she is partly non-Aryan. She claims that her parents' name was STARITZKY, and that she was adopted in Russia by Russians of

German origin called Von Schalbourg, who left that country at the time
of the Revolution in 1918 and settled in Denmark where they assumed
Danish nationality.[4]

An article written by Günther Stiller that appeared in *Hamburger Abendblatt*
on 11 August 2011 claimed that Vera was born in Riga to a Tsarist admiral.[5] This myth appears to have been first perpetrated by Ladislas Farago
(Faragó Ládislás), the Hungarian military historian, who claimed her real
name was Vera or Viola de Witte, 'the daughter of a Baltic aristocrat and
Tsarist naval officer'.[6] The claim was perpetuated by former OSS agent Tom
Moon, who described her as a 'beautiful Nordic blonde … daughter of a
Russian naval officer who died fighting the Bolsheviks'.[7] The idea that Vera
was a 'beautiful Nordic blonde' was continued by renowned author and
expert on cryptography David Kahn in his monumental book on German
military intelligence, *Hitler's Spies*. He refers to her as 'the classic woman spy
… whose name was given as Vera de Schallberg'.[8] Vera was *not* blonde, and,
as we shall see, Farago made other dubious claims about her that were also
ill-informed.

An MI5 report dated 24 February 1942 by Agent U.35 (of whom more
later) shows that Vera had initially refused to tell them where she was born, but
when Agent U.35 pointed out to her that her Russian accent suggested that it
originated between Warsaw and Kieff, she said it was Kieff (Kiev). The report
adds that her reticence in revealing her birthplace may have been due to the
fact that she was 'not pure Russian, but partly "non-Arian"' [*sic*]', implying
that she was actually part-Jewish. It concluded that this may have been a cause
for the German Intelligence Service to blackmail her, and also for the attitude
of her second husband, von Wedel (Dierks) towards her. However, nothing
so far has been uncovered to confirm that she may have had Jewish heritage.
Other facts gleaned from the report were her extensive knowledge of music;
that she was well-versed in history and literature; her knowledge of Latin; her
ability to speak, read and write five languages (Russian – her mother tongue,
German, French, Danish and English); and the impression that she was 'an
intelligent Russian girl of an upper middle class fami[ly] with a sound and
thorough education'.[9]

Vera's father, August Theodor Schalburg, born on 6 July 1879, and who died
25 October 1964 in Gentofte, Copenhagen, was a half-Russian, half-Danish
export merchant. One source claims he was a dairy farmer, another that he
was the manager of Sibirisk Kompagni, a Danish company involved with
agriculture and forestry in Russia and Siberia. Her mother, Elena Vasiljevna

Staritzkaya Siemianowskaya, born 11 July 1882 in Poltava, Ukraine, and died 25 June 1962 in Gentofte, Copenhagen, was half-Russian (Ukrainian), half-Polish, from the 'Army officer class'.

Even the information about Vera's immediate family is contradictory. She had two brothers, Christian Frederik (her MI5 file suggests his name was actually Constantine), born in 1906, and the youngest, August, born in 1909. However, a Registry document in the Copenhagen State Archives dated 1920 gives her father August's birthplace as Nyborg; her mother's date of birth as 24 July 1882 (listed as Helene, the anglicised version of Elena); her brother Christian's as 13 April 1906; her brother August's on 13 August 1909 (yet another document gives the date as 15 August); and Vera's as 23 November 1907.[10]

When the Russian Revolution broke out in October 1917 Vera's family fled St Petersburg for Copenhagen, having lost everything. Her uncle, Ernst (or Ernest) Schalburg,[11] told John Day of MI5's B1b that this was between 1917 and 1918, but Vera contradicts this by saying that they left in 1919. Given their bourgeois background it seems more likely that Ernst's information is correct, and not Vera's. What is known is that, as of 1 November 1921, Vera, her father, and her brother Christian were living in Vibevej, Copenhagen, and at Borups Allé 4, Copenhagen, as of 1 May 1923, which concurs with the Copenhagen State Archives' document.[12] Strangely, the document on the Danish website does not mention her mother or her younger brother August, and neither does the *Geni* website.

Other information about Vera's background came from Major Geoffrey Wethered of B1b on 30 September 1943 when he commented to Edward Blanchard Stamp, also of B1b, that, 'It looks to me that the S.O.E. report from Sweden is founded on some sort of misapprehension.' Writing to Stamp again on 25 October 1943, Wethered referred to the SOE report of 21 September 1943 (listed as 143a):

> The position seems to be that Mrs. Vera COLLIN, referred to in the report from Denmark at 143a is a family connection of Vera ERIKSEN. The relationship seems, from the information on the last page of this file, to be that Vera ERIKSEN's uncle, Ernst SCHALBURG, had a sister, Ellen, who married William KNUDSEN. Ernst Sergei SCHALBURG-KNUDSEN is described as Mrs. COLLIN's brother. It therefore seems probable that Ernst and Vera are children of the marriage between Ellen SCHALBURG and William KNUDSEN. As far as I can disentangle this it seems that as if Vera ERIKSEN and Vera COLLIN are first cousins by marriage.[13]

The report from Denmark (143a), addressed to Wethered from an unnamed source in SOE, refers to Richard Olsen of the 'contre-espionage branch of the Danish Police now in Sweden' who sent it to SOE:

Dr Osier of Copenhagen,[14] who together with several others was arrested by the Germans, has stated in confidence that the information which was supplied to the Germans could have emanated from only one source, namely, Fru [Mrs] Vera Wedel, nee Schalburg who according to him, is now in England.

Within informed circles in Copenhagen, there has been talk of a leakage in England, perhaps this is the solution to the riddle:

Several months ago, there was in Copenhagen, a German by the name of Wedel, this man was described as a German master spy. Perhaps there is a certain connection between these two people ... Please note that the woman mentioned in the report, Fru Vera Wedel, is stated to be born 'Schalburg'. This woman may be Mrs. Vera Collin of 'Heathcote', East Grinstead, Sussex, who may be a German agent. Her name has been given as a reference by two recent arrivals in Denmark, namely:
a) Ernst Sergei Schalburg-Knudsen, a Kornet [Second Lieutenant] of the 3rd regiment's (infantry) 'Kanoncompagni'. This man admits to being related to the late Von Schalburg of Frikorps Danmark. [see below]
b) Vagn Holm, a Lieutenant of the Danish air force.[15]

However, the veracity of the SOE report must be questioned when it asserts that, 'Several months ago [in 1943], there was in Copenhagen, a German by the name of Wedel, this man was described as a German master spy.' It could not have been Hilmar Dierks, also known as von Wedel, because by that time he was dead and Vera was in custody in England.

Originally the two Veras (Eriksen and Collin) were thought to be identical but a letter to Wethered on 23 October 1943 from Major Grassby, the MI5 Regional Security Liaison Officer (RSLO) in Tunbridge Wells, referring to a report received from the Sussex Police, stated, 'it appears that this woman is definitely not identical with Vera ERIKSEN'. The Sussex Police report forwarded by the Assistant Chief Constable, No. 1 District, Lewes on 22 October, provides further background on Ellen Vera Collin (*née* Knudsen) and confirms that she had been born in Denmark on 13 November 1912 and was married to Dr John Olaf Collin sometime in early 1939. He died in 2000 and his wife Ellen in 2001. Their son is now a Harley Street ophthalmic surgeon.[16]

In Copenhagen Vera's brother, August, joined his father's business; little else has been recorded about his life. On the other hand, Christian Frederik joined the Danish Free Corps, and later in 1935 the Royal Danish Life Guards. There he was described as 'unstable and for the army possibly a dangerous man'. Meanwhile, in the Russian Orthodox Alexander Nevsky church in Copenhagen on 18 October 1929 he married Baroness Helga 'Helle' Friderikke von Bülow, the daughter of Friederich August Heinrich Freiherr von Bülow and Frederikke Hedevig Christiane Damm. Helga was born on 2 February 1911 in Wilhelmshaven and died in 1995 in Hillerup, Denmark, although a website states that she died in Frederiksborg Amt, Norsjaelland.[17] Her Wikipedia entry describes her as a Danish-German Nazi. A declassified CIA document suggests that, according to X-2, the counter-espionage branch of the OSS, forerunner of today's CIA, a relative of Helga, Baroness Fritze von Bülow, worked as an agent for the SD (Sicherheitsdienst), the intelligence arm of the SS:

> BULOW, Baroness Fritze von. Dane. Important Sicherheitsdienst agent, living in a well-furnished flat. Employs sub-agents and possesses a direct telephone line to Sicherheitsdienst H.Q. at 'Dagmarhus'. Makes periodic journeys to Germany. Is thought to be relative of Schalburg's wife whose maiden name was von Bulow. Born about 1900. Attractive. Address: Fridtjof Nansens Plads 8, 2nd floor, Copenhagen. Note: Two branches of von Bulow families, the Danish and German. Baroness is German. The Danish branch is patriotic.[18]

According to Vera, Helga von Bülow had lived in Denmark since she was 4 and was 'really more Danish than German'. Helga and Christian's son, Aleksander, was born on 22 November 1934 and died in 2006. His god parents were the Grand Duchess Olga Alexandrovna Romanova of Russia (1882–1960), sister of Tsar Nicholas II and youngest daughter of the late Tsar Alexander III, and her second husband, Nikolai Alexandrovich Kulikovsky (1881–1958). Kulikovsky's name would come up later during various interrogations of Vera by MI5.

In September 1940 Christian joined the *Waffen-SS* and served in the 5th SS Panzer Division *Wiking* as an SS-Hauptsturmführer (captain). It has been suggested that Christian had joined the SS to avenge the gang rape of his sister Vera by the Bolsheviks when she was 6 years old, which he had been forced to watch whilst tied to a chair.[19] Whether this was in fact the case cannot be verified and has not been referred to anywhere else, certainly not by Vera, but the obvious embarrassment and stigma of such an act inflicted on her may explain her reticence. Christian was killed by Russian shrapnel on 2 June 1942 during an attack on the Demyansk Pocket, near St Petersburg. That same day Himmler posthumously promoted him to Obersturmbannführer (lieutenant colonel). Afterwards, a medal, the Schalburgkreuz, worn by officers, NCOs and enlisted men, was struck to commemorate his death.[20] At Himmler's instigation the name of the *Germanic-SS* was changed to *Schalburgkorps* in his honour, something to which Helga initially agreed but later regretted.

In Vera's own words, the family moved from Copenhagen to Paris in 1929, where she studied dance under the great Anna Pavlova in the Trefilova Company.[21] Once again, Vera's account conflicts with that of her uncle Ernst, as well as Gerhard Dierks, who both said that her family moved to Paris in 1924. Yet in the undated MI5 report referred to earlier ('Summary of Information Obtained from Vera Eriksen'), she contradicted herself yet again by stating that she had moved to Paris in 1927. For seven years she 'led a somewhat vivid life as a ballet dancer', performing classical and acrobatic dancing at the Folies-Bergères and with the Russian Opera at the Théâtre des Champs-Elysées. Whether she actually met Serge Diaghilev as has been claimed largely depends on whether she had been in Paris from 1924 onwards as Diaghilev died in Venice in 1929.

One person with whom Vera was aquainted in Paris was the Abkhazian Prince, Aleksandr Konstantonovich Chachba-Shervaschidze (1867–1968) (written as Chervachidze in her file), who worked in Paris from 1920 to 1929 as a scene painter for Diaghilev's Ballet Russes. A note in her file states that, 'Vera danced with him. Probably the Montecarlo [sic] gigolo. Vera showed some interest in his and his wife's whereabouts.'[22]

A letter dated 16 March 2001 from Vera's 84-year-old sister-in-law Regna Schalburg – this must have been August's wife, as Christian's wife had died in 1995 – has appeared on a website created by Michael Dierks, the grandson of Hilmar Dierks, and purports to shed some light on Vera and her life as a dancer:

Dear [Redacted, but obviously Michael Dierks]
   Thank you for your letter and for the articles which I found very interesting. But I still not understand why your great interest in the family Schalburg. Has it got to be a sport[?] for you?
   I [don't] have any photo of August or the rest of the family and I don't know anyone who has.
   Vera had a wishfull [sic] thinking of being a ballerina, and therefore got an agreement with Pavlova and another ballerina about teaching her, but the both died [sic].

Therefore she came to the balletmaster Diaghilev (how to spell it)? and that was the beginning of her remarkable destiny! Because he sold her to the Communists and under threats again her family and herself she was forced to work for them. She got small threating [*sic*] letters and once in the Metro[?] they stabed [*sic*] a knife in to the back for getting her to obey them. Every night after dancing her brother August escort her home after this treachery. Diaghilev's little girl became lamb [lame?] in both her bones and yet Vera took care of her. She was a very good young girl! First she danced on 'Folies Bergeres', but Mistinguette was jealous and spite [?] her off, and so she went to 'Moulin Rouge'.

As anyone could help her to get rid of the Communists her brother Christian managed to send her in Germany with an orderly, <u>but there she fell in love with an submarine captain [*sic*] and got pregnant.</u> However she sailed to Schotland [*sic*] and you know the rest. This history was what August told me and I hope you are satisfied! This is the first letter in English I have wrote since I was 21 years old so please forgive the … [letter ends]

Yours sincerely,

Regna Schalburg [*sic*][23]

The information in this letter must be treated as somewhat unreliable, in part by Regna's own admission that her English was not good, so some things may have been lost in translation, and also old age. Other inaccuracies are:

1. Regna implies that it was Diaghilev who 'sold her to the Communists', yet the new Bolshevik regime regarded him as an 'insidious example of bourgeois decadence',[24] so she must be mistaking him for Ignatieff (see below).

2. Exactly when Vera first went to Germany is unknown. As we shall see in Chapter 3 the most likely contender for the identity of this submarine captain is Hans Meissner, who was a submarine commander during the First World War, known to have met Vera in Copenhagen in 1940, but had she known him before? According to a document produced by CSDIC in 1945, he had re-joined the Kriegsmarine in 1933 when he was recalled to active service. He was also later at *Ast* Angers in France. It is quite possible that Regna Schalburg's memory is confused and she is actually referring to Vera's meeting with him in 1940.

3. There is no reference in any of her files that Vera became pregnant by Meissner, although she was supposed to have been pregnant by von Wedel (Dierks).

4. Meissner's file shows that in 1926 he married Anneliese Osterroth, who gave birth to a son on 30 August 1928.[25] He was still married to her in May 1945 as they went on a trip to Lucerne on the 15th, where he was arrested by Swiss police. Obviously this does not preclude his having had a little dalliance with Vera, if indeed it was him.

Vera's parents were still 'hopelessly poor' and most likely she was the main source of income. Her uncle Ernst managed to get his brother August a job in Brussels as a representative of Danish Agricultural Interests. But it seems that the concept of Vera being, if not a prostitute, a woman of loose morals, persisted when Farago wrote with far too much dramatic licence:

> While she was still in finishing school she became infatuated with a much older Frenchman, and when her mother refused to permit her to marry him, they eloped ... Abandoned by her French lover, she was left to the not inconsiderable resources of a beautiful and charming young woman with a seductive air. But somehow Vera felt more comfortable in the gutter than in the drawing rooms. She drifted from bed to bed, danced in shabby cabarets, and lived with a succession of squalid swains in the wretched poverty of the Montparnasse slums.[26]

Given that Vera's parents were 'hopelessly poor', it is unlikely that she would have attended a finishing school, most of which tended to be (and still are) in Switzerland, and expensive. Exactly who this 'much older Frenchman' was whom she had supposedly met while still at finishing school Farago does not mention, nor is he identified in any of her MI5 files, so it is doubtful whether he existed. Neither is it clear when Farago mentioned 'a beautiful and charming young woman with a seductive air' whether he was actually referring to Vera herself or some other, possibly Mistinguette – Jeanne Florentine Bourgeois (1875–1956), a French actress and singer who appeared at the Casino de Paris, Folies-Bergères and Moulin Rouge – referred to in Regna's letter. That Vera could be seductive is highly plausible, but at this point she probably did not have 'inconsiderable resources'; nor is it likely that she slept around with 'squalid swains' in the beds of Montparnasse or any other part of Paris.

Farago claimed that one of these so-called 'swains' was making a living 'as an Apache dancer in a basement café on rue de Champollion, but was in fact a political agent of the Soviet secret police, spying on White Russians in France'.[27] This café must have been the Théâtre des Noctambules, established by Martial Boyer in 1894, at 7 rue Champollion in the 5th arrondissement

(Latin Quarter). Farago then claims that Vera became a GPU agent under the tutelage of this 'double-barrelled pimp' who later tried to kill her in Brussels. To use the term 'double-barrelled' implies that he had a hyphenated surname, but no one recorded in Vera's files meets this description. The only one having a double-barrelled name was Prince Aleksandr Konstantonovich Chachba-Shervaschidze. There is no evidence to suggest that it was he who tried to kill her.

In the rest of his account of Vera and the Duchesse de Château-Thierry, Farago manages to confuse Vera Erikson with My Eriksson, claiming that they were one and the same, as well as claiming that 'Château-Thierry' was a code name Ritter had assigned to the Duchess Montabelli di Condo. Brian Simpson, in a footnote in his book about detention in wartime, also repeats Farago's allegation, but notes 'there is no such Duke or Duchess'.[28] It is unclear to which Duke and Duchess Simpson is referring, but it must be assumed to be that of Montabelli di Condo, as there is documentation in Château-Thierry's MI5 file on her late husband's title. I have been unable to find any such Duchess Montabelli di Condo. Simpson also ponders on the identity of My Eriksson, suggesting that she may have been the Countess Costenza (see Chapters 7 and 8), which, as we shall see, she was not.

What is known is that while Vera was in Paris she met a White Russian officer whom she knew as Ivan Ignatieff. He styled himself a count and was also referred to as 'Petersen'. How she met him is not known. However, he does not appear to be the same person to whom Farago referred. In the indictment of Walti and Drueke (of which more later) it was stated that in 1930 Vera had married a certain Ivan Ignatieff, a Russian with a Nansen passport who was posing as a White Russian but who was in fact a 'Red' Russian. An anonymous, heavily redacted report in Vera's file states that it was in 1930 that she:

became associated with and married one IGNATIEFF, an unscrupulous blackguard, who appears to have had a strange hold over her. This man was not only engaged in espionage on behalf of the Soviet [*sic*], but also in dope trafficking and was himself a drug addict. He appears to have introduced Vera to the drug habit, but she never became enslaved to it. He used her as a courier in connection with his espionage, and she used to travel round the capitals of Europe, carrying messages on his behalf. Although she only lived with him for one year, her association with him lasted for six, and terminated in 1936 in his stabbing her near the heart in a fit of jealousy. The sordid realities of this glamourous romance have not been fully explored and there is doubt as to whether IGNATIEFF may not still be alive.[29]

What this Svengali-like hold Ignatieff had over Vera was, and what provoked the jealous rage that caused him to stab her, will be examined shortly.

Farago makes reference to Vera's stabbing when he refers to her bumping into Drueke 'in a sleazy nightclub near Place Pigalle in time to rescue her from a dreadful liaison when her lover, a South American gigolo, stabbed her in the chest in true Apache fashion',[30] whatever that is supposed to mean. As we shall see later, there is no record of her meeting Drueke in Paris, nor any mention of a 'South American gigolo'.

Ignatieff's true identity has been cause for speculation and not entirely resolved, nor made easier by the name 'Petersen', which contributed to this confusion. In a note in Vera's MI5 file dated 7 August 1941, R. Pilkington, the head of F2c, responsible for Russian intelligence and the Communist Party, concluded in discussion with Dick White, the Assistant Director of B Division, that it would be pointless interviewing her about Ignatieff, as she was:

> a confirmed liar and there is not in any case any suggestion that she worked for the Russians against this country or has any knowledge of Soviet espionage activities here. It would seem that her work for the Russians in Paris ended at least seven years ago.[31]

Various people speculated on who Ignatieff might be. On 9 October 1940 Millicent Bagot of MI5's B4b, which dealt with Soviet affairs – she is often said to be the model for John le Carré's Connie Sachs – suggested four possible candidates for Ignatieff:

1. IGNATIEFF, Count Alexis, born Petrograd 18.2.77 formerly Military Attaché at the Russian Embassy in Paris under the Tsarist regime, subsequently in 1933 Soviet Military Attaché in Paris and in charge of Soviet espionage and Comintern work.

2. PETERSEN, Peter, aged 40 in November, 1938, Danish who was arrested at the end of 1938 in connection with the PFLUGK-HARTTUNG [sic] espionage case,[32] and was connected with the German espionage system working against Britain, France and the U.S.S.R. in Denmark.

3. PETERSEN, Henry, German, reported in 1935 to be the courier in contact with Martha and Charlotte SCHOLZ of the Strasbourg Soviet Espionage Case.

4. PETERSEN (no initial) of Holsteinhasse 7, Copenhagen who was reported in February, 1940, to be connected with Soviet S.S.[33]

Gerhard Dierks claimed that Ignatieff was Sergei Ivanovitch Ignatieff, 'an unscrupulous rogue engaged in drug traffic and espionage for the Soviet government'. A Count S. Ignatieff is listed as being a captain in the Imperial Russian Guards. Although no date is offered for this post, it must be pre-Revolution (i.e. before October 1917), so he is unlikely to be the same one as claimed by Gerhard Dierks.[34] A report from B4b to Dick White, dated 17 October 1940, suggested that Ignatieff:

> 1. May be identical to Count Alexis IGNATIEFF who went over to the Soviets and worked for the G.P.U. in Paris 1937, or –
> 2. He may be Theodor MALY @ Paul HARDT @ PETERS @ PETERSON @ MANN.[35]

However, the suggestion that Ignatieff was Theodore Mály (1894–1938) @ PETER @ PETERSON @ Paul HARDT @ Fjodor @ Der Lange ('the tall one'), just succeeds in muddying the waters even more. The claim is not supported by any other information in the literature or MI5 files currently available, nor do they make any connection between Vera and Mály. When Vera was shown a photograph of 'Paul Hardt' on 30 October 1940 she failed to identify him as the man she had known as Ivan Ignatieff, although the two men were about the same age (47/48). There are many reasons why Ignatieff could not have been Mály/Hardt, which will shortly become apparent.

2

THE RED MENACE

Theodore (Téodor) Stephanovich Mály (or Mælly) was born in Timişoara, Hungary (now Romania) in 1894. He would later go on to control for a time the 'Cambridge Five' – Kim Philby, Guy Burgess, Donald Maclean, Anthony Blunt and John Cairncross – before being recalled to Moscow and murdered during one of Stalin's purges. 'Paul Hardt', one of his adopted aliases, was apparently born in Odenburg, Austria, on 21 January 1894, according to his registration card for 5 April 1937 in his MI5 file. This file also gives his (Hardt's) wife's name as Lydia, *née* Koch, born in Sereth, Austria, on 18 December 1906, which is also borne out by the date on her registration card of 5 April 1937. Nigel West and Oleg Tsarev's book *The Crown Jewels* says she was his second wife and gives her name as Lidya Grigorievna (Lifa Girshevna) Razba, born in Riga in 1906.[1] Hede Massing described her as a Russian Jewess. Mælly's true nationality, Hungarian, was confirmed by Percy Glading,[2] Walter Krivitsky, Hede Massing, Margarete Charlotte Moos @ Jacoby,[3] and Elsa Bernaut, the widow of Ignace Reiss.[4] In 1923 Mælly's wife gave birth to a son, Theodore Theodorevich. William Duff, Mælly's biographer, writes, 'Nothing is known of his wife and very little of his son.'[5] This concurs with West and Tsarev.

Margarete Charlotte Moos *née* Jacoby (or Jacobi), also referred to as Lotte, was a petite brunette (she was 5ft 2½in), born in Berlin on 9 December 1909, who became a naturalised British subject on 15 September 1947. On 14 October 1932 she married Siegfried Moos, 5ft 10in with brown hair, born in Munich on 19 September 1904, who became a naturalised British subject on 9 September 1947. The couple had fled Germany, first to Paris in July 1933, then to London in December 1933, as Jewish refugees from Germany after Hitler had come to power. A note on Siegfried in Margarete's MI5 file states that he was wanted by the Gestapo.

In April 1937, Siegfried, described as a university lecturer and statistician, had hoped to undertake economic research in conjunction with the Department of Social Biology at the London School of Economics. He had previously been working on the staff of the London office of the *New York Times* in the News Photographic Continental Service. Later he worked at the Institute of Statistics at Oxford University under the British economist Sir William Beveridge, best known for the 'Beveridge Report' on the post-war Welfare State written in 1942.

Described as 'a scholar of International Student Service' and a poet and playwright, Margarete had been studying at University College, London, and at the Institute for Slavonic Studies. She also hoped to enroll on an interpreter course at the Regent Street Polytechnic. She had first come to MI5's attention in February 1934 when she had stayed with Robert McKinnon Wood, a principal scientific officer then working at the Royal Aircraft Establishment at Farnborough who was described as an 'ardent Communist'. During the First World War McKinnon Wood had been sent by the Royal Aircraft Establishment to Göttingen, Sweden, to Ludwig Prandtl's laboratory to study his wind tunnel experiments on the aerodynamics of airframes. Margarete and Siegfried separated in 1935, although they got back together again later as their daughter, Merilyn Anne, was born on 28 June 1944. This separation, according to Siegfried, was:

> entirely due to my attitude. I could not get accustomed to refugee life … I therefore separated from my wife, against her will. It was my neglect which drove her to loneliness and despair and made her thankful for the friendly attitude of Mr. Verschoyle who was a common friend of us and who I esteemed very much.[6]

At the time of their arrest and internment in 1940, 'strongly suspected of espionage on behalf of a foreign power', the Home Office Warrant gave their address as 159 Banbury Road, in the Summertown area of Oxford. Another resident of the house was Isabel Judith Masefield, the daughter of writer and Poet Laureate John Masefield and illustrator of his book *The Box of Delights*. Margarete was arrested on 11 April 1940 and sent to Holloway, then transferred to Rushen Camp on the Isle of Man on 7 June 1940; Siegfried was interned on 29 June 1940 but released on 23 August 1940 'as a useful alien'; he returned to 159 Banbury Road.

The reason for Margarete's internment was that she had been suspected of being an OGPU agent. This was confirmed in a note in her MI5 file by

Jane Archer: 'KRIVITSKY has told us that he is convinced that Margaret MOOS is a member of the Ogpu [*sic*], and he considers that she is very important.'[7] She was also a close friend of Brian Goold-Verschoyle (1912–42), code-named FRIEND, whom she had met at a German class in November 1934 and with whom she later began an affair. She admitted to MI5 that she had been co-habiting with him 'at a time when we know him to have been acting as an Ogpu agent in this country … She admits visiting Russia with GOOLD-VERSCHOYLE and that she had in the past herself indulged in political activity.'[8]

Her MI5 file goes on to note, 'We would have been prepared to permit this woman's release on restrictions, but as Category B. are now all interned, we see no alternative but for her to remain in internment during the present crisis period.'[9]

Various appeals for her release had been launched, by McKinnon Wood, and one by the MP for Oxford Quintin Hogg, later Baron Hailsham of St Marylebone. Siegfried had applied to the Home Office for his wife to be released 'on the ground that the Home Sec. had held out the prospect of interned wives being treated with special consideration where the husbands in Cat. C have been released'. On 17 September Kathleen (Jane) Archer of MI5, writing to the Home Office on behalf of MI5, expressed, 'We have no objection to the release of Margarette Charlotte MOOS [*sic*].' She was released on 8 October 1940 and went to live at 10 Wellington Street, Oxford, according to an entry on internees on the Isle of Man. A letter in her MI5 file to 'Jasper' Harker of MI5 from the Chief Constable of Oxford City Police, Charles R. Fox, refers to it as Wellington Square. Both street and square exist; exactly which is immaterial to this story of Vera, but for our purposes the police account is taken to be more accurate.

Goold-Verschoyle was a member of the Communist Party of Ireland (he was born in County Donegal), and while in London between 1935–36 was being used as an NKVD courier by Henri Piecke and Paul Hardt (Mály); he also served as a contact between Mály and Captain John Herbert King (see below). On 15 April 1939 Krivitsky (of more later) wrote an article about Goold-Verschoyle's disappearance for the New York *Saturday Evening Post*. Goold-Verschoyle had been suspected of being a Trotskyite and was kidnapped in Barcelona while covering the Spanish Civil War. He was brought to Moscow by ship, where he was taken to the Lubyanka, before dying in Orenburg gulag in 1942 as part of Stalin's 'Great Purge'. Officially, he had died during a German air attack on Russia. A Foreign Office enquiry was launched into determining his alleged death in that air raid.[10]

From January to June 1939 Margarete was living at 26 North Dithridge Street, Pittsburgh, employed as a teacher at the Federated Labor School. She had contacted Krivitsky in New York after the *Saturday Evening Post* article's publication. From August 1935 to March 1936 (one document says in early April 1936) she made a journey to Russia; her address in Moscow from April to October 1936 is given as Hotel Novaja Moskowskaja. A report by Special Branch on 31 March 1936 indicates that she left Folkestone on 17 March en route for Vienna. On 30 December 1938 she left Southampton for America, returning on 2 July 1939.

Prior to her affair with Goold-Verschoyle, between 1935 and 1936 Special Branch observed Margarete as being 'in relations' with Jack Rapoport, a member of an Austrian Communist group operating in London led by Engelbert Broda.[11] Broda later worked at the Cavendish Laboratory and was thought to have recruited Alan Nunn May, his son-in-law, the spy later convicted of passing atomic research secrets to the NKVD.

Interestingly, Margarete's address from August 1935 to March 1936 and again from October 1936 to January 1937 was two rooms at 9 Lawn Road, London NW3, shared with Goold-Verschoyle. David Burke's book on Melita Norwood, *The Spy Who Came in from the Co-op*, states that Margarete and Goold-Verschoyle moved in there, a few doors down from Robert and Ruth Kuczynski at number 12.[12] Indeed, the 'Lawn Road Flats' harboured a number of Communist and left-wing sympathisers, as well as writers such as Agatha Christie.

Robert Kuczynski, code-named 'René' and Ursula Kuczynski @ Ruth Werner @ Ursula Beurton @ Ursula Hamburger, code-named 'Sonja', were two Communist spies working for the NKVD. Special Branch observed that Margarete, often referred to by her second name, Charlotte or Lotte, was seen frequenting the address of Edith Tudor-Hart at 158a Haverstock Hill, NW3, where she had a photographic studio. She had been introduced to Tudor-Hart by Dr Edith Bone (1889–1975) *née* Edit Olga Hajós in Hungary, a casual acquaintance of Siegfried's when he was in Berlin. She had hoped to find work in Tudor-Hart's darkroom but without success: 'However, there was hardly any work to be done … we went there mainly to take a bath … and I to wash and to iron my things, and to print photos, also sometimes to have a good meal, for Mrs. T.H. had a very good cook.'[13]

Also of note is that the work Siegfried intended to do at the Department of Social Biology at the London School of Economics was with Dr Kuczynski and Dr Glass. Margarete died on 3 January 2008.

When Vera was supposed to have met Ignatieff, Málly was in Moscow serving under the newly appointed Vlacheslav Rudolfovich Menzhinsky, head of the OGPU, following the death of Lenin in 1924. At that time, Vera may or may not have been in Paris, depending on which story is to be believed. According to William Duff, Mály was in Moscow in 1930 working on a file regarding a farmer sentenced to death, but was sent away on a two-week assignment. Exactly what this assignment was or where, Duff does not record. Part of a redacted document from B2 dated 22 October 1940 states that:

> It was decided between Captain Cowgill and B.2. that the name of IGNATIEFF @ PETERSON (the Russian who directed Vera ERIKSON's activities in Paris on behalf of Russia and whom she describes as her first husband) should be referred to various White Russian contacts of [Redacted] of S.I.S. who came to this country from Paris after the collapse of France.[14]

Captain, later Major, Felix Cowgill was head of SIS's Section V, counter-intelligence. The SIS name redacted from the document was the colourful Commander Wilfred 'Biffy' Dunderdale, RNVR, who had been the MI6 Head of Station in Paris at that time, and long thought to be a possible model for Ian Fleming's James Bond, although Fleming denied it.[15]

Hede Massing stated that Paul Hardt (Mály) whom she knew as 'Der Lange' (the tall one) and not as Mály, was in Paris in the summer of 1933 and again when she met him there in 1935–36. From June 1935 to June 1937 Mály was in Britain as the chief 'illegal' OGPU *rezident*. His presence in Britain during that time is confirmed by his banking records for that period as well as his Travel Index record of arrivals and departures through English ports. A memorandum in the MI5 file on Hardt written by Jane Archer (*née* Sissmore) and dated 23 October 1939, states that:

> The man PIECK and the man referred to as PETERSON in KING's state-ment are both well known to the Military Intellige[nce] Branch of the War Office as Soviet agents operating in the collection of political and mili-tary intelligence in this count[ry] from January 1935 to February 1936, and February 1936 to June 19[?] respectively. It is within my knowledge that both these men handled large sums of money for the payment of agents of the Sov[iet] Intelligence Organization in this country.[16]

Captain John Herbert King (MAG) was a Foreign Office cypher clerk con-victed in October 1939 of passing Foreign Office communications to the Russians between 1935 and 1937.[17] Henri Piecke (COOPER) (1895–1972) was a Dutch citizen working for the Russians to whom King passed his infor-mation.[18] Archer adds:

this man's correct name is Paul HARDT, an Austrian, who took over the
Soviet Espionage Organization in this country from PIECK in February
1936. From that date onwards HARDT paid continual visits to this country
… HARDT left this country in June 1937 for Paris, where he was concerned
in the arrangements for the murder of the ex-Soviet agent, Ignace REISS.
From there he went to Moscow, and has not since returned to this country.[19]

Hardt's record of arrivals to and departures from England for 1935–37 are
shown here in Figure 1.[20]

Figure 1

Arrived/Left	Date	Observations
Arrived	14.6.35	at Croydon from Paris (pleasure)
Left	24.6.35	Croydon for Paris
Arrived	11.9.35	at Newhaven (pleasure)
Left	14.9.35	Dover
Arrived	4.1.36	Dover (textiles)
Left	4.3.36	Dover
Arrived	16.3.36	at Croydon from Paris (textiles)
Left	25.3.36	Croydon for Paris
Arrived	15.4.36	Croydon from Paris
Left	9.5.36	Croydon for Paris
Arrived	21.5.36	Croydon from Amsterdam
Left	6.6.36	Croydon for Paris
Arrived	7.7.36	Croydon from Paris (Described as representative of Gada textiles of Amsterdam, going to Austin and Son, Atlas Wharf, Hackney Wick)
Left	24.8.36	Dover
Arrived	6.1.37	at Croydon from Paris (textiles)
Left	20.2.37	at Croydon for Paris
Arrived	27.2.37	at Folkestone (Described Textiles proceeding to Dandridge and Co., Atlas Wharf, Hackney Wick)
Left	24.6.37	Dover

Flights to Croydon Airport would most likely have been with Imperial
Airways' Silver Wings lunchtime service from Le Bourget, Paris.

★★★

Ignace Reiss (1899–1937) was an ex-OGPU agent who had been their *rezident* in England from 1931 to 1934 and was murdered in Lausanne, Switzerland, on 4 September 1937. Swiss police suspected that Reiss's assassin was a man named Josef Leppin, who had worked for Hardt in London. Christopher Andrew, MI5's official historian, states that Reiss, also known as Poretsky, was killed by a French 'illegal' in the 'Serebryansky Service'[21] known as Roland Jacques Claude Lyudvigovich Abbiate @ François Rossi and code-named LETCHIK ('Pilot').[22]

Abbiate's real name was Vladimir Sergeevich Pravdin (1915–70), code-named SERGEJ, born in Leningrad on 15 August 1915. He was an NKVD assassin who later operated as head of the TASS news agency in the USA (1944–45)[23] and described by Nigel West as 'an impressive, sophisticated opera-tor'.[24] His wife, Olga Borisovna Pravdina, also referred to as 'Margaret' and 'Lucy', was born in Tomsk on 10 May 1915. For a short while she was employed by Amtorg in New York – the Amtorg Trading Corporation, the first Soviet trading organisation in the USA.[25] She was identified by Elizabeth Bentley as a substitute Soviet contact whom she met on five or six occasions.[26] While in New York, the Pravdins lived at 125 Riverside Drive.

It was noted in a letter to Jane Sissmore on 15 June 1938 from SIS's Section V that Abbiate had used the alias François Rossi when he departed Folkestone on 14 May 1937. His MI5 file mentions that FBI records indicate that he entered the USA at Seattle on 19 October 1941 to take up a position as editor of the TASS News Agency in New York. This seems strange, given that Seattle is on the west coast and New York is on the east. This means he would have had to take a ship via the Panama Canal to get to the USA. That being the case, had he stopped off somewhere en route on another assignment? Most likely it was Cuba, as noted below.

A cancelled Home Office Suspects List (HOSI) document in Pravdin's file dated 12 September 1946 states that his name was Abbiate, Roland Jacques Claude; Francois Rossi; Roland Smith; Doctor Benoit; Carroll Georges Quinn. His date of birth was given as 15 August 1905 in London (another document specifies Hampstead) and states that he left the UK at Liverpool for Havana, Cuba, on 18 February 1937 having arrived at Dover from Dunkirk the previous day. Records then at Somerset House confirm his date and place of birth. While in the United States he was also:

> Sentenced to two years' imprisonment in New York for impersonating an immigration officer in 1926 and subsequently deported to U.K. Later visited Mexico on several occasions. Is a Russian agent who, since 1938, has been

sought by the Swiss Police for complicity in the murder of IGNACE REISS, an ex-G.P.U. agent, near Lausanne. No recent information.[27]

Further information on this is provided in a letter from E.L. Spenser of F2a to the Deputy Assistant Commissioner, Special Branch, in which he states that Abbiate @ Francisco Rossi, arrived in the USA on 27 July 1926 on a British passport issued in Nice. (Another document claimed he had a Monaco passport.) On 3 April 1927 he was arrested by the New York Police Department for impersonating an immigration officer and deported to the UK on 22 February 1928. Evidence implicating him in Reiss's murder was his coat found near the crime scene containing a cheque from Salvador Y. Giribar, a prominent Mexican and friend of M. Ligarette, a Mexican banker and Menorcian Minister in Mexico City. A strand of hair from Gertrude Schildbach, 'an aging German actress and Communist trusted by Reiss',[28] and 'short and squat with an oversized head, usually wearing thick-lens glasses', was found in Reiss's hand.[29] Renata Steiner, a Swiss Communist, confirmed Abbiate's involvement. According to Nigel West and others, she had provided a rented vehicle with which to abduct Reiss, a story that was corroborated by Walter Krivitsky.[30] That evening Abbiate had dined with Gertrude Schildbach. As West described it:

> She [Steiner] confessed that, while on a stroll after the meal, Reiss had been forced into a car and shot at point-blank range by Abbiate and another NKVD agent Etienne Martignat. Steiner had been traced when the rental car was found abandoned in Geneva, and her confession served to implicate Schildbach, Martignat, an employee of the Soviet Trade Mission in Paris named Lydia Grozovskaya … and Abbiate.[31]

It seems that there had been a back-up plan with another hit team in Reims in case the Lausanne attack failed.[32] The Pravdins left New York City on 11 March 1946 en route for Moscow.

A letter from SIS Section V (probably Major Valentine Vivian) to Jane Sissmore dated 29 December 1938 stated that their representative in Finland reported a Charles Martignat leaving Rajajoki on the Finnish-Russian border for Leningrad on 11 September 1937, and a Mireille Abbiate leaving the same place on 10 October 1937. The representative in Finland at that time was Harry Carr, later the SIS post-war Controller, Northern Area (CNA). Someone in B4 at MI5 (the name has been redacted, but likely Sissmore) followed this up with a letter to Vivian dated 3 February 1939 stating that, 'The Paris police say that they have some reason to believe that Roland ABBIATE and his accomplice Charles MARTIGNAT may now be in Warsaw, but so far their enquiries have not produced any definite result.'[33]

In a draft note to M. Joseph Lynch, the FBI legal attaché at the US Embassy in London, dated 4 November 1944, Roger Hollis regretted that MI5 had no further information on Abbiate since 1939. At the bottom someone, probably Hollis, has written, 'You will observe that acc. to our information A. was never arrested by the French' – Lynch had claimed in his letter to Herbert Hart of MI5 on 25 October 1944 that he had been. The accompanying report on Abbiate states that he had accompanied an ex-mistress of Reiss, Gertude Schildback [sic] née Neugenbauer, to Lausanne to arrange Reiss's assassination. The report further adds that Étienne Charles Maxime Martignat was born on 24 August 1900 in Culhatt, Puy de Dôme, in the Auvergne, France. Martignat is also mentioned in a letter from Mary E. Hobkirk of MI5 to J.B. Luzmore of the Home Office Aliens Department, dated 5 March 1946, in which it refers to cancellation of his entry in the Home Office Suspects List.

The letter to Vivian also reported that Mireille Abbiate was the sister of Roland Abbiate. The report mentioned above, adds that she was born on 30 March 1901, the divorced wife of Basil Erikalov, a Russian. A letter to Vivian on 3 February 1939 gives her place of birth as Maisons-Lafitte, France. When she left France in September 1937 she reportedly went to live with her cousin, Madame L.A. Kerson, at Rue Fronze No.13, Moscow. (Most likely this is actually Ulitsa Timura Frunze 13.) It was not determined whether she had actually played a part in Reiss's murder, but her departure from France appeared to have been connected with her brother's sudden departure.

Pavel Sudoplatov (1907–96), a long-time member of the Soviet intelligence services and responsible for ordering the assassination of Trotsky, writes in his autobiography that Reiss was shot with a sub-machine gun and dumped by the roadside outside Lausanne by one of his Bulgarian illegals, Boris Afanasiev, and his brother-in-law Victor Pravdin. However, not all of what Sudoplatov has written is now considered reliable. A report from Jacquillard, the Chief of the Police Service in charge of Security Police in Lausanne, sent to the Commissioner of the Metropolitan Police stated:

In the evening of the 4th September, 1937, there [w]as found on the public roads of the suburbs of Lausanne, the [c]orpse of a man who had been killed by nine shots. The [c]rime was committed the same evening very likely in a motor [c]ar, and the body deposited from the motor car where it [w]as found. On the body was found the Czecho-Slovakian [p]assport of the

victim, made out in the name of Hermann [EB]ERHARDT, born on the
1st March 1899 in Opova, Troppo, [do]miciled in Chamitov Komotau.

It has been ascertained from enquiries made [th]at the passport utilised is
a forgery, and its bearer [ha]s been identified as being really Ignace REISS,
born … January, 1899 in Podwoloczyska, (District of Skalat, [Pol]and, a Pole,
married to Elsa Barenhaut, born 25th [Jan]uary, 1898 in Koloma, Poland.[34]

Afanasiev is mentioned in a document classified Top Secret Froth Bride sent to
Ronnie Reed at MI5 from the Government Communications Headquarters
(GCHQ) at Benhall dated 2 September 1954 in which he is referred to as
Viktor Vasil'evich Afanas'ev code-named Sergej when he was in San Francisco.
Coincidentally, Pravdin was also code-named Sergej when he was in New
York.[35] The above-mentioned classification indicates that it is from one of the
VENONA decrypts. A VENONA decrypt, marked Top Secret Bride Suede
dated 16 May 1944, mentions Pravdin as Sergius (Sergej) in connection with
a meeting with VISSON (André Visson). Another VENONA decrypt for
15 June 1944 mentions him reporting on US policy towards Europe.[36] Pravdin
would later meet with Donald Maclean (HOMER) on 25 June 1944 in New
York and Judith Coplon (SIMA) in January 1945. Both Afanasiev and Pravdin
were awarded the Order of the Red Banner. Pravdin later went to work for
the Moscow Foreign Languages Publishing House at 21 Zubovsky Boulevard
(as did Guy Burgess) until he died in 1970.[37]

According to the Swiss police, Hardt travelled back to Moscow via Le Havre,
France, on 22 July 1937. An MI5 report sent to Vivian on 8 June 1938 stated that
Hardt and his wife left Dover on 24 June 1937, as shown in the Traffic Index
(see Figure 1). According to the French police, Hardt was in Paris between
17 and 18 July, where he had met with a high-ranking GPU representative
to arrange Reiss's murder. The French police also stated that he and his wife,
Lydia, had left for Moscow on 28 July, while MI5 reported he and his wife had
left Paris for Moscow on 21 July on the SS *Bretagne*.

Exactly when Mály died poses another question. When Hardt and his
wife hurriedly left London he still owed rent on the flat in which they
were living. However, a typewritten letter dated 'Vienna, Sept. the 21 1937'
addressed to Mr D. Ainslie, 37 Panton Street, Haymarket[38] and purportedly
signed by Hardt was found by the agents for Hardt's flat at 8 Wallace Court,
300 Marylebone Road. The letter stated that he had been prevented from
returning to London in late August owing to a 'bad attack of appendicitus'
[*sic*] and that he would be undergoing surgery 'in a Vienna nursery'. This
letter was accompanied by a cheque to the agents for £36. To Jane Sissmore

the letter looked suspiciously like a forgery; she thought that the use of
the word 'nursery' for 'nursing home' may have been a genuine mistake
on Hardt's part, but unlikely as his English was very good. However, his
bank manager confirmed that the signature was Hardt's. He was later proved
wrong when on 9 July 1938 Jane Sissmore wrote to Vivian informing him
that the letter was indeed a forgery:

> I enclose a photograph of a letter and envelope which has just been received
> at the Midland Bank from Paris. You will see that the signature is an obvious
> forgery, and that the name HARDT is misspelt in the body of the letter and
> in the signature. The address 'Iris', 22 Rue Saint Augustin, Paris is known
> to have been used as a cover address for the W.I.R. [Worker's International
> Relief - Comintern] in 1934 ...
>
> You will see that the letter enclosed was posted in Paris on 6th July, but
> was evidently typed on 5th May 1938. Moreover the original was typed on
> typing paper with a German watermark. That fact together with the discrep-
> ancy in dates looks as if the letter was typed in some place other than Paris,
> probably Moscow, and sent to Paris to be posted.[39]

The envelope also had the address of the Russell Square branch of the Midland
Bank at 1 Woburn Place misspelled, with only one 'l' in Russell, a mistake that
Hardt is unlikely to have made, being acquainted with the bank. The letter,
which also had the word 'address' spelled with one 'd' stated:

> Dear Sir,
> Since last year I have not received any balance of my banking account, as
> I was absent from my home all the time. Will you please send it to me
> according to the last date to the adress [*sic*] as follows:
> 'Iris' 22, Rue Saint Augustin
> PARIS (2)
> Mr. P. Herdt
> Thanking in anticipation, I remain,
> Truly yours,
> [signed] P. Herdt[40]

The English also seems a bit clumsy, and not something written by someone whose first language is English: 'Thanking in anticipation', which should
read 'Thanking you in anticipation'; and 'Truly yours' would have been
better expressed as 'Yours truly'. The misspelling of the word 'adress' suggests

someone French who might have written it, except the French form has an 'e' on the end – 'adresse'.

Sissmore went on to say that the bank manager had no account of anyone with the name of Mr P. Herdt, but would reply to the letter in the hope that further correspondence would ensue. She wondered whether they should approach the French to ascertain who this P. Herdt was using the post box at 'Iris', and posited that perhaps Hardt was still alive. It seemed unlikely, given that his funds had been transferred to the Moscow Narodny Bank in March 1938, the GPU should have bothered to forge his signature for the sake of £25, unless, of course, they didn't know and were trying to trace his money.

On 8 April 1938 the Director of MI5, Colonel Sir Vernon Kell, as he was then (before his dismissal in 1940 he was a major general; the title was redesignated as Director-General in 1941), wrote to the Commissioner of the Royal Canadian Mounted Police (RCMP), Colonel Stuart Taylor Wood, regarding Hardt, mentioning the agents Willy and Mary Brandes;[41] Canadian Aaron Marcovitch (described by Duff as 'an agent of the Hebrew Sick Benefit Association'); the murder of Reiss, and the Glading case, saying that since one of them had a visa for North America (he does not specify which one) he was sending Wood their particulars and photographs. He also stated in a letter to Wood on 15 February 1940:

> GINSBERG [Hardt] has given us most important and valuable information during his stay here, and we are most anxious, for every reason, to do everything possible for him. He is genuinely concerned as to his safety and that of his wife and child, and we for our part are anxious to keep the knowledge that he has been here in as small a circle as possible.
>
> We should be very grateful if you could arrange that a senior officer in Montreal could act as an advisor to him and as a link between him and us.[42]

According to *Caught Red Starred* by Curtis Robinson, a Mr and Mrs Stevens, posing as Willy and Mary Brandes, had been in Canada in 1936 'for the specific purpose of obtaining a Canadian passport'. They left Canada sometime after 2 October 1936. Robinson cites Oleg Gordievsky, the KGB *rezident*-designate in London who had been working for SIS and defected to Britain in 1985, as claiming that the Brandes were in fact Arnold and Josephine Deutsch.[43] However, I can find no references to them in Christopher Andrew and Gordievsky's books on the KGB.

Mály may not have been executed in Moscow in 1937, as West and Tsarev report that he was still alive in 1938: '… Mally was charged in the case heard by the Military Collegium of the Supreme Court of the USSR on 20 September 1938, on an indictment that seemed to rely on Mally's refusal to go to Canada.'[44]

The KGB file on MANN (Mály), quoted in West and Tsarev, elaborates on this:

> Grounds for Mally's arrest were provided by the 5th Department of the First Directorate of the NKVD which discovered Mally's activities harming the interests of the USSR (malicious violation of the security rules, disclosure of state secrets, refusal to carry out orders in combat conditions).[45]

And a further account by Tsarev states:

> Before Mally was sentenced to death by the Military Collegium of the Supreme Court on 20 September 1938 (after he had been found guilty on trumped up espionage charges brought under article 58 section 6 of the Criminal Code) ...[46]

Mály's KGB file referred to above added that, 'Being under arrest, Mally T.S. during the preliminary investigation stated that he was a German spy and in the course of several years had actively worked against the USSR.' The indictment also alleged that he had been in contact with 'the Berlin Centre of German military intelligence' through the *rezident*, Ottó Steinbrück ('Vater Otto' – Father Otto), born in Hungary in 1892 and died in 1937. One of MI5's files on Krivitsky states that:

> HARDT left Moscow after an interview with YEJOFF,[47] successor to YAGODA[48] in 1937. Mr. THOMAS [Krivitsky] had an appointment with Stalin, however HARDT did not see Stalin before he left ... HARDT's landlord received a letter from HARDT while he was in a sanatorium in the Caucases [*sic*]. This was while the O.G.P.U. were deciding what to do with HARDT.[49]

Mály's MI5 file concurs that Hardt was in the Caucasus while the OGPU was determining what to do with him. According to an unverified SIS source in Holland, Mály was shot as a Trotskyist in the Lubyanka prison on 28 September 1938 as part of Stalin's Terror. This is confirmed in an article by John Simkin in *Spartacus International*, although he does not mention the source of his information.[50]

A twist in the tale was added by Krivitsky (MR. THOMAS), who said that when he was in New York in 1938 he met Serge Bassov and two other men in a restaurant on 42nd Street:

1938 [date was changed in the file from 1939] met KRIVITSKY in a restaurant on 42nd St., New York, together with two other men. During course of conversation, KRIVITSKY gathered from BASSOFF that Theodore MALY @ Paul HARDT might still be alive. KRIVITSKY believed that BASSOFF and his companions intended to 'liquidate' him and managed to elude them.[51]

Konstantin Mikhail Basov (also written as Bassoff), then living in the Bronx, was born as Jan Ābeltiņš in Eisk (Yeysk), Latvia, on 5 October 1896.[52] Described as the 'goon type used by the Soviets to scare people', he had been a member of the OGPU recruited in the 1920s and an ex-sailor in the Black Sea Fleet. He was also described in Mály's MI5 file as being an associate of Piecke in Paris and used the Grand Hotel. Krivitsky also claimed he had received a letter from Mály in a sanatorium in the Caucasus in August or September 1937:

[T]he reliability of these reports are questionable. (Since then one or two odd reports showing that he might not have been shot such as: September 1937 in Vienna nursing home – KRIVITSKY stated that he had received a letter from HARDT from a sanatorium in the Caucasus.)[53]

Walter Germanovitch Krivitsky (1899–1941), born Samuel Ginsberg, was a Soviet intelligence officer who coordinated many intelligence operations in Europe in the 1930s, before defecting to the West in 1937.[54] His sudden death at the Bellevue Hotel (now The George) on 15 E Street NW, Washington DC, on 10 February 1941 occurred in a locked room and was made to look like suicide, although his wife and others suspected foul play.[55] It came in the wake of Trotsky's assassination in Coyoacán, Mexico, on 21 August 1940.

A report, 'Soviet Agents Mentioned by Krivitsky' dated April 1941,[56] lists an OGPU agent, Ignatieff, who it states was the service name of a Russian Orthodox priest, recruited in Vienna, who went to a Russian church in France, 'probably Paris'. A document in Vera's file offers to shed more light on Ignatieff, although it may just confuse the issue even more:

Trace for Count Ivan IGNATIEFF, extracted
from PFR.436 IGNATIEFF 59a: a report
from Source BRIT, dated 8.2.42.

(Not likely to be E.'s IGNATIEFF)

(Major.Gen.Count A.A.Ignatieff) [This cannot be Count Alexis Ignatieff, who was killed on 22 December 1906]

Count Ivan IGNATIEFF, nephew of above, aged (?) 35. Described as charming but a coward. Very religious (Orthodox) and originally intended to be a monk but married instead. Wife nee Countess OSTEN-SACKEN,[57] an Orthodox and completely Russianized Balt. This young woman had for some years acted as an informer – reporting to KASEM-BEG on affairs in Russian reactionary circles with which her family was closely connected. Both wife and husband now members of Young Russian Org. They fled from France in Sept. 1939, spent some time in Spain and are now in Tangier.[58] 2 or 3 children.

It is through Ivan IGNATIEFF that, in late 1937, his uncle contacted KASEM-BEG in Paris. It is said that, at first, K-B refused to meet the General but eventually did so 3 or 4 times in company with Ivan IGNATIEFF and another Young Russian.[59]

A typed note underneath states: 'NO ACTION TO BE TAKEN ON THIS REPORT WITHOUT REFERENCE TO MAJOR ALLEY, E.2.'

Stephen Alley (1876–1969) was head of E2, Alien Control, who originally worked for MI6 and was suspected of being one of the organisers of Rasputin's assassination on 30 December 1916. His alleged involvement is cited in a biography of Rasputin by Douglas Smith.[60] In 1918 he returned from Russia and was recruited by MI5, having been sacked by Mansfield Cumming 'for reasons that remain obscure. Alley would later make the sensational claim that he had been sacked for failing to carry out an order to assassinate Joseph Stalin ...'[61] When Krivitsky went to North America it was Alley who escorted him to his ship, the *Duchess of Richmond*, taking him to Canada and then to the USA.

Kasem-Beg, or Alexander Lvovich Kazembek (1902–77), was a Russian emigré of Azeri and Iranian origin who had founded the Mladorossi group, an organization dedicated in part to the restoration of the Russian monarchy but also the adoption of the Soviet system. The von der Osten-Sacken family were of Germanic origin living in Courtland, now Latvia. One previous countess, Alexandra von Osten-Sacken, was the aunt of author Leo Tolstoy.

Vera claimed in a statement she gave to MI5 on 2 October 1940[62] that Ignatieff had told her that he worked for the 'Red Party' (i.e. the Communists) and then blackmailed her into working for him, otherwise he would tell the police and her parents. She said he made her bring some papers to Copenhagen for him, although she does not elaborate on what these papers contained. In a letter written to Jane Archer at MI5's Registry based in Oxford dated 6 November 1940,

Dick White in B2 stated that it was in 1929 or 1930 that Ignatieff approached Vera to work for the Soviet government, which she did under protest for five years:

> The work included taking papers to Denmark and Berlin. They travelled on the same train, but in different compartments and she carried the papers. When they had crossed the frontier he took the papers from her and she did not see him again, but it is difficult to see who [*sic*] this is possible as she later stated that they stayed at the same hotel, the Bellevue in Copenhagen and the Adlon in Berlin.[63]

In other statements Vera gave MI5, the word 'parcel' or 'package' was used instead of 'papers', which may help to bear out the assertion that in addition to spying for Ignatieff he had wanted her to become involved in cocaine trafficking and act as a 'mule' for him. She may well have had a drug problem. From what the Duchesse de Château-Thierry told Maxwell Knight of MI5's B5b, Vera was always ill or drugged and was once in a coma for thirty-six hours from having taken *Sedormid* (also known as *Apronal*), a hypnotic/sedative similar to, but not, a barbituate.

Jona 'Klop' Ustinov's (the father of actor Peter Ustinov) report on Vera dated 11 March 1942 describes Ignatieff 'as charming as he was unscrupulous'. He stated that Ignatieff had used her from their first day of marriage for his drug trafficking and espionage activities, to which she was well-suited because she was:

> Young, attractive, resourceful, courageous, and in possession of a fair number of passports, and the easy life of travel to capitals of Europe (Berlin, Kopenhagen, Brussels) satisfied her spirit of adventure without unduly troubling the sloth of her mind.[64]

This 'sloth of her mind' was also picked up by the graphologist who analysed her handwriting while she was in prison when he identified her as being 'very indolent and lazy'. Klop's observations suggest that they may have been based either on the graphologist's report, or when she stayed with him. His relationship with Vera will be dealt with later on. The full analysis of her handwriting can be found in Appendix 2. Stephens too expressed his view that:

> This woman is essentially a sloth. She cannot be bothered to settle down to a statement divulging all her knowledge, but, at the same time, she is willing to give information always providing specific questions are asked. Professionally she dislikes anyone connected with the Intelligence Services of Russia, Germany and England, and I think she fears some of us.

Ceteris paribus [other things being equal], she prefers to lie, and in order to get rid of us, she not infrequently gives an answer which is calculated to please. With the Doctor [Dearden], I think the position is a little different. She is bored in Prison, and, in giving information which she mistakenly supposes will save de DEEKER, I think, in some curious way, she feels she is getting the better of the regular Intelligence Officers.

Also, in her boredom, she likes being entertained, and she naively asked the Doctor, in the manner of a hostess, to 'come again soon'. The value, therefore, of the information which ERICHSEN is willing to give the Doctor must accordingly be very carefully assessed. It is one thing to give information under cross-examination, with the possibility of checking, and quite another to discuss pleasantly subjects of mutual interest in conversation. There is no doubt in my mind that ERICHSEN does give the Doctor, from time to time, information of value, and, always providing that it is subject to check from our records, all is well.[65]

Klop disputed Ignatieff's background saying:

The story, that Ignatieff was a count and belonged to the wellknown [sic] Russian family of that name, can, I think, be dismissed, as, according to friends of this family, there does not exist a Count Sergei Ivanovitch but only a Sergei Alexandjevitch, who is much older and is married to a wellknown [sic] Russian actress.[66]

Vera's relationship with Ignatieff ended in 1936 when he was reportedly shot by the Bolsheviks. If this were true, then Ignatieff and Málly/Hardt cannot be the same person, as the latter was alive until at least 1937, perhaps later, as previously discussed. In her statement made under caution on 28 February 1941 for the trial of Walti and Drueke, Vera confirmed that Ignatieff had in fact died at the beginning of 1937. She may well have met Málly during this time, and their meeting, if it took place in 1930, may have coincided with his sudden departure from Moscow on his two-week mission, but there are no details to confirm this in his file, nor where he actually went during that time. However, if Málly and Ignatieff were one and the same, Vera would have had to be living in Moscow, not Brussels, and we already know the name of Málly's wife. Nor is there at present any link between Ignatieff's so-called 'death' and Málly's execution.

The question of whether Vera had indeed been married to Ignatieff was noted in a report by John Day of B1b on 21 May 1942: 'It would seem that Vera was not telling the whole truth even to U.35 ['Klop' Ustinov]. Her inveterate tendency to romance appears to have got the better of her in her account of her first marriage to the Russian agent IGNATIEFF.[67]

The fact that she had only *lived* with Ignatieff for a year before they had then separated, only seeing each other for 'business' until 1936, implies a cohabitation but not necessarily marriage. There was even an unsubstantiated claim that she had had a daughter by him, but the child had died in 1939 at the age of 8. Day's report also makes reference to the interview with Vera's uncle Ernst, who said he was 'quite certain that she had not been [married before] and that he was indeed beginning to become quite anxious about whether she would ever succeed in getting married'.[68]

Gerhard Dierks told MI5 that his brother Hilmar had introduced Vera to him in Hamburg in 1936, but he doubted that they had ever married, on the grounds that Hilmar, having had one unsuccessful marriage, always stated that he would not marry again.[69]

In 1919 Hilmar Dierks had married Gertrud 'Nuti' Cordes (1895–1938), daughter of Paul Ferdinand Cordes and Alma Cordes, with whom they had two children, Hans, born in Hanover in 1921, and Klaus-Jürgen, born in Hamburg in 1923. However, the website by Michael Dierks, Hilmar's grandson, claims that Hans was born 'from an extramarital relationship' and was adopted by Hilmar.[70] A daughter also appears to have died from polio at the age of 1, although the same website claims that she was stillborn in 1924. At the same time, Gerhard also conceded that a marriage may have occurred so that Vera could claim money from his brother's estate. He told MI5 that Vera had married his brother Hilmar in October 1937, but later called this claim into doubt when MI5 interrogated him on 28 November 1945. When Vera was reported to have married Zum Stuhrig (an alias of Hilmar Dierks) in October 1937, she was told by one of Ignatieff's friends that Ignatieff was dead. If Mälly and Ignatieff were one and the same their deaths would have freed up Vera to marry Hilmar Dierks, but the evidence so far does not suggest that this is the case. Hilmar's first wife 'Nuti' died in May 1938. Prior to that they had divorced, according to Michael Dierks' website.

On 5 December 1940 Dick White wrote to Felix Cowgill at MI6 asking about Vera:

> You will remember that Vera ERIKSEN stated that she worked in Paris for about five years as an agent for the Soviet Government. She was persuaded to take on this work by a man whom she knew as IGNATIEFF or PETERSEN, with whom she worked as a courier between Paris, Copenhagen and Berlin.

It has occurred to me that KRIVITSKY amy [*sic*] know Vera ERIKSEN
and I enclose two photographs of her which could be shown to him …[71]

Unfortunately, this appears to be the sole reference to Vera in any of Krivitsky's
files now publicly available. If the photographs were shown to him his comments were not recorded, unless they have been redacted from his files, which
is always possible. C.A. Haines (Charles Haines), writing to Helenus 'Buster'
Milmo of MI5's B1b on 17 August 1945, expressed doubt as to whether she
had in fact been married to Ignatieff as:

> … anonymous letters, believed to originate from Ignatieff, were received
> in 1939 by Vera's friend Major Mackenzie, and also Vera herself. These let-
> ters threatened to expose Vera as a Soviet spy … however the probability is
> that Vera never in fact married Ignatieff and that she lied when she said that
> she did.[72]

White's letter of 6 November 1940 to Jane Archer goes on to add that when
the two broke up, as a result of Vera refusing to work for him anymore, Ignatieff
attacked her and wounded her in the chest with a knife. Later, while staying
in London at Dorset House with the Duchesse de Château-Thierry, Vera was
attacked again and injured one night while walking in Regent's Park. She
suspected that the attack had been orchestrated by one of Ignatieff's friends
because she had received letters signed 'Ignatio' threatening to kill her if she
did not return to Paris, leading her to believe that he had been involved.
A report on her interrogation by MI5 on 30 October 1940 states that she had
told the Duchesse about the incident, but played it down and never reported
it to the police, in spite of the Duchesse urging her to do so. Why she did not
leaves open the speculation that she did not want the British authorities to
investigate and learn that she was involved in spying.

Another letter sent anonymously to the Duchesse accused Vera of being a
Russian spy saying: 'Some friend wishes to warn you immediately to get rid
of V.D.S. [Vera de Schalburg], as she is only a Russian spy and dangerous … In
your own interests get rid of this woman.' The Duchesse shed more light on
the attack and the letter at a meeting of the 'Advisory Committee to Consider
Appeals Against Orders of Internment' held in London at 6 Burlington
Gardens, W1 on 9 June 1941:

> … it was only when I had one anonymous letter and she had several letters
> pushed under the door, evidently threatening things, that I got very fed up

and said to her that I must ring the Police and she begged me not to … she had gone out with someone in a motor-car and she said he had cut her face or something … I wanted to [call the Police] and I went so far as to ring up one day and ask for a certain gentleman I had known many years ago in connection with a case when I was also having somebody in the house who was very undesirable for a week … I tried but did not get in touch with that man, and she implored me not to and said she would be murdered. They had already threatened to murder her.[73]

Unfortunately, the Duchesse's contact in the police is not mentioned in any of the files.

A more detailed account had been given by the Duchesse to Lieutenant Colonel Robin 'Tin Eye' Stephens, Major George Sampson and Meurig Evans on 12 November 1940 and is worth repeating in full. Although it does not specify who was doing the questioning, the persistent tone is indicative of Stephens:

Q. You took much trouble to verify this [her reference from Grand Duchess Olga Alexandrovna], that she had been a Russian spy for years.

A. Not at all. You don't think she would admit such a thing, and I would take her into the house. I had an anonymous letter which said such things.

Q. When did you receive that letter?

A. Just between the time when she had 3 letters pushed under her door threatening to murder her.

Q. How long after that did you keep her?

A. Very little. The war broke out and I got rid of her immediately.

Q. Is that a proper answer to a question?

A. A few weeks. It must have been a few weeks I think.

Q. So you kept a spy a few weeks in this country.

A. I questioned her. There was a worse thing said than that in that letter to me. But I questioned her and she gave me her explanation that a man she had been married to had been a spy and wanted her to spy and wanted her for traffic dope and things.

Q. When she told you she had been a spy and that her husband had been a spy (on your own admission this woman had been denounced to you by anonymous letter) you questioned her and she told you she had been a spy – when did you get rid of her?

A. First of all I sent her to Brussels and she came back. I didn't like to refuse her. I wanted to be kind to her. That is the truth. The poor woman had to leave her husband because he was an absolute rotter.

Q. So that on your own admission for weeks afterwards you kept a woman who had been connected with espionage. You have been sheltering people connected with espionage.

A. I wanted to ring up the police.

Q. Why didn't you?

A. She begged me not to. I said I don't want people in the house when people push letters under the door.

Q. You understand now how the story is built up against you? You are connected with the chief of the Western espionage. You have been sheltering a spy. You have been paid to keep Vera SCHALLBURG. [*sic*] She has said that.

A. But she is mad and if she had admitted that the next day she would have been out of the house. She was followed up and had a wound from this man.

Q. When did you finally get rid of her?

A. Directly the war started, first she had to go to Brussels, then she came back.

Q. You sent her to Brussels?

A. Well yes, she wanted to go too, to see her mother.

Q. Who paid for that?

A. She paid herself. She had other things the matter with her.

Q. What were the other things the matter with her?

A. She was not well.

Q. Suffering from an abortion wasn't she?

A. She was in the family way. I only know now that she was marrie[d]. She was in love with a Belgian. I said she must go back to her mother, she must marry this man, I didn't want to keep her.

Q. A very proper decision. She came back?

A. She came back.

Q. What date was that you sent her to Brussels?

A. I can't remember.

Q. What month was it? What season was it?

A. I am very sorry I am terrible about dates, but you can find it out.

Q. I am asking you a proper question.

A. When the war started, the first weeks of the war. She was here about 4 months, 5 months perhaps; maybe 2 months before the war.

Q. How long did she stay in Brussels?

A. About a fortnight. I can't swear to it.

Q. She came back again and you put her up?

A. I put her up until the beginning of the war.

Q. How long was that for?

A. That was for about 2 months.

Q. A woman who is denounced as a spy, she goes to Brussels, she comes back again and you put her up. She says that you were paid by REINHARDT.

A. I certainly was not.

Q. It is no use telling lies.

A. I am known to be a very truthful woman to start with.[74]

That Vera 'was in love with a Belgian' suggests that this could have been Drueke, given that his nationality was Belgian. Yet this precedes her later pregnancy just prior to her return to the UK in 1940.

Yet another account of the attack on Vera came from Major William Herbert Mackenzie, General Manager of the Greyhound Racing Association and a director of Alltools Limited; Precision Toolmakers; Alltools (Aircraft Division); and Alltools (Airframe Division) in Brentford, north London.[75] Mackenzie was born in Victoria, British Columbia, Canada, and had held a regular commission in the RAF for ten years. That being the case, he must have served in the Royal Flying Corps as officers held Army ranks until August 1919; further research indicates that he served in the Royal Naval Air Service.[76] The two services had merged on 1 April 1918 to form the Royal Air Force.

Mackenzie had met Vera at a party at the Duchesse's in the summer of 1939. He told Desmond Orr and Major Gilbert Lennox of MI5's Room 055 that he had got to know her very well and taken her out to dinner. He also told them that he had slept with her at least six times and described her as a 'very beautiful girl, who was also clever, but did not say very much'. On one occasion when he went to visit her she appeared with her face bandaged. She told him that a taxi had pulled up alongside her while she was out walking and a man had jumped out and attacked her with a bottle. Her face had been cut between the left eye and ear, as well as her breast. This was followed shortly afterwards by an anonymous letter saying, 'Tell Vera that unless she returns to Paris, we will get her sooner or later. What happened to Serge will happen to her.' Serge, Vera told Mackenzie, was her husband (meaning Sergei). There was some disagreement between Orr and Lennox as to whether it was actually Brussels or Paris to which the author of the anonymous letter insisted she return, although the letter clearly states Paris. It is also unclear exactly what 'happened to Serge', but it could be taken to mean his expedient demise or a reference to Mally's own death. Since the date of this incident occurred in the summer of 1939, it was her husband Ignatieff who was already dead, at least according to her, so whoever had written the note signed 'Ignatio' must have been one of his friends acting on his behalf.

3

THE IMPORTANCE OF
BEING ERNST

It is unfortunate that many of the documents in Ernst Schalburg's MI5 file have been destroyed. Judging from the considerable quantity indicated on the Minute Sheets, it would seem that MI5 may have had something to hide about his background, or conversely, considered that they were unimportant. What remains, however, still provides a useful insight into the man who was Vera's uncle. Ernst (Ernest) Schalburg was born in Nyborg, Denmark, on 25 February 1888 and died in Denmark in 1974. After he completed his education, Ernst took courses in economic and commercial subjects, and languages, then went off to Siberia. After a six-month apprenticeship, he was controlling milk supplies from four villages, responsible for paying the peasants, and controlling the making of butter in the factories. In the spring of 1907–08 he was in charge of four leather factories in Siberia. After eighteen months of training he became an interpreter, translating Russian into Danish at a salt factory for six months from 1908–09. Finally, he became a clerk, buyer and branch manager at a firm in Barnaoul owned by William Knudsen, exporting butter and importing machinery for the factories.

In 1910, after four years in Siberia, he returned to Denmark where he secured some agricultural agencies for the sale of products to England. During the spring of 1911 he began his business, Schalburg and Co. Ltd., in Birmingham, which later became a sub-agent of the Ministry of Food (Bindal) section that distributed imported bacon during the Second World War.[1] He had offices in Hitchin, Hertfordshire, as well as in London. In 1916 he spent six months in the stockyards of Swift & Co. of Chicago studying working conditions with the aim of securing their agency for Russia. As well as Russia and the USA, he also travelled extensively, to Canada, North Africa, Egypt, Syria, Iraq, Italy, Spain and Europe, including Scandinavia. Interestingly, there is only one entry in the Traffic Index, which shows he left Southampton on 20 May

1939 for Aden, returning from Suez on 23 June 1939. How was it that the other trips were not recorded, or have they been redacted? If so, why? Had he been working for British Intelligence?

Ernst first married Beatrice Ridgeway on 12 November 1920 in St Petersburg, with whom he had two children, Conrad and Annette Augusta. In 1921 Beatrice filed for divorce and the marriage was dissolved on 6 February 1922. There is an allusion in his MI5 file to an incident with a certain Austrian servant girl, the likely cause of the divorce. Beatrice later married Albert Prince, a history professor at Queen's University, Kingston, Ontario, Canada. On 28 April 1922 Ernst married Marion Glover Watson, who was born in the Falkland Islands on 22 February 1898. Together they had three children – Charles Peter Ernesto Schalburg (1921–86), Donald David Ian Schalburg, and Marion Augusta Schalburg, who was born in Worthing, Sussex, on 12 April 1925 and died in 2010. In 1941 his second wife, Marion, also divorced him. According to an extract on Ernst from an Air Ministry file, found in his MI5 file,[2] both his parents were Danish and his mother's name was Jorgensen. As we have seen in Chapter 1, William Knudsen was Ernst's brother-in-law by his sister Ellen's marriage to William. Ernst, it appears may also have owned a yacht (styled a 'Composite Sailing Vessel Cutter'), the *Cintra*, in 1938, as it was registered to him at Warren Road, Worthing, Sussex; by 1940 it was registered to Schalburg & Co. Ltd., Bank Chambers, London Bridge, London SE1.

On 20 October 1941 Ernst applied as a candidate for service in the Marine Craft Branch of the RAF, submitting his CV a month later. On 24 November 1941 he was accepted into the Administrative and Special Duties Branch of the RAF Volunteer Reserve (RAFVR) and commissioned as a pilot officer. On 7 January 1942 he reported for duty at Calshot on the south coast close to Southampton. By this time, Calshot, which had been a pre-war flying boat station, had become responsible for the repair, modification and maintenance of RAF flying boats. From January 1942 onwards he was an adjutant with the Aircraft Dispatch Unit, but on 8 April 1942 he requested a transfer to intelligence duties. A month later, on 9 May, he was informed that he could not work in intelligence owing to his nationality. He later served at RAF Benson in Oxfordshire, which, ironically, from 1940 onwards became the home of No.1 PRU (Photographic Reconnaissance Unit) equipped with Spitfires.

His career change in 1944 comes as something of a surprise. In June 1944 he applied to become an assistant deckhand in DSVP (Director Small Vessels Pool – Royal Navy), which supplied auxiliary ships to the Royal Navy on an as needs basis. It is unclear why he should have wanted to transfer to such a lowly position, having been an officer in the RAF, but H.W.H. Sams of MI5's

C3a, reviewing his application, expressed no objection. On 15 October 1946 he was invested with the King Christian X Liberty Medal for his services to Denmark. In his file, there is also an application to join the Royal Navy Minewatching Service dated 27 February 1952. Joan Chenhalls of MI5's C1a replied to Commander H. Winter of the Naval Intelligence Division (NID) that MI5 had no objection to his employment.

Conrad, his son by his first marriage to Beatrice Ridgeway, served in the Merchant Navy as a first mate for the Indo-China Steamship Company. Annette, his daughter also by this first marriage, worked at the Ministry of Education in Montreal. As for his other children by his second marriage, Charles Peter Ernesto trained as a pilot with the RAF. In 1943 as a flying officer he applied to attend the Combined Arms Staff Course (CASC) at Wimbledon. Donald David Ian served as an officer with the 71st Battery, Bedfordshire & Hertfordshire Regiment, later the Devonshire Regiment (according to the *London Gazette* for 28 May 1943). Marion completed her education at Wycombe Abbey, an English public school for girls. She applied to be a wireless telegraphy operator with SOE (stamped S.O.2 on the form) on 4 August 1943. The form states that she had two months' experience in radio assembly. MI5 responded 'no objection seen'. She applied for a post in Naval Intelligence in 1944, dated 3 May 1944, to which there was also no objection. In 1944 her occupation was given as shorthand typist. On 17 November 1947 she married Edward Dare Stewart Norman Sparkes. On 9 October 1951 she gave birth to a daughter, Sally Ann Sparkes. As of 4 June 1952 she was living in Windsor, Ontario, Canada.

There was some suggestion by Milmo that Ernst had been 'dabbling with espionage on behalf of the Germans in the year 1937 and up to the outbreak of war', and was certainly associated with William Peel Tillotson,[3] a notorious member of the British Union of Fascists from 1937 to 1939. Both men hotly denied this, but Helenus 'Buster' Milmo of MI5's B1b described their relationship to someone in MI6 (most likely Peter Falk, see below) as 'an intimate one'.[4] In 1940 Tillotson, an hotelier, filed for bankruptcy.

Ernst was also associated with a certain Count Morner, an extremely distant relative, who was suspected of working for the German Intelligence Service. John Day, writing on behalf of Milmo, on 11 September 1942 sent a letter to someone at MI6 (the name has been redacted) saying:

SCHALBURG's association with him is, hower, extremely slight since apart from being distantly related to MORNER, all he knows about him is that he was at one time resident in this country and believes him to be of Nazi sympathies.[5]

It also appears that the unnamed MI6 official had written to Cecil Liddell of B1h, MI5's Irish section, on 20 July 1942 regarding Morner. Unfortunately, the serial referred to in Ernst's file (26b) no longer exists, having been destroyed by MI5, and the file on Morner (PF.47325) appears not to have been released by MI5 to the National Archives. Day's letter concludes that Ernst Schalburg 'is also known to the family BANCK, one of the daughters [Else] of which is living in Sweden married to the aforementioned Count HORNER [sic]'[6]. This tidbit of information now gives us a link to the identity of Count Morner.

Warner Wilhelm Hans Anton Gräf (Count) von Mörner was born in Wiesbaden on 30 August 1901. His second wife was Ida Birgit Banck, born 31 May 1913, with whom they had a daughter, Madeleine Birgitta, Gräfin (Countess) von Mörner, born 3 May 1940; there was a son by his first wife, Dorothy Livingston – Michael Hjelmar Krister, Gräf (Count) von Mörner, born 8 June 1942, who appears to be still living. There was also a Helmer, Count Mörner (1895–1962), born in Uppsala, Sweden, who was an artillery lieutenant and equestrian sportsman who specialised in eventing.

Milmo also wondered whether Ernst was in some way involved with De Deeker (Drueke) and Vera's mission to England in 1940. Ernst and Vera also denied ever having anything to do with one another before the war when she was in London. Interestingly, the author of the MI6 letter to Milmo (Peter Falk in VB1) on 26 September 1942 notes that Ernst Schalburg 'was the subject of an M.I.5 enquiry from Inter Services Research Bureau on 2.8.41'. The Inter-Services Research Bureau was the cover name used by the Special Operations Executive (SOE). MI6 told Milmo that they would ask their representative in Sweden to check him out. This would have been Malcolm Stafford, the Head of Station in Stockholm.[7] As of 15 November 1942 they had not received any information.

4

RECRUITMENT

The date and circumstances of how and when Vera was first recruited as a spy for the Germans, as well as who recruited her, are somewhat confusing and contradictory, and continue to attract elements of fantasy, as witness part of a trilogy of teenage fantasy books by Derek Hart set during 1941–42, in which the 'ravishingly beautiful' Vera (*née* Staritzka) is introduced as having fled the Russian Revolution to Denmark with her family; marrying a certain 'Count Sergei Ignatieff'; being recruited by the German 'Secret Police'; then sent to Britain in 1938 to form 'casual relationships with German agents, German sympathizers, and other influential people'. Then, in 1940, she is sent back to England 'under orders issued directly from Reinhard Heydrich [Deputy Protector of Bohemia and Moravia at that time], where she supposedly sneaks into Scotland Yard during an air raid on London.'[1]

While a few of the facts are fundamentally true – she *was* regarded as beautiful; she *was* given the name Staritzka (her mother's maiden name); she *had* fled the Russian Revolution to Denmark; she *may* or *may not* have been married to someone named Ignatieff; and she *did* live in Brussels for a time – there is no evidence to suggest that she ever received orders from Heydrich or managed to sneak into Scotland Yard! The author must have mistaken Heydrich's first name Reinhard.

An online entry about 'Undiscovered Scotland' also claimed that in 1930 at the age of 17, Vera met Count Sergei Ignatieff, who she married later that year. It further claims that in 1932 she was approached by the British Secret Intelligence Service (SIS or MI6) to spy on White Russians for them.[2] So far, none of my research has been able to confirm either of these statements. Nor is there any reference to this in her MI5 files; however, they have been heavily redacted. If she had been recruited by British Intelligence it would most likely have been by MI6. None of their files have been released to the public, except where copies of some of their documents have appeared in MI5 files, albeit heavily redacted.

The first time Vera became involved with the German Intelligence Service (according to the same 30 October MI5 report referred to in the previous chapter) was through Captain Winding Christensen, a Danish engineer, also known as 'Dr Kaiser' whom she met in Copenhagen in 1940. A report dated 13 November 1940 from G. Sampson of B8l (Camp 020) states that:

The German agent, Curt Karl HANSEN, alias Dr. SCHRADER, alias CHRISTIANSEN [*sic*] who contacted BORRESEN, is presumably identical with Dr. KAISER alias CHRISTIANSEN, mentioned by Vera ERICHSEN as occupying an important position in the German Organization at Hamburg. She said she thought he worked in Denmark. Her description of him is as follows:

Aged about 40 to 45.
Medium height.
Sharp face.
Reddish-blonde hair.
No glasses.
Clean-shaven.
Blue eyes.
Good teeth.

The description tallies with that contained in the BORRESEN file.[3]

However, the date given in the 30 October 1940 report contradicts other information in Christensen's MI5 file.

Gunnar Edvardsen, a Norwegian suspected of being an Abwehr agent, had first met Christensen in Oslo while he was working for *Oslo Illustrierte* as their publicity agent, and later just before he arrived in Scotland on 25 October 1940, at the seaplane base at Sula, near Trondheim. The significance of Edvardsen will become apparent later. An extract of an SIS report in Vera's file that mentions Jørgen Børresen gives the following information about Hansen:

HANSEN Curt Charles
Danish national
Aged 40-45

Stated to be leader of the Danish Nazi party

Uses Hotel Hafnia, Copenhagen

Definite German agent

During the voyage HANSEN had become more and more unpleasant. At the commencement he was most considerate and helpful, but once at sea he was constantly praising the Nazis, and on his being asked if he was the well-known Danish Nazi leader of the name HANSEN, he proudly confessed that this was so. This was, according to TVERMOSE, a great shock to him and his companions.[4]

Unfortunately, the MI5 file on Børresen does not appear to be publicly available from the National Archives at Kew, or has not been released to them.

Vera had apparently written to Christensen for help, although the report does not detail any specifics, but it likely relates to his connection with her brother Christian (see below). She described Christensen as about 45 years of age, average height, blue eyes, red hair, 'hatchet-faced', good teeth, clean-shaven, and thin. It was he who had suggested she should stop working for the Russians and work for the Germans instead. To do this, he put her in touch with Egon Fischer, also known as Feldmann, an Austrian born in Vienna in 1903. This would bear out a list of names Vera gave to MI5. As R.L. Hughes of B3b noted in Christensen's MI5 file in 1946, 'It is interesting to note that before he became interested in hormone research he [Christensen] had the distinction of being the original recruiter of Vera ERIKSSON.'[5] On 23 October 1940 Felix Cowgill wrote to Dick White asking whether he had a full description of Christensen, saying that, 'we have traces of about six men of this name in our records, many of whom are German agents'.[6]

Holger Winding Christensen was born on 22 August 1902 to parents who were school teachers, Johannes Berg Carsten Christensen and Dorthea [sic] Marie Christensen née Winding. Holger had wanted to become an engineer, but instead ended up as a captain in the Danish Army Signals Branch. In October 1923 he was recruited into the 16th Battalion, and the following year became an officer cadet at Kronberg. In 1926 he graduated as a lieutenant into the Corps of Engineers, becoming a captain in 1937. In 1938 he was dismissed surrounding disagreements over Danish rearmament and his being out-of-pocket over research he was conducting into transmitting speech over infrared wavelengths.

While still serving in the Danish Army, in 1937 he recruited Vera Eriksen to work for the German Intelligence Service to spy against Russia. After leaving the Army, in 1939 he was on the staff of Siemens & Halske in Berlin. From 20 July 1941 until 1 January 1942 he was listed as a company commander, an SS-Hauptsturmführer (captain) in the Danish Freecorps under Vera's brother Christian, until the latter was killed on 2 June 1942. A declassified CIA file lists Christensen as an agent of *Ast* Kiel in I-N and one of the Abwehr's chief agents in Brazil from 1941 to 1942.[7] This makes little sense that an SS officer should have been part of the Abwehr, long before the Abwehr was subsumed by the SD in 1944.

By 1943 Christensen was a technician (or purchasing officer) for RSHA *Amt*VI-F 'H' at the Havel Institute, under Department VIIa, the technical section of *Amt*VI.[8] From 1944 to 1945 he was working in Prague engaged on hormone research for Danish scientist Dr Carl (Kjeld) Värnet.[9] Värnet, with Christensen handling the technical aspects, later carried out hormone treatment experiments on homosexuals at Buchenwald that he claimed rendered them 'completely normal, whereafter they have got married and had children'. Christensen's connection with Buchenwald is not mentioned *per se* in his MI5 file, but at the bottom of a letter written by him on 4 October 1945 about his research a typed note states that of the 300 so-called 'volunteers' to which he refers, about half of them were from concentration camps. A handwritten note adds 'ADP to see.' MI5's R.L. Hughes noted on 8 December 1945 that:

> It seems far more likely that CHRISTENSEN was being prepared for a long term post-war career for the German G.I.S. [German Intelligence Service] and that his devotion to endochrinology was to be his cover. There might well be a lesson to be learned from this in connection with the present inflow of German experts to the U.K.[10]

Hughes' comment is interesting as it is an indirect reference to the Allies' plans at the end of the war, such as Operation *Paperclip*, to bring German scientists and technical experts to Britain and the USA to avoid their expertise falling into the hands of the Russians. Some of these missions were carried out by Ian Fleming's 30 Assault Unit and 'T' Force. Hughes went on to describe him on 10 December 1945 as a 'thorough-going Danish traitor now trying to evade the penalties by professing to be a medical research worker. How many "scientists" like him are being brought here under various pretexts?'[11]

When Christensen was approached by German Intelligence to work for them he discussed it with Lieutenant von Schalburg (Vera's brother Christian) 'who as an emigrant Russian at once was fired up ... As Danish military he had twice been on secret journeys to Sovjet [*sic*] for the emigrant Russians

[*indecipherable*] one of the times to Pskov.'[12] Christensen told MI5 that a
year after joining Siemens & Halske, in February 1940 he was instructed
by Kapitänleutnant Karl Robert Johannes (sometimes occurs as Johannes
Robert Carl) Meissner @ Hans @ Peter, at Abwehr headquarters in Berlin at
Tirpitzufer 80 to go to an apartment in Palägade, Copenhagen, where he was
to install some microphones for tapping the telephone of the French military
attaché in the apartment upstairs:

> Two persons were in the apartment at my arrival, viz. a German man called
> WEDEL (naval officer) and a lady, Miss VERA von SCHALBURG a sister
> to the chief of the Freecorps … It is furthermore well-known to me from Lt.
> Capt. von SCHALBURG [*sic*] that his sister shortly after my departure was
> attacked in the apartment in question one night, when she was there alone,
> and she was severely wounded by a stab. It is possible that the installation
> at the same occasion was destroyed, as the culprits are said to have ravaged
> the appartment [*sic*] seriously, Miss von Schalburg was brought to a lazarett
> [hospital] in Flensburg at the request of Mr. Wedel.[13]

This last statement in his file implies that he probably already knew her, most
likely through Vera's brother. Christensen's file provides no details of his putting her in touch with Fischer, only the note saying that he had recruited her
in 1937 and that Fischer had started employing her that same year, thus contradicting the MI5 report. What is curious is why 'Mr Wedel' (Dierks) would have
had her taken to a hospital in Flensburg when they had been in Copenhagen.
Flensburg is nowhere near Copenhagen but conveniently closer to Hamburg
and the *Abwehrstelle*. So was Vera at that time already working for the Abwehr
or did Dierks use his influence as her husband? Unfortunately, this is the extent
of any mention of Vera in Christensen's file. The rest of it contains information
relating to his recruitment; various scientific and medical research that the
Medical Research Council dismissed as '… from the medical point of view are
completely worthless'; and an attempt to come to the UK after the war and
MI5's attempts to prevent him, none of which has any bearing on Vera's case.
    An extract from a report by SNOW (Arthur Owens) based on information
received from Jørgen Børreson states:

> The woman you arrested in 1940 on a charge of espionage is known in some
> quarters as the Doctor's secretary, her name is Miss SHALBURG, she is a sister
> of Count SHALBURG, Commander of the German Viking Division on the
> Eastern Front. [*sic*] He was born in Russia and is now a naturalised Dane.[14]

The Doctor in question is probably Nikolaus Ritter, also known as Dr Rantzau, although there is no evidence to suggest that Vera had ever acted as his secretary; nor was Dierks known as 'The Doctor'. Jørgen Børreson, a Dane, had been captured in Greenland while setting up a meteorological station in the Arctic while pretending to be on a hunting trip.[15]

A note in the 'Monthly Summary of Current Cases at Camp 020 and 020R' dated 1 July 1945 indicates that:

> Hans MEISSNER has had a lengthy Abwehr career. He first came to our notice in connection with the spy Vera ERIKSEN whom he had met in Copenhagen in 1940.[16]

Another document in his files adds to this:

> [In early 1940] Vera ERICHSEN, a German agent who was staying in Hambourg [*sic*] paid a visit to Copenhagen. She met MEISSNER who described himself as a journalist employed by the German Embassy. He told her confidentially that he had orders to spy on her movements.[17]

Hans Meissner was born in Dresden on 20 February 1895 – a declassified CIA report gives the year as about 1893. At Easter 1914 he joined the German Navy as a cadet. By the end of the First World War he was an Oberleutnant zur See (equivalent to a sub-lieutenant in the Royal Navy) and a submarine commander, although it seems somewhat implausible that a junior officer of such a lowly rank would be in charge of a submarine. In September 1933 he was recalled to active service and trained in signals. In 1935 he was recruited by a friend, Freegattenkapitän Ruge of *Ast* Kiel, and posted as III-F and III-L to *Nest* Swinemünde with the rank of Kapitänleutnant (lieutenant). At the suggestion of Colonel Bamler, Chief of Abteilung III, in 1938 he was posted to Berlin as assistant to Oberst (Colonel) Rohleder, *Gruppenleiter* III-F. The CIA report states that at the beginning of the war he was with Abwehr III-F in Berlin.[18] In his MI5 file a progress report on his case, dated 20 June 1945 and mentioning Admiral Canaris, head of the Abwehr, states that, 'MEISNER [*sic*] took every opportunity of travelling to Berlin and on these occasions was always received by the Admiral.' This suggests that if Christensen spoke the truth, then Meissner may have received instructions on the bugging operation in Copenhagen directly from Canaris. Interestingly, in Meissner's file an 'Extract from 12 A.G. [Army Group] on Walter SPECK[19] captured FAT 361 official' mentions that Meissner was a friend of Canaris. If this was indeed the case, it seems strange that none of the biographies of Canaris even mention him.

In March 1940 Meissner was *Gruppenleiter* III in *Ast* Oslo, but a note from WRC1d dated c.18 June 1945 mentions that, 'The earliest trace on MEISSNER whose PAIR[20] cover-name was PETER shows him at Brest on 21.6.40. By the end of that month he was reported as Leiter Ast Oslo.'[21] While in Oslo it is likely he travelled to Copenhagen to meet Vera; however, his file makes no specific mention of the operation or Christensen. He remained in this position from July 1940 until February 1941, when he was posted as *Leiter* of *Ast* Angers, according to MI5 Minute Sheets dated 10 and 11 June 1945. Whilst in Angers he also came into contact with Stella Lonsdale. When Korvettenkapitän Herbert Wichmann, formerly *Leiter* of *Ast* Hamburg, was interrogated by MI5 after the war he only mentions Freegattenkapitän von Bonin as being *Leiter* of *Ast* Angers until 1944.

A confidential CIA report on the interrogation of Oberstleutnant Friederich Dernbach *Leiter* III-F of *Ast* Angers lists Meissner as being *Leiter* from August 1940 to July 1941 and exclusive of III-F.[22] Meissner would spend the latter part of his career from March 1942 onwards in Berne, Switzerland, as *Leiter* KO (Kriegsorganization) succeeding Oberstleutnant Waag.[23] During that time he uncovered unauthorised transactions made by Hans Dohnányi, Major Hans Oster, Canaris, Helmut James Gräf von Moltke, and Dietrich Bonhoeffer to help Jews escape to Switzerland, as well as Hans Bernd Gisevius's contacts with the enemy in Switzerland (i.e. with Allen Dulles's OSS organisation).[24]

Hans Dohnányi (1902–45) was the son of Hungarian composer Ernő Dohnányi. In 1934–38 he was aquainted with Hitler, Goebbels, Himmler and Göring. Recruited to the OKW by Hans Oster just prior to the war, together with Admiral Canaris he became part of the resistance to Hitler. He was arrested by the Gestapo on 5 April 1943 charged with breaches of foreign currency violations, and was later involved in Von Tresckow's plot to assassinate Hitler. In April 1945 he was hanged with piano wire for his part in the July Plot and being the 'spiritual head of the conspiracy against Hitler'. Von Moltke (1907–45) was a German jurist and member of the Abwehr who was a founder-member of the Kreisau Circle resistance group opposed to Hitler. He was executed on 23 January 1945. Dietrich Bonhoeffer (1906–45) was a theologian and founding member of the Confessing Church. He served as a courier for the German resistance, using the Abwehr as his cover. He was hanged on 9 April 1945.

According to Ben Macintyre and Nicholas Booth, Freegattenkapitän Reimar von Bonin was head of the Abwehr in Norway. This was actually

Kapitän zur See Udo (Hugo) Wilhelm Bogislav von Bonin, born in Breslau on 5 November 1894; Reimar was Udo's cousin. From 4 July 1940 until 9 November 1942 he served in I-M *Ast* Paris under Colonel Rudolph. A Top Secret U intercept of 13 June 1940 from *Ast* Hamburg to Abwehr I-M Berlin reports that he was appointed to *Ast* Paris effective that day. From 15 November 1942 to July 1944 he was *Leiter* of *Ast* Oslo, confirmed in a Top Secret U intercept dated 21 November 1942, which stated that, 'I took over duties of LEITER of AST NORWAY on 21.11.42.' In 1943 he would brief Eddie Chapman (Agent ZIGZAG) at his office in Munthessgate in Oslo. Prior to that he was listed as being an officer of III-F in *Ast* Angers as an assistant from May 1942 to March/April 1943 – he is shown as being there in May 1942 according to a Top Secret U intercept of 15 May 1942.[25] However, in the Archives de Nantes there is a report signed by him dated 8 December 1941 regarding the arrest of the Prefect and hostages following the assassination of Lieutenant Colonel Karl Hotz (1877–1941), the Feldkommandant of Nantes, on 20 October 1941 by the French Resistance.[26] In all, forty-eight hostages were shot (some accounts say fifty).[27]

The true identity of Egon Fischer/Feldmann is a puzzle. In a list of names Vera gave to MI5 she claimed she couldn't remember his real name, but said that MI5 already had it and that his name apparently ended with 'mann'. A copy of an interrogation report of Vera dated 30 October 1940 stated that she met Fischer in Amsterdam at one of the large hotels, thought to be the Carlton, in 1936. From 1937, for about eight months, Fischer employed her to work against the Soviet government in Belgium by instructing her first to go to Brussels and get in touch with Vladimir Grigorievitch Orloff. His reason for choosing her was that she was Russian. At this point she began operating under the name Schalburg. Vera described Fischer as being:

> Rather tall, long face, wears a monocle when he goes to Restaurants, hair dark blond, blue eyes, gold tooth in upper front teeth, normal build, normal chin, nose rather long and straight, mouth rather large, turning up at the corners, lips medium, eyebrows and forehead normal. He had a sly smile and he wore a ring with a large stone in it. He was well dressed and usually wore sports clothes. He walked quickly with long strides.[28]

The report also states that she claims she did not know anyone who referred to Fischer as Paulson, nor had she heard of Abas; she had, however, heard of Hans Luders, who she believed was associated with Hansen in Hamburg. Rodney Dennys of MI6's VB3 (the section dealing with France, Corsica, Andorra and the Benelux countries – Belgium, the Netherlands, Luxembourg) wrote to Dick White on 21 October 1940, stating:

I enclose 2 copies of a report Graham and I have concocted from our archives on various contacts of Vera SCHALBURG which throws a most interesting light on the whole case. It also gives us definite lines on to the Hamburg organization running the spies sent to this country recently.

I feel it might well repay you to check up again on all contacts of ABAS in the U.K. as he seems to be a much more important German agent than I thought, when I first made investigations about him in Holland.

It is a very long shot but it occurred to us that TEMSCHE may possibly be de DEEKER. Do you think this worth trying?

There seems a possibility that the RANTZAU alias HANSEN, alias RITTER, mentioned by you in your interrogation of Vera may be LUDERS alias LORENZ alias PAULSEN etc. Both seem to have a positive passion for pseudonyms, their methods seem similar and they both work from Hamburg, while HANSEN and LUDERS both appear to be leaders of the Hamburg Stelle. This is a very tentative suggestion but you may care to turn it over in your mind.

I am making further investigations into the whole Hamburg show and will let you know the results as soon as I can.[29]

The report to which Dennys refers also confirms that Abas was von Stuhreck's chief agent in the Netherlands; Dr Harry Luders @ Lorenz @ Egon Paulsen worked from Spaldingstraße 4, Hamburg, and was regarded as being 'a most important member of the German S.S.'. The report also mentioned a Max Richard Augner who was being run by Luders against the UK. At first, Luders and von Stuhreck were thought to be identical, but Luders was later identified as being Hans Lips of I-H *Ast* Hamburg. A diagram of the organisation is shown in Figure 2.

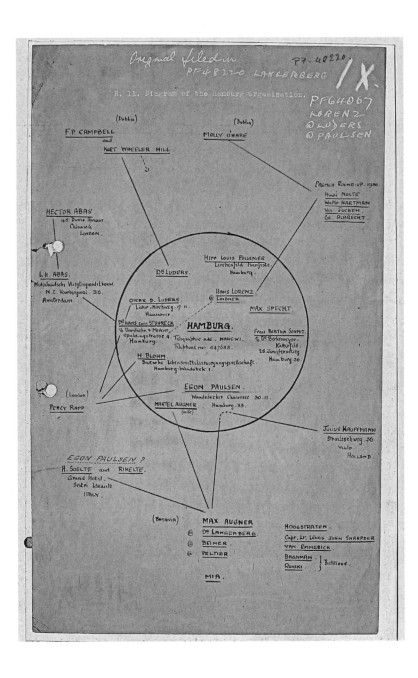

B. 11. Diagram of the Hamburg Organisation.

According to Etienne Verhoyen (and roughly translated from the Dutch), Hauptmann Hans Lips was also known as either Oskar Hans Luders, Luders, Hans Lutz, Hans or Dr Lorenz.[30] A report, 'Officials of IH Ast Hamburg' dated 28 February 1946 in Lips' MI5 file, states that he was *Leiter* of I H Hamburg until 1939, assisted from 1937 by Sonderführer Ernst Moll. Moll was also known as Hans Lorenz or Lorentz, Dr Oscar Luders or Dr Hans Luders, Egon Paulsen, Lindner, and Max Specht.[31] The name 'Egon Paulsen' was attributed to both Lips and Angestelter (civil servant) Moll. Just to confuse things even more, there was also a real A.K.F. Paulsen, as well as a fictitious import-export company 'Egon Paulsen, Wansbeckerchausee 30', which was used by, or the actual address of, a Frau Nohl, one of the mailing addresses of *Ast* Hamburg. A document mentioning Hans Lips included in Vera's file also appears in his file and was referred to earlier.[32] This information was also corroborated by Kapitän zur See Herbert Wichmann, *Leiter* of *Ast* Hamburg, when he was interrogated at Camp 020 in 1945. Further information on Moll was provided in a report to WARREC (War Records) from Brigadier A.L. Grant, who was head of the Intelligence Bureau, CCG (BE), Bad Oeynhausen, BAOR, dated 8 April 1946:

Ernst MOLL, interned in No.6 Civilian Internment Camp [the former Neuengamme concentration camp] has been interrogated on the points mentioned in your letter, with the following result:

MOLL, Ernst was an employee of Ast X [Hamburg] Dept. I H from 37 to Aug 40. He was then appointed Sonderfuehrer in the same Dept, until he left for Nest BOULOGNE in Nov 41.
Whilst employed at Ast HAMBURG, MOLL used the cover name of PAULSEN, Egen. He claims that this was his only alias.
Chief of Dept. I.H. until May 1939 was Hptm. LIPS.
This man had various cover names. MOLL remembers the following:

Dr. LUDERS, H.
Dr. LUTZ, H.
Dr. LORENZ or LORENTZ, H.

MOLL believes that the initial 'H' stood for Hans.

SPECHT, Max, was a Coffee Export Merchant in HAMBURG, Esplanade opposite the Bar of the Hotel Esplanade. This man received letters from a

V Man [*sic*] in BATAVIA whose name was Max AUGNER. He then forwarded them to Ast HAMBURG.

MOLL does not know anyone by the name of LINDNER.[33]

Lindner, according to Ritter's MI5 file was:

A German from BREMEN; was paymaster in the NDL liner BREMEN
and was recruited by prisoner [Ritter] during summer 37 to act as a link
with the agent DUQUESNE in NEW YORK, collecting his reports and
delivering to him all new orders from I L HAMBURG; he served no other
agent or Dienstellen and did not engage in direct espionage. No special
arrangements were made to cover his activities and no one serving in the
liner was aware of his extra-professional activity.[34]

Max Richard Augner was born in Erfurt, Germany, in 1891. In 1922 he first
went to Batavia in the Dutch East Indies to work as a cook at a restaurant in
Surabaya. Prior to 1938 he had returned to Germany and joined the Nazi
Party, becoming a *Zellenleiter* (cell leader) in Hamburg. Early in 1938 he met
Dr Luders, who recruited him as an agent of the *Nachrichten Dienst* (military
intelligence) and in March sent him back to Batavia 'to report on British
troop movements', shipping, and trade of interest to Germany.[35] He arrived
in Batavia in March 1938, where he worked under the cover of various front
companies and visited Penang, Singapore and Kuala Lumpur. He was arrested
on 9 December 1938 in possession of correspondence relating to his espionage activities.

Leo Harry Abas, described as being a Dutch half-Jew, was born in
Hamburg on 16 July 1905, the son of Samson Jacob Abas and Fredrika
Johanna Busch. He married Sara Huner (b. Berlin, 1904) on 17 September
1937; however, a website dedicated to Abas states that his wife was Sophie
Wiener (1908–42).[36] He had two siblings, Ilse Constance Abas and Frauke
Elizabeth Abas. The London edition of *Het Contra Signal* in 1940 lists his
address as Michelangelostraat 13, Amsterdam. Leopold Harry Abas was listed
as Dierks's head agent in the Netherlands (Agent RR 3076) working under
the cover of manager of Nederlandsche Vliegtuigmodelbouw (Dutch Model
Aircraft), Keizergracht 316, Amsterdam, according to an MI5 report on
Dierks dated 19 December 1940.[37] Vera denied ever knowing anyone of that
name, but this information is also confirmed in Rodney Dennys's report:
'Abas worked against the U.K. through the cover firm of Nederlandsche

Vliegtuigmodelbouw, N.Z. Voorburgwal 316, Amsterdam C. His private address was Weeperstraat 811, Amsterdam.'

Abas was arrested by the police in Bourtange, a village in the Westerwolde region of the Netherlands near the German border, on the night of 26/27 February 1940. The arrest was recorded in the *Politieke Recherche Afdeling* (Political Bureau of Investigation) of the Amsterdam police. In his possession the police found a wireless receiver, which was thought to be part of a plan by *Ast* Hamburg to set up wireless operators in Belgium and the Netherlands. It was claimed that Abas was to be Heinkel's representative in the Netherlands and that the address at Michelangelostraat 13 was to be the headquarters of Heinkel Nederland. Nederlandsche Vliegtuigmodelbouw was known to be 'a cover under which the German secret service is organizing a bureau in Holland for transmitting information obtained in the UK concerning Air Defence'.[38] His alleged spying activities had been reported to the British consul in Amsterdam by his assistant. He would also come into contact with Heinrich Walti, alias Robert Petter, of whom we shall learn more in the coming chapters.

Whatever his involvement with espionage at that time, Abas appears to have been released because on 25 September 1941 a certain Karel Christiaan Wessel Hagemeijer, born in The Hague on 30 September 1884, whose profession was given as legal consultant, and living at 55hs Bosboom Toussaintstreet, was called into the police station on suspicion of embezzling fl.100 and insults, accused by Leo Harrij Abas [*sic*], a 36-year-old 'representative' (presumably for Heinkel), living at 13hs Michelangelostraat, Amsterdam. Hagemeijer, the son of Jan Hagemeijer (b.1852), a plasterer, and Jeannette Hagemeijer (*née* Marks) (1845–1922), and brother of Hendrik Hagemeijer (born *c.*1878), was sent away after interrogation due to nothing objectionable being found.[39] Abas is later listed in a register for Buchenwald concentration camp (Prisoner No. 29963) dated 1 February 1944 as part of a new intake of prisoners.[40] However, he allegedly died in Sobibór extermination camp, Poland, although the date is unknown.

Vera's list states that 'Fischer' worked in Holland, Belgium and Switzerland. She also told Major Stephens and Dick White during her interrogation at Latchmere House (Camp 020) on 4 October 1940 that Fischer was immediately subordinate to Rantzau. This means he must have worked for the Abwehr in *Ast* Hamburg.

The only 'Fischer' who appears to at least have had links to Hamburg and the most likely candidate is undoubtedly Hauptmann (Captain) Adolf von Feldmann in III-F of *Gruppe* III for the same period, which also agrees with

Vera's recollection of the name ending with 'mann'. His MI5 file states that on 1 October 1935 he took up duties at *Ast* Hamburg as OC *Referat* III-F.[41] In the late summer of 1938 he was posted to III-C and tasked with vetting a 'Dr Orloff', nationality Russian, who was a *Staatsrat* (state counsellor) in Brussels. Whether this is the same Orloff referred to below has not yet been ascertained, but seems likely. The spring 1939 organisational chart for *Ast* Hamburg shows Feldmann as an Oberleutnant (senior lieutenant); later in the document he is shown as having been with *Ast* Hamburg in 1939–44; as of 1945 he is listed as a major.[42]

Feldmann told MI5 in statements made at CSDIC on 6, 11 and 14 September 1945 that, 'Unsuccessful efforts were made to solve this case. Gruppe I of AST Hamburg put the agent VERA VON SCHALBURG, a Dane, temporarily at our disposal.'[43] According to his file, he was suspended from duty in September 1939 and court-martialled 'over something which had happened many years back', then replaced by Hauptmann Giskes. What this something was he doesn't explain. At this time Vera had not met Baron de Graevenitz,[44] Richard Walter, Arthur Emile Bay,[45] or Wellak, a White Russian believed to be living in Antwerp. In Brussels, Fischer required her to report to him twice in three months. However, he gave her no contact address, saying that if he needed to contact her he would write. The last time she saw him was in 1938 at the Hotel Reichshof in Hamburg where she was accompanied by Zum Stuhrig, who she claimed was now her husband.

Vladimir Grigor'evich Orlov (Orloff), not to be confused with Alexander Mikhailovich Orlov (1895–1973), described as the Russian 'Ace of Spies', was a Tartar born in Riazan, Russia, on 7 April 1882 to a 'family of intelligensia'.[46] A heavily redacted CX report from Felix Cowgill, head of Section V of MI6, to Dick White, dated 21 October 1940, gives his birthplace as 'in the province of Grovno'. A report from B4b to Dick White dated 17 October 1940 stated, 'In 1925 or thereabouts he was regarded with grave suspicion by S.I.S. as an "agent provocateur".' His name has also been erroneously connected with the Zinoviev Letter in 1924, a document purporting to be a directive from the Comintern (Communist International), published on 25 October 1924 by the *Daily Mail* four days before the General Election, which caused the fall of Britain's first Labour government under Ramsay MacDonald.

Vladimir Orlov operated at the same time as Britain's so-called 'Ace of Spies', Sydney Reilly, with whom he liaised, and was an old school friend of Boris Savinkov, whose involvement in 'The Trust' would bring about Reilly's eventual downfall and death. He had intended to become an Orthodox monk but, having abandoned that career, had entered the *Okhrana*, the Tsarist secret police, later the Petrograd (now St Petersburg) *Cheka*, both forerunners of the KGB and today's FSB, but was discovered to be a White Russian spy and forced to flee to Odessa in the Ukraine. There he worked for Lieutenant General Anton Ivanovic Denikin, formerly of the Imperial Russian Army and later one of the principal generals in the civil war that followed the Russian Revolution, in the intelligence department of the Armed Forces of South Russia.

In 1920 Orlov went to Riga to monitor the peace negotiations between South Russia and Poland. From 1921 to 1926 he was on the staff of Baron Pyotr Nikolaevitch Wrangel's (intelligence) 'Committee' in Berlin. Wrangel was the commanding general for the White Russian forces in South Russia. Convicted of forging documents in Germany in 1929, Orlov was expelled from the country and settled in Belgium in 1931. Wim Coudenys's article on Orlov states that he had been sent there on the orders of Vladimir L'vovich Burtsev (1862–1942). In Belgium, he became involved with the Ordre de Pierre le Grand, 'an obscure, quasi-fascist organization that, according to a police report, had set as its goal "the active struggle against the Soviet regime and Communism in all its forms"'.[47] It was also a cover for the Anti-GPU. Orlov also became involved with CILACC – the Centre international de Lutte active contre le Communisme. However, Coudenys does not mention Orlov's recruitment of Vera. Orlov would die under mysterious circumstances in Berlin in 1941 – he was shot in the Tiergarten on 12 January 1941 'by a person (or persons) unknown'. A CX report from MI6 written to Dick White dated 31 October 1940 sheds more light on Orlov's career and family:

We have received a report from one of our officers to the following effect:-
ORLOV is known to us as having been in contact with the following German S.S. agents:-

(a) Baron Von PILKVITZ (Antwerp)
(b) Arthur BAI (Brussels)
(c) Von BAUCHER (? RAUSCHER or RAUFER) (Germany)[48]
(d) Col. FLEISCHAUER (Editor of 'World Thought')[49]
(e) Many members of Russian émigré organizations connected with General TURKUL (Yugoslavia).[50]

ORLOV, it is said, now works conscientiously for the Germans owing to his fear of sharing the fate of his German friend Alexander GUMANSKI [*sic*],[51] who was killed by the Gestapo. He enjoys the confidence of the Germans, as they (Col. FLEISCHAUER) consider him to be an ideological fighter against world Jewry, and to a certain extent a victim of the latter. (The trial of ORLOV in Berlin and his confinement in prison are regarded as having been provoked by the American journalist Knickerbocker).[52]

Further information on Orlov is provided in Nigel West and Oleg Tsarev's *The Crown Jewels*.[53]

The von Baucher to whom the report was referring could be *Geheimrat* Hermann Bücher, a member of the Armaments Council and chairman of the board of AEG Berlin. Born in 1882, he was a prominent industrialist and later a member of the German Foreign Office. From 1925 he was an economic adviser to IG Farben, the company that would later produce Zyklon-B gas used in the extermination of the Jews and others. He died in 1951. I have been unable to find any information on Baron von Pilkvitz or Arthur Bai.

Felix Cowgill's MI6 report of 21 October also states that Orlov was married to Margarita Radomirova. They had two children, a son thought to have been named Vladimir who worked in a bank, and a daughter Nina married either to an Englishman or a Russian. The MI6 report states that in 1920 his wife and children were evacuated from the Crimea to a concentration camp in Egypt. From there they came to England. There is a Home Office Traffic Index record of a Nina Orlov departing from Bergen, Norway, and arriving at the port of Newcastle on 12 October 1939; her UK address was given as 28 Parliament Court, Parliament Hill, London, NW3. As Dick White noted in a letter to Felix Cowgill on 19 November 1940, 'As however, you say Nina ORLOV is married, it seems improbable that the two are identical.'[54] No information is available on the others. Vera's own description of Orlov given to Captain Robin Stephens [*sic*] at Camp 020 (Latchmere House) on 1 October 1940, shortly after her arrest was, 'Age about 60; goatee beard; heavy build; believed to have been a Public Prosecutor in Russia; living in Brussels at 50, Rue Marie Henriette; profession, journalism.' Erikson was told that she might have to follow him to Switzerland.[55]

A document in her file dated 2 March 1942 states that:

I hear from Sabby, that Orloff [*sic*] had close connections with Mrs. Harold Williams, (Tyrkova) here. He used to inform her on Soviet activities. His daughter, now married to Roman Zagowsky, Evesham, as reported, was a frequent guest of Mrs. Harold Williams.[56]

Mrs Harold Williams (Tyrkova) was Ariadna Vladimirovna Tyrkova-Williams, born in St Petersburg on 13 November 1869 (the Library of Congress gives it as 26 November) and died in Washington, DC, on 12 January 1962. She was married to Harold Williams (1876–1928), a New Zealand journalist and polyglot reputed to speak fifty-eight languages and later foreign editor of *The Times*, whom she had met in Stuttgart in about 1903. On 17 March 1917, she was elected to the Petrograd Committee of the Kadet Party and the Petrograd Duma. After the Constituent Assembly, which she ran, was dissolved, she organised anti-Bolshevik resistance in southern Russia. After General Denikin was defeated in late 1919 she returned to Britain in 1920. She became a founder of the Russian Liberation Committee and the author of a biography of Alexander Pushkin. The daughter referred to was Sophia Alfredovna Borman Botcharsky (1896–1982), a Russian nurse on the Eastern Front during the First World War.

While in Brussels Vera mixed with the Russian emigré community in various cafés trying to secure a meeting with Orlov. However, they warned her not to meet with him as they regarded him as a 'bad lot'. When she did finally manage to meet him he was living first at 18, rue Marie Henriette, then on the rue Verri. However, she failed to establish with any certainty whether he was really working for the Germans, the British or the Soviets. Either way, she thought he was a double-crosser. She also got the impression that Kraus, the man working with Orlov, who was half-Italian, half-Austrian, was actually his employer and not the other way round. This she inferred from an altercation the two men had had over some documents that Orlov had not made ready for him. She had overheard Kraus say that he was sending Orlov abroad, probably to England.

Alfred Ignatz Maria Kraus, sometimes referred to as 'Freddy' or 'Freddie', was born in Sarajevo on 28 November 1908, of German, originally Austrian, nationality, and undoubtedly the same man whom Eddie Chapman (Agent ZIGZAG) met at the Paris *Dienststelle* and described as 'slightly built and effeminate so Eddie surmised that he was homosexual', as well as 'sinister'.[57] This is confirmed in Ben MacIntyre's book *Agent Zigzag*:

> Chapman had been allocated a new 'shadow', in the shape of a young, slightly built man from the Lutétia[58] known as Kraus, or Krausner. Von Grönig warned Chapman that Kraus, a homosexual who frequented the Paris underworld, had a reputation as a spycatcher and had trapped more enemy agents than anyone else in German counter-espionage …[59]

In Paris in October 1941 Kraus married Princess Jacqueline Marguerite *née* de Broglie (1918–1965), the daughter of Prince Jean de Broglie and novelist, poet and magazine editor, the Honourable Daisy Fellowes (1890–1962) *née* Marguerite Séverine Philippine Decazes de Glücksberg, who was also involved in espionage with Comtesse Colette 'Coco' de Dampierre, *née* Colette Cahen d'Anvers (1911-69), who married Armand de Dampierre (1902–44) on 5 July 1933. Together they had a daughter, Sophie Charlotte, born 25 June 1936. According to an account in Kraus's MI5 file,[60] the Comtesse, being a Jewess (described in her family tree as an honorary Aryan), was later arrested on 19 December 1941 following the round-up of agents involved with the *Interallié* network and interrogated at the Hôtel Eduard VII. The Comtesse's involvement with Kraus was also connected to the break-up of the *Interallié* network in Paris.

Unfortunately, Kraus's MI5 files are such poor-quality faded photocopies that it is extremely difficult to discern very much useful information from them. Those that are semi-legible record that he visited the UK, arriving at Harwich on 26 March 1938 and staying until 23 September 1938, ostensibly as a commercial traveller representing Siemens. On 18 March 1939 he attempted to re-enter the UK at Folkestone but was refused entry by F.J. Ralfe, H.M. Chief Inspector Immigration Branch. This refusal was brought to the attention of the German ambassador to Britain, Herbert von Dirksen, who went to bat for him on his behalf, but it cut no ice with British authorities. As Colonel Edward Hinchley Cooke reported in his file in 1944:

> The exact nature of KRAUS' [*sic*] activities since the outbreak of war has not yet been fully ascertained but it is known both from his own statements and other sources that at least during the second half of the year 1941 he was employed in Paris by Abteilung III F of Abwehr (the C.E. [Counter-Espionage] section of the German Intelligence Service) and that he played an important part in the penetration and breakup of an extremely valuable Allied Intelligence organization in France.[61]

This 'Allied Intelligence organization' was the *Interallié* network. Mathilde Carré, who was an important member of the network, described Kraus as a 'small employee of the Gestapo'. Kraus is listed in an MI5 file on Herman Giskes – 'Appendix to Personnel of FAK 307' – as being 'Hptm Dr. Grosse @ Dr. Krause. 1939-43 in various Referats with Abwehr Abtg I [Abteilung I], Berlin with Oberst ROHLEDER, as reserve officer'.[62]

Vera must have met Kraus, and therefore Orlov, after 1937. A CX report from MI6 sent to Guy Liddell, Director 'B' Branch at MI5, dated 18 March

1937 reported that a source who had served in the Spanish Civil War that year had found himself sharing a cell in Pamplona with, 'an Austrian Nazi, one Alfred KRAUS of Freudgasse 7/8, Vienna, aged about 31 … employed as a commercial traveler for an Austrian or German firm in Pamplona'. That firm must have been Siemens & Halske; the prison in Pamplona would have been the Castillo (Fort) San Cristóbal, where many Republican prisoners were held.

In 1937, while in Brussels and anxious to return to Denmark, Vera met Hans von Wedel, also known as Zum Stuhrig, through her brother Christian. She had discovered that she was on the Germans' Black List because of her work for the Russians, so enlisted her brother's help (referred to in the anonymous report as 'step-brother') in getting Dr Rantzau interested in her situation. According to a Danish website, it was through Holger Winding Christensen that Vera was introduced to Dr Rantzau. Christensen had introduced her to 'Hans Luders' alias Hauptmann Hans Lips of 1H *Ast* Hamburg[63] who in turn introduced her to Rantzau.[64] Dr Rantzau was, in fact, Nikolaus Ritter of the Abwehr. Ritter saw this as an opportunity to use Vera as a penetration agent of the Russian Secret Service, so he spoke to his agent, von Wedel. However, the anonymous report stated that nothing very much materialised as Vera's only connection with the Russian Secret Service was through Ignatieff and describes her as 'only very minor fry'.

Zum Stuhrig had been a German spy for much of his life, having worked part of the time for German Naval Intelligence during the First World War in England, where he had been arrested. The Dutch had also arrested him in June/July 1915 for his espionage activities in The Hague. Among the agents he recruited were:

Cornelius Marinus den Braber, a Dutch seaman arrested in Britain in 1915, but released for lack of evidence;

Dr Brandt, a German with a PhD in economics who recruited agents for IIIb up to December 1914 and 'N' (German Naval Intelligence);

Louise Emily Wertheim, a Polish-German (also known as Lizzie Klitzke), married to Bruno Wertheim, in 1914, and Jacob Dirkswager in 1915;

Jan van Brandwijk, a Dutch casual labourer @ Agent A51, who may have exposed Dierks;

Fernando Bushman or Ferdinand Buschmann, a Brazilian of German origin who travelled to England in April 1915, was arrested in June, and executed in October;

Heinrich Flores @ Agent 68, a German language teacher in Rotterdam;

Hockenholz, a skipper used to recruit Dutch seamen, including van Zwol; arrested in June 1915 with Dierks;

Haicke Marinus Petrus Jannsen (1885-1915), trained by Dierks and sent to England in 1915, where he was arrested, court-martialled and executed;

Kerstein, a resident of Rotterdam who acted as a cover address (Kerstein Co.) for Paul Daelen;

Klancke, naval agent recruited by Dierks;

Ernest Waldemar Welin, a Swede, sent to England in 1915, who was arrested, court-martialled and executed; and

Willem Johannes Roos (1882-1915), a Dutchman, who was sent to England, arrested and executed, even though he was certified insane.[65]

A summary of his career (no date) prepared by MI6 has been heavily redacted. It reported that, according to Most Secret Sources (ISK decrypt) in June 1940, he had been promoted to Oberleutnant and stationed in Antwerp. A note appended at the bottom adds:

> Vera says zum Stuhreck [sic] also worked at Antwerp, so it seems reasonable to deduce that there was some connection, apart from the fact that both zum Stuhreck and Dierks are reported to be in contact with ABAS.[66]

To Vera he was variously known as Hans Zum Stuhrig, Dierks Zum Stuhrig or Freiherr von Wedel, as well as Oberleutnant Dierks, although he was also referred to as Major. Some of his other aliases were J. Van Dongen, Müller, von Savigny, and Sanders. 'Van Dongen' was, according to Rodney Dennys at MI6, a code name to be used in an emergency to contact Dierks:

> You will remember that Vera stated that an alias used by DIERKS was van DONGEN. I have had our archives searched and find that a certain Carolus Napoleon Jules LEON stated in January of this year that 'dr. Richter told me ... in exceptionally urgent cases I could telephone to Hamburg either 24685 or 525545 and ask for Herr von DONGEN. The name was a sort of password for the telephone girl, because an ordinary mortal got no answer from these numbers ... In future all letters must be written in duplicate and one copy sent to J. van DONGEN, 84 An der Alster, Hamburg and the other to Peter P. PETERSEN, 26 bis Absolongsgarde, Copenhagen, V. This was in case one of the copies should fail to arrive.' From time to time van DONGEN sent him instructions.[67]

An extract in Vera's file from *Wer ist's?* (*Who's Who?*) of 1935 lists two scions of the von Wedel family, but no mention of a Hilmar or Hans.[68] So had he 'borrowed' that name?

Carolus Napoleon Jules Leon, born on 6 November 1884, is listed in population census records for 1913 as living in The Hague, where on 17 October 1934 he married Helena Henrica Ploegmakers (b. 24 July 1898 in Oss and resident of Megen). His profession, given on the marriage certificate as 'handelsvertegenwoordiger' is variously translated as trade representative, commercial agent or sales representative. Exactly who he worked for is unknown, but possibly one of Zum Stuhrig's front companies.

When Vera knew him, Zum Stuhrig had worked briefly in the Netherlands and also had offices in Hamburg at Papenhudenstraße 1; Rothenbaumschaussee 83; Heimhuderstrasse 18; and An der Alster 84. The address at Papenhudenstraße 1 was a boarding house owned by Frau Freese, a family friend of Zum Stuhrig. This was confirmed by the Belgian Sûreté d'État in 1940. Later when she was in England, Vera would write to him at an accommodation address in Amsterdam, c/o Fraulein Sofia Krause, Prinzengraat [*sic*], the number of which she could not remember but thought it was probably around 1,000. An MI6 CX report dated 22 October 1940 mentions an address at Prinsengracht 749, which is most likely the one to which Vera referred. The building is now listed as a national monument because of its halsgevel (neck gable) dated 1701. Kraus's cover was that of an export firm connected with a Richard Gould. This may have been the address in Spaldingstraße 4, given as Reinhold & Co, a known cover address of *Ast* Hamburg, the Hamburg office of the Abwehr.

Hilmar Dierks, as he was also known, established a safe house in The Hague at a boarding house run by Hanne/Hanna Fiehne at 1st de Riemerstraat 24 to which Vera would go after a visit to England in 1939. In Appendix I of a report in the MI5 file on Werner Unversagt, she is listed as MARGOT or Hanna Fiene:

Known slightly to UNVERSAGT. A cleaning woman or housekeeper run by KRAZER. First seen in the Spring of 1944 in Paris at the house in the rue Copernic [in the 16th arrondissment] which was used by officers of Group I, Brussels, and their drivers. MARGOT could obtain extra parcels of food. Last heard of as having been ill and sent back to Germany.[69]

Ritter's MI5 file mentions 'Hanny Fiehne' of Riemenstraat, 24, The Hague:

An old cover-address and rendezvous used by the late Htpm DIERKS (I H HAMBURG) and 'lent' to Prisoner [Ritter] at the outset of his Abw career, when he had no connections of any kind. Prisoner used her sparingly, giving the address to only one agent: ODENWALD, at AERDENHOUT (HOLLAND). He met her in 1940, when she was working for Kap Lt BENDIXEN (I M) at ANTWERP.[70]

Whatever her real name, she was employed by *Ast* The Hague, then later by *Ast* Brussels as a *Forscher* (talent spotter).[71] According to Kluiters and Verhoyen she was later moved to Paris, where she ran a boarding house for their agents being sent to England, under the name Margot Pertnini.[72] In Paris she lived at the Maison Pax, 52, rue Copernic, which was also the address of the Paris *Aussenstelle*, as listed in Werner Unversagt's MI5 file. In 1944 she was sent to Wiesbaden as an agent of FAK 130.[73] She is likely the MARGOT referred to above and listed as an agent of Major Karl Krazer (also known as Rudolf, his other Christian name and spelled Kratzer in his MI5 file) who worked for *Ast* Brussels, later in 1942 as Leiter (chief) Gruppe I.[74] Curiously, she is not listed in his MI5 file.

Odenwald was a German who was a representative of Krupps, Essen, in Aerdenhout introduced to Ritter by his cousin, Dr Ernst Ritter, in The Hague in 1937. Odenwald's mission as a *Forscher* (talent spotter) was to keep an eye out for prospective recruits during his frequent visits to England. However, he was a complete failure and was dropped in 1938. Thorwald Hans Bendixen @ Bertrand @ Bertram @ Dias was I-M2 under Erich Pfeiffer at *Nest* Bremen, later posted to Antwerp. In late 1942 he was sent to KO Portugal as *Leiter* I-M until late 1944 and then became Chief of a FAT in Denmark.

Kratzer was also known as Onkel Carl (Uncle Carl) or Dr Kruger. His agent, Leutnant Werner Alfred Waldemaar von Janowsky (also spelled Janowski) @ BOBBY (or Bobbi), late of the Brandenburg Regiment, was sent on a mission to Canada, code-named 'Watchdog' by the RCMP and dates back to 9 November 1942 when he landed in Canada; later they ran him as a double agent.[75]

After the invasion of the Netherlands in May 1940 Zum Stuhrig set up yet another office in Antwerp at 24 rue de l'Étoile (Sternsgrat). Some of these addresses are confirmed in a document prepared by Rodney Dennys of MI6's VB3 dated 16 October 1940:

1. Dr. Hans Zum STUHRECK was reported in Sept. 1938 by a most suspect source to be working L.H. ABAS, who was said to be his chief agent for Holland. Dr. Zum STUHRECK was reported to work from the cover address DAVIDSOHN & MERCIER Spaldingstrasse 4, Hamburg. It will be noted that this is also the address of Dr. Harry LUDERS @

LORENZ @ Egon PAULSEN etc. STUHRECK also has an address at Papendrectstrasse, Hamburg.[76]

What comes as a surprise is that Vera was unable to tell her interrogators at MI5 the location of the registry office where they had allegedly got married in Hamburg in October 1937. Nor did she know Dierks's exact age, which she thought was between 53 and 55. She put this down to his telling her not to be too inquisitive. All he would tell her is that he had worked for the German Secret Service during the First World War. She finally admitted that perhaps they had never really been married. This seems a likely explanation as it is most unusual not to remember such a key fact as where one got married! That the marriage was unusual had also been noted by the author of the anonymous report:

> There is something strange about this marriage, and it would appear that VON WEDEL in view of Vera's non-Aryan blood rendered himself guilty of race 'pollution', and thereafter was at pains to keep Vera in the background. She did, however, accompany him on his travels, but no attempt was ever made to set up a home. Attempts were made to employ Vera against the 'Reds', but they met with no success.[77]

That there was 'something strange' about their marriage was also remarked upon in a report prepared by U.35 (Klop Ustinov), who tells of how von Wedel was regarded as the 'black sheep' of his family, a family Vera had never met, and ventures that:

> This may explain the strange marriage of Hans Friedrich von Wedel, Intelligence officer of the Third Reich to Vera Ignatieff, Soviet agent. Wedel, no more from the top drawer, some 27 years older than the attractive Russian girl, may have felt that he is not the loser in this match. It must moreover not be forgotten that Vera through her step brothers, the Schalbourgs, had good contacts with the German and Danish nobility, and if Wedel did attach any importance to social standing and breeding, Vera was at least his match.[78]

Ustinov went on to say that at the time of their marriage von Wedel must have been in love with her. He had even faked the questionnaire that Vera had to complete before they were married, so as to prove her 'arian' [sic] descent. Klop posed the question, 'If you know nothing about your parents, let alone your grand parents [sic], how could you satisfy the German authorities on this point of 'arian' descent?' To which Vera replied, 'Wedel filled the dates in for me. I do not know what he wrote,' adding, 'These officers of the Geheimedienst can do that sort of thing, just as they can arrange for illegal operations, forbidden to other people under heavy penalties.' Klop opined that perhaps the reason for Vera's marriage to von Wedel might have been caused by her being pregnant by him, adding wryly, 'Germans sometimes suffer from sudden attacks of decency.' He was convinced that their affair had begun when they were both in Brussels.[79]

The date of Vera's marriage to Zum Stuhrig is also disputed by John Day of B1b. In his report of 21 May 1942 he stated:

It will be seen that SCHALBURG [Ernst Schalburg, Vera's uncle] is quite sure that Vera's marriage, which is clearly that with von WEDEL [Zum Stuhrig/Dierks] took place after the outbreak of war and not before, at a time when she was living in Brussels.[80]

The truth is, as Klop surmised and as we shall see later, Vera was pregnant when she returned to the UK but the father of her unborn child was apparently not her so-called husband.

VERA AND THE DUCHESSE

Clues to Vera's life in London before the war can be found in the files and interrogations of the Duchesse de Château-Thierry by Maxwell Knight of MI5's B5b, as well as the interrogations of the Duchesse's daughter, Anne Valeska Uhlig. The only information relating to Uhlig can be found in the Duchesse's and Vera's MI5 files, and Uhlig's Home Office file, which tends to focus on her internment.[1] If there are any MI5 files on Uhlig they are currently not available.

The Duchesse was born in Nijmegen in the Netherlands on 16 March 1877 of Dutch parents. Her maiden name was Anna Sonia Salamonska – her father was A. Salamonski, of Polish extraction, her mother's name Lichenski. It has also been suggested that she was of Jewish extraction.[2] She was first married to Kurt (Curt) Oscar Uhlig, who was involved in insurance and first came to Britain in 1896, where she gave birth to a son, Richard, and a daughter, Ann Valeska Uhlig, at 23 St John's Wood Road on 21 November 1898. Her daughter died in Sutton, Greater London, in December 1973. In 1916 the couple divorced, with Kurt Uhlig citing Léon Armand Joseph de Rais-Bouillon, Duc de Château-Thierry, pretender to the French throne, as co-respondent.[3] From 1905 to 1915 a Madame Lucie Van Spoor (later also known as Jeanne Anthonis and Jeanne Guliano) had been living with the Duc, but the Duc left her as she continually made a nuisance of herself. On 2 September 1914 she was bound over and later arrested for trying to force her way into his flat.

On 27 July 1916 the Duc married Anna Sonia Salamonska. At that time he was living at 40 Buckingham Gate, SW; Anna's address was given as Chiselhurst, Kent. The Duc was, however, issued with a Deportation Order in 1916 having refused to serve in the French Army. Eventually the Order was quashed since he claimed to be a political refugee in Britain. He died in June 1936, having filed a petition for bankruptcy in 1924.[4]

The Duchesse lived at a variety of addresses in London – prior to 1937 she lived at 46 Chiltern Court, Baker Street, NW1 – and from January 1939 at 102 Dorset House, NW1, after she had returned from Switzerland. Her various residences for the period covered in this book are listed in Figure 3 below:

Figure 3

Date	Address
2.11.1916	32, Lower Belgrave Street SW
28.2.1924	41, Chester Square, SW1
17.3.1924	Flat 50, Westminster Palace Gardens (Artillery Row), SW1
20.5.1924	51, Cleveland Square, Lancaster Gate, W2
22.10.1924	41, Leinster Gardens, Bayswater, W2
28.11.1924	1, Cornwall Terrace, Regent's Park, NW1 (Note: the house sold for a record £80m in 2013)
31.1.1928	22, South Street, Mayfair, W1
30.7.1928	2, Granville Chambers, W1
8.8.1929	23, Upper Berkeley Street, W1
24.6.1932	22, Park Crescent, W1
8.6.1933	28, Seymour Street, W1
9.9.1933	46, Chiltern Court, Baker Street, NW1
28.1.1939	46, Chiltern Court, Baker Street, NW1
24.2.1939	102 Dorset House, NW1
4.3.1940	Savoy Court Hotel, Granville Place, W1
9.4.1940	17, Swan Court, SW3
15.8.1940	99, Chesterfield House, Curzon Street, W1

The Duchesse's life can be largely divided into her association with Vera; her involvement with the German Secret Service and Dr Rantzau; and her circle of friends, hangers-on and fellow-travellers, many of whom were implicated in some way with her and Vera's espionage activities. For her part in these activities the Duchesse was issued with a Detention Order under Defence Regulation 18B on 16 October 1940 and sent to Holloway Prison.[5] On the same day, her daughter, Ann Valeska Uhlig, was also detained. Under the 'Reasons for Order' sent to the Advisory Committee on 21 May 1941 it was stated:

The said Anna Sonia DUCHESSE DE CHATEAU-THIERRY

(i) Was, between May 1938 and September 1939, in constant touch both personally and by correspondence, with the Head of the German Secret Service at Hamburg.

(ii) Received sums of money from the Head of the German Secret Service at Hamburg or his representative.

(iii) Between March and September 1939 harboured an agent of the German Intelligence Service at her flat at 102 Dorset House, N.W.1.

(iv) Is suspected of having acquired information and transmitted the same to an agent of the German Secret Service.[6]

Vera was first sent over to England in early 1939 by Dr Rantzau to stay with the Duchesse de Château-Thierry at Dorset House. Rantzau believed that the Duchesse could use her social position to put Vera in touch with important people from whom she could obtain information. This Vera later regarded as a joke because the Duchesse lived 'in an atmosphere of incessant impecuniosity and make-believe, spending most of her time avoiding her creditors'.[7] While in Hamburg in February 1939, Vera was sent to learn photography from the photographer Krueger at Rantzau's offices at the Oberkommando. She probably suffered from what is now known as 'attention deficit disorder' (ADD) as she was quite disgusted to have to wade through a large manual and learn how to use a tripod in order to photograph documents. Robin Stephens at Camp 020, in his inimitable way, described the Duchesse as 'quite evidently a low grade agent on the threadbare fringe of High Society, which she was to have exploited for espionage purposes'.[8] Vera's instructions were:

1. Not to mention his [Rantzau's] name to the Duchess.
2. To report what the officers who were supposed to come to the Duchess's flat and other people said about the possibility of war.
3. To get hold of any documents belonging to officers visiting the Duchess and photograph them.
4. The films were not to be developed in England and were not to be sent by post, but were to be taken personally to RANTZAU by Vera.
5. To find people who would be prepared to work for RANTZAU, preferably people who were financially embarrassed or in trouble.
6. Air matters were to be given first place.[9]

It strikes me as odd that she was not supposed to mention Rantzau's name to the Duchess.

When the Duchesse travelled to Switzerland in 1938 she was in touch with 'Reinhardt', one of Rantzau/Ritter's aliases, who instructed her to advertise for an au pair and select Vera out of 200 applicants.

Vera was given a list of names of people who allegedly would be helpful to her, as well as others in the Duchesse's circle whom she suspected were working for German intelligence. One of these was a Russian, Colonel From, and an 'instructor' who Rantzau said was a British captain of German origin who she supposed must have been in the RAF, since that was Rantzau's prime area of interest.

Colonel Vladimir Charles From @ MORE, born on 8 March 1878, was a Russian with a Finnish father and Russian mother, married to a Polish woman. In 1917 he was living in Petrograd and working as an engineer specialising in armaments. In 1918 he came to England and demonstrated a night sight to the War Office. Since then he had lived in England and had become involved with selling his military inventions, and the arms trade. In 1934 he corresponded with the French government about aerial torpedoes. During the Spanish Civil War he was involved in arms trafficking and interested, from 1937 onwards, in high explosive anti-aircraft bombs and torpedoes. He died on 21 February 1939, survived by his wife who was living in Kensington. As John Day notes in his report of 14 April 1942:

Apart from his background of arms racketeering, there is no real indication of espionage activities with the possible exception of the following. On 19.12.36. S.I.S. received a report to the effect that a certain Madame J. de KEUKELAIE, 106 Rue de Jourdon, Brussels, was in the habit of making frequent visits to England where she met FROM at 95 Sinclair Road, London. This woman was stated by S.I.S's informant to be in touch with the German Secret Service. At the end of June 1937 FROM wrote a letter to Oscar GILINSKY in the following terms:-

'Please inform our Second Bureau that the name mentioned here is entered in my records belonging to our friend. In no circumstances do I wish that all the things should be in one basket, and so I send you this by virtue of my counter-espionage, because I treat you as a friend.'

It does not appear whether this incomprehensibility lies in the original Russian or in the inadequacy of the translation, but it possibly indicates that both FROM and GORLINSKY were interested in more than mere racketeering. In this connection it will be remembered that GORLINKSY described FROM on 8.1.42 as a slightly mad Russian inventor with whom he had had some dealings connected with the sending of arms to Spain, which however subsequently came to nothing.

It is suggested that, as in the case of HOOD, RANTZAU may have meant in giving FROM's name to Vera, as a person who may be useful, no more than he would be a useful source of information in his capacity of inventor. It has been seen that FROM's speciality appears to have been bombs and torpedoes in which RANTZAU as head of the Air Department would naturally hav[e] been most interested. On the other hand, the possibility that FROM really was an agent of the German Secret Service, cannot o[f] course be set aside.[10]

Another contact was Tibor Weber, connected with press matters at the Hungarian Legation, who Dr Krueger[11] described as a 'Damned little double crosser'. Weber asked her to steal documents from a certain Vassilieff connected with the Soviet Embassy in London. No actual list of contacts is in her MI5 files, but these have been heavily redacted. Vera's entire mission came to naught because she claimed that none of the people who she was supposed to meet had turned up at the Duchesse's house; nor had she been given a camera or money with which to purchase one. It stretches the bounds of credulity that the Abwehr should have been so parsimonius, so inefficient or so incompetent, but this seems to have been symptomatic of many of their espionage operations. When Vera returned to Germany shortly after the outbreak of war on 5 September 1939 she vowed to 'get out of the racket'.

In May 1937 the Duchesse went to Leysin, Switzerland, to the Clinique La Valerette to visit her ailing son Richard, sometimes referred to as Dick, who had pneumonia. However, she was short of money and unable to raise the £100 deposit to enter Switzerland. She therefore wrote to her brother-in-law in the Netherlands asking him to sell some property in Germany that had been left to her by her father. While in Leysin in 1938 she received a letter from a Dr Nikolaus Reinhardt of Mittelweg 117A, Hamburg XIII, saying that he had heard via a mutual friend of her financial difficulties and suggested that he might be able to help out in a way that was to their mutual advantage. Reinhardt, also known as Nikolaus Ritter, was at that time head of the Abwehr in Hamburg. She assumed that this mutal friend was My Eriksson, which was confirmed when Reinhardt alias 'Dr Rantzau', wrote to My Eriksson on 3 June 1938:

I wanted to let you know that I have been in touch with your friend in Switzerland. She actually seems to be in a very difficult position on account of her son's sickness. I told her that I might be able to help her and she is willing to meet me. I did not know whether I should mention your name but she guessed that the suggestion came from you.[12]

On 9 July 1938 Reinhardt wrote again in response to a letter he had recently received from My Eriksson saying that, 'Your lady friend from Switzerland, I shall meet in the course of next week. I shall speak quite openly with her and hope that everything will be settled to mutual satisfaction.'[13] The Duchesse's movements for 1938-9, according to her Travel Identity Card, are shown in Figure 4:[14]

Figure 4

Date	Observations
?.5.1938	Went to Germany.
13.7.1938	Went from Leysin to Munich.
17.7.1938	Returned to Leysin.
25.9.1938	Went to Germany again, returning on some date which is not revealed by the card.
21.10.1938	Left Leysin for Germany.
24.10.1938	–
23.12.1938	At Wiesbaden, where she drew out 1,150 R.M. from the Deutsche Bank.
25.12.1938	It seems that on this date the DUCHESSE unsuccessfully attempted to get back to Switzerland via Basle, as the Swiss-Basle station stamp is cancelled and the words appear 'Turned back because no visa'.
28.12.1938	Passed from Germany through Basle on the way to Leysin.
14.1.1939	Left Leysin for Germany.
27.1.1939	Passed through German passport control at Bentheim on the way to this country.
28.1.1939	Arrived at Harwich.
21.4.1939	Went to Flushing.
22.4.1939	At The Hague.
24.4.1939	Returned to this country via Flushing.
14.7.1939	Went to Flushing and thence to The Hague.
17.7.1939	Returned to this country via Harwich.

For most of her early life the Duchesse had found herself in dire financial straits and received the occasional small sum of money from her stepsister, Ellen Duwell, who had married a Swiss, Robert Duwell, and then become a naturalised German. Other funds also came from the USA. In 1936 the Duwells had settled in Wiesbaden. Later, in 1940, their address was Sweerts de

Landasstraat, 30, Arnhem, in the Netherlands. In 1943 the house was shown to have a certain Louis Israël (1884–1943) as a resident. The Duchesse told the 'Advisory Committee to Consider Appeals Against Orders of Internment' that her late husband had had an income of only £600 a year, which was reduced to £150 when the franc collapsed. She and her stepsister also had an allowance of £25,000, which was managed by someone in America, although she had had problems accessing that money. To supplement her income, the Duchesse acted as a chaperone to foreigners who she would introduce into London society using her title and social connections.

My Eriksson, not to be confused with Vera Schalburg's other names (Erichson, Eriksen), was one of Reinhardt's agents. She was born Josephine Fillipine Emilie (or Emmeline) Karpp in Kassel, Germany, on 20 October 1892, although she claimed to be Swedish, the daughter of Josef Karpp of Hasselbrucke Straße 14, Hamburg, a director of a chemical works. From 1927–28 she worked as companion-housekeeper to a Mrs Helen (Nellie) Neumann of The Hague. Farago refers to her as 'May Erikson', 'Lady May', the 'Countess', and ' … a gay divorcée in her mid-forties … a handsome, voluptuous woman with dark hair and sparkling brown eyes, obviously fond of a good time'.[15] She had been married to Erik Viktor Erikkson but had divorced him in 1926. The Duchesse's daughter, Anne Valeska (Valescka) Uhlig, described My Erichsson as 'over 40, tall, biggish, she is darkish, pleasant looking', whereas Vera was 'a dark good looking girl' and 'under 30, very good looking … of the Slav type, hair is parted in the middle'.

Eriksson had arrived at Southampton on 16 February 1930 from Hamburg and began employment as a domestic servant for Mrs E.G. Macphie, Kingsmead, Dover House Road, Roehampton, London, SW15, on a conditional twelve-month Ministry of Labour Permit. She worked in a domestic capacity for a number of influential families, as shown in Figure 5 below. Later, in 1939 she went to work for the Duchesse as a cook-housekeeper for a few months.[16]

Figure 5

Date	Observations
1 February 1936	To 25 Berkeley Square, W1, from Godalming.
31 July 1937	To Lord Derwent, Hackness Hall, Scarborough.
10–13 November 1937	To Lady Elvedon, Gloucester Lodge, Regent's Park.
15 May 1938	To Hon. Mrs F. Cripps, 71 South Audley Street, W1.[17]
30 July 1938	To Lord Derwent, Hackness Hall, Scarborough.

19 December 1938   To Sir Walter Wyndham, 'Warren Mere', Thursley, Surrey.

2 January 1939   To Steventon Manor, Oakley, Hants.

2 June 1939   To Mr Campbell Davis, Neuadd, Fawr, Cilyewm, Llandovery.

29 July 1939   To Lord Derwent, Hackness Hall, Scarborough.

8 November 1939   To Lady Eden, Fritham House, Lyndhurst, Hants.

4–5 December 1939   To 102 Dorset House, Gloucester Place, NW1. [The Duchesse's residence]; Of no occupation; N.B. Suggest possible flat of contact.

An entry in the diary of Herman Walter Christian Simon @ Carl (Karl) Andersson, indicates that she met him for the first time on 20 December 1937 at Marylebone Underground Station at 2 p.m, while she was working for Lady Elvedon. The following day Simon recorded that:

> I met Mrs. Erikson [*sic*] and as she was leaving tomorrow for Hamburg I gave her a letter for Dr. Regler to deliver at the Sailors Home in Hamburg. He calls there for letters sometimes. He is a lawyer. I know Dr. Regler yet I don't know him. I couldn't say what there was in the letter. It was telling him how I feel, how I am doing, they are all interested how I am getting along.[18]

A report provided by Dr Friederich Karl Praetorius claimed Simon, formerly a Merchant Navy officer, had been recruited by Eins Luft (I-L) of *Ast* Hamburg in 1939–40. However, Simon's entry in the report on Ritter, 'Agents despatched to or controlled in the U.K.', dated 24 January 1946, states that Ritter had first contacted Simon at the Seemansheim (Seaman's home) in Hamburg 'in Autumn 1937':

> He agreed at once to work under RITTER's direction and signed a pledge of secrecy. Shortly afterwards he was instructed by RITTER at the Stadtburo in the Konigstr in meteorological observation, description of airfields and identification of aircraft ... Twice during 1938 – the first time at the beginning of the year, the second in the summer – the agent was despatched via the Hook of Holland to the U.K., where he was given the name and address of My ERIKSSON as a contact in case of need.[19]

Simon was a tall, slender man with an oval face, blue eyes and light brown hair turning grey. His right forearm bore the tattoo 'WS'. He was born on

12 December 1881 in Elberfeld, Germany, to Christian Simon and Louise Anna Simon *née* Dapper. He had first arrived in England on 25 July 1937, having left Hamburg the previous day and travelled via Flushing to Harwich, departing from there on 14 August. On 26 September 1937 he returned to England, arriving at Folkestone and staying until 4 October, when he left from Dover. His third and final visit was on 25 October, again arriving at Harwich, and he stayed until he was deported on 16 July 1938.

When he came to the UK in the summer of 1937 Simon claimed that he was in England looking for a boat to purchase for a Dr Schliebitz of Altona (a district of Hamburg) and a Mr Willy Naumann of Hamburg. He also said that My Eriksson was acquainted with Naumann, who was a friend of her uncle. Could this have been the husband of Mrs Neumann for whom she had worked in The Hague? The spellings are so similar that it is hardly a coincidence. He described someone called Regler as a 'commission agent in Hamburg for boats and other things'. Simon's statement says that a letter brought over by My Eriksson dated 12 January 1938 and signed 'R' was from Regler, whereas another dated the same day was signed 'Rantzau'. During his first stay in England, Simon had carried out reconnaissance visits to various RAF air-fields in the areas of Stroud – Cirencester, Minchampton, Hullavington – and Southampton – Portsmouth, Lee-on-Solent, Calshot, Hythe. During this latter visit he handed over at least one letter to be passed on to Ritter.

MI5 had first become aware of him in August 1937 when a Mrs Duncombe (her first name is unknown), known to be acting as a post box for the German Secret Service, received a letter from *Ast* Hamburg instructing her to pay him £15 from someone named 'Campbell'. Mrs Duncombe's address was given as 90 Broadhurst Gardens, London NW6 (close to Finchley Road Tube station). Simon later explained that:

> George Campbell, Hamburg 20, Edgar Ross Str. 5, is not a man at all. It is an address to which letters for Dr. Rantzau are addressed. That was the address I was supposed to use for Dr. Rantzau.[20]

An extract from Mrs Duncombe's file appears in Simon's file in which it states:

> D.S.S. (through B)
> Mr. Kelsey, (G.P.O.) called up to say that a letter had been seen going to Mrs. Duncombe from Hamburg, saying that a sum of money was being sent to her and that she had to send it immediately to the following address:-

H.W. Simon,
c/o Harmon Visger,
France Lynch,
Stroud,
Glos.[21]

A Home Office Warrant (HOW) was instituted to intercept any mail being sent to that address. As a result, the Director of Public Prosecutions (DPP) directed that Mrs Duncombe's flat be searched under the Official Secrets Act (OSA).

Simon also met Eriksson on 22 January 1938. An entry in his diary mentions 'Mrs E. £6', referring to £6 she had lent him when he was short of cash. But this was not the first time he was without any money. On 8 November 1937 Klop Ustinov, reporting as Agent U.35, informed MI5 that Simon had called at the German Consulate in London asking for money, giving the names of Rantzau and Braun of Hamburg as references. A letter containing £18 in £1 notes was sent to him c/o the German Consul-General by Kol & Co., Amsterdam from a Mr van der Valde on 5 November 1937. (Another entry in his file states that he acknowledged receipt of this money to a Madame L. van der Velde.) Simon refers to a 'Ludwig Van der Velder' in a statement given to Inspector John Reynolds of the City of London Police on 5 February 1938. In January 1938 he received a further £10 from Kol & Co. by a P. Straaten at the Salvation Army hostel, Liverpool House, Aldgate, where he was staying.

On 5 February 1938 he first went to Kidbrooke, Kent, to a detachment of the RAF's barrage balloon section,[22] then in the afternoon to Hendon aerodrome. Upon his return to Liverpool House he was arrested and charged with contravening the Aliens Order, 1920 (7) for failing to sign the hotel register at The Chequers Inn, High Street, Tonbridge, while staying there from 10 December 1937 until 8 January 1938, and not providing information about his whereabouts. In his possession the police found notes and sketches of various aerodromes, names of contacts, and materials for sending secret messages. On 6 February 1938 he wrote to Willy Naumann at the Seemannshaus in Hamburg from 1 Pembury Road, Kent County Constabulary, Tonbridge, informing him of what had happened:

My dear Naumann,
    This surely is an S.O.S. They got a hold of me here and charged me with not registering as an alien – having been three months in the country. Kindly see to it that I get a lawyer to defend my case immediately and if you can't arrange it, let me know in any case. They looked through all my papers etc.

and somehow, it appears, they [*illegible*] one such suspicion, and out of the manner of the gentleman enquiring, I believe there is an other charge [*sic*] pending, and a lot more serious. I do not consider myself too guilty but it appears that I acted against their laws. This means a good lawyer without a doubt. I do not know what to say, else, <u>but see to it</u>, old man, that I get a lawyer. I know it is a question of getting the money across, for which I have no possibilities; only you are in a position to arrange that, as you have property outside of Germany.

What else can I say? That's all.

Kindly inform all the friends, so that they are not astonished not to see me during this week, as I promised.

With all best wishes,

Yours

H. W. Simon[23]

On 7 February 1938 Eriksson wrote from 'Farmleigh', Castleknock, County Dublin, where she had gone with her employer, Lady Elvedon, to Grete Müller, another servant, referring to 'S', from whom she had received a letter, saying that she was:

really astonished with its contents. Certainly one doesn't like helping more than one must – especially as we have already helped him.

I gave him your address in case he sometimes felt lonely – but never thought that the poor fellow was in such difficulties again. Certainly I told him that there was no hurry about <u>my</u> money, but I never expected him to want more so soon – I am very annoyed with Rantzau, for he promised to transfer £20 to £30 to my account – and as I am informed by the bank – so far nothing has come …

You see, apart from S I have <u>two others</u> I must think of – of whom he of course does not know anything and must not know anything for each of them works alone …

Write S that, much as you would like to, you are unable to help him any more. Believe me, if S makes his application punctually, he always gets it, but he relied on me – and as I said, if I had it, I would very gladly give it, for D [i.e. Germany] is sufficient reward,

But he must know that we haven't got much to spare.[24]

Clearly 'S' is Simon, looking for Eriksson to provide him with money. Müller wrote to Simon from 18 Porchester Terrace, London W2, on 4 February 1938 in response to his letter of 1 February saying that she was not in a position to help him. It seems that in his letter Simon had asked her to lend him £9, saying that, 'I had not expected to get into difficulties, but this has unfortunately happened.' The 'two others' to whom Eriksson referred may be 'two dangerous individuals who must be traced' – a certain Dr Rollin whom Simon was supposed to contact in Stroud or Cirencester, Gloucestershire, and Guido Mutz, who may have been mistaken for Greta Müller when she mentioned 'G.M.' to Hinchley Cooke. Entries in Simon's diary suggest that this may be the case:[25]

30 July 1937: 'Dr. Rollin mal aufsuchen' (look up Dr. Rollin)

17 March 1937 when Simon was in Germany: 'bei Dr. Rollin – zufrieden' (met Dr. Rollin – satisfied)

8 April 1937 when Simon was still in Germany: 'War bei Dr. Rollin (zuerst Prof. Kering)' (Visited Dr. Rollin (first visited Professor Kering))

However, Eriksson's letter was dated 7 February 1938 and the entry in Simon's diary for 9 May 1937 clearly states: 'Guido MUTZ dem Dr. RANTZAU vorgestellt' (Guido MUTZ introduced to Dr. RANTZAU). So 'G.M.' may not be Mutz, but Greta Müller, unless, of course, Eriksson did not know that Ritter (Rantzau) had already been introduced to Mutz by the time she wrote the letter.

It is possible that Willy Naumann was related to Helen (Nellie) Neumann of The Hague, who had once been My Eriksson's employer. Whether Naumann managed to obtain a good lawyer for Simon or not, he was sentenced to three months' imprisonment and deported once his sentence had been completed. Yet in spite of the detailed statement prepared by the Kent Police and signed off by Detective Sergeant Heathfield and Superintendent S.W. Pollington, in which they stated that Simon had been questioned by Hinchley Cooke and 'further more serious charges will be preferred against <u>SIMON</u>', 'for various reasons it was decided not to prefer charges under the Official Secrets Act, 1911 and 1920'.[26] Exactly what these reasons were is not revealed in his file, but could not have been on the grounds of national security as all such trials would have been held in camera. A conviction would almost certainly have led to internment; the Treachery Act, which would have carried the death penalty for anyone found guilty, would not be passed until May 1940; Defence Regulations would not come into effect until 1939 and 1940; and the

Double-Cross System had not even been dreamed up. Given that he had so obviously been caught spying, why the reluctance on MI5's part not to convict him? Whatever their rationale for granting his freedom there is nothing anywhere to indicate that he was later turned as a double agent. Or was he?

Shortly after Simon's arrest, Mrs Duncombe committed suicide. Simon was arrested again on 13 June 1940 in Eire and charged on 8 July with illegally entering near Dingle, Co. Kerry, and sentenced to three years' penal servitude. From June 1940 until June 1942 he was interned at Mountjoy Prison, Dublin, after which he was interned at Athlone Detention Barracks until October 1946. In 1941 he was still in touch with Rantzau when he wrote on 28 July informing him of his internment. It appears from MI5's interrogation of Ritter (Rantzau) in 1945 that he had sent Simon to Ireland, and he had been trained in W/T under Major Werner Trautmann, as well as in cipher and secret writing. Upon his release on 1 November 1946 Simon lived in Dublin until 8 January 1947 when he was sent back to Germany and promptly rearrested.

The report on Ritter also states that he could not remember how Eriksson was first brought to his attention but thought that he must have recruited her in the summer of 1937. His impression was that she had good connections with well-to-do people in the UK so she might prove useful as a *Forscher* (talent spotter). Her agreement to do any work for him must have been based on ideological reasons as she did not ask for any payment. She provided as an accommodation address that of a Mrs Lund in Stockholm, the wife of a former major in the Swedish Army and a friend of hers, who would act as a cut-out for communications.

It was through Eriksson that Ritter was first introduced to the Duchesse, and Mrs Editha Ilsa Hilda Dargel, a German-born amateur pilot born in Franstadt on 7 July 1900 who was then living in Parkstone, Dorset, with her adoptive mother, Mathilde Caroline Marie Krafft, code-named CLAUDIUS.[27] According to a CCG (B)E Bad Oeyenhausen report on Major Friedrich Hugo Bernard Theodor Lieber @ Dr Friederich Bauer,[28] dated 15 October 1946, Ritter recruited Dargel for *Ast* Hamburg in the late autumn (probably October) of 1938 while she was in Hanover, Germany; however, an extract from a CCG (B)E Bad Oeyenhausen report on Ritter dated 31 May 1946 notes that it was in September 1939 that Ritter was put in touch with her. When Ritter found out Dargel had been deported to Germany on 18 May 1939 he dropped her as an agent. While living in England she had acted as a *Forscher* for southern England as well as providing information on Ipswich and Southampton (Eastleigh) airfields.[29] Eriksson would act in the capacity of courier, passing messages to Ritter on a number of occasions.

In January 1938 Eriksson was living at Gloucester Lodge, Regent's Park. A Home Office Warrant (HOW) had been issued to intercept and open any mail being sent there 'or any name at that or any other address if there is reasonable ground to believe that they are intended for the said M. ERIKSSON'. In April she was living at 'Farmleigh', Castleknock, County Dublin, judging from a letter she sent to Gretel Müller. However, in May 1938 she was back at Gloucester Lodge, Gloucester Gate, NW1, working for Arthur Onslow Edward Guiness, Viscount Elvedon (1912–45), the son of the 2nd Earl of Iveagh – Rupert Edward Cecil Lee Guiness (1874–1967).

On 12 June 1938 Elisabeth Simon, Walter Simon's sister in Köln (Cologne), wrote to Eriksson enquiring after her brother, asking if she had any news of him as she had not heard from him and wondered whether he was either ill or had embarked on another voyage. Eriksson replied from Castleknock, County Dublin, on 15 June explaining that she had been unable to find out what had happened to him. The last time she had seen him was on 22 January when he had been talking about how much he was looking forward to going to Köln on his way to Hamburg. She explained that before she went to Ireland Simon had said he would telephone to arrange a last meeting, but had never done so. Clearly, he had been released from prison by that time. In fact, he had written to her on 1 February from the Golden Cross Hotel in Oxford saying that he was leaving at once for Cologne but was prevailing on Gretel Müller to lend him the £9 he needed for his passage from London–Cologne–Hamburg.

In June Eriksson was living at 71 South Audley Street, London. When the Duchesse was in Switzerland she was working as her housekeeper at her flat at 22 Park Crescent. Gonne St Clair 'Toby' Pilcher of MI5's Legal Section described her as:

> an educated and intelligent woman who appears to have had little difficulty in acquiring the friendship of most of her employers. She has always been extremely efficient in the performance of her duties and is also an extremely convincing liar.[30]

The Duchesse said of her:

> She was a woman I liked immensely and everybody liked … [I] told her about my son's illness, about wanting a night nurse. I wrote to her also about my German property. She wrote back and said she had relations in Hambourg [*sic*] who knew someone who had great power to do things in the matter of finance and money and would like me to get in touch with

them. She felt sure they could help me out of my German money. I was pleased about that and I wrote. Then I got a letter from Dr. Reinhardt.[31]

The Duchesse told Maxwell Knight how, when she went to meet Reinhardt in Munich in July 1938, she was pleasantly surprised to see that he was not as old as she expected but a 'perfectly honest looking' fair-haired man of about 40 with a ready smile. Reinhardt obviously charmed the Duchesse with his easy-going manner as she admitted to being 'favourably impressed' by his being a doctor of law and a legal advisor to banks and international commerce: 'I had confidence in him,' she said. In Ritter's MI5 file he claimed that because the Duchesse was short of money she 'practically forced her services on him'; he was not impressed with her and 'at some loss to suggest any possible employment for her'. He further reported that, 'She proposed to establish a salon in LONDON to which German agents might be invited to meet such persons of interest as she counted among her social contacts.'[32] In the same report he apparently gave her a sum of money to cover her expenses but initially did not accept her offer to work for him as he was convinced that she was only in it to make some 'easy money'. When he returned to Germany, he wrote an *Aktennotiz* (action report), which he circulated to all interested parties at *Ast* Hamburg. It was after this that Dierks approached him and suggested that she might be used as a cover for his agent, Vera. They then discussed it with Vera, who agreed to their proposal.

When Ritter had offered to get the Duchesse's money out of Germany, he cautioned her about not confiding any of their dealings with My Eriksson, which she found strange. And contrary to her wish to have it all taken out, he insisted that some must remain in Germany so as not to arouse suspicion. More likely, it was his way of ensuring that she continued to work for him. When she offered him a percentage of it he said he would take a percentage of her American money. In addition, he would obtain beauty preparations and ladies' underwear, which he wanted her to sell using her connections. In a letter written to her daughter on 18 July 1938 she told Valeska that:

> Dr. R … promises to send me that (2,500 Rm) [Reichmarks] at the rate of about £25 a month until the whole is paid me … The work for R. will be difficult and expensive for me to handle, so must see what remuneration he can offer …[33]

Overall, the amount of her German money she said she actually received from him was about £300–£350 from 1938 to 1940; a further £6 a month came from America. When Knight interviewed her she claimed Reinhardt still owed her £60 or £70.

Exactly why Vera was in London is connected with Dierks (Zum Stuhrig) and Reinhardt (Ritter). It appears that some time shortly after her return from Hamburg on 4 February 1939, acting on Ritter's instruction, the Duchesse inserted a notice in *The Times* for a companion 'au pair' and, as noted earlier, told to select Vera out of a total of 200 applicants. The Duchesse claimed that she knew nothing about Vera's character but had selected her because she had brought with her a letter of introduction from Princess Olga of Russia – actually Grand Duchess Olga Alexandrovna Romanova (1882–1960), youngest daughter of Tsar Alexander III. At Holloway on 12 November 1940, where Vera was confronted with the Duchesse, she denied having supplied any references, but the Duchesse contradicted her. Vera arrived in March and lived with the Duchesse at Dorset House, NW1. The Duchesse admitted to MI5 that she was made aware of Vera's espionage activities:

> yet apart from a period of fifteen days when she returned to Brussels and saw RANTZAU, ERICHSEN continued living with her until a few days after the outbreak of war.
>
> ERICHSEN has freely confessed that it was RANTZAU who sent her to CHÂTEAU-THIERRY and paid the latter £60 a month in consequence. In return for this CHÂTEAU-THIERRY was to give her board and lodging [and] pay her £10 a month. This was not regularly paid, but RANTZAU was also irregular in his payments to CHÂTEAU-THIERRY.[34]

This had apparently caused the Duchesse to describe Rantzau to Vera as a 'bloody dog', although she always denied it. As an MI5 report dated 27 December 1940 stated:

> When she last left London in September 1940 she had been requested by the Duchess [*sic*] to go to the address Riemerstratt 24 [*sic*] to make contact with a woman there named Heine TINI. VERA states that she does not believe that the Duchess knew this woman but that she had been given the address as one at which to apply for money.[35]
>
> I said I could not get in touch with anyone, I wanted to get in touch with my sister to get some money and to get in touch with Miss Sormani and say the flat had definitely been let, and somebody else; all sorts of things.[36]

The Duchesse told the Advisory Committee that Vera had gone to visit her parents in Brussels and that she was glad to get rid of her. When asked whether Vera had told her that she knew Reinhardt, the Duchesse said that Vera at first denied knowing him, then later admitted that he was a friend of a great friend and that he was dishonest about money. As she freely admitted when MI5 asked her whether she had complained about him not sending her enough money: 'I do not know why he keeps £80 which he says is at the bank, he should send it in a lump sum.'

Even though she was in possession of a Swedish passport and an Exit Permit (No. 122303) issued on 11 September 1939 valid until 11 January 1940, My Eriksson was arrested by Gravesend police on 16 December 1939 while attempting to leave the country, purportedly to visit her son and daughter in Sweden via Holland. (She also had a Dutch visa issued on 14 December 1939 valid for two months.) The immigration officer later determined that her children were actually in Hamburg but she had neglected to mention this to the Permit Office because she knew that she would not have been granted an Exit Permit.

She was later interned in Holloway Prison before being transferred to Eastfield, Port Erin, on the Isle of Man on 31 August 1943. Interestingly, Guy Liddell originally expressed objections to her being sent to the Isle of Man. In response to a note from R.K. Renton of E3 on 6 January 1942, on 13 January he wrote:

I do not feel that Josephine F.E. ERIKSSON should be allowed to go to any camp from which women may at some time be repatriated. Since our letter of 20.2.40 she has been closely associated with Vera ERIKSON and also with Mrs Jessie JORDAN at Holloway.[37] We should be very much opposed to any information she has obtained as a result of conversations that she has had with these women going back to Germany. There is absolutely no doubt whatever that My ERIKSSON is a German spy, although it would be impossible to obtain a conviction against her. She has in fact certain knowledge about espionage activities in this country which she has resolutely refused to divulge.

The real trouble in all these cases is that the Home Office have never really faced up to the problem of the internment of women. To begin with they had no places of internment and all women were sent to Holloway. The Germans then said 'If you are going to imprison our women we will imprison yours.' This led to a suggestion from the H.O. that we should release all the women who had been interned at the outbreak of war, and later that they should go back to Germany. The lesson was not learned, however, and Holloway was allowed to fill up again, until the moment came for general internment, when something really had to be done. It was then decided to start a camp for women in the Isle of Man ... I feel very strongly that unless and until some camp is established for women which is reasonably secure, the problem of My ERIKSSON and others of her kind cannot satisfactorily be solved.[38]

6

A TASTE OF FREEDOM?

Somehow My Eriksson had got wind of Vera Erikson and her voyage to Britain. On 2 February 1943 she wrote to Hinchley Cooke from Aylesbury Prison asking him for the return of photographs and letters taken from her when she was arrested, and for a transfer to the Isle of Man. In her letter she also queried why Vera was 'at liberty':

> I really cannot see any reasons why you purposely confused my case with that of Vera v. Schallberg or Schallburg which you recorded in to Holloway prison under my name. As your representative told me himself last year – she came over here in a German seaplane. Why is she at liberty on the Isle of Man? Why have I been kept for over 3 years in prison and under detention when I have committed no act against this country? – I know from people you did this deliberately – for what reason I don't know?[1]

On 8 February, My Eriksson continued her campaign by writing to Richard Stokes (referred to as M. Stokes in her file), the Member of Parliament for Ipswich. Exactly why she singled him out is not clear, but Stokes was an independent Labour MP who had been a critic of the government's policies of bombing and Allied tank design. He had also asked questions about Defence Regulations and internment in 1941, to which the MP for Gravesend, Sir Irving Albery, had replied.[2] The wording of her letter is much the same as the letter sent to Hinchley Cooke (above), except that she asked Stokes to raise the questions in the House of Commons about Vera's arrival, the confusion between her and Vera, and what if anything was being done about it. J.L.S. Hale in SLA, MI5's Senior Legal Advisor, wrote to A.I. Tudor at the Home Office Aliens Department on 16 February to clear up the misconception created by Eriksson about her being confused with Vera, 'There is of course no truth in the suggestion that there has been any confusion between My ERIKSSON and Vera von WEDEL @ ERICHSEN.' He went on to explain exactly who each one was and how they came to be detained, adding, 'We are of course anxious, so far as possible, to avoid any unnecessary publicity both about these ladies who are at Aylesbury and about Vera von WEDEL who, for your information, is being of some assistance to us.'

Eriksson's letter caused a flurry of correspondence between Sir David Petrie, the Director-General of MI5, and Sir Alexander Maxwell, Permanent Under-Secretary at the Home Office. On 3 March Maxwell wrote to Petrie regarding Hale's suggestion that her letter to Stokes be stopped 'to avoid any unnecessary publicity'. He pointed out that the Home Secretary had said in the House of Commons that detainees were free to write to MPs, 'subject to the general requirement that all correspondence is censored', but that any letter containing secret information not in the public interest would be within the power of the Home Secretary to suppress, regardless of who it was sent to. He added:

> I am not very clear, however, whether this particular letter from My Eriksson falls into this category ... and I imagine it is of no importance at the present time to conceal from the enemy the fact that she has been arrested. As regards Vera von Wedel is it of any importance to conceal from the enemy her arrest, seeing that the arrest of her companion Drücker and his subsequent execution has been announced?
> ... but on the information contained in Hale's letter I ~~find it difficult to understand what~~ am not quite clear whether real harm would be done by sending on the letter to Stokes or indeed ~~what~~ whether much harm would be done if Stokes should, as is not very likely, put down a Question in the House, as he is asked to do in the letter.[3]

Petrie replied to Maxwell on 5 March, a draft of which is available in Eriksson's file, in which he outlined his reservations:

> The difficulty which we feel about the delivery of this letter to Mr. Stokes lies not so much in any information which it expressly sets out as in the facts which would naturally be gathered by inference from any discussion of it. I agree at once that the fact of both My ERIKSSON's and Vera von WEDEL's detention must be presumed to be known to the Germans, but I am not so happy that the Germans should learn that, whereas ~~her~~ Vera's accomplices WALTI and de DEEKER were duly executed, ~~Vera von WEDEL~~ she

is living comfortably in the Isle of Man. At the best, this news would be a gratuitous encouragement to prospective female spies, while at the worst it would suggest that Vera von WEDEL has since her capture come over to our side. As you will remember from my letter of the 14th March 1942, this is what has happened, but it seems hardly fair to Vera von WEDEL, ~~to advertise the fact~~ who may want to go back to Germany, to make public this fact.

As for My ERIKSSON, we are anxious to avoid publicity not so much about her case as about her present place of detention at Aylesbury. She forms, as you know, one of a small group of ladies who were sent there largely so that they could be company for Madame CARRE, who in view of the information in her possession could not be allowed to meet the ordinary run of female detainees who come and go in Holloway Prison. The fact that some at least of these ladies are in Aylesbury is no doubt known, but this we regard as an unfortunate necessity, and we should deprecate any avoidable publicity as to their names or the reasons for their segregation.

We do therefore hope that it may be thought proper to stop My ERIKSSON's letter to Mr. Stokes. If the Home Secretary feels that this would be ~~impossible~~ undesirable, and if Mr. Stokes does ask questions, we should be grateful if the answers could be framed in the light of the considerations to which I have referred.[4]

Madame Carré was Mathilde Carré, also known as 'The Cat' and code-named VICTOIRE, who was accused of betraying members of the *Interallié* network in Paris to the Abwehr, and was now in custody in Britain. Maxwell's reply to Petrie on the 9th stated that Herbert Morrison had agreed that 'it is justifiable to suppress the letter addressed by Mrs. Eriksson to Mr. Stokes, M.P. on the ground that there are security objections to the publication of the information contained in the letter'. It is not clear whether the letter was suppressed, but there appears to be no record in *Hansard* of any such questions being asked by Stokes in the House of Commons, so it must be assumed that it was.

During the spring of 1943 the subject of My Eriksson being repatriated had been mooted. From Aylesbury Prison on 5 April she had petitioned the Secretary of State for the Home Office, Herbert Morrison, regarding her status as a prisoner. An extract of that petition requested that she be transferred to the Isle of Man:

Herewith I kindly ask you if you could see any possibility for my transfer to the Isle of Man or another suitable camp – as I rather would prefer to go to a prison as prisoner – as as stay here with the present Detainees. [*sic*]

Whatever I do, whatever I say everything is wrong and everything is so exaggerated as always some deaf people understand the wrong things and like to hurt, whenever there is a possibility and make my life those last weeks extremely miserable, as happy I have been, so for that goes – so unhappy I am now. I know I am not faultless but even, I always try to be as much for myself and going out the way by stopping in my cell.[5]

Her handwritten letters on 16 April to the Swedish Consul-General and Hinchley Cooke about conditions in prison are quite revealing:

Dear Sir,

Herewith I kindly will ask you to go in contact with the Home Office for my eventl [sic] transfer to another camp or Isle of Man as really as much as I tried to bear up with my lot my strength is failing in the daily life, with some rather funny girls wich [sic] make my daily life a great misery – as I don't want to have anything to do with them – they go out their way deliberately to make my life a real hell.

As I don't like to go complaining to our government I have kept patience but I yuste [? sic] finished and can't go on any longer therefore I have also written by the same post to Colonel Cooke War Office, rather to put me back to prison again as I have to go on here any longer to live in this misery – Perhaps you would find the convenience to come and see me so I could make things clear to you.

Please try to understand I have tried hard to bear up with my lot and 3½ years does the telling.

I beg you of all my heart to try, to give me a little help and in that hope I await your kindly soar[?]

Dear Col Cook [sic]

As life here is now really unbearable as the young girls deliberately go out their way to make my daily life a great misery and I don't like to go complaining to Miss Mellanby [the Governor of Aylesbury Prison].

Even when I was in prison I had a more happier life [sic], as I have had here, since Xmas and as I cannot go to another camp or Isle of Man I rather prefere [sic] to go to prison again as live here between this hate & strife.

Therefore I really don't mind if you will put something on to me, only out of this present misery – that is my greatest wish.[6]

It seems that there were moves afoot not only to transfer My Eriksson, but possibly to exchange her for a British agent. A note by Tar Robertson marked 'Urgent' written on 9 May 1943 stated that Colonel (Redacted, but likely Maurice Buckmaster of SOE) had rung up to say that one of their women agents who had been instrumental in helping over 100 RAF personnel to escape through Occupied France had just been captured and was under a death sentence by the Germans. Robertson reported that the unknown colonel was 'hoping that we may be able to get her released by the Germans if we offer in exchange a German agent who is at present held by us in this country.' Dick White appended a handwritten note, adding, 'I spoke Col. Hinchley Cooke who does not raise objections to the proposal to exchange My Eriksson but thinks Vera Eriksen would be more suitable.' A flurry of letters was exchanged between MI5, SIS and SOE, with opinions bouncing back and forth as to the feasibility of such an exchange.

A letter marked 'Secret' from SIS Section V/PA (Robert Cecil) to 'Buster' Milmo on 29 June 1943 stated that the German government had requested more information about Eriksson and whether she wanted to return to Sweden or Germany, as well as asking why the Swedish Legation was not dealing with her repatriation. There was also correspondence between the Swedish Consulate-General and E.N. Cooper of the Home Office Aliens Department regarding Eriksson and two other Swedish nationals – Karl August Hansson and Hugo Ludvig Laurentius Jonasson – and their repatriation to Sweden. On 28 July Mrs K.G. Lee of the Home Office Aliens Department wrote to Guy Liddell asking what the security objections were to the repatriation to Sweden of Eriksson. It took until 2 August for him to respond in a draft letter to Mrs Lee, in which he said:

> …this woman is and was over a period of several years the trusted agent and friend of a high officer of the German Secret Service who was at the material time principly [sic] engaged upon the direction of espionage against this country. This woman, although technically a Swede, is German by birth and it is significant that at the time when she was arrested in December of 1939 when about to leave the country she pretended that she was going to Sweden but subsequently admitted that she was going to Hamburg to contact the German Secret service officer to whom I have referred.
>
> It is our view that, whilst the war continues, the repatriation of an enemy agent such as My ERIKSSON must necessarily involve the country in some degree of risk which we would not be justified in incurring unless some compensating quid pro quo were to enter into the matter. Thus we would

be prepared to exchange My ERIKSSON on the terms indicated in our minute of 8.7.43. on Home Office file, no. E.323/6.

Quite apart from the foregoing considerations, if you would be good enough to refer to the Director General's letter of 5.3.43. to Sir Alexander Maxwell, you will see that, in the second paragraph additional reasons are set out for opposing this woman's repatriation on security grounds.[7]

In the meantime, on 30 July Tar Robertson, in a report to Guy Liddell, commented on a letter from Air Commodore Archie Boyle at SOE:

There is one other point which you mentioned to me and that is that S.I.S. and S.O.E. have agreed to offer My ERIKSSON in exchange for an S.I.S. agent who was captured by the Germans. I suppose Boyle realises that My ERIKSSON has been in the closest possible touch with VICTOIRE during her stay at Aylesbury. I have discussed the mechanics of this exchange with Mr. Milmo wh[o] says that the whole matter is in the hands of [Redacted] S.I.S. As to whether this exchange can be stopped, I do not know, neither is Mr. Milmo in a position to advise me as it is an S.I.S. responsibility.[8]

As Boyle had noted in his letter to Liddell on 26 July:

We have lately had evidence of the harm that can be done by prisoners with special information being allowed to mix with others who may be released. Dr. INGRAO[9] has addressed a letter to the American Press giving details of those 'unjustly detained' by the British. The list is a long one and includes Admiral MUSELIER![10]

On 5 August, in a report written by Tar, 'Removal of detainees from Aylesbury back to Holloway', he discusses a meeting he had had with Captain Christopher Harmer of MI5's B1a, SOE's Air Commodore Archie Boyle, and Lieutenant Colonel Buckmaster involving the removal of five special women detainees, one of whom included My Eriksson. As Tar pointed out:

I also reminded the meeting that S.O.E. had taken no exception to the repatriation of My ERIKSSON in exchange for an agent of S.I.S. who had been captured by the Germans. This point came up some four months ago and various aspects of this exchange were then discussed. It was pointed out that My ERIKSSON had been in constant touch with VICTOIRE since their earliest days of internment. Commander Senter said that he thought

it was important that My ERIKSSON should not be told in advance
that she was to be repatriated for fear least this information should get to
VICTOIRE and that between them VICTOIRE should then be able to
get information to the Germans through My ERIKSSON. I undertook to
look into this and it suggested that if My ERIKSSON is to be repatriated
she should, as soon as this became apparent, be removed from the other
four internees. [11]

When he and Commander Senter went to visit Holloway on 7 August, Tar
reported that the Deputy Governor informed him that Eriksson was 'agitating
to be repatriated to Sweden'. A further draft minute by Liddell on 8 August
1943 for the Home Office file on Eriksson went on to express that:

I am afraid that there was a slight misunderstanding between Sir Alexander
Maxwell and me on the question of Mrs. ERIKSSON's suggested repatriation. We still feel that there are some security objections to the release
or repatriation of Mrs. ERIKSSON and we should be most unwilling for
her to be released or repatriated unless some substantial quid pro quo was
received. The position however is that a certain very important British
agent is detained by the Germans and an exchange of this man for My
ERIKSSON has been suggested. In view of the great importance which is
attached to the safety of the British agent we are, subject to the approval of
the Home Office, ready and willing to waive our objections to the repatriation of My ERIKSSON if such an exchange can be arranged. I should add
that the repatriation of My ERIKSSON only came up for consideration in
connection with the British agent above referred to.
     If the present exchange proposal falls to the ground we submit that the
repatriation of My ERIKSSON to Sweden should only be considered with
a view to the release and repatriation to this country of some British Agent
detained by the Swedish authorities in Sweden. [12]

On 11 August 1943 Tar wrote a note to the R3Y secretary (Registry) saying
that he was sending over papers relating to Eriksson and asked that since they
were of a secret nature they be made into a Y Box file. A 'Y-box' file is that
reserved for the most confidential documents, containing sensitive information that is marked inside the front cover with a yellow card known as the
'Yellow Peril': 'All MI5 agent and informants are Y-boxed, and so are suspected spies, defectors, MPs and ministers. Officers may only gain access to this
material with the permission of the agent-handler.' [13] Writing to Guy Liddell

on 16 August 1943, Air Commodore Archie Boyle, Director of Security, Intelligence and Personnel at SOE, expressed that:

> … we are naturally concerned over the prospect of her being repatriated and, as Buckmaster and Senter pointed out at our meeting on 5th August, when this came up in April it was put to us as a matter of extreme urgency and on the basis that her repatriation would result in the release of a very important S.I.S. agent. [14]

On 10 September 1943 Milmo wrote to Robert 'Robin' Cecil at MI6 regarding Eriksson's possible repatriation, saying that he felt it inadvisable to speak to her about whether she wanted to be sent back to Sweden or to Germany, but thought probably Germany, 'and in any event she would be extremely unlikely to say that she would go anywhere other than Sweden'. That being the case, '… it might well prejudice the chances of the Germans agreeing to the proposed exchange'. The Foreign Office sent a telegram to Bern on 17 September 1943 to that effect:

> Secret
> Your telegram No.4197 [of 2nd September: exchange of Miss de Jongh].
> You should reply that Mrs. E. when last questioned admitted that she intended to go to Hamburg where her children were understood to be living.
> 2. For your own information, Mrs. E. has not since been questioned on this point. It is probable that she intends to go to Germany, but if asked she would most likely assert a wish to go to Sweden, which might make the Germans less inclined to agree to this exchange. [15]

A document dated 18 November 1943 to B4a (Major Whyte) and D4c (Miss Fisher), recommended her removal from the Central Security War Black List (CSWBL):

> This woman has been detained under Order 12 (5a) and will continue in detention until the end of the war unless she is specially exchanged for a British agent of value (see 302x 316a). She will doubtless, as a known spy, be included in any post-war Black List. [16]

On 7 December 1943 Mrs K.G. Lee of the Home Office Aliens Department wrote to Guy Liddell to inform him that the Swedish Legation had written to her department asking whether Eriksson could be repatriated to Sweden:

'They suggest that this might be justified on health grounds as Mrs. Eriksson is complaining of severely impaired health.' While on the Isle of Man, Eriksson had been visited at Port Erin by Miss Ethel K. Houghton of the Society of Friends (Quakers)[17] on 17–19 November 1943, who reported:

> This woman said she had been ill and cannot eat. She does not like being in Port Erin.
>
> Two men from the Swiss Legation came to see her but knew nothing of her case. She has written to the Legation but receives no reply and she wonders whether the letters are kept in Liverpool.
>
> If she cannot be repatriated, she would like to go back to Holloway. She groused about the Isle of Man climate and said 'Our air is dry'.
>
> Also, she cannot stand being closely togeather [sic] with other people and prefers the privacy obtained in Holloway.
>
> She receives encouraging letters from her home in Germany. The children are in good health and well looked after.
>
> She asked Miss Houghton to convey her greetings to people in Hollowa[y]. A Margaret Nolan was a friend of hers.[18]

An indication that British authorities might be willing to exchange her for someone can be seen in a letter sent to Guy Liddell from an unknown writer in MI6's Section VB, possibly Cowgill or Rodney Dennys, on 27 June 1944, in which it stated that:

> You will recall that a trusted agent of ours, by name Andree de JONGH, was caught by the Germans, and during the course of last summer diplomatic negotiations for her exchange were begun through the medium of the Swiss. On that occasion, the name of Frau ERIKSON was put forward as a suitable exchange. The negotiations came to nothing.
>
> We are anxious to reopen the negotiations offering this time either Frau ERIKSON or Ernst FRESENIUS as a suitable candidate for exchange. We realise that such an action in the case of the latter may, and probably will, blow BEETLE, but we feel that it is more important to save the life of Andree de JONGH rather than protect the future of BEETLE as a controlled agent.
>
> Could you please let us have your observations on the above urgently, so that if you are in agreement negotiations may be immediately begun through the Foreign Office for such an exchange.
>
> Alternatively FRESENIUS could be offered in exchange for Jean Francois NOTHOMB mentioned in the attachment to your letter under

reference. From the point of view of work done, Andree de JONGH and NOTHOMB are almost equally important to us.[19]

Andrée Eugenie Adrienne de Jongh, known as Dédée, was a member of the Belgian Resistance who had set up and run the *Comet* line, which helped Allied prisoners escape over the Pyrenees to neutral Spain. Dédée had been captured by French police on 15 January 1943, and after imprisonment in the Château Neuf prison, Bayonne and Fort du Hâ, Bordeaux, was taken to Fresnes prison in Paris, where she was brutally tortured by the Gestapo. Later she was sent to Ravensbrück and Mauthausen concentration camps.[20]

Fresenius was Ernest Christoph Fresenius @ Faber @ Holger @ Resenius, a German naturalised Icelander recruited by the Abwehr in 1943 and captured on 30 April 1944.[21] Baron Jean-François Nothomb, DSO (1919–2008), known as 'Franco', became leader of the *Comet* Line after Dédée was captured. He was arrested on 19 January 1944, but was released by the Americans on 23 April 1945. He died on 6 June 2008, aged 89.

Guy Liddell wrote to an unnamed major in SIS on 3 July 1944 saying that, 'As regards FRESENIUS we are not particularly anxious to send him back as he has been associated with certain recent arrivals at Camp 020. We might, however, be able to stretch a point if you were really stuck. The matter must finally rest with the Americans, whose prisoner he is.'[22]

BEETLE was Petur Thomsen, an SIS double agent run in Iceland and a 'professional radio operator … who arrived by U-boat in September 1943'.[23] In his letter Liddell also says that:

A short time ago S.O.E. were strongly opposed to My ERIKSON going back because she had at one time been associated with VICTOIRE at Aylsbury [*sic*] Gaol. They have however now agreed to waive their objection. She is therefore available for exchange.[24]

A Top Secret note from an unknown source, but likely SIS, dated 27 June 1944 but referring to a Foreign Office telegram of 12 July (?), was copied to Milmo at MI5 saying that:

We have heard nothing further on this projected exchange and it is possible that the negotiations lapsed because of the arrest of Mlle. de JONGH's father [Frédéric], who was connected with the same escape organization. Meanwhile Mlle. de JONGH has been moved to Berlin and, according to our latest information, is due to stand trial there very shortly. We are anxious to do all we can to save her and should be grateful if a telegram might be sent to the Minister at Berne, asking him to raise once more with the Swiss the question of exchanging her against My ERIKSSON, who is still detained in this country and available for the purpose.[25]

On 24 July 1944 Peter Loxley at the Foreign Office sent a letter marked 'Top Secret' to Robert 'Robin' Cecil, PA to 'C', Sir Stewart Menzies, and also the MI6 Foreign Office Advisor, concerning the resumption of negotiations of a possible exchange of My Eriksson for Andrée de Jongh. Loxley's letter stated that the Belgian embassy had also approached them about the possible exchange. He explained that the Foreign Office had serious reservations about any such exchange:

As far as the Foreign Office records of this case are concerned, the last paper on our files is Foreign Office telegram No. 3466 to Berne of 17th September, 1943, giving some particulars of Mrs. Ericksson for which the Germans had asked. No reply was received to this communication and after that the case apparently lapsed.

We have lately reconsidered our general attitude regarding these exchanges. So far as I know, only in two or three cases have we ever agreed to make an exception to the established principle not to enter into any individual exchange of British and Allied against German nationals or agents. Exceptions were made quite recently on account of the outstanding services they had rendered to the Allied cause, in the case of two Belgians, Andree de Jongh and Jean Nothomb. Only in the former case, however, did the proceedings reach the stage of an actual offer of a particular person in exchange to the Germans viz. Mrs. Eriksson.

When the question of producing a suitable body arose in Nothomb's case, Guy Liddell, in a letter to me, put forward some very cogent reasons why these individual exchanges should not be encouraged. He listed some of the difficulties, both on political and security grounds, of producing a body for the Germans and he also mentioned some of the risks that would clearly be run if we none the less persevered in our efforts. Over and above these considerations, there is the very important fact that, once exceptions are admitted, it is extremely difficult to know where to draw the line. This might easily lead to trouble with and amongst the Allies. In this connection you should know that the Dutch have also just asked us to make a special case of a Captain Thomson, who has apparently done excellent work and was recently sentenced to death as a spy. We have refused. Finally, it seems pretty clear that, whatever we do for individuals, we shall not succeed in preventing the Germans from sentencing and executing prominent patriots or important agents. On the contrary, the chances are that they will behave with even greater barbarity and ruthlessness and on a far greater scale as the hour of their doom approaches.

In the circumstances, while we fully appreciate the extent to which these people deserve our gratitude and sympathy, we have reluctantly come to the conclusion that we must abide strictly by the rule of 'no exceptions'. This means that we do not feel able to proceed with the cases of either Andree de Jongh or Jean Nothomb. I enclose copies of letters which we have written to Vicomte de Lantsheere[26] and Jonkheer Teixeira.[27]

I am sending copies of this letter with enclosures to Guy Liddell and to Commander Johns of S.O.E.[28]

While all this had been going on there had been other correspondence to Special Branch about Eriksson's passport. MI5 took the view that since the passport was Swedish it should be returned to the Swedish Legation. A summary of a letter sent from Mathilde Krafft to Eriksson dated 6 June 1944 reported that Eriksson expected to be released soon.

7

A STRANGER CALLS

While Vera was staying at the Duchesse's flat, she was visited by a man, reputedly a naval officer named Wilkinson, asking to see her. Peter Wilkinson[1] had shown up early one morning in July, according to Dorothy Winifred Morrish, who was employed by the Duchesse as a cook from the end of June until the end of October 1939. However, he left about a quarter of an hour later. As MI5 noted in 'Summary of the case against the Duchesse of CHÂTEAU-THIERRY':

… if ERICHSEN's story is true it is extremely unlikely that he had called to see her only, and that C.T. [Duchesse de Château-Thierry] was ignorant of the purpose of his visit. This, according to ERICHSEN, was to 'see how they were getting on'.[2]

In a note dated 3 December 1940, the Duchesse had informed Morrish one evening that:

a gentleman would call fairly early the following morning and ask for Vera. MORRISH was to tell the Duchesse when he arrived and if Vera was not up the Duchesse would see him. The man called at about 10 a.m. on the following morning and asked for Vera. MORRISH cannot remember his description or his name, but would recognise him again if she saw him. The Duchesse saw the man and MORRISH went downstairs to call Vera, but does not know what happened after that.[3]

Vera later denied ever knowing a Lieutenant Peter Wilkinson during an interrogation at Holloway on 24 December 1940, even though she also said she had only met him once. So who was he? The Advisory Committee investigating the Duchesse concluded that whoever he was 'there can be little doubt that

Wilkinson also was an agent of Dr. Reinhardt and that the Duchesse was concealing the real truth about this matter'. The Committee came to this conclusion when they stated in paragraph 10 of their report that:

> ... in or about June or July 1939 in the flat at 102 Dorset House. On that morning about 10 o'clock a man called who gave the name of Wilkinson and who was seen by the DUCHESSE and by Vera. Vera alleged that when she came into the room Wilkinson turned to her and said, 'Kind regards from Reinhardt', and then, observing that Vera did not appear to understand, added 'Hansen'. The DUCHESSE admitted that she had seen the man Wilkinson but denied that he had addressed Vera in the terms referred to.[4]

When questioned by the Committee, the Duchesse claimed to have never seen him before in her life, but described him as being English and a 'perfectly gentlemanly looking fellow', and not someone with a foreign accent. She denied his ever mentioning the names Reinhardt or Hansen, as well as the fact that she had forewarned Mrs Morrish to expect a visitor. When Norman Birkett KC, the chairman of the Committee, persisted with this line of questioning, the Duchesse insisted that at no time did she ever ask what Wilkinson wanted with Vera, even though it was unusual for her to receive visitors. At the same time she admitted that she may have teased her about it saying, 'She was the most reserved girl, the kind of girl you could not ask things at all.' During the Duchesse's appeal she changed the time of the visit from 10 a.m. to 8.30 a.m.

Dick White, writing to Stephens at Camp 020 on 11 November 1940, asserted, 'the real thing that must be discovered from her [the Duchesse] is the identity of WILKINS or WILKINSON, if that man exists'. Meurig Evans of B8l listed him as a 'suspicious contact'. It was further discussed in a report prepared by MI5's B21 (the signature cannot be deciphered, but possibly White):

> Another individual who had not yet been traced, is a man who visited the DUCHESSE when Vera ERICHSEN was living with her before the war, and introduced himself as Mr WILKINSON or WILKINS. He has not yet been identified, and in view of the dangerous work on which he was engaged and of the German habit of using aliases when engaged on Secret Service work, it seems doubtful whether WILKINS or WILKINSON was the name under which he commonly went in this country... It must be borne in mind that this visit was made unexpectedly at about 8.30 a.m. before either the DUCHESSE or Vera ERICHSEN were dressed. It therefore seems unlikely that the man WILKINS or WILKINSON had slept in

London, and had got up for the purpose of making this early morning visit so as to give Dr. RANTZAU's kind regards. The whole picture makes it much more likely that the man WILKINS or WILKINSON was an individual who had come across from Hamburg after seeing Dr. RANTZAU, and who had disembarked at Harwich and had just arrived at Liverpool Street on the boat-train. An individual just having arrived might very well drive straight to the DUCHESSE's flat without realising that it was much too early for a call to be made. In the circumstances it is proposed to get a list of Germans who arrived at Harwich on the date in question, and to trace up the movements of those aged about thirty.[5]

The author of the report proposed that Richard Butler of B2 check with Mrs Morrish to verify when this visit occurred as well as to put pressure on the Duchesse and Vera to try to remember the date.

Wilkinson was first thought to be Robert William Wilkinson, a member of the British Union of Fascists, or Dr John Douglas Wilkinson, FRCS, LRCP, 'a crook doctor' and allegedly a British Union of Fascists district leader for London. Vera was shown photographs of Robert William Wilkinson and Robert Jacob William Wilkinson, the British Union of Fascists District Leader for Lincoln, interned on the Isle of Man, but failed to identify either. He was subsequently identified as Paymaster Sub-Lieutenant Anthony Peter Wilkinson by Major Robin Stephens and Meurig Evans[6] of Camp 020 in their report on the Duchesse dated 23 and 25 November. At that time Wilkinson was stationed at HMS *Ganges*, a centre for 'Hostilities Only New Entry Training' at Shotley in Suffolk, across the River Stour from Harwich. Stephens' 'Yellow Peril' of 25 November addressed to Guy Liddell wrote that:

A main, if not the primary object of the investigation was to establish the existence and identity of WILKINSON, the reputed right-hand man of RANTZAU in this country. In my judgement, the existence of this enemy agent in England has been established, but further investigation is necessary to connect his identity with that of Paymaster Lieutenant A.P. WILKINSON of H.M.S. Ganges, Ipswich. I so distrust CHATEAU-THIERRY, Vera ERICHSEN and COSTENZA, that I naturally suspect connivance to lead us away from an agent indiscreetly revealed by ERICHSEN. On the other hand, the search of COSTENZA's property in B.8., dating back to her arrest ten months ago, provides outside and independent corroboration. Again, independent descriptions are uncannily close, while, lastly, there is evidence of overspending at places such as the Dorchester and the Kit Kat Club by a Junior Officer in the Paymaster branch of the Navy. Lines for immediate investigation are so obvious as to render suggestions perhaps unnecessary.[7]

Anthony Peter Wilkinson, aged 23, was educated at Bramcote School, Scarborough, and had entered the Royal Naval College at Dartmouth in 1931, serving on HMS *Frobisher* until 1937 when he was commissioned into the Royal Navy and posted to the battleship HMS *Royal Oak*. On 14 October 1939 it was attacked and torpedoed at Scapa Flow by U-boat U-47. Wilkinson survived the attack but the ship sank with the loss of 833 men and 414 survivors.[8] As a result of this attack and the shock suffered (nowadays called 'post-traumatic stress disorder' or PTSD) he was posted as Secretary to Captain Fallowfield at HMS *Ganges*.[9]

Richard Butler of B2 reported on 17 December 1940 that he had been down to HMS *Ganges* to interview Wilkinson the previous day, which was conducted in the presence of Commander Mallett, the Harwich SO (I) (Staff Officer Intelligence). Wilkinson had first been told to report to the Captain, Walter Herman Gordon Fallowfield, who instructed him to fully co-operate with MI5. Wilkinson said he had never been to Germany and did not speak German. He had first met the Duchesse at a cocktail party on Christmas Day 1939 at the Normandie Hotel, 96 Sussex Gardens, London, W2, with some friends called Clench, notably their daughter, June. There he also met the Countess Costenza, who he dated until she was interned. Another possible guest was Lady Mayo. He did not remember ever visiting Dorset House where the Duchesse and Vera lived, nor could he remember Costenza's address until it was retrieved from his address book. Stephens and Evans described him as being 'vague and secretive' when they interviewed him earlier, giving them the impression that he was concealing something regarding his relationship with Vera and the Duchesse. Butler's conclusion was that:

> Commander Mallett and I are fairly confident that this young man has not been used as a German agent. We are, however, equally confident that he is concealing something and we are disturbed by the fact that, if it is true that he was seen with the Duchesse de Château-THIERRY and her friends prior to Christmas 1939, he was at that time serving on the '*Royal Oak*' and was serving on it when it was torpedoed.[10]

The Duchesse (and later Vera) also denied that Wilkinson had ever attended a luncheon party at her flat, yet Mrs Morrish stated that, according to a note in her diary, on 21 August there had been a party of three composed of the

Duchesse, Vera and Wilkinson. An account of this event is included in Simon's MI5 file, recorded by Richard Butler of B2 who interviewed Mrs Morrish on 8 December 1940:

On August 21st 1939 she noted there was a luncheon party of three. She had put a ring around this date. She remembered that the party consisted of the Duchess, Vera and the unknown gentleman [someone has written 'possibly WERNER' above it] who had called to see Vera one morning a short while previously. The Duchess told her the night before the luncheon party that the gentleman who had recently called to see Miss Vera was coming to Lunch on the following day. He arrived between half-past twelve and one. MORRISH thought he was very rude, because he did not say good morning to her, he did not offer to give her his name, he put his hat down and walked straight into the sitting room where the Duchess was waiting for him. The Duchess never gave MORRISH his name, but she was very often in the habit of not telling her the names of the people who called to the flat. The only names which she used to mention were those of Lord and Lady Mayo.

MORRISH remembers that the Duchess sat in the dining room with her back to the windows, with Vera on her left and the man on her right. Her recollection is that he wore a dark civilian suit; he was fairly tall and very broad; he had thick hair, well brushed back, inclined to be fair, but with so much oil on it that it looked dark. He had a fresh complexion. He appeared to be starting a small moustache. She would think that he was in his early thirties.

MORRISH carried the food into the room, and left it on a side table. She did not wait at table. The little conversation she did hear seemed to touch mostly on the fact that Vera was not getting news from her people and the strange man seemed to be anxious to help her about it. He stayed in the flat for about an hour after lunch, and did not leave until at least 3 o'clock. MORRISH is quite certain that he was the same man who called on the previous occasion. She thought that he spoke rather clipped English, as if he was a foreigner. She remembers being so struck by his apparent rudeness when he arrived at the flat that she commented on it to s[ome] friends of hers whom she visited that evening.[11]

Whoever this guest was could not have been a naval officer as the wearing of a moustache is forbidden by King's (and Queen's) Regulations. Only a beard, or 'full set', as it is referred to in the Royal Navy, is permitted.[12]

On 1 October 1940 Vera told Stephens that Wilkins/Wilkinson was half-English, half-German, but maintained that she had never seen him. When Stephens questioned her about this, she told him that perhaps Wilkins/Wilkinson had seen a photograph of her or had been following her in Brussels. She gave as a reason that the Germans didn't trust her because she worked 'for the Red' i.e. Communists. She told him that, on Hansen's instructions, she was to await a visit from Wilkins/Wilkinson at the Dorchester within a few days or weeks of her arrival in England. She was to sit in the tearoom or elsewhere from 4 p.m. and 5.50 p.m. Her mission was to try to obtain information on aircraft and air force officers and report it to Wilkins/Wilkinson when he arrived. For this she was paid £300. An interrogation report of Vera on 4 October 1940 found in one of Ritter's files explored the circumstances of Wilkins'/Wilkinson's visit and his identity and is worth repeating in full as it is more revealing. She was questioned by Dick White, Tar Robertson and Stephens at Camp 020, with Stephens likely taking the lead (Part of Serial No.434):

Q. Now then, a very peculiar thing about this WILKINSON story. You know, I still don't believe it.

A. You don't believe it?

Q. I don't believe that WILKINSON story at all.

A. But he exists.

Q. He exists possibly, but I don't think he's in England.

A. That's possible. I know nothing about it, if he is in England now or not.

Q. Whether he exists as WILKINS or WILKINSON is beside the point, but the person you described – how did you describe him?

A. Tall, very, very – like that – long and thin, and a little moustache, and blue eyes. Rather a long face, blond hair.

Q. What was your reason for thinking he was in London?

A. Because I know that from RANTZAU he was in London.

Q. From RANTZAU?

A. Yes.

Q. Why should he mention another agent to you like that? Very bad technique.

A. No, I don't know, very bad technique. He said he may come to us.

Q. And how was he to come to you, if he didn't know where you were?

A. Probably he knew the address of the Duchess.

Q. So you were to go to the Duchess.

A. He?

Q. You were.

A. No, not now. I am speaking from last year.

Q. Last year WILKINSON was to meet you at the Duchess's?

A. Yes, then he had to come there.

Q. It was not before you came here this time, that he sent you to WILKINSON, but the time before.

A. No, he spoke again about WILKINSON. But I hadn't to meet him now.

Q. Ah, I see. But he might have got in touch with you while you were staying with the Duchess of Chateau Thierry?

A. Yes, that's the position.

Q. But why?

A. To bring news from RANTZAU or something like that.

Q. Instructions from RANTZAU, and to take your information back. You've got it, have you?

A. No, just to ask if we have got the money and things like that. It was nothing about – we shouldn't see each other.

[Part of Serial No.435]

Q. Are you absolutely certain that WILKINSON never came and saw you while you were at the Duchesse's?

A. No, she came on a morning. (N.B. ERICHSEN appears to refer to WILKINSON as 'she')

Q. He did come?

A. Yes, a morning.

Q. And brought you money?

A. No.

Q. Did he call himself WILKINSON then?

A. Yes, he did.

Q. He came to see the Duchess, did he?

A. Yes.

Q. And did you see him when he came?

A. Yes. I just come as he went away [*sic*].

Q. Yes, and you saw him? So the description you gave of WILKINSON is the description of a man you have seen?

A. Yes.

Q. Did the Duchess say it was a WILKINSON [*sic*]?

A. Yes, she say it was a gentleman with the name WILKINSON.

Q. His name is WILKINS or WILKINSON?

A. I don't remember, WILKINS or WILKINSON, I can't say.

Q. But she did say that – that is Mr. WILKINSON?

A. Yes.

Q. Who has come here from Dr. RANTZAU.

A. No, no. He didn't spoke so about Dr. RANTZAU. I know that she should come, a man of this name. He just asked how we are going on, and thing like that. But nothing about business [*sic*].

Q. Well now you saw him. What language did he speak?

A. English, very good English.

Q. Would you have mistaken him for an Englishman?

A. Yes.

Q. What else can you tell us about him? What type of man was he, was he well-dressed?

A. Yes, well-dressed.

Q. What did he strike you as – a British Army officer?

A. Yes, he could be.

Q. He could be a British Army officer?

A. Yes.

Q. Captain Peter EYRE?

A. No, Freddy EYRE.

Q. Freddy EYRE.

A. Oh no, he is much older.

Q. He's older than WILKINS?

A. Yes. Oh, he had nothing to do. I suppose he's the most innocent man in the world. Freddy EYRE.

Q. WILKINS' name wasn't Major MACKENZIE?[13]

To add yet another twist to the story, in a document relating to the Duchesse's daughter Anne Valeska Uhlig, dated 19 October 1940, when she was asked about Wilkinson and given his age (26 to 30) and description, Uhlig replied 'That's Major Ayres', but then stated that it couldn't be Ayres as he was 36.

Ayre(s) could not have been Alfred Jules 'Freddie' Ayre (1910–89), who was educated at Eton and Christ Church, Oxford, then the University of Vienna where he studied logical positivism. After a spell of teaching philosophy at Oxford from 1933 to 1940, on 21 September 1940 he was commissioned as a Second Lieutenant into the Welsh Guards from the Officer Cadet Training Unit. Later, he joined SOE (the Special Operations Executive) and then became an agent for MI6. On 27 December 1940 when Richard Butler questioned the Duchesse about the visit she thought it might have been Major Ayres, 'A very old friend I have known for about 30 years.'

Alfred Ayre the philosopher was 29 in 1939, but not yet a soldier; the rank is also wrong – as stated above, he only became a junior officer in September

1940, while the other was already an officer of field rank. Therefore it must have been another 'Freddie' Ayre and not the philosopher. Nor can Wilkinson have been 'Freddie' Ayre. When shown a photograph of Wilkinson the Duchesse said that whoever came to lunch on that particular day was not the man in the photograph. She thought that he could have been Leslie Stokes, a playwright and BBC radio producer and director, another old friend.

What confirms conclusively that Ayre(s) was not the philosopher is a letter from the Director of Military Operations and Intelligence at the South African Defence Ministry, dated 24 January 1941, to MI5 in Oxford regarding the Duchesse, Vera, and Wilkinson:

> Another friend was a man whose name was FREDDIE AYRES. He was an Officer in the Regular Army, believed to be an Adjutant, and after war was declared he got his majority [promoted to Major].
>
> He was a man about 45–50 years of age, tall, slim, light blue eyes, bloated face and dissipated appearance.
>
> The DUCHESSE informed Mrs. KAPLAN [Lili Kaplan] that AYRES and his wife had been very good to her during the years she had been in England.
>
> After war was declared, AYRES often visited the DUCHESSE in uniform with a very young man (name not known) also in uniform.[14]

This Major Ayres is most likely Brevet-Major Alfred Henry Rammell Ayers of the Royal Regiment of Artillery, and formerly the Royal Field Artillery in the First World War,[15] who was awarded the Bronze Star Medal by US President Harry S. Truman in 1948 in recognition of his services to SHAEF as a Prisoner of War liaison officer attached to G-1 section, 12th Army Group from 29 March 1945 to 8 May 1945 and 'Gazetted' on 17 September 1948. The official citation reads:

> Major Ayers' sincere and constructive work in connection with recovered British prisoners of war, his assignment and relief of British Prisoner of War exchange officers attached to armies, and his assistance in connection with Allied prisoners of war and and liaison officers of other nationalities contributed materially to the efficient handling of a large volume of Allied Prisoner of War work by this headquarters. Major Ayers' actions reflect high credit upon himself and the Allied forces.[16]

A summary report made on 16 January 1941, following on from Richard Butler's 29 December 1940 observations, shows that he had made some small progress. He started by saying that, 'no further steps have been taken with regard to A.P. WILKINSON' and concluded that section of his report by saying, 'My feeling is that it is unlikely that he is RANTZAU's agent,' although he does not venture how he came to that conclusion. He proposed confronting Wilkinson with Mrs Morrish and the porters at Dorset House; interviewing his friends, the Clench family; and checking his bank accounts. He was also going to follow up and check on Ayres. He reported that he had spoken to Wilkinson's brother, Lieutenant John Valentine Wilkinson. A check with the Admiralty and an unofficial Home Office Warrant to intercept A.P. Wilkinson's mail had both yielded nothing.[17]

Maxwell Knight, Major Stephens, Major George Sampson (Assistant Commandant of Camp 020), and Meurig Evans[18] reported that after Wilkinson had met the Countess Costenza at the Christmas Eve cocktail party, he had taken her out to lunch, probably at the Berkeley in Mayfair. The following day he met her at the Piccadilly Hotel, where he was accompanied by two men and a 25- or 26-year-old actress who had made a name for herself in a play or film called *Behind the Bars*.[19] He frequently took Costenza out to the Dorchester and Grosvenor Hotels in Park Lane, the Kit Kat Club in the Haymarket, and the Embassy Club,[20] spending a lot of money and was apparently always drunk. This profligate overspending was likely an attempt to impress the countess. On the surface this looked suspicious, given his position as a paymaster and very junior officer. He later told Richard Butler his spending was on account of a legacy of £1,000 that he had come into. Whether MI5 ever attempted to verify this is not recorded. His club was between Athenaeum Court, Piccadilly and the Berkeley, which would make it the Naval and Military, known as 'The In and Out' at Cambridge House, 95 Piccadilly (now at 4 St James's Square). Later in the same report Stephens wrote, 'I have already ventured to suggest that a main objective is the arrest of WILKINSON, and it may well be considered that the investigations in the subsidiary cases might be held in abeyance until this objective is achieved.'[21]

It appears that when Vera later returned to Hamburg, Rantzau told her that Wilkinson was, in fact, his principal and best English agent, so MI5's suspicions were confirmed, although they perhaps did not know this at the time. Vera described him as being aged twenty-eight to thirty (Butler said Wilkinson was twenty-three), tall, fair-haired, with light-coloured eyes, a small fair moustache, a biggish head, and 'typically English in an ordinary indistinctive sort of way', but of mixed blood, and appeared much like a banker. However, she failed to identify any of the thirteen photographs shown to her by Richard Butler as being Wilkinson. As noted earlier, the wearing of a moustache would have been unusual and against regulations by a naval officer, unless he was in the Royal Marines, or it was a false one, which seems highly unlikely. Stephens reiterated his suspicion that:

> The fact that ... CHATEAU-THIERRY and COSTENZA had had the opportunity of putting their heads together naturally raises a suspicion of connivance to direct investigation on to a false trail. Nevertheless VERA ERICHSEN's repeated assertions that WILKINSON exists carry conviction. COSTENZA's acquaintance with a Paymaster Lieutenant WILKINSON is established by her address book. The descriptions of WILKINSON by the two women are sufficiently similar to make it possible that they relate to the same man and CHATEAU-THIERRY provides a further link.
>
> That Paymaster Lieutenant WILKINSON may be identical with RANTZAU's agent must therefore be regarded as a serious possibility.[22]

Meurig Evans went on to recommend interviewing the Duchesse's maids: Dorothy Morrish, who was by that time serving in the ARP (Air Raid Precautions); Mrs A. Baker, an Austrian by birth but British by marriage; and Mrs Lockwood, a charwoman. There were other 'long shots', who were ruled out as being contenders: Edward Haliburton Bourke @ Wilson, the son of Lord and Lady Mayo; Ransom Markham; and an unnamed member of the Secret Service.

During the 12 November interview of the Duchesse, conducted by Major Sampson and Meurig Evans, they confronted her with Vera, to whom they posed the following questions:

> Q. Do you remember you said that on October 30th RANTZAU had told you when you returned to Germany that he was paying WILKINSON £25 and the DUCHESS [sic] £60 a month?
> A. No. I only told you about WILKINSON. I told you that the DUCHESS got money from Holland - £60. RANTZAU said the DUCHESS got £60.
> Q. That he was paying her £60 a month - I see. WILKINSON was getting how much?
> A. £25.
> Q. Wasn't he supposed to give you some?
> A. Sometimes I got some because I was always hard up.[23]

This suggests that Wilkinson was indeed involved with Rantzau as his agent, but was he the young naval officer or someone else entirely? Later they asked

Vera about where she had first met Wilkinson. She told them it had been at Dorset House in June or July 1939 and reiterated his description – tall, blond moustache, blue eyes. Vera and the Duchesse confirmed that they were both present at the time, but that it was her he had come to see; the Duchesse had appeared just as he was leaving. Exactly why Wilkinson had come to see Vera was not explained, but, as noted earlier, it appears that she had been given instructions to contact him after she had returned to Britain in September 1940. Later the line of questioning continued about Wilkinson, and it is worth repeating verbatim:

Q. But when you came into her flat and found WILKINSON there – they'd been talking together for some time you told us before.
A. Yes, he was just going as I came.
Q. She appeared to know him?
A. If she knows him or not I can't say. I think she asked him about this address or something like that, but she didn't say it.
Q. Duchess [*sic*] appeared to know WILKINSON.
A. She doesn't seem to know him. I don't know whether she knows him.
Q. Weren't they engaged in conversation?
A. He was just saying goodbye. I think she asked him about his address [...] he didn't say it.
Q She said that he came there to ask for you and you were in the flat below and he came down and you went up about a quater [*sic*] of an hour later.
A. Not at once, not dressed.
Q. What time?
A. May be a quater [*sic*] of an hour.
Q. Don't you think it strange that if he came to see you he went after a quater [*sic*] of an hour without seeing you?
A. He just asked my maid. She said it was a strange man who wanted to see me.
Q. You just guessed that he came to see you? He may have come to see the Duchess and asked to see you at the same time.
A. Yes.
Q. Did anyone say that this is Mr WILKINSON?
A. He said himself.[24]

During the questioning Vera mentioned a certain Major Mackenzie, which it is worth noting was also an alias sometimes used by Maxwell Knight (also Captain King). She thought that because Wilkinson was very young, he couldn't be important. When asked about his nationality, she said Wilkinson was half

English/half German. Rantzau had apparently told her that, 'WILKINSON was his righthand [*sic*] man in England and that he had done much more than anybody had done for me and you, and the Duchess has done nothing at all and I used to pay her very well':

> Q. When you came to stay with the Duchess you were expecting to be called on by a man representing HANSEN [Rantzau]?
> A. He told me only that some people of his might come. No names.
> Q. Didn't you ask the names?
> A. No.
> Q. First time you heard the name WILKINSON was when he called on you.
> A. Yes.
> Q. When you went back to Brussels.
> A. When I went to Hamburg.
> Q. Did he call on you after your return or before that WILKINSON came to call on you?
> A. Before, but I am not quite sure if it was before I went to Brussels.[25]

So here we have an admission from Vera that he *was* a contact person. But what had he come to tell her? Most likely that she was being recalled to Europe to prepare for her future mission in England. This seems a somewhat circuitous way of doing things – to send her over to work for the Duchesse, establish herself in the Duchesse's *milieu*, then have her return to Europe, only to return a short while later, with the inevitable prospect of being captured. Why did the Abwehr not prepare her for the mission the first time around? Or have someone in England brief her? Most likely this was what is known in intelligence circles as 'establishing her bona fides'. The Advisory Committee, reporting on the Duchesse's case, stated that:

> We feel reasonably certain, however, that the DUCHESSE is not telling the truth and that Vera's account of WILKINSON's early morning visit is probably true. It is, moreover, probable that the man in question was an emissary of RANTZAU who had been sent to see how things were getting on at 102 Dorset House with the object of reporting to RANTZAU. Alternatively, he may have come to pay the DUCHESSE some money.[26]

Maxwell Knight, accompanied by Norman Himsworth and Joan Miller, questioned the Duchesse in Holloway Prison about Wilkinson on 2 November 1940. She responded that she thought she knew the name from somewhere but seemed vague. It seems implausible that Sub-Lieutenant A.P. Wilkinson could be Rantzau's agent. What could have motivated him to work for the Germans, and if so, how long had this been going on? After all, he had nearly lost his life in 1939 as the result of enemy action, which was hardly a motivation for working for them. Whatever the case, his file was destroyed by MI5, so it may have contained embarrassing information which they did not want to be made public. On the other hand, MI5 may have considered it as containing nothing of any significance. Perhaps, after all, they had not caught all the spies working for the Abwehr, although they were keeping a check on him. Was he arrested and charged at some point? We will probably never know.

The Camp 020 report suggested that Wilkinson's description tallied with Werner Ulm, except for the absence of a moustache, and agrees with the note scribbled in Butler's report. According to his MI5 files[27] his name is given as Sonderführer Werner Unversagt, born c.1912 and based mainly in I-H at *Ast* Brussels, described in 1945 by Helen Osmun in WRC1 as 'undoubtedly the "brain" behind the spate of agents directed towards the United Kingdom in 1940'. The photographs show a man with a high forehead, his hair combed back and a smear of a fair moustache. The age also looks about right. A check of these files reveals that he was called up into the 2nd Army Reserve around July 1939 and trained as an interpreter. Until 29 September 1939 he was in Limburg, near Bad Ems, at the 12th Army's prisoner-of-war (POW) cage. On 25 May 1940 he reported to *Ast* Brussels and worked under Walter Sensburg[28]. He was still in Brussels from August until the end of September 1940 and was *Leiter* of the Kommando in Le Touquet at the training school where he instructed Sensburg's agents. This would seem to preclude his being a visitor to the Duchesse in 1939 or 1940, unless he popped over for a brief visit, and also not A.P. Wilkinson.[29] What all this means is that the Germans must have already had an agent based in Britain, and not someone parachuted in or who had arrived by sea, as they had all been rounded up.

Another person MI5 interviewed was Countess Costenza, who claimed to have seen the naval officer in the company of the Duchesse and admitted to knowing him.[30] Deputy Head Porter Michael Smith and porter Cecil Swain at Dorset Court both identified him as someone who came to the flat on at least three or four occasions in 1939, while Mrs Morrish said he came at least once towards the end of June 1939. Both Vera and the Duchesse told MI5 different versions of the same story: Vera that an emissary of Dr Rantzau's had come to the flat; the Duchesse that such a visit took place, but that he was *not* an emissary of Dr Rantzau. The question is, how would she know? That the visit took place was considered an important piece of evidence against Vera if she were ever brought to trial.

When Richard Butler interviewed Mrs Morrish again on 13 December 1940 she identified the man in the photograph he showed her as the one who had come to the Duchesse's flat on 29 July 1939, and she was 'absolutely certain' that he was the one who had previously come to see Vera. This was because it was the only time that the Duchesse and Vera had had anyone alone to lunch. She said that the man had told her that the Duchesse was expecting him, and that he seemed to know his way around the flat. He also stopped talking if she were around. According to the description given, the man's hair was very heavily oiled and he had the makings of a small moustache. Butler queried the fact that the Duchesse had told Morrish the night before to expect a guest for lunch, but had she told Vera? He wondered what they talked about and if the man was there on Rantzau's behalf; were there any messages, or money that he conveyed from Rantzau? Morrish told him that the conversation appeared to be to the effect that Vera had not heard from 'her people'. Butler found it convenient that this luncheon had taken place just two weeks before war was declared and posed the rhetorical question, 'Were the Duchesse and herself [Vera] given any instructions about wartime activities?'

We now turn briefly to another person with whom the Duchesse came into contact – Lily Sormani. Described as 'very wealthy and eccentric' and closely associated with Dr Rantzau, she was a Dutch woman living in Wiesbaden who the Duchesse's stepsister had introduced her to and who claimed to have known the Duchesse's family when they lived in Holland. The Duchesse described her as 'Fat and middle-aged. About 50 with greyish hair. Frumpish looking always. Not nice looking or bad looking. Glasses generally.' She said Sormani was looking for a flat in London as well as an English companion who would accompany her to America, where she planned to write 'political books'. One requirement was that the companion could speak Russian. The Duchesse thought that Vera 'would be useful for that'. Miss Sormani agreed to pay Vera £10 a month.

The Advisory Committee examining the Duchesse's case expressed doubts as to Miss Sormani's existence based on the advertisement the Duchesse had placed in *The Times* after her return to England, and a letter she had written to her daughter on 23 April 1939. In the letter she had written: 'I succeeded in getting the lady who sent Vera to me to give me £30 a month, that is £80, for a few months anyway as she seems satisfied with what I do for the girl.'[31] The Advisory Committee then appears to have changed its tune and assumed this lady to be Miss Sormani:

it is plain that this new arrangement must have been made by letter, for the DUCHESSE had not seen Miss Sormani since January of 1939. No letters to or from have ever been found and it seems fairly clear from this extract, and from the whole correspondence, that the DUCHESSE was deceiving her daughter, who was extremely anxious about the money her mother was receiving, and the trouble which appeared to be brewing for her mother in consequence.[32]

There is contradictory evidence about whether Vera ever actually met her. However, in an interview with MI5 on 12 November she described Sormani as a middle-aged woman who was quite fat, with blonde hair and blue or grey eyes. She even said she'd met Sormani once in Copenhagen in December or January at the house of Max Bodenhof, prior to March when she went to England. This is possibly Max Bodenhoff, born in Copenhagen on 21 February 1887 and who died in 1954. One contender for Sormani was Hildina Margaret Sormani, a British-born widow, French by marriage, who arrived at Dover on 18 June 1937, giving her address as 108 Carshalton Road, Sutton, Surrey. Enquiries by Special Branch in 1941 at that address revealed a Rubina Margaret Sormani, widow, who had died on 26 May 1940. Her son was Paul Sormani of Merrow, near Guildford, Surrey. However, Special Branch was unable to make any connection with Lily Sormani. No further information has come to light about the true identity of Sormani, if indeed she really existed. A website to the Pockley family mentions a Countess Sormani who had lived in Switzerland with Edith Muriel 'Gill' Pockley, the twin of Eustace Mitford Pockley (1873–74) who was born in St Leonards, New South Wales, Australia, in 1873 and died in Chatswood, New South Wales, in 1951/52 aged 79.[33] In a history of the Pockley family, R.V. Pockley describes Sormani as 'a little old woman' in 1975, which by then she would have been. Could this be the same Lily Sormani?

The Advisory Committee further concluded that there must have been some collusion between the Duchesse and Reinhardt in which Vera had been deliberately sent to her and not, as the Duchesse had suggested, that she had picked Vera quite randomly out of 200 applicants. The Duchesse would therefore allow her flat to be used as a rendezvous for German agents. A series of letters she wrote to her daughter Valeska are quite revealing. For example, on 14 June 1938 she wrote that Reinhardt had written to her suggesting a meeting in Freiburg; she countered it with Basel as an alternative. The following day she told Valeska that she was now living all expenses paid in the lap of luxury and that Reinhardt was 'charming and young and quite OK'.

In July 1938 a check had been placed on any mail sent to the Duchesse at the Clinique La Valerette, which turned up a letter from Arnold Louis Chevallier. Included with it was a note written by the Duchesse asking him about Belgian defensive fortifications. Chevallier replied with answers to her questions. MI5 reported that in 1938 he had sent the Duchesse a long report on general political and commercial matters 'and it is probable that she thought he might be of use to her in introducing her to some of his industrial contacts'. At the time of the report (undated) his whereabouts were unknown. On 10 August she asked her daughter to enquire at the Colonial or Overseas Club of Chevallier's address. Two days later she emphasised that, 'It is of great importance to me to get in touch with that clever lunatic Chevallier.' Also that same day she told her daughter that:

> I do not think that Dr. Reinhardt will succeed in sending me before September. He is not sure about that at all, only trying. Why I want Chevallier's address is that he has an article for sale which they want me to buy … He can submit his drawings and they can manufacture abroad. Chevallier did ask me several times if I knew of a purchaser, but I did not then, but I do now. It would mean a good profit.[34]

Send her where?

8

THE DUCHESSE'S CIRCLE

The motley assortment that made up the Duchesse's circle was comprised of 'a collection of people as odd and as mixed as Vera had ever met in her life' – members of the British aristocracy, mad scientist inventors, military officers, and young women hoping to be introduced into London society. Some members have already been mentioned, but there were many others, such as Dr Frederick Henry whom the Duchesse had met ten years before in 1930.[1]

When he was interrogated at Brixton Prison on 30 October 1940, Henry said that their first meeting was in connection with his wanting to become an FRGS (Fellow of the Royal Geographical Society). The Secretary of the Society informed him that he would need a proposer and a seconder to become elected. A month later, he was duly elected, having answered an advertisement placed by the Duchesse offering to make social introductions for a fee of £20 per person. Two years after their first meeting she asked him for money, but he declined and referred her to some of her rich friends. While in Switzerland visiting her son, the Duchesse wrote to Henry sending him a thirty-page letter regarding an invention relating to guns by one of her protégés, and asking for his assistance. This protégé must have been Chevallier. Henry turned down the Duchesse's request, replying that he was not a financier. Unperturbed, she went to him to complain, so he put her in touch with Serge Karlinsky, a Russian Jew who was an old friend of his and a distant relation of his wife (of more later). However, that was the last Henry heard of it.

In 1939, shortly after the war began, Dr Henry was attending English classes put on by Hampstead Borough Council. There he met a young woman named Bauer whose father was an expert on growing seeds and sugar beet. It appears that Bauer was using some sort of hydroponic process that Henry thought might be useful to the war effort. He passed on Bauer's name to the Duchesse, who sent him to Captain Drummond of Drummonds Bank.

However, Drummond apparently was not interested in Bauer, so the Duchesse never received her fee. When Maxwell Knight had asked the Duchesse about Bauer she replied:

> This Bauer was sent for by the English Govt to lecture at Cambridge. He was thought to be the greatest authority in this world on sugar and seeds and things. He had been an expert in Czechoslovakia and Hungary. He though [*sic*] the Govt should grow these seeds in this country and save millions of money. This man was growing tomatoes and cauliflowers (on) under water. I was supposed to tell him of some people in this country, ad [*sic*] to get about 100 acres here and there to get Bauer to cultivate. First of all I turned it down. This man was recommended by three people from the Ministry of Agriculture, and then Dr. Henry said there was an enormous lot of money to be made for the future.[2]

Henry told MI5 that the Duchesse was always surrounded by women of all ages:

> whom he assumed to be connected with her activities as a professional introducer into society. Amongst others whom he met with her were Lady MAYO. He also met a young American girl who he described as 'very stupid' and also a young Danish-Russian woman whom he described as 'tall, dark, with black [eyes] and a very Russian appearance. He could not [remember her name at f]irst but she had obviously made a considerable impression on [him] … He also remembered ab[out h]er that she was [en]gaged to a French soldier and that s[he] was very se[nt]imental.[3]

Much of the remainder of the page has been obliterated. When asked, he identified the young Danish-Russian woman as Vera de Schalburg, but at 5ft 6in Vera could hardly be described as 'tall'. The American girl may have been Jane Lawrence, referred to by Major William Mackenzie when he told MI5 about a group of friends she had proposed bringing round to his flat at 39 Bruton Place for drinks. The others in the group included Lady Mayo, an Army officer, and a 'Russian girl', who was almost certainly Vera, although Mackenzie said he couldn't remember the names.

Henry's first meeting with Lady Mayo was in the spring of 1939 when he and his wife were invited to a ball at Claridges in aid of birth control. He also identified someone named Barbara as Mrs de Froberville, married to a broker dealing in South American stocks, who lived in the same building as the Duchesse and was an old friend of hers. A meeting had taken place between

Karlinsky and the Duchesse's daughter at Madame de Froberville's flat (she often styled herself as 'Madame') to provide the necessary background as the Duchesse was not available. Valeska Uhlig also said that Philip de Froberville was in the RAF (in 1940 he was a squadron leader, according to Nigel West and Guy Liddell),[4] 'who appears to travel about the country with his wife visiting aerodromes.'[5] Henry claimed he had never heard of Hansen or Rantzau or Major Mackenzie. Henry's wife, Raissa *née* Halberstadt, whom he had married in Warsaw in 1925, claimed she had never met Wilkinson or Philip de Froberville.

During his interview with the Duchesse on 2 November 1940, Maxwell Knight asked her about Dr Henry and whether he had been connected with Dr Reinhardt. She denied this and replied:

> I got an awful shock when I heard about Mrs Henry [she was interned in Holloway Prison]… I was wondering whether these poor wretches have called on me once or twice while Vera Schalburg was with me, and I wonder whether she got them into trouble.[6]

Lady Mayo was Geraldine Sarah Bourke *née* Ponsonby (1863–1944), the Dowager Countess of Mayo, widow of Dermot Robert Wyndham Bourke (1851–1927), the 7th Earl. The Duchesse's daughter described her as being 'definitely crackers; and always has been'. Lady Mayo was a passionate gardener and kept a diary of her plantings at Palmerston House in County Kildare, which was destroyed by fire during the Irish Civil War.[7] Lady Mayo's illegitimate son, Edward Charles Bourke-Haliburton, had been given certain papers about Chevallier's invention by the Earl of Mayo, who had passed them on to the Duchesse. This must have been the 8th Earl, Walter Longley Bourke (1859–1939). A report by Stephens and Meurig Evans dated 25 November 1940 states that according to Major Peter Perfect, the MI5 RSLO in Edinburgh, Lady Mayo 'appears to be consorting with officers in Scotland and encouraging some shady young women who are with her to relieve these officers of all their worldly wealth. She is a drunken and dissolute woman'.

Countess Costenza, mentioned earlier, was an Austrian countess who was staying with a Miss Eileen D'Orne. The Duchesse described Costenza as a 'decent girl' who Eileen D'Orne had brought to her to launch into society. Stephens described her as 'another international hanger-on to London Society … [who] appeared to have a certain personal attraction, but … was no Mata Hari'.[8] The Duchesse told Stephens, Sampson and Evans at Holloway on 12 November 1940 that she had refused to help Costenza as 'she was not the style of girl I wanted to take about'. As noted earlier, the countess's Home Office file is not available from the National Archives at Kew but she is described by Nigel West as 'another Abwehr agent'.[9]

What is known about Costenza comes from two articles that appeared in the *Ottawa Journal* in 1940.[10] Her full name was Edeltrud Claudette von Costenza, a beautiful red-haired, 22-year-old Austrian refugee who had come to England in 1936 to take up a film career. She is also mentioned by Brian Simpson as Edeltrud C.L. Newirth @ von Costenza in context with Defence Regulation 18B.[11] Her other aliases, as listed in the National Archives entry for her Home Office file, are Stein, E; Neuwirth, E.C.; Neurith; Cosowxi, Countess M Von; Costenza, Countess E.C. Von; Costowzia, M; Wharton, E.C.; Waldhasven, C.; Stein, E.; Hanson, H. Stein. Her date of birth is given variously as 1904, 1914 and 1927.[12] Stephens, the Commandant of Camp 020, refers to her in his own inimitable way as 'the spurious Contessa von COSTENZA'. If the article in the *Ottawa Journal* giving her age as 22 is correct, that would make her birth date 1914. Certainly, from the photograph found online (no date given) she looks very young and very pretty. It may not be purely a coincidence that one of her aliases is Hanson, as Hansen is also an alias of Nikolaus Ritter.

The countess was cited in a court case at Marylebone Register Office involving Frederick George Wharton (1905–84), a 34-year-old clerk of Braemar Avenue, Wembley, accused of bigamously marrying her on 4 June 1937. She told the court that she had wanted to marry an Englishman to escape ending up in a concentration camp. When cross-examined by Mr R.L. Jackson, the countess told the court emotionally, 'For five years I tried to escape from my people, but they followed me to Holland and Germany.' She claimed to have met Wharton in a café:

> I asked Wharton if he thought it would be right for him to marry me, as I was not in love with him. I wanted to make a marriage of friendship, and I said I would do my best to help him if he would help me. He agreed, and a day or two later I went with him to St. Marylebone register office to give notice of the marriage. I went through a form of marriage with him on June 4, 1937. After the ceremony we went to a friend's flat in Holland Park Road for tea, and I gave Wharton £25. He left me after supper and did not return.[13]

Wharton, who had married 21-year-old Emily Whemay (born c.1906) in Manchester on 26 December 1927, and with whom he was still living in Newton Heath, Manchester, denied ever going through a ceremony with the countess. He alleged that his birth certificate had been obtained from him under false pretences. When asked from whom she had obtained the money to pay Wharton, the countess told the magistrate that it had come from an American friend, Charles Reisner, who was a film producer and was interested in bringing her to Hollywood. Charles 'Chuck' Reisner was a German American born in Minneapolis in 1887 who had appeared with Charlie Chaplin in *A Dog's Life* and *The Kid* and was responsible for directing the Marx Brothers in their final film for MGM, *The Big Store*. He died in California in 1962; Wharton died in Blackpool and Fylde in 1984.

The countess's mother was apparently present at the so-called 'marriage', but since she was currently in Nazi Germany during the court case, she could not be called as a witness. When war broke out Wharton was visited by a detective sergeant from Special Branch to enquire about the countess's correct nationality. He told the police that he was not married to her and that he believed his birth certificate had been stolen by a gang. He further alleged that he had been standing at the meeting ground in Hyde Park (probably Speaker's Corner) when he had been approached by a man with a foreign accent who said he might be able to help him get a job:

> I went to an address in Paddington where I met a number of people, all of whom appeared to be foreigners. Among them was the countess. They discussed the formation of a society to aid foreigners in London, and said I was to be secretary. They asked me to learn German, and they also asked for my birth certificate, as they wanted to get me a passport in case I had to travel abroad I took my birth certificate. After three weeks, during which I received about £10 salary, they said that they could not get sufficient backing, and I was no longer wanted. My birth certificate was not returned. The countess gave me an introduction to a member of an engineering company, and I got a post as a storekeeper, which I held for about twelve months. On October 2, 1939 the countess phoned me at work and made an appointment to meet me at Wembley L.M.S. station at 6.15 p.m. I kept the appointment; and she said: 'Hello, Fred.' We went to a restaurant in Kensington High street (I did this with the approval of the police.). She paid for our dinner and a bottle of port. She said I might expect a call from the police, and she urged me to tell them I was Count von Costenza, her husband, and to refuse to answer further questions. I have never gone through a form of marriage with her.[14]

The address in Paddington could not have been the Duchesse's because at that time she was living in Chiltern Court, NW1, not W2. Nor is it known

whether the engineering company to which Wharton referred was anything
to do with Chevallier; the member of the company could have been J.S. Hood
or Dr Root (also written as Proot), who were two other inventors (of more
later). According to a letter written by Richard Butler to Major H.J. Baxter,
the RSLO in Manchester, on 18 January 1941,[15] Root had been trying before
the war to dispose of an invention to the War Office, and that 'all the circumstances relating to him make him gravely suspect'. He went on:

2. Sir Stafford Cripps had informed the War Office that 'any delay in interviewing HOOD would 'increase the possibility of the invention getting into
the hands of our 'potential enemies'.

3. The duchesse de CHATEAU-THIERRY receives HOOD's address from
RANTZAU and writes to his [sic] with regard to an invention. She is careful
not to mention the name of the friend who gave her HOOD's name and
address, and endeavours to suggest that she really wanted his help with regard
to American Funds. HOOD apparently is no [sic] sufficiently interested in
the progress of his invention to reply to this letter, and the Duchesse is not
sufficiently worried about her American funds to follow the letter up.

4. HOOD has a laboratory at Croydon from 1932 to 1937, and frequently
meets Schmidt REX.[16] HOOD when asked by REX how he is progress-
ing with one of his inventions, tells him that he is proposing to turn it to
some commercial use. On the suggestion of REX, he then interview [sic]
a member of the staff of the German Embassy, who turns out to be the
Assistant Air Attache there.

5. At the commencement of the war, HOOD applies for membership of the
War Department Constabulary, and for some reason which is not at all clear,
leaves the body and transferred to the Passive Defence Dept. at the Royal
Ordnance Factory at Hooton. He is now being recommended as an assistant
to a Security Office[r].

6. You state that HOOD is positive that the Duchesse's letter was addressed
to him at the Westminster Club. So far as I can trace, you have not sent us
the envelope of the Duchesse's letter so I am unable to confirm that this is
the case. It is perhaps a coincidence, but it is all the same interesting, that the
Westminster Club premises were situated in the basemen[t] of Broadway
Buildings, Westminster, and as you are aware a certain very important body
has its London offices on one of the upper floors [The headquarters of SIS
and GC&CS was at 54 Broadway Buildings, under the guise of the Minimax
Fire Extinguisher Company].[17]

Butler requested further particulars about Hood, including a full description, with a photograph; his marital status; his bank account; and whether he still lived at 63 Grange Road, Birkenhead. His summary on 16 January 1941 indicated that he had not yet heard back from Baxter. He had read all the Deutsche Lufthansa files but could find no record of Hood knowing Schmidt Rex. He was rewarded with a reply from Manchester on 23 January in the form of extracts from a report relating to the Duchesse that sheds much light on John Samuel Hood's unwitting involvement with German Intelligence:

I interviewed this man yesterday at some length. He gives the impression of being most anxious to have this whole matter cleared up, and is obviously trying hard to give any information which may be helpful. It is just possible, of course, that he has slipped up in the past and is now trying to bluff. I do not, however, think that this is the case.

This man is employed at the R.O.F. HOOTON.[18]

I discussed with him, at some length, his relationship with Schmidt REX at Croydon. HOOD had a laboratory on the factory estate, near the Croydon aerodrome, from 1932 to about 1937, and even after that date he constantly visited a laborator[y] at Croydon, where he was engaged on his experimental and research work. When there, he used frequently to visit the Aerodrome Hotel. He was a member of a small snooker Club that played at this Hotel. He met Schmidt REX very frequently there. He said that REX was a very popular person with everybody at the Hotel. Among other persons who were friendly with Schmidt REX were a man named ROBINSON, a pilot of the Imperial Airways and a man named 'Swank' ROGERS a former pilot of the Imperial Airways on the Cologne-Croydon Service, but who more recently ran an air taxi service at Croydon.[19] HOOD could not suggest that either of these men were likely to be engaged in espionage. Another person at the snooker club was PARMENTIER,[20] the K.L.M. pilot, regarding whom I know you have a file. HOOD was meeting Schmidt REX, and these other people very frequently. I have no doubt that he used often to talk about his invention to Schmidt REX and any other persons whom he could persuade to listen. It is very difficult to prevent him talking about these inventions even now.

At one time a certain amount of newspaper publicity was given to one of his inventions, relating to incendiary bombs. Shortly afterwards, Schmidt REX asked him how he was getting on with this invention. He said that he was turning it into a welding process for commercial use. Schmidt REX told him that he thought he could put him in touch with somebody who could

hel[p] him. Schmidt REX left him for a moment, while he telephoned and
then came back to tell him to go to the German Embassy at Carlton House
Terrace[21] and ask for Herr SPIELER. He went the next day to what he
thinks is the Commercial office of the German Embassy, in Carlton House
Terrace. My original reference to the Embassy Club was an error of the
Police Officer who took the message. HOOD had met SPIELER once
before, at the Aerodrome Hotel at Croydon, but only for a few seconds,
and this latter meeting had no connection with the earlier one. SPIELER
appeared to know the type of invention in which HOOD was interested,
and had presumably been told by Schmidt REX. He explained that he was
not a technician, but after a few minutes conversation he said that he would
get in touch with a steel corporation, who would undoubtedly help HOOD
and would ge[t] into communication with him. HOOD has not, in fact,
heard anything from the steel corporation or from SPIELER since that
interview. He has never been to the German Embassy since then. He cannot
fix the date of this connection with POSTNIKOW[22] and consequently it
was some time in 1938. He thinks that it must have been in March, as it was
some time before the Munich Crisis. HOOD said that he saw Schmidt REX
a day or two after the interview with SPIELER, and REX said that he was
returning to Germany within a few days. HOOD has not seen Schmidt
REX si[nce]. He said that if REX left this country just before the war, he
must have come back to England after HOOD last saw him.

At first it seemed to me reasonably certain that the information had come
to the Duchesse of CHATEAU THIERRY via SPIELER, although it is difficult to see why the Intelligence Service should have been employed where
it would have been simple to obtain the information about the invention by
commercial investigation. Moreover, Duchesse of CHATEAU THIERRY
refers to inventions while HOOD stated that he only discussed one invention with SPIELER. The more important reason for doubting this theory
is that HOOD is positive that he only gave SPIELER the address of 10
Broad Green, West Croydon, whereas the Duches[se] wrote to him at the
Westminster Club. He is convinced that he did not tell SPIELER about the
Westminster Club, nor does he think that he ever told Schmidt REX.

I am afraid that this is as far as we can take the matter. HOOD told me
that EWERTZ was another person who used to play snooker at Croydon [a
ground engineer for Lufthansa, spelled ERTZ in Baxter's report]. I enclose
another letter, somewhat mutilated, which HOOD received at one time
from POSTNIKOW. HOO[D] thoroughly realised that he is in an awkward
position, and [i]s anxious to help. One possible line of inquiry might be if

he could be given the names of any other persons who are known to have been in touch with the Duchesse of Chateau Thierry or with RANTZAU.[23]

In Baxter's 1 January 1941 report of his interview with Hood on 19 December 1940 he stated that Hood was engaged in 'chemical research' from 1927 onwards, which Baxter thought had been something of a hobby. Even so, Hood had managed to obtain a 'certain number of minor academic qualifications', such as F.I.C. [Fellow of the Royal Institute of Chemistry], indicating professional competence. When he retired from the Liverpool Police Force he continued in a professional capacity to pursue chemistry as a student, consultant and inventor. Baxter claimed it was difficult to pin him down to anything specific, but Hood had at one time been involved with waterproof clothing and had become a director of the British Proofing Corporation. Another director was Carlos Otto Gaetjens,[24] whose brother-in-law Dr D.F. Bernauer was also a director, as well as an accountant named D. Cavill Evans.[25] At one point the company was proofing fabric against mustard gas.

Sir Stafford Cripps employed Hood as a 'tame technical expert' investigating a variety of subjects such as 'refractory matters', artificial silk, and the cause of silicosis. Hood claimed to have invented an aerial torpedo, the details of which he had given to Cripps and Emmanuel Shinwell, Independent Labour Party MP for Linlithgowshire, later chairman of the Labour Party in 1942, and was in negotiations with the War Office.[26] At the end of 1937 he was negotiating with Alexander Alexandrovich Postnikow (see above) of the Industrial Facilities Corporation Ltd., of 33 Cornhill, London EC3, who had claimed to be able to sell any kind of patent such as Hood's. According to Baxter, Cripps had dissuaded Hood from continuing his negotiations with Postnikow and tried to attract the War Office's attention. Spieler and another man named Hauptmann were involved with some sort of welding process for the Mauser Steel Corporation. Baxter commented that Hood was 'conceited an[d] considered himself in possession of expert knowledge and abilit[y] in matters in which he is probably only semi-skilled. I think, however, that he is patriotic and has not knowingly been in touch with the German Secret Service.'

Other information about Hood came from Richard Butler on 29 December 1940 quoting a report by Meurig Evans to Robin Stephens on his interview with the Duchesse on 23 and 25 November, discussing her various associates. He refers to Baxter's report and states that Hood was the son of a Liverpool police officer, who was also in the Liverpool Police Force at one time, but had left to set up an enquiry office. Hood was 'now doing some kind of A.R.P. work'. Hood had produced a letter from the Duchesse that said:

A mutual friend gave me your address, telling me that I would be interested in some of your inventions – indirectly so to say. I have been successful now and then in being instrumental to bring inventors together with people who are able to launch various inventions.[27]

The Duchesse confirmed during those interviews and one on 29 December by Richard Butler that Rantzau (or as she had put it then, Rheinhardt) had given her Hood's name as he might be able to help her out with regard to her money tied up in America. She claimed not to have known Hood before, but seemed to think there was some sort of American connection with him. When shown her letter she also confirmed that Hood was interested in inventions and that she might be able to help him get them produced. She had not mentioned the matter of her American funds in her first letter to Hood because she considered it 'a very delicate matter', which Evans found to be a 'most unsatisfactory' explanation, and was convinced that she was lying to him. She also denied knowing Schmidt Rex or Spieler, or anything about either of them. As Butler put it:

It is just possible that this is true and that RANTZAU got HOOD's name from Schmidt REX and was proposing to use the Duchesse to obtain particulars from him. *On the other hand* [added, handwritten; Butler's italics] I cannot believe that RANTZAU would not have made use of a more businesslike person than the Duchesse.[28]

In a note to Major J.R. Whyte of B4 on 24 March 1942, John Day concluded that Hood's name *had* been given to the Duchesse by Rantzau when she visited Holland. Vera had confirmed that the Duchesse had written to him but did not know whether Hood had ever called the Duchesse (he hadn't). She also claimed that she had never met Hood or been to the Curzon House Club with the Duchesse. As Day said:

I think the inference is that the Duchess's account of her relations with HOOD is probably true, since it tallies exactly with what she appears to have told Vera at a time when there was no reason why she should have lied to Vera. I think you will agree that the complete innocence of HOOD is thereby upheld?[29]

Dr Proot was a Belgian consulting chemist on the technical staff of Cyclax Co. living in Edgware, north London.[30] The Duchesse said that he lived at 35 or 36

Manor Park Gardens, Edgware, and described him as a 'small man, pleasant face, clean shaven, brownish hair, funny sort of teeth', Proot's wife had apparently started a shop in Bond Street, which later went out of business. The Duchesse was to go into business with Proot and sell her products through his wife's shop.

It seems possible that the 'society to aid foreigners' may have had something to do with the Duchesse. When Valeska, the Duchesse's daughter, was interviewed by Maxwell Knight, she told him that she had only known Costenza since their incarceration in Holloway. Knight was curious about what attracted the Duchesse to Costenza. Valeska told him:

> I was curious myself. She was very young and very kind. I couldn't tell you anything about her except what I read in the papers. She had been kind to a woman named D'Orm [*sic*] who had died in hospital, and it was there that she met Costenza.[31]

Knight referred to a letter Costenza had written to the Duchesse on 27 February 1940 in which she spoke of her alleged perjury, of which more shortly. When Knight asked Valeska whether Costenza was 'a bit crackers' she replied: 'She is slightly hysterical; has brain storms I imagine, but she is quite a kindly thing in spite of that.'

The Duchesse's MI5 file (KV2/357) refers to Costenza @ Editrud Neuwirth being interviewed by the Advisory Committee on 24 April 1940 regarding her continued detention under a Home Office Warrant. According to the Duchesse, 'the young lady was anti-Nazi and resented the Hitler regime. Whether Costenza and the Duchesse had been well acquainted is not known.' It appears that Costenza did know Stella Lonsdale when they were in 'E' Wing at Holloway, as a letter dated 27 July 1942 from Dr Matheson, the Governor at Holloway, to Cyril Mills confirms when he referred to Stella trying to get hold of a quantity of moth balls for Costenza's clothing and furs, but, 'I don't think they were wanted for any other purpose.' This related to a letter from Cyril Mills to Dr Matheson on 17 June 1942 when he refers to:

> … in the postscript at the head of page one you will see that Lonsdale asks for 'a lot of moth balls'. As Lonsdale presumably has very few clothes in prison the request seems a peculiar one. I am told, although I do not know if it is true or not, that certain types of moth balls contain Naphthalene, which in certain circumstances can be used for making explosives; I believe they are also poisonous if taken. At least the request seems to be a very peculiar one in the circumstances.[32]

An extremely effusive letter from Stella to Costenza, dated 18 July 1942 addressed to 'Countess Manna von Costenza' refers to her as 'Darlingest Manna' (found in KV2/735). A previous letter from Costenza to Stella in Aylesbury Prison on 10 July had referred to her as 'Ma petite cherie'. Stella also added that the Duchesse, Mathilde Krafft and My Ericsson all send their love and best wishes, and indicated that Ericsson would be writing to her in a few days.

A Source Report in the Duchesse's file,[33] dated 4 April 1945 and extracted on the 27th from KV2/3800 (PF.64307) on Mary Marita Margaret Perigoe @ Brahe, stated that Costenza had recently married a Czech Jew, 'and although it was correct to express disgust one need not really feel it as COSTENZA was still a Nazi at heart and had married for convenience. It was assumed that this meant that COSTENZA had married to obtain British nationality.' The document went on to state that the Duchesse had said that Germany would stage a *revanche* (revenge), and while the British Union of Fascists had proved to be a disappointment, that friends of Germany in England were stronger than was believed, and that 'something far better is on the way'. This, she alleged, was the formation of a new movement of which she was being kept informed. Perigoe was the wife of one of Mosley's British Union of Fascists.

On 12 November 1940 the Duchesse was asked about another acquaintance in her circle: a certain 'Grenade' or 'Granaad'. She told her interrogators that a friend, a Mrs Coleman who was a friend of Lady Mayo, had suggested to her that since she was looking to do Dutch translations, there was a man staying at the Savoy who might be able to help her.

A list of deleted documents in the Duchesse's file indicates that this was Siegfried Granaat, born on 21 December 1891 in Amsterdam, whose occupation was given as manufacturer and jeweller,[34] and not Siegfried Joseph Granaat, born Amsterdam 18 September 1900, who died at Sobibór on 23 July 1943. He also apparently illustrated books (caricatures) as a hobby, such as *The War in the Picture* (1915), *From Times of War Gain* (1918), and *The Peace in Picture* (1924) by Jan Feith. His ex-wife was Wilhemina Ptasznik (1901–88); they married on 16 May 1922 and divorced on 31 August 1932. A Home Office file lists his application for naturalisation;[35] parts of that file are closed until 2030 and 2057 respectively. At one point he was arrested as a suspected Fifth Columnist. A Metropolitan Police Special Branch report on the Duchesse's contacts, dated 22 January 1941, refers to Granaat:

Siegfried GRANAAT, Dutch, also referred to in M.I.5. letter, is no doubt identical with Segfrid GRANAAT [*sic*], who was interned under Art.12(5)

(a) of the Aliens Order 1920 on 2nd. August, 1940 (correspondence 79/40/9171 refers).[36]

A further reference signed by Richard Butler, 'London Region 29.12.40' notes that:

> This man is, in fact, one Siegfried GRANAAT, a Dutchman whose case has been before the Lindley Committee. I understand he is about to be released. He has been questioned with regard to his association with the Duchesse and cannot give much assistance. He is, however, most emphatic with regard to the pro-Nazi sentiments of one of the Duchesse's friends, Countess COLLOREDO, who lives in Great Cumberland Place. He says that he left her flat because of the pro-Nazi and anti-Semitic views he heard expressed there. He also says that there was a photograph in the Countess's flat of a very good-looking fair young man. I feel that the Countess should be approached in some way and I am proposing to ask Special Branch to devize an excuse for seeing her.[37]

A pencilled note in the margin says 'B17 to make enquiries'.

Indeed, a question was asked in the House of Commons by Colonel Josiah Wedgwood about Granaat on 7 November 1940:

> **Mr. Wedgwood** asked the Home Secretary why Siegfried Granaat, a Dutch diamond merchant and an anti-Nazi, who fled from Holland, has been interned in Pentonville Prison?
>
> **Mr. H. Morrison** The detention of Mr. Granaat was ordered on security grounds. I am referring this case to the appropriate Advisory Committee.
>
> **Mr. Wedgwood** How long is it likely to be before the case is heard by the appropriate committee?
>
> **Mr. Morrison** I could not say, but I do not think there will be any undue delay. It must, of course, take its turn with other cases.[38]

A Siegfried Granaat is listed as dying in the UK in 1952, but without the deleted documents on him or his MI5 file (PF.48929) it has not been possible to establish with any certainty whether this is the same person. The Duchesse described Granaat as 'good medium height ... dark hair, complexion pale ...The main thing was that he was so fat he could scarcely walk – a monster.' He had been looking for accommodation, so she sent him to see Countess Colloredo.

Exactly who this Countess Colloredo was has yet to be determined. There is mention in 1931 of a Countess Colloredo-Mannsfeld, *née* Nora Iselin, in the *New York Evening Post* 'who will arrive on the Veendam from Paget, Bermuda, where she has been stopping at the Huntley Towers'.[39] This was Eleanora 'Nora' Iselin Colloredo-Mannsfeld, born 27 December 1881, died 25 February 1939, who married Count Ferdinand Jean Jerome Marie Colloredo-Mannsfeld, an attaché of the Austrian embassy in Rome, in 1909. The Colloredo-Mannsfeld family was a prominent Austrian family; the Iselins, a rich banking family described as 'one of the first families of New York'.[40] Richard Butler, writing on 16 January 1941 and referring to her as Colloredo, states that, 'I have ascertained that Special Branch have some papers with regard to this woman, and I am seeing them today.' That being the case, this cannot be the same countess mentioned above, as she was already dead by then, unless of course Butler didn't know that.

On 2 January 1944 Tar Robertson wrote to John Senter at SOE informing him that the Duchesse's case was coming up for review by the Birkett Committee, saying that:

We have told the Committee and the Home Office that we think she should stay in, but if we are pressed we will have difficulty at this stage of the war maintaining that the continued detention of CHATEAU-THIERRY is essential on the merits of her case alone for security reasons.[41]

He added that, 'The possible repercussions on the VICTOIRE case are another matter, but these obviously cannot be stated to the Birkett Committee.' Still on the subject of VICTOIRE, he said that:

… I am informed that so far as our information goes VICTOIRE and CHATEAU-THIERRY have not been freindly [*sic*] during their detention; on the contrary, they dislike each other intensely, and in our view CHATEAU-THIERRY is unlikely to be in the confidence of VICTOIRE.[42]

The Duchesse's case came up for review by the committee on 14 January 1944 as the result of a request by solicitors Messrs. Marsh & Ferriman on 25 November 1943.[43] In a note to J.L.S. Hale at MI5, the Home Office wrote on 12 April to say that the Home Secretary had decided to maintain the Detention Order.

Further developments in 1944 regarding the Duchesse's possible release appear in the form of various reports in her Home Office file. One of these

by J.L. de la Cour on 19 December 1944 about the Duchesse's medical condition stated:

> Medical report dated 9.12.44 by Dr. Mills which states that she is not in good
> general condition and it is thought the indigestion is of cardiac origin. Her
> heart is slightly enlarged. There is at present no heart failure but her liver is
> a bit enlarged. 'She is entirely absorbed at present with her various ailments,
> and is I should say deteriorating, both mentally and physically'.[44]

He goes on to say:

> The Society of Friends have recently drawn attention to what they con-
> sider the unsatisfactory quarters occupied by this woman in Holloway. If
> detention is to be maintained some steps will, I suggest, have to be taken to
> provide some extra heating in the passages in the married quarters.
>
> The Duchesse is now 67½ years of age and not in good health; her case is
> similar in many respects to another elderly woman, KRAFFT, whose release
> has been approved. I think on the whole that having regard to the arguments
> advanced by the Committee the present war situation, her age and state of
> health, that the slight risk of her release subject to suitable conditions might
> now be taken.[45]

He suggested that Dr Matheson, the Governor of Holloway, be asked to interview her, but without indicating that her release might be imminent, and what
arrangements would be made if the Home Secretary decided to release her.
On 29 December Hale responded with the following:

> While we have had no reason to alter our previous view of this woman's past
> conduct, we do not feel we need, in view of the considerations set out in
> Mr. de la Cour's minute of 19.12.44, recommend her continued detention
> at the present time.
>
> If she is to be released, we recommend that an order be made against her
> under Article 11 of the Aliens Order, imposing in effect the restrictions set
> out in Article 6A of that Order.[46]

On 6 February 1945 Herbert Morrison revoked the Detention Order and on
12 February the Duchesse was released from Holloway Prison. On 20 February
Mrs D. Spring of B1b requested that D4 remove the Duchesse from the Stop
List. A handwritten note by W. Shay asked that, 'With reference to Minute 249

[deleted from the file] we have placed the Duchess on the P&PO Stop List in respect of exit permit applications. In future will you please complete W.S. Form 17 for this type of request.'[47]

Someone else implicated with the Duchesse was Lady Mosley (Diana Freeman-Mitford). As a result of her right-wing views and marriage to Sir Oswald Mosley, leader of the British Union of Fascists, telephone checks were being carried out on her (and no doubt the Duchesse). On 18 February Enid Riddell rang Lady Mosley at Crux Easton 37, a hamlet in the parish of Ashmansworth, Hampshire, where the Mosleys lived, to say that 'Almost' (a code name assigned to the Duchesse most likely by the British Union of Fascists), had returned on Monday the 12th, having been released from detention, and that the two of them were now sharing rooms at 9 Cheyne Row, Chelsea. The Duchesse had been unwell but had now recovered. Lady Mosley suggested that they come down and stay soon. On 13 February 1945 the Duchesse had been taken from Holloway Prison, where she had been served with a copy of the order under Article 6a of the Aliens Order 1920, and then to the Aliens Registration Office at Piccadilly Place, W1, from where she proceeded to her current address at 'More House', 52 Tite Street, Chelsea.

A telephone check on Lady Mosley on 12 March 1945 revealed that the two women were coming down to stay on Thursday afternoon (the 15th). Enid Mary Riddell, described as a striking blonde, was a member of the Right Club and a close friend of Anna Wolkoff and Tyler Kent, the American diplomat, who were both convicted under the Official Secrets Act 1911 in 1940 for passing secrets to Germany; Riddell was interned under Defence Regulation 18B in 1940 and released from Holloway in 1943.[48] According to Cyril Mills in B1a, the Duchesse had written to her from Aylesbury in 1942 asking for 'certain things left behind to be found and forwarded';[49] a copy of her letter was forwarded to Major Jock Whyte in B4a. A further check on 14 March has Riddell asking if the two women can come down on Friday instead. In another check on 15 March the Andover Police rang Sir Oswald Mosley to say they had received an application from 'Miss Sonia Bouillon' to visit Crux Easton. The police said they had no objection, but because she was French she had to register her arrival and departure with them under Alien Restrictions. Sir Oswald told them that as far as he knew she had no interest in English politics, but she was definitely not a member of the British Union of Fascists.

A telephone check by F3c on Lady Mosley on 30 November 1945 revealed that Enid Riddell had told Diana Mosley that ALMOST (the Duchesse) was in a terrible state. It appeared that a Miss Sharpe had an American lawyer staying with her who was going to take up the Duchesse's case of her money still tied up in America: ' ... he has written to say the old man is alive and there is hope of getting the money. I wanted to lend ALMOST the money to get a lot of papers copied but she wouldn't hear of it.' The 'old man' referred to was likely Sir Oswald Mosley. Certainly the Duchesse was still exhibiting her pro-Fascist tendencies as she was present at a social and ball held for 18B Detainees (British) Aid Fund at the Royal Hotel, Woburn Place, on 6 October 1945, where several people shouted anti-Jewish slogans and declared that if the 'Old Man' (Mosley) didn't lead them they would take matters into their own hands.

WHAT HER
DAUGHTER KNEW

In 1924 Valeska Uhlig became engaged to be married to Lieutenant Somerled Hamilton Watson (1899–1938) of the Welsh Guards Reserve of Officers but for some reason this did not take place and Watson later married Elma Mary Walker in 1925.[1] Elma died in 1983. Valeska's father's bankruptcy may have been a contributing factor to the break-up of the engagement. Since 7 September 1939 Valeska had been employed as a car driver by the Auxiliary Fire Service (AFS) at Station 2.Z, Grammar School, 248 Marylebone Road. According to the document on file, she was also known as Anne Curtis when she ran a small car hire firm at 6 Berkeley Mews, W1, and travelled as Anne Curtis-Uhlig when she went to the USA in 1939. She stated that she and her brother, Theodor Uhlig, known as 'Dick', were Wards in Chancery from 1914 to 1921 and that she had not lived with her mother since 1914.

On 15 October 1940 'Toby' Pilcher of MI5's SL1 wrote to Sir Norman Kendal, Assistant Commissioner, Metropolitan Police, stating that he was applying for a Detention Order for Valeska. That Detention Order was signed by the Home Secretary, Herbert Morrison, on 16 October; the following day, the 17th, she was interned under Defence Regulation 18B, suspected of association with German agents. The Detention Order stated that, 'Valeska UHLIG is the daughter of the Duchesse de Chateau-Thierry by her first marriage to a German subject. She is therefore of hostile origin.' Remarks attached to the Order stated that:

> We have information which leads us to believe that Valeska UHLIG was almost certainly in her mother's confidence and was at least aware that her mother was in receipt of money from Dr. RANTZAU. Valeska UHLIG was also aware that her mother received money from Dr. RANTZAU as the price of affecting the introduction of Dr. RANTZAU's friends to prominent

diplomats and other influential persons in this country. It is also clear that Valeska UHLIG had some suspicion that her mother's activities in this connection had a sinister background.

…

In the circumstances, therefore, we recommend that Valeska UHLIG, who is of hostile origin, should be detained at least until such time as her own case, that of her mother and that of Dr. HENRY can be investigated.[2]

At the time of her arrest Valeska was sharing a flat at 6 Berkeley Mews, Portman Square, W1, with a Miss Winifred Elwina Mary Davis, a nurse at the Middlesex Hospital, although one of the Duchesse's files states that she was a clerk with the ARP at the hospital annexe.[3] The flat was also occasionally occupied by a Miss K.M. Walsh and a Miss Llewellyn, friends of Miss Davis. When Valeska was arrested, a quantity of correspondence was seized, along with a .320 calibre gas pistol. That correspondence, which Valeska later requested be returned, was examined by William Skardon of B27 who 'found nothing there of interest to this department nor of a later date than 1934'. William James 'Jim' Skardon would go on to become MI5's top interrogator and involved in the 'Cambridge Five' investigation, as well as interrogating Klaus Fuchs, the atomic spy.

On 2 November 1940 Maxwell Knight, Norman Himsworth and Joan Miller went to interview Valeska and the Duchesse separately, which took the best part of the day. Knight's list of questions, taken from the same file on the Duchesse, as referenced above, are quite revealing about Uhlig and the Duchesse's relationship, and are worth quoting in detail. He began by asking Valeska about her own loyalty:

Major Knight: I take it that you claim to be loyal to this country?
Miss Uhlig: I definitely claim to be loyal in thought and deed.
Knight: Then you will naturally wish to assist me in every way. You consider, I suppose, that your detention was a mistake?
Uhlig: Definitely a mistake.
Knight: That being so you wont quarrel with what I said just now?
Uhlig: I am willing to tell you all I know, but it is probably so little that probably you wont believe me, but that also I can explain.
Knight: I am going to refer to a letter you wrote to your mother on Feb 6th, 1939?
Uhlig: I wrote that from America.
Knight: In the course of that letter you said 'I do hope, mummie darling, you are going on with Dr. R's plan. I know Dick [the Duchesse's son Richard]

would want you to, although I expect you feel too miserable and dazed like I do to think properly.' Who was Dr. R?

Uhlig: The man I understand was going to smuggle mother's money out of Germany. I don't know whether 'smuggle' is the right word.

Knight: What was his name?

Uhlig: I don't know. Presumably Dr. Rheinhardt. These letters are going back two years. They were written just after my brother died on January 11th. Of course it sounds terrible now, but it was nothing at the time. I don't even remember the name.

Knight: When you wrote that you didn't know who Dr. R was?

Uhligh: I hadn't the slightest idea.

Knight: He was just referred to as Dr. R?

Uhlig: By my mother. All the letters were nearly all about my brother's illness. Frankly I don't really take much interest in what mother says. There have been so many schemes in her life with business propositions. She referred to Doctors like that after my brother's illness, like 'Dr. R.' or 'Dr. W'. I was terribly sorry for her as she saw my brother suffer after the agonies of the damned. I don't know who introduced the man to her, or why she knew him.

Knight: What was Dr R's plan?

Uhlig: It must have been in one of the letters. I don't remember exactly what it was, but it was something to do with some business proposition. I think it was with this Belgian chemist who worked at Cyclax. He was always inventing patents.

Knight: What was his name?

Uhlig: I think his name was Proot. Even that I would not have remembered except that among the letters was something he had written. I though[t] it would take her mind off my brother's death to do something. But as to there being any plan or any real way – mother has always had schemes which were going to make money. If you look through her papers you will find millions of schemes.[4]

When Knight asked Valeska about another letter she had written on 18 May from France, saying, 'Hope your business is being successful,' she claimed not to know what that was about. He suggested to her that Rheinhardt had another name, but she said she didn't remember. In her letter of 21 July 1938 she wrote, 'I can't make head or tail of your letter as to what you expect from Duwell' (most likely the Duchesse's brother-in-law Robert, rather than her sister Ellen), 'And what you expect from Rheinhardt.' She took this to mean Rheinhardt getting her mother's money out of Germany, and for him to pay her bills while she was in Switzerland. She told Knight that her mother had asked her to telephone 'the Eriksson woman' when she got back. Valeska said she neither knew her name nor had met her before. When she tried looking her up in the telephone directory she couldn't find her, so was unable to ring her up.

'The Henry proposition' referred to Dr Henry, someone she had only met once who 'had some relation who wanted to be introduced into high society to get married or something'. A pencilled note written next to it says 'Put this to Duchess'. When Knight asked Valeska about it saying, 'I only hope Rheinhardt's is a better one', she explained that this was 'definitely ordinary business'. Knight persisted in this line of enquiry about Rheinhardt when he referred to the letter she had sent from New Orleans in February 1939:

Knight: You say you didn't know who Dr. R was, but in 1938 you referred to him?

Uhlig: I didn't remember who he was. I don't know who he was beyond the fact that he was introduced by a man who apparently thought he could get mother's money out of Germany. I still didn't know who he was until the C.I.D. told me who he might be.

Knight: When you talk about smuggling your mother's money out of Germany, what money had she in Germany?

Uhlig: On her father's side – her father was a Dutchman – and the estate was divided between her and her sister, and he had a lot of property in Germany. This property was being sold, I understand, by Duwell, and she was entitled to her proportion of it.

Knight: But she was not allowed by German laws to get it out?

Uhlig: I expect it was done by one clearing house and sacrificing so much. That is a thing I don't approve of because I don't believe in going against the law.

Knight: Not even against the Nazis?

Uhlig: With a Gestapo in the country who will stick you in prison, no. But I would get everything out if I could.

Knight: If Dr. Rheinhardt is in Germany, and he is in a position to get your mother's money out of Germany he must have some sort of official standing to be able to do that?

Uhlig: Presumably he must [ha]ve.

Knight: He was not a Jew?

Uhlig: To the best of my knowledge, no; I thought originally that he might be a Jew. I haven't lived a life with my mother for 15 or 20 years, and expect for the illness of my brother, our communications have been very slight.

Knight: I take it that you don't ~~entirely~~ get on well?

Uhlig: We lived different lives. I should never have been hawled [sic] into her circle.

Knight: What was it that attracted you into her circle?

Uhlig: Simply my brother's illness. Watching him die was pretty grim.[5]

Valeska said she knew nothing of the other aliases used by Rantzau – 'Hansen', 'Ritter', or 'Reinken' – to which Knight referred. She admitted to having had a few rows with her mother since she had been in prison, when she had asked her 'what the Hell she had been up to'. When asked whether she had any ideas or theories about her mother's dealings with Rheinhardt, she told Knight that:

> my mother was on one of her usual mad business propositions which would probably end in her getting nothing except that some of the money was got out to her. It was definitely her matter. I didn't really feel happy about it. I thing [sic] mother has just got herself tangled up in a foolish thing.[6]

She added that her mother was not a good judge of character: 'She just believes what she is told.'

Knight asked her about a number of other people: Philip de Froberville and his connection with Madame Aliventi, who Valeska said had borrowed money from her mother; Dr Henry, who she had introduced to Barbara de Froberville, and William Mackenzie. Her reply, 'I don't know. Is he on the greyhound track?' surprised Knight, who scrawled a note on the transcript of the interview, 'Why did she say that?' indicating that she did indeed know Mackenzie. She then admitted that she knew him through their interest in greyhound racing. Another person of interest was Arnold Louis Chevallier, who she said was a mad Frenchman and a friend of her father's, who 'had been inventing things since the year "Dot", mainly guns'.

The fact that the Duchesse had in her possession typewritten specifications for some of Chevallier's inventions was because he had wanted her to introduce him to people who would put them on the market. Unfortunately, the MI5 file on Chevallier (PF.27057) in which it mentions his dealings with Whitehall, and a summary of his inventions initialed 'E.C.H.B.' is not available from the National Archives at Kew. Nor is MI5's file on the Countess of Mayo (PF.53295), whose son, Edward Charles Bourke-Haliburton – 'E.C.H.B.' [sic] – was associated with Chevallier. Bourke-Haliburton married Mairi Wilson Stewart of Aberdeen in 1949; they were divorced in 1954 on account of his misconduct.

Arnold Louis Chevallier, a Swiss living at Moss Side House, Rampside, Lancashire, is listed in the *London Gazette* for 2 June 1896 as being an alien who had been granted a Certificate of Naturalisation on 1 May 1896. He also shows up in patents as being an inventor of various sporting guns, some in connection with Robert Churchill, the well-known gunsmith, as well as a Martini-Henry grenade discharger, and the author of *A Treatise on the True Dynamic Flight of Projectiles*.[7] He was the son of Elizabeth Chevallier *née* Langtree (c.1818–90) and Adolph Chevallier.

A man named Karlinski was 'another man who wanted to be introduced about some pictures. It is another of those mad and daft schemes. I imagine he was a friend of Dr. Henry's, but I may be wrong.' Serge Karlinski was a Sephardic Jew who, in 1934 was described as a banker's broker, had no nationality, and was living at 24 Brent Street, Hendon.[8] In 1938 he was elected to the London Committee of Deputies of the British Jews. An interrogation of Dr Henry in the Duchesse's file carried out on 30 October 1940 states that she had informed MI5 that Karlinsky [*sic*] was a distant relation of Mrs Henry and that he had started off buying and selling Russian Bank drafts, before setting up in business at 33 Cornhill in the City. At that time he had made 'a very substantial sum of money' out of a confidential deal with the government. However, what this deal was, or exactly how much money he made are not available.[9]

Valeska said that, 'The only thing that strikes my mind is that someone said he lived in Belgrave Square which had a "b" or an "a" to the number, and I couldn't think of a house in that Square could have anything but a number.' In fact, Karlinski lived at 11a Belgrave Square.[10] MI5 records that after the Duchesse had met Rantzau:

> her daughter Valeska wrote to say that Dr. HENRY was to introduce her to KARLINSKI and added 'There seems to be no definite proposal or definite statement of what the man really wants or that he really wants anything at all and is willing to pay for it.' It is not clear whether 'the man' is HENRY or KARLINSKI.
>
> Our records of this man show that he is a naturalized British subject of Russian origin. He has been manager of P.P. BOECKEL of 33, Cornhill, who act as brokers for the Export Credits Guarantee Dept. of the Board of Trade, and in this connection KARLINSKI helped to secure the contract between Westinghouse Brake and Saxby Signal Co. of London and the Polish Government. He is also said to have been successful in arranging loans for Rumania and to have been interested in the supply of arms to China. We have no record of his being directly in touch with the Duchesse.[11]

On 6 June 1939 Major-General Sir Alfred Knox, MP for Wycombe, Buckinghamshire, asked a supplementary question in the House of Commons in which he named Karlinski as being chairman of Trade Facilities Limited:

> Is there any truth in the rumour that the Export Credits Department advised the Chinese Advisory Committee to deal entirely with the organisation called Trade Facilities, Limited, of which the chairman is Mr. Serge Karlinski: and why were the interests of British traders in China, who have recently been hard hit, disregarded?[12]

To which R.S. Hudson, Secretary, Overseas Trade Department, responded that '…I have looked into it and find that most of the statements arc [sic] entirely unfounded and a large number are deliberate misrepresentations.' Robert Boothby (later Lord Boothby), Conservative MP for East Aberdeen, replied:

> I am a director of the Industrial Facilities Corporation, of which Mr. Karlinski is chairman. The hon. and gallant Member was aware of that when he put the question, bue [sic] he gave me no notice that he intended to ask it. He gave notice yesterday that he intended to raise the matter on the Adjournment, and, personally, I sincerely hope that he will do so; but, in case he should think better of it, I desire to assure the House without further delay that there is not the slightest foundation for the imputation cast not only against the company with which I am associated, but also that against the Civil Service which is contained in the supplementary question he thought fit to put.[13]

A website for burials at a Jewish cemetery at Veyrier, Switzerland, lists a Serge Karlinski (1896–1979) and Muriel Karlinski (1896–1979) both buried in the same plot.[14] However, it has not been confirmed that this is the same person.

Turning to the subject of Vera, Valeska said she was 'a girl who stayed with mother, and I saw her three or four times' when she was staying at the Duchess's [sic] at 102 Dorset House, but was an entirely different person to My Eriksson, who she said she had met once at her mother's very briefly – 'You cannot possibly mix Eriksson and Vera up together.' Knight asked what on earth the Duchesse had been thinking getting involved with the Countess Costenza. Valeska said she was also curious and had met her at the hospital where a Mrs Orm [sic] had died. As Knight put it:

Knight: On the 27th Feb, 1940 this woman writes a letter to your mother in
which she confides that the crime alleged against her was in fact committed,
and it was quite clear that everyone committed perjury in the courts?
Uhlig: Well she has never told me about that.[15]

The remainder of that exchange and Costenza's situation have already been
dealt with in the previous chapter. Knight returned to the subject of Rantzau:

Knight: I suppose when the Police officers talked to you when you were detained
they did say something about Rheinhardt being identical with Rantzau?
Uhlig: No they told me he was in the German Intelligence.
Knight: Does the name Rantzau convey anything to you?
Uhlig: The only other R. I met was Von Rintelen. [A handwritten note next
to it says, 'Where did she meet him [illegible] often? Put to Duchesse']
Knight: What do you think of Von Rintelen?
Uhlig: The Dark Invader.
M.K: Would you say he was that?
Uhlig: Yes.
Knight: I don't think you were far wrong.
Uhlig: I think it was a scoundrel he was out loose [sic].[16]

It seems that the Duchesse was also somehow involved in a sort of marriage
bureau, although Valeska said that there were two girls who actually ran it. One
of their clients was a Mrs Jane Martin.

Knight: You know there are certain undesirable aliens who would certainly
make it worth-while to be introduced to Englishmen?
Uhlig: Yes, it is disgusting and they are the people who turn round and say
they are badly used.[17]

Knight continued through his list of the Duchesse's contacts: Captain Freddy
Ayres was a friend of her mother's and a very nice man, according to Valeska
(the adjective is actually illegible, but that was what Knight supposed it to be).
Mrs Stern was a Christian Scientist who was 'also a bit crackers' and lived at
Chiltern Court where the Duchesse had lived in 1933 and 1939, although
Valeska did not specify in which year the Duchesse and Mrs Stern had first
met. She told Knight that she didn't know Tibor Weber, but Mrs Osborne
Smith was someone her mother had stayed with in Swan Court in 1940. She
was unsure who Bauer was and whether he was a Belgian chemist, or why her

mother was interested in him but supposed it was 'someone putting up money and building a factory or running a firm'.

Richard Butler interviewed Valeska in Holloway Prison on 8 November 1940. Then she claimed that she did not know William Mackenzie and had never met him, although her mother had. Nor had she been to Mackenzie's residence at 39 Bruton Place, thus contradicting what she had told Knight on 2 November. The Duchesse had told her that Mackenzie was something to do with Harringay [sic], but this must have been after 24 March, since Valeska had not returned from America until then.[18] She also denied hearing the name Rantzau until a few days prior to her interview with Butler.

It was her understanding, she explained, that Rheinhardt was helping her mother to get her money out of Germany. The Duchesse always referred to Rantzau as Rheinhardt in her letters; however, Valeska had only been interested in the parts of the letters pertaining to her brother, Richard, also known as Dick and Theodor. When Butler asked her about why the Duchesse should discuss with Rheinhardt about chaperoning people in London, she said she thought it was because her mother seemed to think she could do some business with him, although she had no idea what that was.

In her letter to her mother on 23 August 1938, Valeska had mentioned about her mother getting into danger in her relations with Rheinhardt. When asked to explain what she meant by that, she told Butler that she didn't think it was anything. He formed the opinion that Valeska had a suspicious mind and was worried that her mother would get into trouble. She said that her mother 'never sees further than her nose' and 'she did think that there was something a bit fishy about someone who could smuggle things out of Germany, and they might have put the Duchess [sic] in a concentration camp'.[19]

As to Valeska's visits to Germany, she told Butler that she went there annually to visit her father in Munich, the last time being at Christmas 1938 prior to going to America. Whether her mother knew that she had gone there she didn't know, but the two had never met there. She refuted the suggestion that the Duchesse would have introduced her to Rheinhardt, or described him to her, largely because, 'UHLIG loathes all Germans, her father being the only one that she respects'. This contradicts the fact that she *had* in fact met von Rintelen (Rantzau) twice at the Duchesse's, but was not a close friend of his, so obviously hadn't realised that they were one and the same. Valeska hardly ever mentioned her mother in the presence of her father as the two were separated, and she lived apart from her.

John Day's report of 14 April 1942 on various people connected with Vera states that Mrs Stern is identical to the woman mentioned in My Eriksson's files (PF.47928). Her connection with the Duchesse had been known to MI5 since 27 January 1942 when Special Branch had interviewed some names mentioned in My Eriksson's diary. One of these was William Weiss, who described himself as an expert on cattle breeding. Weiss had been born in Topolcany, Czechoslovakia, formerly Hungary, on 25 July 1893.[20] He had been a cattle breeder with his brother Hermann in Vienna and came to England on 19 February 1939. There he was introduced to Mrs Stern at her flat, where he was told he might make introductions to people likely to be interested in his business projects. He continued to call on her at her flat until February 1940, when she moved from Chiltern Court to the Red House, The Grove, Ilkeley, in Yorkshire.

According to Day, she appeared to be the wife of Alfred Stern, who moved at a date unknown to MI5 to Canada (see below). It has not been confirmed whether there is any connection between him and a Dr Alfred Stern who in 1947 accepted a position at Caltech's Humanities division, but it seems unlikely.[21] Nor is he the Chicago millionaire Alfred K. Stern, an NKVD agent married to Martha Dodd, described by *Top Secret* magazine as 'The Reds' Mata Hari in the US',[22] as that particular Stern fled to Prague in 1953.

In March 1942 Mrs Stern moved again, this time to Troutbeck Hydro, Ilkeley. However, Weiss stated that he had met her and had had conversations with her at Chiltern Court, where the Duchesse was also present on two or three occasions. During one such meeting, My Eriksson was also present. Stern's case was currently in the hands of B4, the Espionage, Country Section under Major Jock Whyte.

When Richard Butler asked My Eriksson on 22 February 1940 about William Weiss, she said he was a friend of the Duchesse's friend 'Miss Stein' (probably she meant Mrs Stern) who she said had taken refugees under her wing;[23] Weiss's address was given as 4 Hyde Park Place, W2.[24] On 7 August 1942 Guy Poston in OB2 (also B5b) prepared a report for Judith Cotton of B4a, the section involved with suspected cases of espionage by individuals living in the UK, which now provides as much information on the Sterns as we are probably likely to ever know, in which he says:

Have now seen Mr. Henry P. Arnholz of Russell & Arnholz, Solicitors, 5/6 Great Winchester Street, E.C., who told me that he had known Alfred STERN for about twenty-seven years. STERN's father was a rubber merchant and the son was employed in the business. During the last war, however, the father left this country for America and Alfred carried on the business. He is understood to have served in the British Army in France for a while. After the war, he devoted himself to the business, which he turned into a most thriving concern, with a turnover of something like £3,000,000 per annum. In due course, he turned the business into a Limited Liability Company and retired to live on his invested income, which, according to Mr. Arnholz, must be considerable.

Arnholz knew that STERN went to Canada about two years ago, but did not know the reason. He thinks it might possibly be connected with his health, which had been very bad for some years. He was apparently very well-known and popular on the Rubber Exchange and was a most generous man. Arnholz said he knew that he had helped some of his wife's relations. Mrs. STERN's maiden name was CURZON, and her family came from the Liverpool district. Prior to living at Chiltern Court, the STERNs had a large house in Harlesden, and as a result, he took a great interest in the Willesden Hospital, to which he gave a lot of money.

Mr. Arnholz expressed absolute confidence in Alfred STERN's integrity and loyalty to this country, and added that his pre-war views on European policy would have commended themselves to the Prime Minister! He does not know Mrs. STERN as well as her husband, and when he last saw her she was still living at Chiltern Court. He described her as 'quiet a nice person, who is fond of company', but added that STERN had told him that he was not very pleased with his wife's friends, though he never mentioned anyone by name. Mr. Arnholz remembers once meeting Maria NERMI,[25] whom Mrs. STERN introduced to him when she was endeavouring to interest people in her singing. He thinks that subsequently his wife went to a concert at which NERMI sang.

Mr. Arnholz feels quite certain that neither Alfred STERN nor his wife would knowingly have anything whatever to do with anyone who was not completely satisfactory from the security angle, but thinks it possible that their hospitality and generosity may have been abused when they were assisting lame dogs at Chiltern Court. He knows nothing about their travels abroad prior to the war, and I gathered that he had not heard from Mrs. STERN since she left London.

I found Mr. Arnholz, who incidentally is well-known to several members of the office in the legal profession and is well thought of by them, most anxious to help, but he pointed out that he saw most of Alfred STERN when he was actively engaged in business. He mentioned, in fact, that the consultations which he had with him were so long and numerous that he had to arrange a special fee – at the rate of 2 guineas an hour! In the course of conversation he mentioned that he was senior executor and trustee to Lord Northcliffe.[26]

Judith Cotton added in other notes on 24 July 1942 that Mrs Stern was born Lilian Henrietta Curzon in Birkenhead on 13 November 1880; Alfred Stern was formerly Austrian, but was born in Liberec, Czechoslovakia (now the Czech Republic), on 15 November 1888; he became a naturalised Briton in 1897.[27] It was thought that Mrs Stern had intended to join her husband in Canada where he had been for about a year, but a letter from Miss Cotton dated 18 April 1942 has a handwritten note added saying, '... but has not yet applied for a permit'.

Both Sterns had travelled extensively in Europe between 1928 and 1937, with Alfred being issued a visa for the United States on 6 October 1928. Their passport application received on 23 May 1938 stated that they wished to travel to, 'All countries in Europe including U.S.S.R., Turkey, Egypt and U.S.A.' for pleasure. Henry Arnholz had witnessed their application as having known them for ten years.

While Alfred Stern was in Canada Mrs Stern had moved from Ilkeley to 'The Flagstaff', Whitesmith, Chiddingly, in Sussex. Enquiries were also made of the West Riding Police, who confirmed the known facts about Mrs Stern's addresses in Yorkshire and that Alfred Stern had never lived there. Whether she ever followed him to Canada is not clear but probate/estate files for the Victoria Supreme Court in the names of Alfred Stern and Lilian Henrietta Stern exist in the British Columbia Archives at the Royal BC Museum in Victoria, as well as a death registration certificate (59-09-003789) for Alfred Stern of 1472, Beach Drive, Oak Bay, BC, which shows that he died on 17 March 1959 and gives his wife's name as Lilian Henrietta Curlon [sic].[28] The cause of death is given as carcinomatosis as a result of carcinoma of the neck, and his profession as retired rubber broker. It also states that he had been in Canada for twenty-one years and the province of British Columbia for fourteen, making the year of his departure from England as 1939. His date of birth was given as 15 November 1888. These records would seem to confirm that Lilian Stern did indeed follow him to Canada, although the date is unknown. Most likely it was towards the end of the war or afterwards as Atlantic crossings were dangerous during the war due to U-boats.

Discreet enquiries had been made by the CID in Lewes, Sussex, and a report forwarded to Major Grassby, the SLO in Tunbridge Wells, by the Chief Constable of East Sussex, Reginald Breffit stated that 'The Flagstaff' was a house in its own grounds some distance away from neighbouring houses, and belonged to a Mr Saulz, 'a wealthy Jew … who controls the "Ambassador Hotel", London'. Since Mrs Stern did not appear to go out very much it was consequently difficult to ascertain from any of the locals anything about her. A tradesman had remarked that Mrs Saulz had said that Mrs Stern would be staying for a long time, and appeared to be there as a guest.

Tibor Weber, according to a report by John Day of B1b dated 12 April 1942, was a Hungarian born in Budapest on 21 October 1895 who had come to England in 1928 and stayed until just before the war broke out. He worked as a correspondent for the *Pester Lloyd*, a German newspaper from Budapest 'with a focus on Hungary and Eastern Europe' dating from 1854. Later he became an emissary of the Hungarian National Bank instructed to discover whether Jews were transferring illicit money from Hungary to Britain. As of 1940 he was employed by the Anglo-Hungarian Bank in Budapest. Day writes that:

It appears that he is an expert in Economics, Scientific Research and Statistics, and in this capacity was in 1929 sending back to the National Bank of Hungary monthly reports on the economics and financial situation in the United Kingdom. In 1931 he applied to reside permanently in London.

As bearing on a possible espionage interest the following facts seem to be of significance. In 1936 information was received that WEBER was employed as London representative of the Dresden newspaper Internationale Finanz und Wirtschaftzeitung.

In 1940 it appeared that he was a fairly intimate friend of Doctor Eugene WIESER, P.F.48182,[29] who was ex-secretary to the Hungarian Military Attache, and apparently suspect.

It appeared on 8.2.41 that WEBER was a great friend of HUBRICH; a search and interrogation of HUBRICH on this date revealed a letter written to him by WEBER in August 1939 from Vienna, ending with a 'heil'. HUBRICH also stated that he believed WEBER to be extremely pro-Nazi.

His association with the circle of the Duchesse de CHATEAU THIERRY has been known since October 1940 from a previous statement by Vera ERIKSEN, who recognised him as attache to the Hungarian Embassy in London. She stated, that she met him at Mrs. STERN's flat and also at the Duchesse's house, where he used to call with de HADASHY, who was the Hungarian Ambassador to Spain. It is clear that this is the Mrs. STERN she refers to elsewhere and that de HADASHY is the diplomat referred to in the report by U.35 as de HEVESSY.

It also appears that Tibor WEBER was a friend of Elsa SCHULTZ, also mentioned in the U.35 report. SCHUTZ is mentioned in the interrogation of CHATEAU THIERRY on 2.11.40 as a hunchback, 'very much trusted by the Hungarian Legation'.[30]

Aristid Gedion Hubrich was interned under Defence Regulation 18B on the Isle of Man. On 3 April 1942 Day was able to shed more light on this person:

Vera's HUBRICH is clearly identical with the subject of P.F.46614. This man is a thoroughly dangerous case as the following very brief summary of his career may indicate. He was born on 17.11.86, Hungarian, and was formerly a captain in the Austro-Hungarian army, and in 1917 held the position of military attache in Berlin where he was highly commended for his tact and energy. After the war he remained in Berlin until 1925 where he was associated with UFA Films and in this year came to England as their representative. He has lived in England ever since although his visits to Germany have been frequent. During his residence in England he has also been engaged in the cinema industry and SATTLERS METAL, Limited. HUBRICH had been subject to the attention of the Security Service since 1936 and he was finally interned early in 1941 [on the Isle of Man]. The principal reasons for this were as follows:-

(1) There was incontrovertible evidence that he had been for some years persona grata in Hungarian Diplomatic circles in this country and was taking advantage of this position to send reports on air-raid damage in London through the diplomatic bag in the summer of 1940.

(2) His own sympathies and contacts were notoriously pro-Nazi, and at the time of the search of his living premises early in 1941 there were discovered a German revolver and a German Nazi badge, the latter the property of his son [called Aristid Gedion Hubrich Jr.] This boy himself was arrested in September 1940 for taking advantage of his membership of the Air Cadet Force [Air Defence Cadet Corps] to interfere with traffic and for the unhealthy interest he was known to have in details about British aerodromes. He also was well-known as being of violently pro-Nazi sympathies.

(3) And for these purposes most significant, it is clear that he Aristide [*sic* – handwritten] was known to RUTER,[31] a former member of the German Embassy in London and in 1938 described as knowing a good deal about German Secret Service Intelligenec and Espionage in this country. RUTER acted as the courier between London and Berlin for the diplomatic bag and

secret party documents. According to the report by U.35, dated June 1938, RUTER said that he remembered HUBRICH very well and said that he used to do film propaganda work for the Germans. It will be noticed that ERIKSEN has mentioned the name of Dr. RUTER as one she heard mentioned in the circle of Dr. RANTZAU, and it would seem that he is certainly the same man.

As has been seen, Aristide [*sic*] HUBRICH is now in internment, but it appears that his son, Buddy HUBRICH is still at large. It is also noteworthy that HUBRICH admits to having been a close friend of Tibor WEBER.[32]

An extract from an interrogation report of Hubrich at Camp 001 on the Isle of Man on 29 April 1942 revealed little about what he could tell MI5 about the Duchesse's circle as he was unable to give any names. When questioned he said that the Duchesse was generally surrounded by a 'number of people of all sorts and kinds'. He found the Duchesse's society 'somewhat too Bohemian and pinched for his gentility and thus had not been sufficiently struck by any of them to be able to retain a lasting impression'. Nor was he questioned specifically about Vera.[33]

À propos of Hubrich, in a House of Commons debate on 18 May 1944 Sir Irving James Albery, Conservative MP for Gravesend (1924-45), posed the question to the Home Secretary, Herbert Morrison, whether he would make arrangements to have Hubrich's son moved to 'P' camp on the Isle of Man so that they could be together, or at the very least to be able to meet since the two camps were adjacent. Morrison replied that such arrangements had been made for the two to meet, but that placing them in the same camp was something on which, 'I am not at present in a position to make a statement.'[34]

During Knight's 2 November interview he suggested to Valeska that this circle of contacts had increased since the Duchesse had met Rheinhardt, and wondered where all the money came from. Valeska refuted this by telling him that the money her mother received for the parties she hosted was from the people who wanted their daughters to be 'brought out' into society during the London Season. But as Knight countered:

Knight: People pay, I know quite considerable sums, in normal times, for girls to be 'brought out', and be presented at Court, and people in reduced circumstances make a aliving out of it. But normally they are British subjects and people well-known in Society. I don't think it is right to say your mother was in that position?

Uhlig: She had not a lot of social gatherings, and what she had were cheap ones. I despised it utterly myself. That is why she has never got her paws on me. That may be why she did it to other people. They think that if they have the name 'Duchesse' in front of them it means something ... they paid quite a lot, £1,000 a season [in return for a husband in 1924 or 1925].

Knight: What were the circumstances under which your mother met Rheinhardt?

Uhlig: I understand through Mrs Eriksson getting her an introduction to some man in Switzerland who again gave her an introduction to Rheinhardt.

Knight: Mrs Eriksson was really the means of your mother meeting Dr. Rheinhardt?

Uhlig: I think so, but I wouldn't like to swear an oath on it.

Knight: I don't think there is any doubt, from what you have told me and from documents I have got, that Dr. Rheinhardt asked your mother, invited your mother, to introduce some of his friends in London to people in London whom he selected. Do you think, from your knowledge of your mother, during the whole of the period she was in touch with Rheinhardt, that she really thought that that was an ordinary social racket?

Uhlig: I think he absolutely fooled her. I don't think that she thought she was doing anything. She wanted to get her money out and was prepared to give a certain amount of service for that. I really think he must have put things up very cleverly, and actually he found a beautiful fool in mother. He must have been extremely well stung, because it was not her line.

Knight: Don't you think after a little time anybody with your mother's experience and savoir faire, would have begun to smell a bit of a rat?

Uhlig: Whether she did or didn't I don't know. I think she was one who was fooled by a name.[35]

She told him that, 'Mother is so used to introducing people that she wouldn't think anything about it. Her sense of proportion doesn't exist.'

Knight: What are your mother's views about Germans?

Uhlig: She has no love for them.

Knight: As Germans or Nazis?

Uhlig: She hasn't even any love for either.

Knight: Has she a political mind?

Uhlig: Yes and no. Quite cockeyed. She always thinks she can read the happenings between the lines in the papers.

Knight: Have you any idea what are her politics?

Uhlig: I think as a whole she is anti-war may be. She is pro-British. ~~Possibly she is anti this war but~~ Definitely she has no love for Germany and is true British. Probably her heart is in Holland which, in the last war had beautiful neutrality.

Knight: If it could be shown reasonably to your mother that Rheinhardt was a German agent, do you think your mother would disclose everything even ~~though~~ if she imagined she would not come out very well in the ~~answering~~ telling of the story?

Uhlig: I do not know the workings of her mind ~~very~~ well enough. I think she will definitely give what she thinks is a frank explanation, but her idea on that and mine may be different.[36]

Knight's conclusion was:

I first interrogated Miss Uhlig … I formed a very good impression of Miss Uhlig, and I am convinced that she neither has much knowledge of her mother's dealings with Rantzau nor does she sympathise with her mother's various financial ventures. In fact she has been doing war work which involves her in considerable danger. I think it would be a great injustice for her to be kept in detention, and if possible, the fact that she has been detained ought not to prejudice her resumption of her war work.[37]

Valeska was clearly an articulate woman who knew her own mind and was contemptuous of her mother's misguided activities. Following the interview she wrote a letter to 'The gentleman who questioned me', which was forwarded to Knight by the Governor of Holloway, Dr John Campbell McIntyre Matheson:

Sir,

When you questioned me yesterday, you asked me if I had used any other names. I said 'no' and at that moment it absolutely went out of my head and I didn't tell you that for business purposes i.e. Carhire Services and advertisement I use the name 'Anne Curtis'. I don't think this fact is of any importance to you but I would [not] like you to think I deliberately withheld it from you, though in any case I did tell the C.I.D. when they came to detain me.

Please accept my apologies for troubling you with this.

Yours faithfully,

A.V. Uhlig[38]

Richard Butler in B2 was clearly not convinced that Valeska Uhlig was telling the truth, the whole truth, and nothing but the truth, when he wrote to 'Toby' Pilcher on 18 January 1941:

> The position with regard to UHLIG now is that she gives a not very convincing explanation of the letters which she wrote to her mother as to the possibility of getting into some trouble by her association with Dr. RHEINHARDT. On the other hand, in my own personal opinion, we have at the moment no evidence of any sort which shows that she had the remotest knowledge of the true nature of her mother's association with 'RHEINHARDT'. She is constantly pressing for a hearing before an Advisory Tribunal, and subject to your better knowledge of these Tribunals and their methods, I do not see how we can hope to make certain of her detention after such a hearing. B.2. has not considered these documents in detail, but has left it to myself, after discussion with you, to decide whether we should not immediately recommend UHLIG's release. B.8.(L), Major Stephens, on the other hand takes the view that this woman should be detained indefinitely on the ground that her mother has been in active contact with members of the German Secret Service. I gather that he also takes the view that we should inform UHLIG that we cannot accept her explanation with regard to the letters, and that in view of her suspicious contacts, we are recommending that she be detained indefinitely. He feels so strongly with regard to the matter that he is of opinion that if the Advisory Tribunal were to recommend her release, this is a case which should be fought strongly by us and a personal explanation offered to the Home Secretary.
>
> Whilst I am in favour of detaining as many people as possible against whom there is the slightest ground of suspicion, I cannot believe that in this case we have any hope of keeping UHLIG detained indefinitely, and at the moment I cannot say that we have any real evidence on which to recommend her continued detention. I would like to have an opportunity to discuss the matter with you.[39]

Stephens' views on the subject were expressed in his inimitable way in his 'Yellow Peril' of 25 November 1940:

> Relying on the pleasant precedent set by the Judges who see fit to dissent from each other from time to time, I am sure I will not be misunderstood if I disagree violently with Major Maxwell Knight's view that this woman is innocent. Myself, I find it quite impossible to believe that the recipient

(UHLIG) of such incriminating letters from her mother can be innocent herself of subversive activity. In a word, if the daughter is innocent, then she must have found all the letters from her mother entirely incomprehensible. And if anything were required to clinch her complicity I would refer to the letter of February 6th, 1939, from UHLIG to her mother, in which she persuades her mother to proceed with 'R's' plan.[40]

The relevant extract of Valeska's letter from New Orleans to which Stephens referred has already been quoted in Maxwell Knight's interview. Others tended to take a more positive view. In 'Notes on the Property of Anna Valeska Uhlig' [*sic*] dated 27 October 1940, the author of the report, Miss E.M.B. Hall of B2, concluded that:

> Although it is obvious that UHLIG was fully aware of her mother's connec-tion with Dr. R., and probably realised what this connection entailed on her mother's side, there is no reason to suppose that she was in any way a party to the Duchesse's activities on dr. R.'s behalf. The Duchesse made no sort of attempt to hide her payments from Dr. R., but all her letters are full of sordid financial details – the lack of money, the possibility of obrtaining small sums from various friends, her debts, the inhuman behavior of the Swiss authorities on his account – all these are recounted in the Duchesse's flowing Victorian style, so that clearly when such an important thing happened as the payments from Dr. R. she found it physically impossible to keep such a thing to herself. It seems possible that UHLIG may have remonstrated with her for in one letter, dated 29.8.38, the Duchesse writes: 'I feel like a figure in Oppenheim's novels the way you write' [E. Phillips Oppenheim, 1866-1946]. The examination of UHLIG's property has tended to clear her and the HENRY's of the suspicion of complicity in the Duchesse's activities, and to establish still further the case against the Duchesse herself.[41]

On 25 November 1940 Meurig Evans wrote:

> The case against her daughter ANNE VALESKA UHLIG should be re-examined. There is abundant evidence in the correspond[ence] that she knew something dangerous was afoot, and yet, in a letter written from New Orleans, in February 1939, (X) she ur[ged] her mother to go with 'Dr. R's plan!'
> Similarly on page 2 of her first interrogation she says her mother never wrote REINHARDT in full. There yet are plenty o[f] letters from CHATEAU THIERRY to UHLIG disproving this.[42]

However, Butler's note to Pilcher and probable discussion obviously changed MI5's tune. A letter to Sir Alexander Maxwell, Permanent Under-Secretary at the Home Office, from Pilcher MI5 SL (1) on 19 January 1941 but signed by 'Jasper' Harker, stated:

> Valeska UHLIG was originally detained because of several passages in let-ters which she had written to her mother which indicated that she knew of her mother's association with RANTZAU ... my officers who are satis-fied that she never had any personal contact with RANTZAU and did not know the real nature of her mother's transactions with him. She also offered an explanation, which we are prepared to accept, of the passages in her letters to her mother which originally led us to regard her with considerable suspicion.
>
> If the Home Secretary sees fit to revoke the detention order against UHLIG we should be prepared to consent to her release without being called upon to appear before the Advisory Committee.[43]

Remarks in her Detention Order outlined the so-called incriminating evidence:

> 2. definite evidence that between March and September 1939 the Duchesse de Chateau-Thierry was entertaining a woman who now turns out to be a German agent.
> 3. Information which leads us to believe Valeska UHLIG was almost certainly in her mother's confidence and was aware of money received from Rantzau. Received money as a price of effecting introduction of R's friends to dip-lomats and other influential persons. Had some suspicions of her mother's activities had sinister a background.
> Ref letter 23 August 1938 when mother was in Switzerland. 'Am glad R (? Dr. RANTZAU) sent you something. What are you doing for him? I hope to goodness you are not running yourself into danger?'
> 4. 23 Aug 1938 letter to Duchesse from Dr Henry: 'Your daughter said it would be wise to introduce my friends to one or some Ambassadors and then it could be decided what should be done further.'
> 5. Anyone connected with the Duchesse should be regarded with consider-able suspicion. Valeska UHLIG must have no opportunity to communicate with anyone after she knows her mother and Dr Henry have been detained.

Valeska UHLIG said in letter dated 17.12.40 that she couldn't remember the contents of her mother's letters but did not attach anything of interest or importance to them… their very existence surely is proof enough in itself that I certainly considered them harmless and of no account to anyone else.[44]

Further insight into what this incriminating evidence was and what Valeska may have known can be seen in extracts from the letters the Duchesse wrote to her daughter:

La Valerette, Leysin, Sunday
I had hoped to get a letter from that man RHEINHARDT and that is why I waited until today.
…

RHEINHARDT may be and may not be a Jew name. I should not think that he is one if he is a friend of Mrs. Eriksson.
…

She [Eriksson] says that her relations in Hamburg want to help me but that things are so strict there that nothing can be sent me direct but if given time, something they hope can be arranged.
…

I don't think he wants me to do anything extraordinary as he mentions the Belgian chemist (I had explained to him that a proposition was put up to me, to co-operate in that business) and says that he represents a big firm and that with my connections I may be able to help them as much in London as the Belgian chemist. He speaks of our mutual advantage, etc.
…

P.S. How can RHEINHARDT get me the money for fare etc. I can't think.

La Valerette, Sat. May 14th, 1938
I am terribly busy with correspondence re DUWELL – to the Amsterdam people also I have a mysterious offer from the representative of a German firm from Hamburg to meet him at the border and discuss possible business and his firm offers to pay my expenses for journey etc!!!!
…

It is all very mysterious and this man (a Dr. NIKOLAUS RHEINHARDT) of Mittelweg 117a, Hamburg 13 offers to be of help in my difficulties to our mutual advantage! and cannot write about it, but must discuss – he says a mutual friend (a lady) asked him to communicate with me. It can either be BARBARA (ask her whether she knows him) or Mrs HO[** illegible] or Mrs. ERIKSSON – probably the latter as she is very keen on helping me …

La Valerette, Leysin, May 30th, 1938
She [Eriksson] writes that Mr. R. is a friend of her relations in Hamburg and that no doubt they have told him about me. That he is very infleuential [*sic*] and a nice man who had also gone through a lot of trouble. He is of an old officers family… Have not heard again from RHEINHARDT and wonder whether it is all nothing again.

La Valerette, Leysin, June 14th
Also I had another letter from RHEINHARDT who wanted to meet me in Freiburg …

La Valerette, Leysin, Monday 18th (July)
Mr. R. is young and very good looking. I had a fit when I saw him and thought he was his own son! … He is more than Aryan … Dr. R. who is a very high government official promises me to send me that at the rate of £25 a month until the whole is paid me.
…
The work for R. will be difficult and expensive for me to handle so must see what remuneration he can offer and it would mean entertaining a bit too … Dr. R. sent some money in English notes from Switzerland he seems to be very clever.
…
Had a letter from Mrs. ERIKSSON. She heard from R. and was put some questions about me – I don't know what – One must be very nice to her darling – as she has done me a good turn indeed.
…
P.S.S. (Page 1) The work for Dr. R. would be most interesting … (Page 3) R. was impressed by names I knew and invitations I had had. Hope he won't be disappointed!!!???
…
[Letter continued on part of telegram] … May come on business for R. to London and Hamburg in between.

Le Mont Blanc, Leysin, Aug 10th, 1938
Sorry you don't understand the affairs of DUWELL – RHEINHARDT, etc. To put it briefly a very small amount will come to me …
…
Dr. R. who is an authority on financial and economical matters over there has assured and promised me that he will, when this money is deposited by

DUWELL for me – send me <u>every month</u> about £25 or so here, until the money is finished. I have no doubt that he can do so – as for my expenses of journey etc. over there – he sent me <u>English £ notes</u> – posted from Lucerne – so I have no reason to doubt his word.

Le Mont Blanc, Leysin, Aug. 29th
Up till now there is no danger my child – I would not be surprised though if there <u>might</u> in time be some things asked me, which I am unable or unwilling to answer. Still – <u>not yet</u>.
…

Please let me know what 11a Belgrave Square looks like – it sounds like a maisonette … [Reference to Serge Karlinski's residence]

Pension Arndt, Bluemenstrasse 1, Wiesbaden, Oct. 26th
Of course the fact that I could not meet Dr. R. when he wanted me a month or so ago did me out of a good deal … I had a terrible shock Mrs. Eriksson wrote me that Dr. R. had gone to America for an indefinite time – but thank goodness <u>today</u> he wrote me here from Hamburg that he is back and going to put his mind on my affairs.
…

I shall know for certain on the 20th whether all the propositions are accepted. R. thinks 90% will be o.k.

Blumenstrasse 3, Wiesbaden, Nov 17th.
I had a very satisfactory letter from the person I am dealing with and arrangements in London will start on Jan. 1st but he hopes Leysin etc. will be arranged <u>before</u> that so do I – as I want to go and see Dick and settle matters in Switzerland. P.S. I never came across such arrangements as R's money for jam.[45]

Here we see that Valeska certainly knew about 'Rheinhardt' and the Duchesse's dealings with him although she did not appear to know the exact nature of them. All she knew was that they were financial dealings related to the Duchesse's money tied up in Germany. She was also aware of the collusion between her mother and My Eriksson in these dealings. That the Duchesse should have alluded to things having the potential to get dangerous later on may simply be that these financial dealings with Rheinhardt would be detected by others in German Intelligence and that she (and possibly him) would be punished. Or did he have in mind other activities not related to finances that the Duchesse sensed when she said 'there might in time be some things asked me, which I am unable or unwilling to answer'? A secret mission somewhere, perhaps?

It is clear that the Duchesse was a naïve and gullible woman, as Valeska had said when she told Maxwell Knight, 'She just believes what she is told.' She was so concerned with not only retrieving what was due to her, but also making money 'for jam' as she put it, and was prepared to go to any lengths to get it, even if that meant collaborating with German Intelligence (although the Duchesse claimed she was not aware of that at the time). Her ex-husband, Curt Uhlig, living at Wilhelmstraße 6/1, München 6, went much further in denigrating her as 'a dishonourable and dishonest woman, who has failed in most of her mother's duties, and says that "her character is so bad that almost any low deed may be expected of her."'[46]

That the Duchesse was also allowing her so-called social status in London to be used as a means for the Germans to make influential connections suggests she was indeed guilty of conspiracy, something that in itself could not be punished under the Official Secrets Acts of 1911 and 1920, nor the Treachery Act (1940), since in 1938 when the acts took place, Germany was not yet the enemy since war had not yet been declared, and the Treachery Act did not exist. Nor had any secrets been betrayed.

What is slightly puzzling is why, given that Valeska and her mother did not get along well, lived separate lives and had not lived in the same house for a number of years, should the Duchesse have bothered to confide so much in her daughter in the first place? Had the Duchesse meant to implicate or incriminate her by association, or was it that she could not help but have to tell somebody as Miss Hall implied? Indeed, as Knight pointed out in his report:

The Duchesse acted the part of the broken-hearted mother when her son died in Switzerland in January 1939, but actually her first act after his death was to ransack through his private papers and she was very annoyed to find that he had left everything to his sister, Valeska … 'A new confirmation of her blend of mind, outwardly a desolate mother, and inwardly thinking of her benefit, if possible, immediately after the sad event.'[47]

The suggestion that this may indeed be the case seems implicit in one the Duchesse's letters, which she wrote on 10 August 1938:

I wrote Henry [Dr Henry] with this post and said I would like your opinion and judgement on the matter and although you yourself were fed up with and cared nothing about my social 'humbug' etc. <u>yet you</u> had if you wished or were <u>very</u> interested – some good social strings to pull etc. So you know what cards to play.[48]

Was this an attempt to co-opt Valeska's assistance in this affair using her social contacts as well? The Duchesse was certainly not talking about Dr Henry's contacts. Whatever the reason, Valeska was not fully aware of, and did not condone, her mother's activities. As MI5 stated later, 'Enquiries since her detention exonerated her of suspicion and MI5 will not oppose her release (19 January 1941).' A Revocation Order was duly made ready for approval; her detention was revoked on 16 February 1941 by Herbert Morrison, the Home Secretary, and she was released the following day to 6 Berkeley Mews, Portman Square. Valeska then resumed her duties as an Auxiliary with the fire brigade on 5 March 1941. A letter to F.W. Smith stated that she is an 'extremely loyal, patriotic person'. Indeed, Richard Butler had added a handwritten note scrawled at the bottom of his 8 November 1940 report, 'She also stated she hated all Germans except her father.'

On 12 March 1941 the Deputy Assistant Commissioner, Special Branch wrote to MI5 saying that Valeska had written requesting the return of papers taken from her residence when she was arrested. The following day, Richard Butler wrote back saying that all the papers were being returned to Special Branch.

10

'THE ALIVENTI GROUP'

While neither Madame Aliventi's nor Chevallier's files are currently available from the National Archives (PF 45802 and PF 27057 respectively), a note to Dick White received from the SCO Shoreham in Sussex and signed 'K.S.W.'[1] provides plenty of snippets of information about Aliventi that he obtained during the course of a conversation with Hester Harriott Marsden-Smedley *née* Pinney (1901–82). Marsden-Smedley, the 38-year-old *Sunday Express* journalist was, according to Ben Macintyre, 'as tough as teak'. While on a train before the Second World War she had met Kim Philby and obliquely suggested to him that he join the Secret Service.[2] She later became mayoress of Chelsea (1957–59) when her husband, Basil Futvoye Marsden-Smedley, was mayor.

Ester Aliventi was a Romanian woman born on 16 January 1903 at Chisinau, Romania (written as Roumania, a common spelling then), then living at the Mayfair Hotel and Claridges. Marsden-Smedley said that she had 'become suspicious of a Roumanian lady by the name of ALIVENTI staying at the Hotel de l'Ermitage, Brussels, and thought she would be well worth watching should she come to this country, as a possible enemy agent'. A question was posed of SIS as to whether they could tell MI5 anything further about Aliventi and if it would be possible to interrogate Marsden-Smedley. Further evidence revealed that Aliventi had been blacklisted on 15 January 1940: 'Refuse visa. Refuse leave to land.' A few points of interest about Aliventi mentioned in the SCO's report are worth repeating in full as they shed more light on who she was and how she was connected to the Duchesse's circle:[3]

1. Vague indications of connections with Andre ROSTIN[4] and THOST[5] which are not clear from this file, but I am getting up others. [There is nothing to indicate in either man's files of any connection between them and the Duchesse or Aliventi.]

2. On 16.7.37. S.11 reported on Philip de FROBERVILLE of 46 Chiltern Court, Baker Street and the Duchesse de CHATEAU-THIERRY. If this is not on the file with you, but has been burnt, would you see whether B.6 has any record of the S.11 report.

3. ALIVENTI used the initials E.A.P. on books of matches specially made for her. The P. appeared to refer to her maiden name which was PRIVER.

4. On 6.7.37. ALIVENTI put through a twenty minute call to Rome.

5. Other details are that in conversation with HEYWORTH DUNNE's[6] friends she said that the Monico was below her style; that she was dining on a certain night at the Dorchester. She did not go to the Dorchester, said that she must ring there to phone up a number which proved to be that of the Hunting & Racing Magazine of 12 Queen Street.

6. On other occasions she has said that she has three hunters [horses] at Maidenhead.

7. On 10.8.37. Lana NEWNES, apparently the wife of Sir Frank NEWNES,[7] wrote hoping that ALIVENTI had enjoyed the Dublin Horse Show.

8. On 13.12.37. there is the following entry on the file:-

Mr Heyworth-DUNNE who came forward with information re Mme. ALIVENTI has again mentioned to me the names of de FROBERVILLE and Duchesse de CHATEAU-THIERRY – alias RAIS-BOUILLON.
    His information is that their flat at 46 Chiltern Court is frequented by a number of 'funny people' – foreigners. Friends of Heyworth-DUNNE who live in the same block think there is 'something fishy' going on there. (sd.) R.S. [Robin Stephens?]

Can Sinclair [Derek Sinclair, SLB] get in touch with HEYWORTH DUNNE and find out anything about this, including the alias RAIS-BOUILLON.

20.4.37. Mrs Georgina BLOIS,[8] Guards Club, Brock Street [Probably should be Brook Street] W.1 wrote to the War Office to the effect that the description

of the woman mentioned in the press appeared to agree with a Mme.
ALIVENTI, whom writer regarded with some suspicion.

22.6.37. M.I.1.a. telephoned to say that HEYWORTH DUNNE, one of the
Arabic teachers at the School of Oriental Studies had an interesting story to
tell about an Italian woman named ALIVENTI, residing at the Mayfair Hotel.

23.6.37. B.6., Mr Ottaway [John Ottaway], informed us that it seemed possible that Mme. ALIVENTI was engaged in espionage.

24.6.37. HEYWORTH DUNNE was interviewed by Mr Robertson
[T.A. 'Tar' Robertson, B1a] and Major Sinclair. [Derek Sinclair, SLB]
During a reception at the Hyde Park Hotel, given by the Saudi Delegation,
HEYWORTH DUNNE had noticed a woman of foreign appearance
who seemed anxious to get in touch with him. She eventually asked him
a number of very personal questions. She told him that she was staying for
another three weeks and was anxious to learn Arabic. In conversation with
an Arab HEYWORTH DUNNE was told: 'We know her; she is a spy.'

A few days later Mme. ALIVENTI telephoned HEYWORTH DUNNE
regarding Arabic lessons and asked him to call and see her. HEYWORTH
DUNNE noticed in her room a number of invitations from families of good
standing in this country. In the course of conversations she mentioned tha[t]
her husband was in the Italian Diplomatic Service. She mentioned that she
knew a number of Mohammedans in England.

HEYWORTH DUNNE said that he had been invited to accompany Mme.
ALIVENTI to a cocktail party and it was arranged that he should go and
out-of-pocket expenses wou[ld] be paid by this office.

24.6.37. HEYWORTH DUNNE telephoned to say that Mme. ALIVENTI
had excused herself from keeping the appointment on the plea that she had
a number of air mail letters to write and had to post them that day to reach
the continent. Her manner was said to be suspicious.

26.6.37. At an interview with HEYWORTH DUNNE the latter said
that Mme. ALIVENTI had used letters from the Russian alphabet which
suggested a knowledge of that language. Her languages were as follows:-

English – fairly good; French – good but not perfect; Italian; Russian (?); Roumanian (?). He had ascertained that Mme. ALIVENTI had lived for 4 years in Cairo and had travelled in Palestine, Syria and Turkey. She declared herself extremely Germanophobe.

HEYWORTH DUNNE ascertained from Mme. ALIVENTI that she was born in Italy (her registration card shows place of birth as Chisinau, Roumania), had a house at Longetevere situated on the Tiber in Italy; her husband died 18 months earlier leaving a considerable sum of money; she had permission from the Italian Government to export £200 a month; that she was living at the rate of 6 guineas a day; that she was shortly going to Denmark.

25.6.37. H.O.W. imposed.

9.7.37. HEYWORTH DUNNE gave further information regarding Mme. ALIVENTI. She would be leaving for the Continent in a week's time; she knew the Duce personally; when he had telephoned her she was speaking on a long distan[ce] call to Rome. When he mentioned this to her she had replied that she frequently put through long distance calls to Rome.

15.7.37. The following names were given as members of the 'Aliventi Group':-
    Philip F. de FROBERVILLE and the Duchesse de Chat[ea]u-Thierry.

15.8.37. Intercepted letter from Lady NEWNES. Asked whether ALIVENTI had enjoyed the Dublin Horse Show.

30.10.37. Mme. ALIVENTI left Croydon for Paris. Add: Claridges Hotel.

4.2.38. 'M' reported that a Pole named Alexander RYGER, with a large circle of foreign acquaintances in London, had mentioned Mme. ALIVENTI, who he referred to as a spy. He said that he had heard through a friend that the War Office were taking an interest in her.[9]

Contacts:-
Sir Frank and Lady NEWNES
The Hon. Dudley LEACOCK[10]

Francis William RICKETTS (Abyssinian concession)
Philip de FROBERVILLE
The Duchesse de CHATEAU-THIERRY
Renee PANNELL (29 Upper George St., Luton) (?)
Stuart MACWATT, 28, Bar Way, Wembly Park [*sic*]
Alexander RYGER, 11 Belsize Park, N.W.[11]

Stuart MacWatt is possibly Major Stuart Logan MacWatt, DSO, MC (1894–?) of the Royal Garrison Artillery, married to Beatrice Sybil Edith Rider (1901–53).

James Heyworth-Dunne, also known as Gamal-eddine Heyworth-Dunne, was a senior lecturer in Arabic at the School of Oriental & African Studies (SOAS) at the University of London and author of *An Introduction to the History of Education in Modern Egypt* (1938). Aliventi appears to have left Britain in 1937 or 1938.

11

DR RANTZAU,
I PRESUME

Nikolaus Franz Adolf Ritter was born at Rheydt, a suburb of Mönchengladbach in the Rhineland, on 8 January 1899, 'the pampered scion of an aristocratic family from Lower Saxony' and described as 'Fatty by at least one of his future spies'.[1] He attended gymnasium (school) in Flensburg and Verden. In 1917 after graduating from school in Verden he entered the infantry, in which he served until the end of the First World War. After his discharge from the army he worked in the textile industry at Laubau, Silesia (now Lubań, Poland), until 1921. At Sorau in Silesia he attended a textile school for one year and became business manager of a textile factory in Laubau until the autumn of 1923.

Ritter made many trips to the USA. On 1 January 1924 he went to New York on a permanent resident visa issued, he believed, in Breslau, aboard the SS *Bremen*. This information is confirmed in a report in his MI5 file dated 22 May 1944 based on a report from the American Consulate-General in Hamburg to the US State Department in 1938, when his presence in the US was first noted. In New York he obtained employment with the firm of H.R. Mallinson of Long Island. Hiram Royal Mallinson was a Polish immigrant who had established a high-end textile manufacturing company producing innovative designs, mostly on silk.[2] Ritter stayed with the firm for two years, until 1926 when he found alternative employment at J.J. Sussmuth of West New York, New Jersey. The firm was taken over by Manhattan Textile Works but filed for bankruptcy in 1935, at which time Ritter returned to Germany. His intention was to go into business in Silesia, but when that fell through after three or four months he returned to the USA, this time with William Meyer, with whom he formed a small loan company. This only lasted six months, with Meyer loaning Ritter $300 to pay for his return trip to Germany. He also tried to go into business with his brother Hans Walter, forming the Brush

Importing Company at 70 East 11th Street, New York City, but when that proved unsuccessful he returned again to Germany in August 1936. A report dated 22 May 1944 notes that both brothers also worked for the Consumer's Credit Corporation in New York City. According to Ritter's MI5 file, Hans was also in the USA in 1926 or 1927, and Mexico. The FBI reported that Hans was later part of Abwehr II and Frontauflaerungstrupp No.249 as an Unteroffizier.[3] It is possible that Nikolaus's various financial dealings and contacts in New York enabled him to assist the Duchesse in obtaining some of her funds from the US.

Ritter adopted many aliases and was known to each person by a different one. Hauptmann Georg Sessler @ George Sinclair 'the trusted courier of RANTZAU's [*illegible*]' thought that Ritter's real name was actually Jantzen. In fact, Dr. Janssen was one of his aliases. One of My Eriksson's files[4] provides a comparative description of him, all of which pretty much concur, shown in Figure 6:

Figure 6

By:	Special Agent (reliable)	W. Schmidt	Chateau-Thierry	Erichsen
NAME	RANTZAU	Maj. RITTER	REINHARDT	HANSEN
AGE	About 50	50	About 40	40–45
HEIGHT	6ft	1.74 [m] [5ft 7in]	medium	medium
[B]UILD	Well-built broad shoulders	Broad sturdy		Slightly stout. '[rot]und'
HAIR	Fair	Fair	Fair	Dark blond
EYES		Grey, no glasses	Light	Slit eyes
FACE shape	Oval	Clean shaven	Round, little fair moustache	Clean shaven
NOSE			Snub	Very short
TEETH	Gold upper tooth on right side of jaw			

[MA]NNER	'Looks like an American'		ready smile. young and very good looking. Not typically German-looking	always smiles 'quite unreal[istic]
UNIFORM		Luftwaffe Iron Cross 1st class		

Copies of a photograph found in the possession of My Eriksson when she was arrested at Gravesend and published in the *Sunday Pictorial* and the *Sunday Express* on 2 April 1939 show Hitler arriving in Wilhelmshaven to launch the pocket battleship *Tirpitz* taken the previous day. These were shown to 'a number of B.2.a. agents with interesting results'. According to a letter to Robin Stephens at Camp 020 from Helenus 'Buster' Milmo of B2c, TATE identified the man on Hitler's left as being identical with Rantzau (Ritter). He also said that since Ritter resembles Goering, at the Berlin headquarters of the Abwehr he was referred to as 'small Goering' ('der kleine Goering'). TATE's identification was confirmed by agent FRANK, who said he was identical with the man he had met in Lisbon known as the 'Doctor'; FRANK, an MI5 informant of Maxwell Knight, was known as McCarthy while in Lisbon. In a letter to Milmo from J.C. Masterman, chairman of the Double-Cross Committee, CELERY also said the man in the photograph 'was either the DOCTOR or someone who bore an extraordinarily close resemblance to him ', while bearing in mind that he had never seen him in uniform, and the cap was pulled too far down 'to make positive recognition difficult'.[5] Robin Stephens' report to Dick White on 23 February 1941 sets out to clarify why it could not be Ritter:

In so far as the uniform is concerned I am relying on a pamphlet 'Uniformfibel', von Geschichtsmaler Knötel d.J., dated 1933, and on page 32 thereof there are fairly clear reproductions of cap badges and collar badges which correspond. Indeed, there seems considerable reason to suppose the uniform is that of a Reichsführer der S.S. bis Brigadeführer. In general corroboration, the photograph indicates the man stands high in the comic German hierarchy, for he is jostling close to Hitler, while both his collar and collar badge are edged with braid. Furthermore the chinstrap is in heavy braid also. It is difficult, of course, in the blurred photograph to speak exactly of the cap badge, but that the impression is that of the scull [*sic*] worn by the S.S. It is not a Luftwaffe badge, for that spread widely across the cap.[6]

However, if the person concerned was a Reichsführer then this could only have been Heinrich Himmler, who held that rank from 1929 to 1945, which from the photograph clearly it is not. That being said, from what can be made out of the SS collar badges, they more closely resemble a Reichsführer. It is not clear why Eriksson had these photographs in her possession.

Further descriptions were provided by four double agents: SNOW, CELERY, BISCUIT, and TATE, seen in Figure 7. However, it is interesting that only one of them (SNOW) mentioned the gold tooth; nor did the Duchesse when she met Ritter. The age varies from one agent to another, with the Duchesse ascribing the youngest age to him (40), and calling him 'young and good look-ing, a more than Aryan type'. The height also tends to vary. Everything else appears to pretty much concur. It is a well-known fact that witnesses at police identity parades do not always identify the right person. Clearly, appearances can be deceptive, and descriptions not always reliable.

Figure 7

Characteristics	SNOW (Arthur Owens)	CELERY (Walter Dicketts)	BISCUIT (Sam McCarthy)	TATE (Wulf Schmidt)
Age	About 50	46	41	50
Height	6ft	5ft 10in	5ft 8in	1.74m [5ft 7in]
Build	Good, broad shoulders	Broad		Broad, sturdy
Hair	Fair	Ash blond, wavy, very thick	Fair, parted on right hand side	Fair
Face	Oval, clean shaven	Round	Round, florid com-plexion, high cheek bones	Clean shaven

| Teeth | Gold tooth in top right side | Perfect | Irregular – no gold ones visible. Has one tooth on left side which pro-trudes | |
| Other | Looks like an American, speaks good English with American accent | Speaks English per-fectly and colloquially with a strong middle-west American accent | Speaks with broad New York accent. Likes dirty stories and is very common | Eyes: grey; Iron Cross 1st Class, Luftwaffe uniform |

The agents' identification is in marked contrast to when the photograph was shown to Finckenstein, K.C. Hansen, Josef Jakobs, and Karel Richter, all at Camp 020, none of whom identified Ritter. SNOW observed that the man is wearing an SS uniform, something that Ritter never did, and is too tall. This uniform can be seen more clearly in another photograph in the collection of the Imperial War Museum.[7] It seems unlikely that Ritter would have been front-and-centre at the launch of a battleship when he was a Luftwaffe officer.

Ulrich Graf zu Finckenstein of Sonderkommando 'Finckenstein' and Kurt Carlis Hansen were among a party of meteorologists aboard the *Hinrich Freese*, a German weather ship collecting intelligence, captured by HMS *Naiad* of the Royal Navy off Jan Mayen Island in the Arctic Ocean on 12 November 1941.[8]

According to author and journalist Peter Duffy, Ritter's return to Germany was at the behest of the German military attaché in Washington, Lieutenant General Friderich von Boetticher (1881–1967).[9] Ritter was offered a commis-sion in the Wehrmacht as an auxiliary officer with the rank of Hauptmann (captain), effective in May 1937 and assigned to *Ast* Hamburg, where he would remain until June 1941, when he was in Libya. In the autumn of 1937 he again returned to the US. Exactly when is difficult to ascertain. Various reports in his file state that it was on 29 October, staying there until 27 December 1937; another report states that it was between 8 September 1937 and 15 February 1938, while the information provided by the FBI states that his last entry into the US was actually 11 November 1937. His visa stated that he was an engineer, but by that time he was employed as an intelligence officer. In a letter provided by his wife supporting his visa application she stated that 'to the best of my knowledge, my husband is not connected with any subservient movement and is not a member of the National Socialistic Party' [*sic*].[10]

While in New York in 1926 he had married an Irish-American, Mary Aurora Evans, born on 31 October 1900 in Clayton, Alabama. Together they had two children, Nikolaus Haviland (Klaus), born on 21 December 1933, and Katherina, born on 13 December 1934. Finding out that her husband was actively engaged in spying, Mary divorced Ritter in 1938. According to Duffy, Mary came from 'hardy, Bible-preaching stock' from the backwoods of southern Alabama, so the fact that he was having an affair with one of his clerical assistants, Irmgard von Klitzing, whom he later married in Hamburg in 1939, likely had as much influence on her decision as his spying activities.[11] His file states that the affair started after his return from the US in December 1937. Irmgard gave birth to a daughter, Karin, on 2 January 1940. In the meantime, Mary gained custody of their children but was forced to remain in Germany because of the war, living at Othmarschen, Klaus Groth Strasse 39. She eventually moved to the USA in 1946 and died in Alabama in 1997. Nikolaus Jr., trained as an electrical engineer, but eventually moved to Berlin, where he died on 25 October 2009; Katherina remained in the USA and worked for NASA and the US Navy.

When Ritter was assigned to I-L (I Luft) in *Ast* Hamburg in 1937 it was under Ic/AO of the Wehrmacht.[12] *Leiter* (Chief) of Gruppe I and head of I M was Korvettenkapitän Herbert Wichmann. Two of the agents Ritter would go on to control were SNOW (Arthur Owens) and CELERY (Walter Dicketts), as well as William Sebold (code-named TRAMP) who was part of the Duquesne Ring in the USA. Ritter claimed he first met Duquesne in 1934, although some sources say it was as early as 1931. Frederick (Fritz) Joubert Duquesne reported that he had received a letter from Ritter requesting information on aviation-related subjects. One of the members of the Ring, Hermann W. Lang, an inspector for Norden, was responsible for delivering to Ritter the plans for the Norden precision bombsight – an innovative design by Carl Lukas Norden intended to improve the accuracy of bombing. However, the Luftwaffe's Technical Office in Berlin initially dismissed the plans as the work of a charlatan. It is not necessary to go into details about this case as Duffy has dealt with it extensively in his book *Double Agent*, and it is not relevant to our story.

Ritter's other contacts were Ultric Thompson in 1934, and Axel Wheeler Hill, whom he met in 1938 at *Ast* Hamburg when Wheeler Hill came to see (this part of the document is missing but possibly Heino (Hans) Lips) in *Referat* H. This was Kurt Wheeler-Hill, who met an Irish bicycle salesman named Francis P. Campbell and his wife who came to Hamburg in 1937 and agreed to spy for the Abwehr.[13] These two men are shown in the diagram of the Hamburg Organisation from Lips' file (Figure 2). In 1937 Campbell had answered an advertisement inserted in an Irish newspaper by Kurt Wheeler-Hill, 9 Mount Pleasant Square, Dublin, regarding German lessons: 'Kurt WHEELER HILL, who is a German, was subsequently identified as a brother of one WHEELER HILL who is a Nazi leader in the U.S.A. – Deutscher Amerikanischer Volksbund.'[14] This was James Wheeler Hill (b. 1905), secretary of the German American Bund, and brother of Axel. There was also an unknown woman in 1940 who, coincidentally, was hoping to have some of her money released by the Germans – but this could not have been the Duchesse because of her age (the unknown woman was aged 24-25, the Duchesse much older). Another contact was Elsa Weustenfeld – a friend of Nikolaus Ritter's brother Hans, with whom she lived, and a member of and allegedly the paymistress for the Duquesne Ring.

An article appeared in the *New York Herald Tribune* on 16 September 1941 about the trial of the Duquesne Ring in which Weustenfeld admitted that she had been living with Ritter's brother for five years. Hans told her that 'Nick was a Gestapo agent', but 'to leave her out of it' when his brother had approached her in 1938 to become a spy.

Herbert Hart in MI5's B1b, Special Sources, wrote to someone in MI6 counterintelligence (Section V) on 25 September 1941 to say, 'There are good grounds, I think, for the conjecture that JUERGENSEN, who has recently appeared on the Madrid to Bilbao service, is our old friend Major RITTER alias Dr RANTZAU.' Hugh Trevor-Roper of the Radio Security Service (RSS) at Barnet replied on 29 September 1941:

RITTER is obviously a man of great importance. He runs agents in England and is so important that their messages are relayed to him personally as far as CYRENAICA. He seems to be the highest personage that we know of in the whole Hamburg system. When he visited Africa, it was clear that he was going to set up a large organisation, probably in preparation for a large-scale German campaign in the Near East; although this was suddenly switched off after the preparations had begun (cf. the withdrawal of Obladen from Athens although he was undoubtedly destined to go on to Africa). RITTER also (or a namesake of his) organised in person the whole network of W/T spies in North America.

It is thus clear that RITTER, more than anyone else, is the Hamburg system; and so far, we have never come across him outside that system.[15]

The assumption that Ritter and Jurgensen were one and the same was based on messages intercepted by Bletchley Park from *Ast* Stettin to Spain via Bilbao between 7,13,14 and 17 August and 9,12,13 September where Jurgensen was the subject, also known as MARTIN, as well as:

SNOW saw on the 'Doctor's' Diplomatic passport in August 1940, the name von JORGENSEN. On th[is] occasion he had travelled to Lisbon by plane via Madrid, so this may be a Spanish alias;

a) JUERGENSEN, according to the message on 13.8.41, was ill and we know that RITTER had an operation in June 1941 as a result of injuring his arm in Cyrenaica;
b) RITTER was of course [connec]ted with a MARTIN when he was in Cyrenaica, who functioned in Cairo.

My impression is that RITTER, after a period of partial convalescence in Berlin in June was sent off to AST STETTIN to help in work agains[t] Russia during the campaign and is now turning his attention to Spain ...[16]

Point (a) above was also reinforced by FRANK, who reported that when Ritter was in Lisbon for twelve hours on 12 August 1940, returning the following day, he was travelling on a diplomatic passport under the name of von Jorgensen. JUERGENSEN was Kapitänleutnant Just Hans Jurgensen, *Leiter* I M in *Ast* Stettin. Clearly, at that time MI5 was unaware of the role played by Herbert Wichmann in *Ast* Hamburg, who was Ritter's superior officer. But it is unlikely that Ritter/Jurgensen/Martin are one and the same judging from earlier ULTRA intercepts marked 'Top Secret U' such as:

7.5.41.
4965 Hamburg informs RITTER of movements of 'Friend A' ?ALMASY. Icf.I/40-5044- 1.5.41) MARTIN and JOHANNES. Also re LENA enterprise and suitable area for landing agents.

7.5.41.
4995 RITTER informs HAMBURG that he has arranged with MARTIN (who is known to have been operating a W/T set in CAIRO) for a W/T set to be delivered to a Hungarian priest with the password 'Alma Mater'.

10.5.41.

5095 RITTER reports to HAMBURG that MARTIN's portable set with instructions in English have been deposited with the Hungarian priest DOEMETEOR, Church of St. Therese, CAIRO, Schukra. Password ALMA MATER. Hptm. v. ALMASY arrived TAORMINA 9.5.41.[17]

All of these, taken from Ritter's MI5 file, would seem to separate him from Agent MARTIN.

In August 1940 Ritter was reported to have been in Lisbon meeting with Agent 3504, better known as SNOW (Arthur Owens) by the British, and again in February 1941. In the meantime, Rodney Dennys of MI6's section VB3 wrote to Dick White on 21 October 1940 about the identity of Ritter/Rantzau:

> There seems a possibility that the RANTZAU, alias HANSEN, alias RITTER, mentioned by you in your interrogation of Vera may be LUDERS, alias LORENZ alias PAULSEN etc. Both seem to have a positive passion for pseudonyms, their methods seem similar and they both work from Hamburg, while HANSEN and LUDERS both appear to be leaders of the Hamburg Stelle. This is a very tentative suggestion but you may care to turn it over in your mind.[18]

In the summer of 1940 Berlin decreed that all agents to be sent to Britain for *Unternehmen Seelöwe* (Operation *Sea Lion,* the German invasion of Britain) were to be coordinated by *Ast* Hamburg, with Hauptman Gartenfeld, a Luftwaffe officer of OKW, handling the logistics by air. These agents were part of Operation *Lena*. Julius Boeckel's MI5 file provides a list of the agents to be dropped:

> ROSE. A young German born in SOUTH AFRICA, the first of the LENA agents dropped in Jul or Aug 40. TORNOW took him to France to superintend his departure. He was given the address of 3504 [SNOW]. Contact was not established with him.

> 'SUMMER' A Swede, agent of I Wi of Ast HAMBURG, despatched [sic] in Sep 40 from an airfield near BRUSSELS or in Southern FRANCE. He landed safely and was assisted by 3504 [SNOW]. After he had passed a few messages, he wirelessed [sic] that he was in danger and would endeavour to leave ENGLAND. Nothing more was heard from him.

DRUCKE, KELLER, Vera von SCHALBURG. Agents of I M, Ast HAMBURG, sent by seaplane from STAVANGER, in Sep 40 and arrested immediately after arrival.

KROPF. An agent of Ast BREMEN, despatched in Nov 40 by TORNOW from a BRUSSELS airfield. He was instructed to go to ASHBORN, LIVERPOOL. 3504 reported at this time that a man was drowned in the MERSEY, though according to the GARTENFELD-Staffel, KROPF was dropped further SOUTH. KROPF was to have received a WT set from 3504 [SNOW].

JAKOBS. A BERLIN dentist dropped early in 1941, arrested and shot.

Karel RICHTER. A Czech, dropped in May 41 and immediately arrested. Prisoner [Julius Boeckel] first met him in autumn or winter 40. He denies having recruited RICHTER from FUHLSBITTEL Concentration Camp, stating that RICHTER was passed to I L by I Wi, for whom he had already undertaken a mission to SWEDEN. RICHTER's mission to BRITAIN was primarily for I Wi and secondarily for I L. He was given a sum of money to pass to 3725.

'TATE' An agent of I Wi, BERLIN, dropped in Sep 40. He hurt his foot on landing and was assisted temporarily by 3504 [SNOW]. Further details on his activities will be found in para 4.

All these LENA agents were in HAMBURG for training, most of them accommodated in the Hotel Phoenix, and all were known to Prisoner. None of them spoke perfect English, but BERLIN insisted that they be despatched [*sic*] as rapidly as possible.[19]

MI5 never managed to identify Agent ROSE, as this note from Joan Paine in WRC-1 to Major Vesey in B1b dated 23 March 1946, which appears in Ritter's file, bears witness:

We have been unable to identify ROSE, described by both BOECKEL and RITTER of I Luft Hamburg as one of the agents dispatched by air to the UK as part of the 'Unternehmen Lena'. He may well be the South African whom RITTER told BISCIUT [*sic*] in July 1940 he was sending as an assistant to SNOW, and who never materialized.[20]

Boeckel was sure that:

ROSE was dropped over ENGLAND;

a) he had received no sabotage training (he had been trained by TORNOW
and Prisoner had given him instruction in map reading for 2-3 days);

ROSE was definitely an agent of I Luft Ast Hamburg, recruited by
TORNOW, possibly from another Referat of the Ast.
    Prisoner cannot give a complete description of ROSE since he only saw
him for a brief period during his apprenticeship. He describes him as slim,
about 1.65 m in height, with blue eyes. He thinks that he was younger than
the 25 years previously attributed to him, being probably only about 21.[21]

The CSDIC report on Ritter states that:

ROSE was a young merchant from JOHANNESBURG of South African
nationality. Prisoner, [Ritter] who was absent from HAMBURG during Jun
40, states that he cannot recall any details about this 'LENA' man, who was
handled exclusively by Kap Lt TORNOW; he received the usual 'LENA'
training in an intensified form. The agent was despatched to the UK by
aircraft in Jun 40 and baled out over SW ENGLAND. He had been provide
with a large sum of money and a special WT transmitter/receiver, but had no
identity or food ration cards. He was not heard of again.[22]

The mention of ROSE in George Sessler's MI5 file is identical to that in
Boeckel's.
    Although some details about ROSE could be applied to Jan Willem Ter
Braak (1914–41), alias Engelbertus Fukken, it is unlikely that they are one
and the same. Jan Willem Ter Braak was born at 's Gravenhage on 28 August
1914, and was found to have committed suicide in 1941 in an air raid shelter
in Cambridge. He was dropped on the night of 2/3 November 1940 around
Haversham, Buckinghamshire, which, ironically, was close to Bletchley Park,
whereas ROSE to whom Ritter referred, was dropped in about June 1940 –
another source (see below) says July or August. Ter Braak was the only agent
not captured by the British authorities. When his body was found he had an
out-of-date ration card in his possession, although he did carry a Dutch passport, whereas Ritter's ROSE had no identity papers or ration cards. Ter Braak's
nationality is sometimes given as Dutch, but this may be on account of his

adopting false papers and claiming to be a member of the Free Dutch Forces working on a Dutch newspaper.[23] Someone having South African nationality could easily pass for Dutch as their accents when speaking English can sound very similar. Both were young – Ter Braak's age was 27, and Boeckel gave ROSE's age as 21-25. But when CSDIC showed Ritter a photograph of Ter Braak on 12 June 1946:

> RITTER could not identify the subject with any degree of certainty. He is emphatic, however, that the man was <u>NOT</u> a LENA agent. After close study of the photograph, RITTER stated that he believed he might have seen the man either in the I/Wi offices at Ast HAMBURG or in ANTWERP, when he visited that city with BOECKEL towards the end of 1940 ...
>
> When stressing the fact that the man in question was <u>NOT</u> a LENA agent, RITTER suggested that he might have been an agent of Major SENSBERG of Ast BRUSSELS.[24]

The MI5 file on Ernest William Carl Rose, a South African born in Johannesburg on 6 January 1914, may help to shed more light on the identity of Agent ROSE.[25] Ernest Rose worked as a stress calculator for the Parnall Aircraft Company at their base in Surbiton, Surrey, before the war. A letter from Captain Archibald Frazer-Nash to Captain S.L. Pettit (ret'd), a higher clerical officer at the Air Ministry, dated 3 August 1939, confirmed that Ernest Rose had worked for Parnall but had left them two months beforehand. Frazer-Nash developed hydraulically-operated gun turrets, such as the Frazer-Nash (Parnall) FN5 later installed on Wellington, Stirling and Lancaster bombers.

In 1939 Ernest Rose moved to Germany, leaving Southampton for Hamburg on 11 June on the SS *Pretoria*, according to a report from Special Branch. His reason for doing so was because at the end of June 1939 the rest of his family, living in South Africa, had sailed to Germany for the Golden Wedding anniversary of Mrs Rose's parents. However, there may have been an ulterior motive on Ernest's part. He had travelled to Germany frequently between 1937 and 1938 and while there had learned gliding. This is confirmed by an anonymous source calling himself 'a true Englishman', writing to Scotland Yard from Johannesburg on 15 March 1938 who stated that when Rose had arrived in Germany in 1938 he was sent to a gliding corps for six months, then sent to England. He had also been 'in touch with some office in BERLIN who had offered him assistance should he ever need it', according to a report by Sir Vernon Kell, Director of MI5. Kell's report, sent to Colonel I.P. de Villiers, Commissioner of the South African Police on 8 September 1939. The report states that at that time Parnall held secret contracts with the Air Ministry and that the company had also stepped up production. It was also suggested that this unknown Berlin office was going to find him work in an aircraft factory.

Another MI5 report states that during a visit to Germany in 1938 Rose had taken courses in unarmed combat 'somewhere in Hamburg', but was very mysterious about his movements and activities. Consequently, his mother, Hedwig Augusta Rose, suspected that he was working for the 'Geheime Dienst' (German Secret Service). Kell added that two reliable sources alleged that Rose was 'an ardent Nazi and supporter of Hitler' and that he 'took with him data relative to aircraft'. A eulogy for his late father, delivered by Pastor Halder on 13 February 1942, suggests that Rose was 'in military service', which prevented his being able to attend the funeral service and cremation. That absence may be explained by a statement in his MI5 file that in August 1940 he was sent on a mission overseas, thought to have been to the USA, and was never heard of again. That mission could equally have been one to the UK as part of Operation *Lena*.

Boeckel's description of Agent ROSE, mentioned above, gives his height as 1.65m, which equates with the height of Ernest Rose (5 ft 4–5 in) given in a document sent to the Home Office Immigration Branch by H.M. Perks, H.M. Chief Inspector. Unfortunately, Boeckel did not give any other physical details so it is hard to say whether Agent ROSE was well-built, with light brown curly hair, slightly protruding ears, longish face and a sallow complexion, as in Perks's description. Boeckel gave Agent ROSE's age as 25 or possibly even 21; Ernest Rose was born in 1914, which would make him 25 and put him as the same age as Agent ROSE. There is also the connection with Hamburg – while in Germany Ernest and his family lived with Mrs Rose's brother-in-law, Dr Gloede, at 27 Zimmermanstraße, Hamburg. Whether this is the same Dr Heinz Gloede of 22 Wangelstraße [*sic* – it should be Wrangelstraße] who was sympathic to the Nazi cause and with whom Klaus Barbie, 'The Butcher of Lyons', had sought refuge in November 1946, has not been confirmed.[26]

While this new information may not confirm beyond a shadow of a doubt that Agent ROSE was none other than Ernest Rose, there are too many similarities to discount and it is hoped that it may be a step in the right direction. The fact that they both share the name Rose only serves to show the Germans' lack of imagination or creativity with code names.

Agent SUMMER was Gösta Caroli (1902–75), who parachuted to England on 6 September 1940. JAKOBS was Josef Jakobs (1898–1941), who parachuted into England on the night of 31 January/1 February 1941 and was shot in the Tower of London by a military firing squad comprised of eight Scots

Guards on 15 August 1941, the only German spy to be executed in this way during the Second World War; all others were hanged. Karel Richard Richter (1912–41) was convicted under the Treachery Act (1940) and hanged at Wandsworth prison on 10 December 1941. TORNOW was Korvettenkapitän Tornow of I M *Ast* Hamburg. This is possibly also the same Kapitänleutnant Otto Heinrich Tornow (b.1886) who had served in Das Keiserlich Deutsche Marineoffizierkorps (the Imperial Naval Officer Corps) as a U-boat commander (U-39 and U-42) during the First World War and responsible for sinking ten ships. As far as Kropf is concerned, Terry Crowdy makes reference to an agent dropped on 7 September 1940 who drowned in the Manchester Ship Canal, citing Ladislas Farago as his source:

> He was sent to Lancashire and came down in the Manchester Ship Canal near the Mersey estuary above Birkenhead. He drowned, helpless and alone, on the night of September 7 1940. He was never missed. His loss was never felt.[27]

This is most likely Kropf, sent by Tornow, but unless Boeckel's memory is playing tricks, which is always possible, it is Farago who once again has got his facts wrong.

Josef Starziczny,[28] code-named LUCAS (or LUCASSEN) and head of the organisation connected with Radio CIT in Brazil, also said there was an agent 'Schmid' sent to England who was under Ritter's control. This was Wulf Dietrich Christian Schmidt (1911–92), later known as Harry Williamson, code-named TATE by the British and 3725 by the Germans, who became a Double-Cross agent for MI5.[29] A War Room WRC-1 telegram dated 10 October 1945 gives the following information about some of his later activities:

PAIR

A. Major Ritter alias Dr. Janssen first reported May 1940 when he was connected I Luft espionage in U.S.A. and worked for AST Hamburg.

B. February 1941 was in Barcelona, returning to Berlin end of month.

C. March 1941 established unit called Sonderkommando Ritter with w/t station in Libya, location Tripoli. Interested running agents primarily in Egypt and to some extent in French North Africa.

D. April 1941 had lengthy dispute with Obladen, then in Greece regarding immediate transmission captured British General Staff maps of Egypt and Tripoli.

E. May 1941 informed Hamburg he had arranged deposit set and instructions for agent cover-name Martin in Cairo with Hungarian priest.

F. Martin apparently transmitted about this time from Egypt with some success, and later returned to Germany via Budapest.

G. A Hptm Almasy of Hungarian intelligence was connected with above affair.

H. About same time Ritter complained to I.M Hamburg that he was not consulted about setting down agents in Tunis and that relations with Italians were jeopardised.

I. Planned send Agent Aliquo Renato alias Hassan to Egypt. Plan abortive and Hassan ultimately used in Myth Network north Italy.

J. Beginning June 1941 went to Berlin for consultations, flying back end month; plane crashed in sea Ritter breaking arm.

K. As result returned Berlin beginning July.

L. Interested results interrogation I Luft activities North Africa and Egypt and any details Agent Martin.

M. Further brief and questions follow by pouch.[30]

Count Lászlo Ede Almásy Zsadány et Törölszentmiklós (1895-1951), better known as Count Lászlo Almásy, was the character who formed the basis of the novel *The English Patient* by Michael Ondaatje. He was recruited by Ritter in Budapest. The description of him in MI5 files bears no relationship to the character played by Ralph Fiennes in the movie: 'a hunchback ... shabbily dressed, with a fat and pendulous nose, drooping shoulders and a nervous tic'.[31] Michael Smith also refers to him as 'a bungling Nazi intelligence officer' and 'no hero'.[32] A book by John Bierman published in 2005 reveals that Almásy was also a homosexual.[33]

The operation in which Ritter was injured was the first Operation *Condor* in 1942. OBLADEN was Kapitänleutnant Friederich Wilhelm Michael Obladen, a Hamburg businessman and director of Schulke and Mayer of Hamburg, born in Bonn on 18 December 1902 and recruited by the Abwehr in 1937 to provide intelligence from his contacts.[34] He was recruited by his friend Fregattenkapitän Herbert Wichmann. Both Tornow and Obladen were intended to become part of Wichmann's *Ast* zbV (in *Abt* 1) which was to operate in Britain following the invasion in September 1940.

In early 1941 Ritter was assigned by Abwehr I L to fly to Egypt to look into the possibility of inserting agents behind the British lines with the help of the Luftwaffe. The trip was unsuccessful and when he flew back on 17 July 1941 his plane crashed into the sea and he broke his arm, spending five months in hospital. The crash occurred when the aircraft in which he was travelling had taken off from Taormina, Sicily, en route to Derna in Libya. As the aircraft was approaching Derna the pilot received a warning of enemy air activity and he was redirected to Benghazi. Low on fuel and its W/T put out of action, the aircraft was forced to make an emergency landing in the sea 50km off the coast. One of the agents, Gefreiter (Corporal) Feiertag (or Freitag) was killed, while Gefreiter Klein was badly bruised, and Ritter broke his arm.[35] Feiertag was a sailor aged 40 who had been recruited by *Ast* Kiel and who had spent some time in Suez. Klein, who may have been Obergefreiter Walter Klein (2 September 1903–30 January 1945), aged 45, from Hamburg, had lived for several years in Alexandria. He had been trained in espionage and W/T by *Ast* Hamburg. Both men were given training in parachuting with the intent that they both be parachuted back to Suez (Feiertag) and Alexandria (Klein).[36] The report on Eppler's interrogation stated that Ritter was actually piloting the aircraft, believed to have been a Junkers Ju 88 (it was actually a Heinkel He 111, according to Ritter's file), and that it crashed 3–4km from the coast:

> RITTER flew one machine alone, and the second plane was flown by another G.A.F. [German Air Force – Luftwaffe] officer. They arrived at the place indicated by ALMASY but could not see any chance of making a safe landing. They consequently turned back without having achieved their object. They lost their way; one plane landed safely at DERNA, but the other, piloted by Major RITTER, made a forced landing on the sea. S.O.S. signals were sent out and the A.C. [aircraft] was discovered about 3–4km from the coast. The EGYPTIAN was killed, but RITTER and the Jew were saved. RITTER had a broken arm.[37]

EPPLER was Johannes Eppler @ Hans Eppler @ John Eppler @ Hussein Gaafer (1914–99).[38] According to the report, 'The EGYPTIAN' was called Ahmed, his last name is unknown; 'the Jew' was presumably Klein. Interestingly, Eppler's book, *Rommel's Spy*, does not even mention Ritter or any of his aliases.

Following his recovery in a Berlin hospital, Ritter was reassigned to an anti-aircraft unit and later promoted to Oberstleutnant (lieutenant colonel). He was captured on 21 August 1945, and made himself available to the Allies as a translator and consultant. For his services he received a certificate signed by Lieutenant Colonel (CAC) V. Rapp, Headquarters Air Defence, Investigative Liaison Officer, 21st Army Group. MI5 appears to have initially written him off, as a letter in Herbert Wichmann's file from Joan Paine in WRC-1 to John Curry on 21 August 1945 states that, 'RITTER, who should have proved a fruitful source of information regarding Hamburg activities against this country, is also thought to be dead ...'; and in another also from Joan Paine to J.L.S. Hale, MI5's senior legal advisor in SLA, the following day states that, 'Both

DIERKS and RITTER have most inconsiderately escaped interrogation. The former was killed in 1940 and the latter is believed to have died in 1943.'[39] In fact, Ritter died in Germany on 9 April 1974.

At first, MI5 decided not to bring him to the UK for interrogation, even though a War Room telegram of 15 September 1945 stated that he was 'a character of great interest to us', but that 'the field should be given an opportunity first to conduct at least a preliminary interrogation'. On 12 November 1945 a telegram from the War Room to GSI(S), BAOR, requested the following:

C. First obtain from R. a full statement on agents despatched or controlled in U.K.

D. On receipt of this we would brief in detail on points omitted or not fully covered.

12

THE MISSION: 'A SULLEN DISPIRITED GROUP'

Early on the morning of 30 September 1940 two men and a woman came ashore in a small 4ft x 10ft rubber boat near Buckie on the Moray Firth in Scotland. They had been landed by a Heinkel 115 seaplane of *X Fliegerkorps* from Stavanger, Norway.[1] For whatever reason, the group had decided to split up. At 8.10 a.m. Vera Eriksen @ Vera Schalburg, and François De Deeker (Drueke) arrived at Portgordon station and bought tickets to London via Forres, while Werner Heinrich Walti separated from them and made his way to Edinburgh's Waverley Station, where he was later arrested. However, it was Vera and Drueke who attracted the most attention when the stationmaster became suspicious of their presence there, noticing that Vera had frost marks on her shoulders, and the bottoms of her trousers were wet when it had not been raining. They had also asked the name of the station. He reported them to the police, who arrested them and took them to Portgordon police station.

At the police station Lieutenant Mair, the MI5 Scottish Regional Security Liaison Officer, was contacted, who in turn called MI5 headquarters in London. They instructed him to send the pair to London with all their confiscated equipment, which included a W/T transmitter in one of their suitcases. A wireless set was also later found in Walti's briefcase, along with eleven maps of parts of England and Scotland; various identity documents, including his Swiss passport; a code book; some food; and a Mauser pistol containing six rounds of ammunition, plus a box with an additional twenty rounds. Two pieces of paper were found: one with the name of the OC (Officer Commanding) the German Air Force in Norway, written on it – 'Major Harlinghausen, Chief of the General Staff', and then 'Felf, 10th Air Force Corps', and 'Andersen, Bergen, Hotel Nord'. Felf must have been someone other than Heinz Felfe (1918-2008) who worked variously for the intelligence agencies of Nazi Germany (SD), Britain (MI6), the Soviet

Union (KGB) and West Germany (BND), because the latter does not appear to have had any connection with the Luftwaffe. At the time of this operation he was working for the SS. The 10th Air Corps (X *Fliegerkorps*) specialised in coastal operations.

Martin Harlinghausen was born in Rheda/Westfalen in 1902 and died in Gütersloh (later a post-war and Cold War RAF Germany airfield) in 1986. After serving in the Spanish Civil War, in 1940 he was a major on the General Staff and Chief of Staff of the X *Fliegerkorps* (10th Air Force Corps). On 30 January 1941 he received the 8th Oak Leaves to accompany his Knight's Cross as Oberstleutnant on the General Staff and Chief of Staff of the X *Fliegerkorps*. In June 1942 he was appointed *Fliegerführer Tunisien*. He was to end the war as a Generalleutnant (lieutenant general).[2] The other piece of paper had the address 23 Sussex Gardens in Bayswater, London, on it. The maps, listed in the Appendices, were loaned to a Captain M. Holroyd of MI14, a branch of Military Intelligence specialising in Germany.

While Vera admitted to being a spy, she and Drueke both claimed that they had no intention of spying on England. She was simply escaping from the Germans, intending to make her way to London, where she would contact her friend Major Mackenzie, aged 39, who she said lived at 39 Broughton Place (it was actually 39 Bruton Street). When she was interviewed by Stephens, Sampson and Evans on 12 November 1940 she told them that she had once told Drueke that she knew a Major Mackenzie who 'would help me because he knew someone in Scotland Yard of the Secret Service. Because he asked me if he could something for me about those anonomous [sic] letters. He told me he had a friend in Scotland Yard of the Secret Service.'[3] Could she have been referring to Maxwell Knight's alias? She had been instructed to buy some clothes and baggage and to take a room at the Dorchester Hotel. There she should await contact from 'Mr Wilkinson', who we have already come across. Wilkinson would come to the hotel any day after the fifth day of her arrival between 4.00 p.m. and 5.30 p.m. and ask for her as Vera Eriksen. It is interesting that when Ritter (referred to as the Prisoner) was interrogated at the end of the war he disclaimed:

> any knowledge of 'WILKINSON', the mysterious caller at Dorset House, who allegedly conveyed to von SCHALBERG 'Regards from REINHARDT (or HANSEN)'. He states that he had no other agent in the UK at that time other than 'X', who does not answer the description, and was not instructed to visit the house anyway. Prisoner believes that if an Abw contact was made in LONDON in the circumstances described, the visitor

could only have been an agent of Hptm DIERKS who he never disclosed to Prisoner.[4]

Drueke claimed he was a refugee who was simply escaping from the Germans because of a crime committed against some German soldiers in Brussels. He told his MI5 interrogators that, for the price of 3,000 kronen, he had managed to persuade a Captain Andersen to take him on a Norwegian fishing boat across to Scotland. Andersen had insisted that he take a suitcase containing a W/T transmitter and hand it over to a man at the ABC restaurant near Baker Street station at 7.00 p.m. on Tuesday, Wednesday or Saturday of that week. Their recognition signal would be that Drueke would be carrying a copy of the *News Chronicle* and have the suitcase standing by his chair.

The MI5 interrogators were not buying their stories. They had discovered that Vera and Drueke had known each other for two years, and that under an alias Drueke had been connected to the Hamburg and Brussels *Abstellen*. Indeed, they would later learn in an entry in a chronology of Ritter's activities in a CSDIC report dated 16 January 1946 that Ritter, accompanied by Dierks, had gone to Brussels in the spring of 1938 to contact him. Drueke had been originally recruited by Dierks as a *Forscher* and given training with I M in 1940, as well as a LENA course. MI5 concluded that:

Instructions for Mission to England.

It would seem that the German Intelligence decided, at short notice, to plant a number of agents in England. Apparently it was not until the end of August that the project was mentioned to Vera. At that stage she and DRUCKE [*sic*] were in Brussels. They were recalled to Hamburg where RANTZAU met them a few days before they left for Norway. RANTZAU instructed Vera that she was to proceed to the Duchess's establishment in London with DRUCKE, taking with them the wireless set. They were to wait there until someone came to fetch the set. If the Duchess was no longer there they were to go to Soho and find a room. The Duchess would get in touch with RANTZAU by letter via Portugal. Vera states that DRUCKE was never intended to use his set, and did not know morse [*sic*]. She also says he did not know English. It was intended that Vera and DRUCKE should remain in London for the duration, which meant no more than a few weeks, as invasion was said to be imminent and to be bound to be successful [*sic*].

WALTI, on the other hand, was intended to use the wireless set which he carried, and was to send messages 'probably about aerodromes in Scotland'.

Journey to London.

In the first week of September 1940, the party set out from Berlin, and were presented with false passports, identity cards and ration books at the station. They were escorted by a HAUPTMANN [Captain], who treated them like dirt. DRUCKE remarked to him 'We are like beasts being taken to the slaughter'. They were handed over in Oslo to a representative of the local Dienstelle. An abortive attempt was made to dispatch them by fishing smack from Bergen, but when this fell through a plane was procured with great difficulty, in which they were flown to the Scottish coast.

Conclusions.

It is now considered that we have been told substantially the whole truth by Vera, and it would seem that she and her companions were not more important than any of the other operational spies who arrived roughly at the same time. They were obviously thrown to the wolves. Doubtless the satisfaction which the directors of the German Intelligence responsible received from the venture was their ability to report to the High Command that they were dispatching spies to the United Kingdom in preparation for the invasion, which was then the practical intention of the enemy.

The unhappy feeling that Vera, DRUCKE and WALTI arrived in this country with some particular mission, the nature of which would always remain a mystery to us, has now been removed.[5]

A similar report mirroring this one was written by Dick White (ADB1) on 26 February 1942, in which he states that U.35 (Klop Ustinov) was also convinced that Vera had given them the whole truth. Two days later the Director-General, Sir David Petrie, appended a scrawled note at the bottom:

It is an interesting statement and may well be correct. Certainly for all the chance these three people had of getting away with it, they were in Druckers' [*sic*] words a 'cargo of meat'? One cannot but think that if they had been of great importance more care and forethought would have been devoted to their 'planting'.[6]

When Vera left the Duchesse's residence on 9 September 1939, she had been instructed by the Duchesse to go to Riemerstratt 24, Brussels, an accommodation address where Rantzau received his mail, and make contact with a certain Heine Tini, (referred to by Klop as Heine Fiene but crossed out and Tini added) 'a woman of about thirty-five, not pretty but with a pleasant and homely manner'. There Vera was to tell her that she was from 'Uncle Richard'. Klop's report states that she had 'originally intended to travel via Ostend and to proceed to Brussels, but she had had to make a detour via Holland and arrived in The Hague without any money'. The Home Office Traffic Index on Vera's movements for the period 1938–89, shown in Figure 8, indicates that she departed London and arrived in Rotterdam.

Figure 8

Date	Observations
29.06.38	Arrived London from Göteborg, Sweden
10.09.38	Departed, Harwich to Esbjerg, Denmark
23.03.39	Arrived, Dover from Ostend, Belgium
10.06.39	Departed, Dover to Ostend, Belgium
19.06.39	Arrived, Dover from Ostend, Belgium
09.09.39	Departed, London to Rotterdam, the Netherlands

The latter likely means that she must have taken the boat train from Liverpool Street station and left from Harwich, arriving at the Hook of Holland, thence to Rotterdam and The Hague. Apart from the two movements in 1938, Vera gave her address as 102 Dorset House, London, the home of the Duchesse. For the 29 June 1938 entry she gave her address as 12 Durham Avenue, Bromley in Kent (the house is now divided into flats); for the 10 September 1938 entry she gave it as 'Bedforda', Pennington, Hampshire, a village near Lymington and close to the Solent. This latter was also conveniently within relatively easy reach of Editha Dargel. Was this a coincidence?

According to Vera's MI5 file, she had gone to a boarding house in The Hague used by von Wedel. From there she proceeded to Hamburg, where in February 1940 she was introduced to Karl Theodore Drucke (sometimes written as Druecke, Drueke, Drücke or Drucker) @ De Deeker, and Werner Heinrich Walti (also written as Waelti) whose real name was Robert Petter.

However, the account in Vera's file written by Klop states that she was introduced to Drueke in The Hague.

Vera soon became aware that Drueke and the proprietress of the boarding house, Heine Tini, had been having an affair, something that was confirmed by Tini herself when the three of them were having dinner in Scheveningen one evening. Not wanting to come between the two of them, Vera made arrangements to move to another pension. Drueke, who appeared to be unaware of

Vera's upcoming mission, made arrangements for her to return to Germany. He bought her a ticket to Hamburg and helped her with her luggage. Yet in spite of her qualms about making trouble for Drueke and Tini, and attracted by this act of chivalry, Vera fell in love with him because 'he was nice to me'. In fact, according to Vera, he was 'the only man I have ever loved, and shall ever love'. The very mention of his name during interrogations brought tears to her eyes.

Her journey to Germany was not without problems. No one had thought to forewarn the German authorities, so when she crossed the border at Bentheim she was initially held by the Gestapo as a suspected English spy, holding a Danish passport and coming from England so soon after war had been declared. This was soon sorted out when Vera told them to call the Oberkommando in Hamburg. Drueke had recently been released from prison in France, after serving three years for 'political propaganda', for which he claimed he was innocent. However, he did not confide in Vera the real reason why he had been there. More about this later.

13

'A BOYISH INTEREST IN DETECTIVES'

A notebook and diary belonging to a certain Kenneth C. Howard of 128 Durham Road, Bromley, Kent, found in Josef Jakobs' MI5 file (KV2/27) open up a mystery relating to Druecke and makes reference to his imprisonment. Exactly who Kenneth C. Howard was, or his association with Drueke, has never been fully established. What little is known appears in Drueke's MI5 file (KV2/1701) and that of Josef Jakobs (KV2/27):

> The diary entry for 13 May 1936 reports that 'Today my frien and ally [*sic*] Karl Theodore Drucke, 30 yrs old was today sentenced to 3 yrs imprisonment + 10 yrs banishment'.[1]

This is made all the more curious by the fact that MI6 reported on 14 December 1940 that Druecke had been sentenced on the 12th May 1936 by the 14th Chambre Correctionnelle in Paris to three years' imprisonment, 2000 francs fine and 10 years banishment from France for espionage (see Chapter 15). How could Kenneth Howard have known so soon? It is unlikely, although not impossible, that he would have read about Drueke's conviction in a French newspaper as foreign newspapers were not as generally available in Britain at that time as they are now, and certainly unlikely to have been read by a teenage boy. Assuming he had been following the case, what would have been his interest in it, unless Druecke actually was his friend? That then presupposes that the two had met either in France, Belgium or England sometime prior to 1936, but there is no evidence to suggest that Druecke had ever visited England. Given that Kenneth's father was essentially a shopkeeper (see below), it seems unlikely that Kenneth would have visited him. It also seems unlikely that Drueke would have written to him so soon after his conviction. But if he did, how did he know about Kenneth Howard, unless they had met somewhere? There is no mention in Druecke's MI5 files of any connection between the two.

The existence of the diary and the investigation into its contents were first reported in a letter from the Birmingham City Police CID dated 5 June 1941:

> I have to report that on Sunday 1st June 1941, a communication was received from the Chief Constable, City Police Headquarters, Leicester, enclosing a diary dated 1936 and an address book. These apparently belong to Kenneth C. Howard, sometime of 17, Evelyn Road, Sparkhill, and contain a number of German references, also two addresses in Birmingham.
>
> I have made enquiries at 17 Evelyn Road, Birmingham, but there is no trace of Howard ever having lived there. Enquiries at 86, Durham Road reveal that Eric Porter, whose name is mentioned in the address book, left this house about four years ago. His present whereabouts are unknown.
>
> I visited 45 Shepherds Green Road, Birmingham and interviewed Mr. S.F. Philpot, whose name is also mentioned in the address book. He told me that he did not know Kenneth C. Howard, neither did any of the names contained in the address book convey anything to him. He is unable to explain how his name and address became known to Howard.
>
> It will be seen on page 64 of the diary that Howard at one time lived at 120 [*sic*] Durham Road, Bromley, Kent.
>
> I respectfully suggest that this report together with the address book and diary, be forwarded to the Commissioner of Police for the Metropolis, New Scotland Yard, London, S.W.1., for any action he may deem advisable.[2]

The letter was signed by Constable Maurice Bennett and C.C.H. Moriarty, Chief Constable.[3] But as Giselle Jakobs, granddaughter of Josef Jakobs, has pointed out in her blog, Josef Jakobs was never in Birmingham and there is no indication in the report from Birmingham CID or the Metropolitan Police Special Branch of exactly how the diary and notebook came into their possession in the first place. Further developments would ensue, with a report from Special Branch on 23 June 1941, signed by a sergeant, an inspector, and a superintendent, which provides more information on the persons mentioned in the diary and is worth quoting in full:

> With reference to a letter dated 5.6.41 from Birmingham City Police – Ref: C.I.D. 958776 – regarding Kenneth C. HOWARD, with which was forwarded a diary for 1936 and a notebook containing names and addresses etc, for any necessary action:-
>
> Enquiries have revealed that a family named HOWARD lived at 128 (not 120) Durham Road, Bromley, Kent from 2.5.1931 until 17.6.1936. The rated

occupier was Frank HOWARD, who lived there with his wife, Flora, nee MITCHELL, and son Kenneth Clifford.

Frank HOWRAD [sic] was a blouse merchant and had a business under the style of 'Flora Mitchell' at 21, West Street, Bromley, where his wife assisted in dressmaking. I was informed that towards the end of his stay at 128, Durham Road, HOWARD was in some financial difficulty and took employment as a salesman with 'Hoovers'. Enquiries of Messrs. Hoovers Ltd, Westway, Perivale, fail to show that HOWARD was ever so employed.

On leaving Bromley, Frank HOWARD gave as his intended address 17, Evelyn Road, Spark Hill, Birmingham – the address which appears in the notebook mentioned above. No member of the family is known to have returned to London.

Kenneth Clifford HOWARD was born on 4th June 1921 at 3, Leigham Court Road, Streatham [as indicated in the diary]. He attended Bromley County School, Hayes Road, Bromley Kent [its successor, Ravensbourne School is actually in Hayes Lane]. From the fact that he could have been no more than 15 years old when he lived at Bromley, it would appear that he was impelled by a boyish interest in detectives in making several of the entries in the notebook. [Someone has written in the margin beside this paragraph, 'schoolboy rubbish']

Examination of the diary bearing Kenneth's HOWARD's [sic] name revealed the entry made in pencil, for Wednesday, 13th May, 1936, as follows:- 'TODAY MY FRIEN & ALLY(?) KARL THEODORE DRUCKE [sic], 30 YRS OLD WAS TODAY sentenced to 3 yrs imprisonment & 10 yrs banishment.' DRUCKE would appear to be identical with Karl Theodore DRUCKE born 1906, who was sentenced to a term of imprisonment in France some years ago, and on 16.6.41 was sentenced to death at the Central Criminal Court for treachery with intent to assist the enemy.

The following names and addresses (within the Metropolitan Police District) are shewn in the notebook and recorded below together with the results of enquiries:-

1) DICKINSON, L.J. 23 Eardley Crescent, S.W.5. This address was damaged by enemy action some time ago and is vacant. Enquiries in the vicinity failed to reveal any person who could identify DICKINSON.

2) De SOLLA, 22, Aylesford Avenue, Upper Elmers End. Mr. E.R. De SOLLA, of this address, who is employed by a firm of typewriter dealers in the City, has been seen, but has no knowledge of HOWARD or his family and does not know how the latter came into possession of his name and address.

3) FULLER, H.A. 24, Fitzroy Street, W.1. This address is now untenanted owing to enemy action and efforts to trace FULLER have proved unsuccessful.

HAMPSON, James, 'Heathpool', 31, Mollison Way, Edgeware. No person of this name resides at the above address nor is he known to persons in the near vicinity.

4) C.A. HARRISON, 56, Oakwood Avenue, Beckenham – identical with C.HARRISON, Amery, Oakwood Avenue, Shortlands – has been seen. This person's full name is Catherine Aston HARRISON. She stated she has no knowledge of HOWARD or his family and cannot identify him with anyone she has met. She wrote several articles about 1936–37, on Greece to which her name and address were appended, and HOWARD may have culled his information from this source.

5) R.K. PILLAY, 638, Green Lane, Ilford, Essex, is identical with R.K.PILLAY, M.R.C.S., L.R.C.P., of Grange Court, Manor Road, Grange Hill. He is now serving with H.M. Forces, outside the M.P.D. Neither he nor his wife have any knowledge of HOWARD. [As of 5 December 1940 he was with the Royal Army Medical Corps]

6) George WARDEN, 'Edenholm', London Lane, Bromley, left that address some time ago, having rented the premises from Messrs. Levens, estate agents, 3, High Street, Bromley. I have been informed that WARDEN is serving with H.M. Forces – present whereabouts unknown.

7) H.J. WOODLANDS Waterloo 5600. This man is now employed at Cornwall House.[4] At the time during which the HOWARDs were at Bromley, WOODLANDS was engaged as salesman of telephonic apparatus in Bromley district and may have called or left his card at F. HOWARD's business address. He has no knowledge of Kenneth HOWARD.

8) Detective Service, 86, Strand. This concern has been defunct for some years. It was owned and run by a Belgian named MEAGUS (now deceased) and no information regarding HOWARD can be learned from this course.

None of the above-mentioned persons (with the exception of DRUEKE) can be identified in Metropolitan Police records.[5]

A check of *Kelly's Directory* of Bromley for 1933 shows a George Warden living at 19 Wanstead Road; later, in 1937 *Kelly's* shows him living at 3 London Lane or 3 London Road – the two entries contradict one another – but he is not there in 1940. The two locations are very close to one another (3 London Lane is close to the intersection of London Road, now a modern block of flats, while 3 London Road is further down, opposite the cemetery), so one may have been a misprint. There is also a G. Warden in the *Army List* for 1941 as being a temporary major (GS02) on the General List, under the Director of Public Relations, having been commissioned as a second lieutenant on 3 September 1939. Whether this is the same George Warden has not been confirmed, but it would explain his absence from Bromley. A Lieutenant Colonel George Warden, Chief of the Press Censorship Branch, which would likely fit with the *Army List* entry for Major Warden of 1941, is mentioned in an entry in Guy Liddell's wartime diaries for 5 June 1944, where Warden had written 'an extremely badly worded and ambiguous directive' which had been forwarded to SHAEF by an American officer of the Associated Press in America. The message to be cabled to America stated that 'Eisenhower's troops have landed in France today', and had been put out prematurely.[6]

Exactly why any of these names were included in the diary of a teenage boy, none of whom appear to have any connection with him or his family, remains a mystery. Was there some connection between the persons listed in the diary who were all within the Metropolitan Police District, although not all living in the same town? If so, what could it have been? Had they all served on a jury? If so, for which trial? The names of jury members are typically not made public so why would Kenneth Howard have taken such an interest? Besides, there are only nine names mentioned, not the customary twelve. And what is the connection with the detective agency? Was it just, as the Special Branch report suggests, 'a boyish interest in detectives'?

Could the address in the diary (128 Durham Road) and the one given by Vera in June 1938 (12 Durham Avenue) actually be the same? The missing number 8 may have been an error on the part of whoever completed the Traffic Index, or by Vera herself, who may have mistaken which one was her old address. Google Street View shows 128 Durham Road as a semi-detached house in a typical 1930s Tudor-style. Durham Avenue runs perpendicular to Durham Road in a neighbourhood known as Shortlands. The only problem is that 128 Durham Road is right at the very end, while 12 Durham Avenue is close to the intersection of Durham Road. However, there is unlikely to be any connection between Vera and the Howard family because they had already moved out by the time she was apparently living there. In searching *Kelly's Directory* of Bromley for 1933 and 1937 I can find no one named Frank (or Francis) Howard listed for that address in Durham Road or anywhere else in the Bromley area. With respect to Catherine Harrison in the Special Branch report, she was living at 56 Oakwood Avenue, Beckenham (Shortlands). It appears that, according to her Registration Card, the Duchesse lived at Shortlands House, Shortlands, between 25 July and

22 October 1924, when she moved to 41 Leinster Gardens, Mayfair.[7] Both addresses were less than a mile away from each other. Maybe a coincidence, but not conclusive of anything.

Further examination of all the other entries in the diary and notebook reveal a few items worth mentioning:

The Diary

The entry for Thursday, 6 February mentions: 'Ship "Nirvana" made water in No 1 hold at Malta.' This refers to the SS *Nirvana*, belonging to the British India Steam Navigation Company, a general cargo liner launched in 1914 at West Hartlepool. On 6 January 1936 she, 'Fractured a plate below the water-line while in the Mediterranean causing a leak in the No.1 hold. She was forced into Malta to discharge her cargo before repairs could be completed.'[8] It is unclear why Kenneth C. Howard should be particularly interested in the SS *Nirvana* and its mishap in Malta, unless he knew someone onboard. The entries for wavelengths of wireless stations worldwide may simply indicate that Kenneth was listening to a shortwave radio on the BBC World Service.

The Notebook

On Page 4, he mentions:

'National Broadcasting Co. / Central Tower, Rockerfeller / Center N.Y. U.S.A.'

The National Broadcasting Company (NBC) was and is at the Rockerfeller Center in New York.

'Empire flying boat Capricornus / crashed Ouroux, Fr / March 24 – with loss of / five lives' /

The Short Empire flying boat *Capricornus* (G-ADVA) belonging to Imperial Airways crashed in a snow storm in the Beaujolais Mountains near Ouroux 15km south-west of Mâcon, France, on its maiden flight from Southampton (Calshot) to Alexandria, Egypt, on 24 March 1937, killing its Captain, Alexander Paterson, First Officer G.E.Klein (an Australian), flight clerk

D.T. O'Brien, steward F.A. Jeffcoate, and passenger Miss B.M. Coates, who was fatally injured.[9] The Australian newspaper *The Western Mail* for 21 April 1936 reported that Klein and his wife were visiting Perth from 'Kenya Colony'. Two days later it reported that Klein, the son of the Director of Education, J.A. Klein, was on leave from Imperial Airways, and intended to 'leave for the Eastern States in a fortnight, where he will study commercial aviation in an unofficial capacity.'[10] It is not clear whether this meant the eastern states of the USA or the eastern states of Australia.

'New worry for England' / 'Musso[lini] claims New Bomber / Speed record. Make Breda 88 / Speed 325.5 (5½ m.p.m.)'

Mussolini's new aircraft may have been the Savoia-Marchetti S.79 Corsa.

'Rt.Hon. S.M. Bruce, High Com / for the Commonwealth.'

The Rt. Hon. Stanley Melbourne Bruce (1883–1967) was Australian High Commissioner to the UK, 1939–45.

It is unknown why any of these facts are mentioned, other than perhaps the boy's curiosity.

On Page 5 he quotes a rhyme:

John Nuttall lives here and that's enough,
The candle's out and so's the snuff.
His souls [*sic*] with God, you need not fear
And what remains lies buried here.[11]

It is unknown what the significance of this rhyme was or how he came to know it, given that its origin is somewhat obscure and unlikely to have been found in the average compendium of poetry.

On Pages 6-8 he is preoccupied with the Dukes of Norfolk, including a potted history of the noble Howard family. Perhaps, having the same surname, Kenneth hoped that he might have been descended from them.

On Page 15 he mentions that on 2 May 'the King will review the Fleet', and the Port of London Authority founded in 1908. He also mentions Ignatius Timothy Trebitsch-Lincoln (1879–1943), the missionary, priest, Member of Parliament (as Timothy Lincoln), and Nazi collaborator, and Sir Roger Casement (1864–1916), the British diplomat hanged in 1916 for his part in the Easter Rising of that year. In fact, George VI reviewed the fleet at

Spithead on 20 May 1937. Why he should mention Casement twenty years after his execution is unknown, neither is his fascination with Trebitsch-Lincoln easily explained.

On Pages 15–16 he mentions various police officers, *inter alia*:

Captain Stephen Hugh Van Neck, CVO, MC [Chief Constable of Norfolk (1928–56)]

Chief Constable John Edward Horwell [head of the CID of the Metropolitan Police in 1935, and later Assistant Provost Marshal of the RAF]

Chief Superintendent William Trigg, MBE [Deputy Chief Constable of Lincolnshire, who was later suspended from duty pending an investigation of 'certain accounts']

Superintendent Harry Battley [a fingerprint expert]

Chief Inspector L. Burt

Detective Inspector Phelan [of Special Branch]

Inspector J.H. Giles [Queen Elizabeth's personal bodyguard]

It is not known why these particular officers were singled out for mention in the notebook.

Leonard Burt, later to become superintendent, was one of a number of Special Branch officers attached to MI5 during the Second World War, and headed B5, Investigations. After the war he headed Special Branch from 1946 to 1958 and arrested Klaus Fuchs, the atomic spy. Phelan is mentioned by intelligence historian Nigel West (writing as Rupert Allason) as being a detective constable in 1929 and able to speak Gaelic.[12]

On Page 36 there are various German references – the *Katholische Volkesreitung* (*Catholic People's Daily*), followed by several basic German phrases:

'Lang Live der König von Englande'
'George der Sechte ist der König von Englande'
'Londre ist der Capital von Englande'
'Berlin ist der Capital von Deutschland',

These can be translated as: Long live the King of England'; 'George the Sixth is the King of England'; 'London is the capital of England'; 'Berlin is the capital of Germany'.

They are followed by a couple of lines from a German Christmas carol:

Nachten und Tagen:- Stille Nacht heilige Nacht, Nur das troute locheheilige Par [should be Nur das traute hoch heilige Paar] ...

which is translated as: 'Nights and days: Silent night, holy night, Only the faithful sacrosanct couple ...'

A 'Frau Elfriede Klosse – Bad Kreuzenach, Deu[tschland?] (9)' cannot be traced.

Der Deutsche Volkswirt (*The German Economist*), also mentioned, was a leading German economic weekly founded in 1926.

It is not known why the *Katholische Volkesreitung* and *Der Deutsche Volkswirt* should have been of interest to Kenneth.

On Page 49 he lists two radio call signs and what appear to be their frequencies – W8XK 19.72, 31.48; W2XAF 19.57 respectively. The station 8XS in Saxenburg, Pennsylvania, was owned by Westinghouse and first broadcast on 19.72 kilocycles in 1923; it was all religious content. W8XK was 'Dr Frank Conrad's old experimental call from 1916 it was cancelled in 1917 and re-licensed as 8XK in 1920 [*sic*] ... All experimental calls consisted of the letter "W" followed by a number representing the "radio district" then an "X" then two or three letters.'[13] W2XAF was a General Electric shortwave broadcasting station in Schenectady, New York.[14]

On Page 50, four names that stand out are:

William R. Forder, 177 Third Ave, West, North Bay, Ont. <u>Canada.</u>

Forder (1915-2002) was a photographer active in North Bay, Trout Lake, Sturgeon Falls, Callender, Corbeil, South River and Mattawa in northern Ontario 'from at least 1948 through the 1980s'.[15] Clearly, he was known beforehand, but how would a teenager in England have known of him, let alone his address?

Count du Berrier, Bank of Ethiopia, Addis Abbaba, Abyssinia.

This is likely Hilaire du Berrier (1905–2002), not a count, who went to Abyssinia (modern-day Ethiopia) in 1936 to work as a mercenary pilot for

Emperor Haile Selassie. He was arrested as a spy during the Spanish Civil War.[16] How would a teenager know who he was?[17]

Enid Jannaway, Devonia, Huntermans Corner, Chatham, Kent.

Enid Olive Barbara Jannaway was listed in the *London Gazette* in 1932 as a writing assistant at the Admiralty; and as Enid Olive Barbara Jannaway Fairbrother in 1945 as an acting third officer, WRNS.[18] The Fairbrother name appears to have been added sometime between these two dates, so she must have got married. How would he have known her?

T. Owen James, 54 Manor Road, Camborne, Cornwall.

Another photographer. A photograph by James of a beach scene depicting a young boy came up for sale on *eBay* in December 2017 and sold for just £2. It seems that Kenneth must also have had an interest in photography.
On Page 53 he mentions:

Lady Mary Millais of Leacon Hall, Warehorne, Ashford, Kent.

Mary St Lawrence Millais *née* Hope-Vere (1861–1948) was married to Sir Everett Millais, the second baronet (son of the Pre-Raphaelite painter Sir John Everett Millais) and a close friend and neighbour of writer Joseph Conrad and his wife Jessie. The Grade II listed house was described by architectural historian Sir Niklaus Pevsner as 'a perfect example of a Queen Anne house'.
On Page 56:

Lady Beryl Groves of Revesby Abbey, Boston, Lincolnshire.

Beryl Fransziska Kathleen Bianca Groves *née* Le Poer Trench (1893–1957), the daughter of the 5th Earl of Clancarty, William Frederick Le Poer Trench (1868–1929). Lady Beryl married (1) Lord Richard Philip Stanhope (he was killed on the Somme on 15 September 1916 during the First World War); (2) Lieutenant Commander Walter Raleigh Gilbert (1889–1977); and (3) Francis Edward Selby Groves (d.1957). She was mentioned in the *Lincolnshire Echo* on 11 February 1936 and the *Nottingham Journal*, 24 March 1937, as having been badly burned when her dress caught fire in the library at Revesby Abbey on 9 February 1936. Why would a teenage boy be interested in her?

Coincidentally, one of the Duchesse's associates was the 8th Earl of Clancarty, William Francis Brinsley Le Poer Trench (1911–95).

The remaining entries are addresses in England, Scotland, Abyssinia, Australia, Egypt, Ireland, Canada, the USA (Florida), South Africa and Denmark. Apart from those investigated by the police and already mentioned above, none of them appear to be significant or make any sense. So is this miscellany simply a hodgepodge of 'schoolboy rubbish', the random jottings of a teenage boy with a wide interest in many things, or is there any more to it than meets the eye? Not on the surface, at least, but the entries raise a number of questions, to which there are no satisfactory answers:

How did the diary and notebook come to be in Jakobs' file? They only became known to MI5 in 1941 after they had been sent to them by Birmingham City Police. As noted by Giselle Jakobs, Josef Jakobs was never in Birmingham so, since the diary mentioned Drueke, did Hinchley Cook put them in Jakobs' file by mistake? It would seem so as they were not recorded as being amongst Jakobs' possessions when he was captured.

Were all or any of the names and addresses in Kenneth Howard's notebook known to him? Who were they? Since most of them are men's names, they are unlikely to have been clients of his father. How would he have obtained them, and for what purpose?

Could they have been contacts for someone? The only contact Jakobs claimed to have known in England was a Mrs Lilli (or Lily) Knips of 9 Compayne Gardens, West Hampstead, London, NW6. A trawl through his MI5 files does not reveal any of the other names in Kenneth Howard's diary or notebook.

Could the phrases from *Stille Nacht* be some sort of code?

Was the German phrase 'Lang Live der König von Englande' and others, codewords or 'paroles' to be used at a meeting?

Why were the countries in the addresses listed underlined?

Were the German journals *Katholische Volkesreitung* and *Der Deutsche Volkswirt* to be used as code books?

Why were Lady Mary Millais and Lady Beryl Groves mentioned? They appear to have had no German connections.

Why were the policemen mentioned? Were they simply because young Kenneth was interested in detectives?

Why the interest in all the radio frequencies? Was Kenneth also a radio 'ham'?

Was Jakobs intending to contact him and use his radio? Except Jakobs was equipped with his own wireless transmitter.

Lastly, was the name Kenneth Howard a case of stolen identity in the same way that deceased persons' identities were used by spies? But why use a live person unless, of course, Kenneth Howard had actually died in his mid-teens?

There is no mention anywhere of the diary or notebook being sent by MI5 to the Government Code & Cypher School (GC&CS) at Bletchley Park for examination and possible decryption. Nor were they sent for forensic testing. Perhaps they should have been.

14

'SOMETHING PARTICULARLY ODD'

Klop Ustinov suspected that Drueke and von Wedel were already acquainted, by the way they had referred to each other, with von Wedel calling Drueke 'Karl Theo' and Drueke calling von Wedel 'Herr von Wedel' in deference to his superior status. Drueke had certainly met Ritter by 1938 as it is recorded in a report prepared by CSDIC (WEA) on 16 January 1946 that in the spring of 1938 Ritter had visited Belgium to meet with him. In the CSDIC (WEA) report a list of 'Agents Despatched to or Controlled in the UK' one agent mentioned is described as 'Belgian Homosexual' who was contacted by Drueke in the summer of 1938. His identity remains unknown. The same report also records that Ritter had travelled to Sweden in the autumn of 1938 to meet V-Leute My Eriksson and Lund.[1] Lund was a Mrs Lund, a friend of My Eriksson, and not Lieutenant Colonel Ragnvald Alfred Roscher Lund, OBE (1899–1975), a Norwegian military officer who was the military attaché at the Norwegian legation in Stockholm in 1940, who had been closely associated with Swedish signals intelligence before the war.[2] As mentioned earlier, Ritter used Mrs Lund as a cut-out.

Drueke kept an office at 5 Rue Feider in Brussels that he shared with someone called Spitzberg. After a while Vera became good friends with him and he took her to night clubs in Brussels. On 13 September 1939 she left for Hamburg. She would not see him again until she was in Hamburg in March or early April 1940, but always accompanied by her husband, von Wedel (Dierks). One day, she was walking past a restaurant where Drueke was having lunch but although he saw her, he made no attempt to reconnect, as he was angry that she hadn't written to him. Instead, he contacted von Wedel and the three of them went out to dinner at the Reichshof Hotel. It was only after von Wedel went away shortly afterwards at the end of April that Vera and Drueke began their affair. Obviously von Wedel must have realised Vera's affection for

Drueke, became jealous, and forbade her to write to him. However, she would maintain regular contact with him in Brussels and Antwerp throughout June, July and August 1940. Klop's report states that Vera had remembered distinctly the meeting on 20 July 1940 in Brussels and suspected that it was the day she had suffered a miscarriage. Vera denied it, saying that she hadn't told anyone and would have taken the secret to her grave.

In August 1940 Rantzau (Ritter) had come up with the idea of sending Vera and Drueke to England on an espionage mission, although it has been claimed that it was actually the brainchild of Generalmajor Erwin von Lahousen-Vivremont (1897–1955), head of the Abwehr's Abteilung II, Sabotage, who was later implicated in two attempts to assassinate Hitler (13 March 1943 and 20 July 1944).[3] Drueke thought the operation hopeless and, with a certain prescience, thought he would never return. Von Wedel (Dierks) also shared this view, saying, 'Rantzau is again at it,' and decided to go to Admiral Canaris in Berlin to get him to countermand the order. It was during this journey that he was killed in a car accident with an oncoming car (one source suggests the car hit a tree). Drueke, who suffered concussion and a broken nose, was at the wheel. As with everything in this case, the circumstances of Dierks's death have become obscured. A so-called account of the crash is related by Farago, but since nowhere in the files of Vera, Drueke or Walti does it describe exactly what happened it must be assumed that Farago made this up for dramatic effect:

Major Dierks arranged a farewell party that promised to be especially gay. He took his beautiful mistress [note: not wife] and her two companions to the restaurant of the Hotel Reichshof for dinner, and then, for more drinks to Jacobs, an elegant wine restaurant that was one of the favorite hangouts of the Abwehr crowd. The party became a wild shindig ...

It was a dark night with heavy clouds, the streets slippery from a steady drizzle. Dierks was taking the car down the broad Elbchaussee when Druecke cried out: 'Left, Hans, we've got to turn left here!' Dierks tore the wheel to the left, the car jerked sideways on two wheels, plunged against the curb [sic], bounced back and, careering out of control for some twenty yards, turned over with a crash of metal and the sound of tearing from the fabric top.

Druecke was the first to climb out of the wreckage. He crawled to a phone booth and called the police. When the squad cars and the ambulance arrived, they found Druecke and Waelti sitting numbly by the wrecked little car. The woman was weeping uncontrollably as she bent over her lover, stretched out in the gutter, his blood mingling with the rainwater. Dierks was dead. The party was over.[4]

There was also supposedly a mystery woman in the car with whom Drueke was 'intoxicated'. Who this woman was, if indeed she existed, is unknown. Whether it was Vera herself is hard to say. During an interview at Camp 020 with Stephens and Dick White on 4 October 1940 she denied being in the car at the time, but when asked whether there was someone else in the car, she said she thought there was. However, she hesitated when she said 'somebody' and claimed not to know her name, saying 'it was a friend of he', [sic] as if trying to hide something. When asked whether the woman was badly hurt, she said, 'No, not all.' How she knew this was, 'Because I asked about STURECK, and they said he's dead because he's fallen out, and other people who were there, he said a friend of his – a lady – and two gentlemen, they weren't hurt at all.' Then she admitted she'd only overheard it, but couldn't remember exactly when but said it was the day before she went to Norway, 'Because then after he was dead HANSEN sent me away.'[5] Later, she claimed that Drueke had been driving the car and it was he who was responsible for killing Dierks – 'That's why he wants to be shot.' The time of the accident was around midnight, according to Vera, which is what she had been told first by the woman in the pension at Rothenbaumchaussee where her husband had stayed, then Hansen (Ritter).

Vera was first denied seeing the body before it was buried, but when she did noted that von Wedel's head was heavily bandaged, so she could not confirm her theory that he'd been shot at close range. But if so, by whom? One possible scenario is an argument between Drueke and von Wedel over Vera. She also thought that the 'accident' had been staged by Rantzau, as we shall see later. It is interesting to note that Dierks was originally intended to accompany Vera, Drueke and Walti to England. When Dierks died, Korvettenkapitän Dr Erich Pfeiffer had proposed sending Kapitänleutnant Fritz Jonetz, at that time I-M of *Nest* Brest, in his place, according to a letter sent to Herbert Hart in B1b from someone in SIS's section VB7.[6] This is confirmed in an 'Ultra' decrypt for 5 September 1940:

5.9.40
402   PFEIFFER hears of DIERKS' death. Suggests Kptlt. JONETZ as substitute for the special enterprise.[7]

A further reference to this appears in Korvettenkapitän Herbert Wichmann's file:

5.9.40

402   PFEIFFER informs WICHMANN of his regret at the news of
DIERKS and suggests Kptlt. JONETZ as substitute for the special enterprise.[8]

Wichmann's response is not recorded, but the suggestion was obviously
rejected.

As for Walti, Vera believed he was Swiss, who spoke German, French and
English. His file contains no biographical information, other than to say that
he was aged 25 and he was born in Zurich on 14 December 1915. The rest of
the documents are photographs showing a man in his twenties or thirties, high
forehead, hair combed back, and a beard. Most of the serials in the file were
destroyed by MI5, including the maps and other documents. A report prepared
by B1b on 14 October 1940 states that:

WALTI had proved most stubborn under interrogation and gave the mini-
mum of information. There is reason to believe that he was a thoroughly
experienced German agent who had operated in Paris prior to its fall, and
had on one occasion narrowly escaped apprehension by pretending to be
an idiot when the Police made a sudden swoop to search for a transmitter
in his room.[9]

All that is known about him derives from an interrogation report prepared
by Meurig Evans on 4 October 1940. Those conducting the interrogation
(Meurig Evans, Mr Short, and Dr Harold Dearden) mistakenly offered to spare
him his life in return for a full confession, although this was declined:

The whole position was put very clearly to WALTI and he was asked if he
understood. He appeared to do so and replied he could give no more information at all. On being told he would therefore be shot, he replied that he
would be shot for nothing. On being told that there was a possibility that his
life might be saved if he would comply with propositions put to him and tell
the whole truth, he repeated that he could not say anything more.[10]

What his interrogators learned was that after the death of his parents he was
brought up in Zurich by an aunt; that he had a girlfriend, a Walloon named
Betty; and that he had been found unfit for military service because he had a
narrow chest and a weak heart. In Zurich he had been employed as a chauffeur to a Mr Bagliano but in the summer of 1936 he left his employment to

travel to Geneva with a Monsieur Dreyfus to seek work and to learn French.[11] However, he had been unable to obtain a permit, so hitched a lift to France, first to Paris, then to Boulogne, and then returned to Zurich via Basel, having done a few odd jobs around the harbour in Boulogne. Between October 1936 and the summer of 1938 he worked again for Bagliano; sometime in 1937 he was also in Friederichshafen.

In the summer of 1938 he decided to emigrate to Brussels, staying at the Hotel Touriste. From there he went to Antwerp and worked for a Monsieur Rosenthal, a connection he had made through Bagliano. In Antwerp he lived at 80, rue Van Dyck (Frans Van Dijkstraat). In June 1939 he left Rosenthal, purchased a Ford truck and set himself up as a haulier. While he had no business premises, he hauled a lot of coal in Charleroi. In May 1940 he made a lot of money transporting Jews to the French border. On or about 17 May he drove to Ostend and lived in his truck for three weeks. Around 15 June he went to Brussels for a couple of days to see Betty. After that he went back to Antwerp, returning for short visits to Brussels, presumably to see Betty, and stayed in Antwerp for six or seven weeks.

Enquiries made to the Swiss authorities through the Foreign Office and the Home Office told another story, as did examination of Walti's Swiss passport. It was first thought by D4 and Passport Control to be genuine; however, correspondence between Milmo and Hinchley Cooke, and Hinchley Cooke and Philip Allen of the Home Office regarding its authenticity, revealed that it was a forgery and that the so-called 'Walti' did not really exist. MI5 sent photographs of the used pages of the passport to the Swiss. A letter sent from Derek Sinclair in SLB to Milmo on 17 June 1943 stated that the Swiss expressed 'that it was a very skilled imitation of a Swiss Passport'. It quoted from a report by Inspector Hess of the Swiss Federal Attorney's Office sent to the Head of the Swiss Federal Police Service in Bern, dated 9 October 1941 in which it highlighted the following reasons why this was so:

The said passport bears Federal No. 636723 and was issued at Zurich on the 5th January, 1937, by the State Office of Zurich Canton under Zurich cantonal No. 26,435. This passport was renewed under the cantonal No.4924 on the 5th January, 1938, by the State office of Zurich Canton until 5th January, 1941.

  Enquiries in this connexion of the State office of Zurich Canton (Passport Office) have produced the following:

  Walti, Werner, particulars from the passport mentioned below, does not appear in the records of the above mentioned Zurich Passport Office.

Federal passport No. 636,723 was issued on the 7th August, 1936, cantonal No. 17,657 by the State office of Zurich Canton to Hedwiz Elise Alice Fritschi-Müller, born on 16th March, 1899, of Zurich, residing at 109 Stampfenbachstrasse, valid for one year.

Cantonal passport No. 26,435 was issued on the 2nd October, 1937, on the passport with Federal No. 854,872 by the State office of Zurich Canton to Robert Spiller, born on 1st September, 1904, of Elgg, Zurich, conductor on the Swiss Federal Railways, residing at Zurich, valid for one year.

Cantonal renewal No. 4,924 (on Walti's passport, page 7) was granted on the 5th April, 1938, on the passport with Federal No. 505,861 (of the year 1934) by the State office of Zurich Canton to Alma Olga Kiener-Ehlich, born on 10th May, 1904, of Vechnigen, Berne (?), coiffeuse [hairdresser], residing at Stäfa, Zurich, valid until 5th April, 1941.

The renewal stamp on page 7 of Walti's passport 'The validity of the foregoing pass is etc.' was no longer used in the year 1938. It was replaced by a new stamp with the wording 'Renewal of period of validity until, etc.') The other stamps must likewise be forged.

It was also established at the civil registry of the so-called Walti in Horgen, Zurich Canton, that he is quite unknown there.[12]

At twilight on 20 August Walti had set out for Oslo with the 'Captain' and 'other people', landing there seven days later. All the time he was in Oslo he had been confined to a room and not allowed out. This isolation continued when they set out for England, where he was not allowed out on deck. The 'Captain' had taken away his luggage and returned it later, together with a briefcase. Walti denied knowing that inside the suitcase was a wireless transmitter, saying that the 'Captain' had told him it contained chemical products. He was also given a gun (the Mauser) and some bullets. He had climbed down from the boat into a rubber raft. There were two other men, one large and one small, with him in the raft, but he later denied ever meeting them. They had paddled to the shore and he had gone off on his own. A further report on 6 October by J. Russell-King of B8l to Major Stephens concluded that:

WALTI did not seem disposed to be any more informative than on previous occasions and apart from the following points this interrogation did not reveal anything of interest.

An appeal was made to WALTI to be more open and to help himself a little more as it was desired that he should have every opportunity but that he must realise that at the moment the evidence against him was overwhelming.

However, this evoked no response except for his continued adherence to his original story, i.e. that he was not a spy, had no connection with Germany and had received no money.[13]

At 6.30 a.m. he had shown up at Buckpool station carrying a suitcase and wearing a raincoat that was wet. There he had been directed to Buckie where he was to take a train to Aberdeen, but instead took one to Edinburgh. Enquiries regarding the other two agents led the authorities to him. As was reported in the *Scottish Daily Express* for 7 August 1941:

> He was a bit queer-looking, that stranger on a Scottish station platform. It was 7.30 in the morning when there aren't many people about, so the railwaymen waiting for a train gave him a bit more attention than usual.
>
> The man looked at a time-table for a while, then asked for a ticket to a neighbouring town. 'And,' says the stationmaster, 'at that moment I noticed something particularly odd. I had a word with one of the men about it, and found he was suspicious, too.'
>
> So the village constable was called in. He took the stranger into the waiting room …[14]

According to railway porter Thomas Cameron, aged 17, that afternoon Walti had deposited his suitcase at the cloakroom at Waverley station (other reports refer to it as the left-luggage office), having arrived from the Aberdeen train at around 4.30 p.m. Detective Inspector Alexander Sutherland, Detective Constable Alexander McCowan and Police War Reserve Constable James Fair searched the suitcase and found the wireless transmitter. They then waited until he returned. The MI5 report on Walti's arrest dated 25 November 1940 from Captain Hancock Nunn in B8l[15] reads as follows:

> At 8.58 that night, the Prisoner came from the vicinity of the Waverley Steps, and after hesitating at the Left Luggage Office, he continued on to the Book-stall some 20 yards distant. A minute or so after he had taken up his stance at the Book-stall, keeping his eye on the Left Luggage Office, Detective Superintendent William Merrilees was joined by Thomas Cameron. Just then the prisoner approached Cameron who asked if he wanted his case. The prisoner replied: 'Yes' and handed Cameron Cloak-room ticket No. H.5221. Detective Superintendent Merrilees was immediately joined by Detective Lieutenant [*sic*] Cormack, Detective Inspector Sutherland and Detective Sergeant Swan, and the prisoner was held. He, however, made an effort to

resist, but was overpowered while in the act of trying to put his hand in his left hand trouser pocket. He was then searched and a Mauser automatic pistol was found in his left hand trouser pocket …

Bearing in mind the circumstances of WALTI's arrival in this country and the exhibits found on him, notably the wireless set, code, money [£190] and Mauser revolver, together with the statement attached hereto, it is submitted that there is a clear prima facie case against this prisoner.[16]

During his interrogation by MI5 Walti was not very forthcoming with information but they thought that he was an agent working for the Germans who had been active in Paris before it fell in 1940. The report from B1b dated 14 October 1941 suggested that:

In view of the documents carried on WALTI and the time at which he arrived it seems probable that he was intended to act as a short-term operational agent whose function it was to supply information about aerodromes on the east coast to the invading German forces.[17]

Walti told his MI5 interrogators that at the end of August (thought actually to be the 20th) he had travelled on a 'motor vessel', the *Boreas*, from Belgium, arriving at a Norwegian town about a week later. The ship lay at anchor for two weeks in a fjord before proceeding further. About two weeks after that the voyage was abandoned and, 'After a few days, I was put in the evening in an aeroplane, and put down near the Scottish coast where I landed in a rubber boat with two other persons.'[18]

A report written on 7 October 1940 stated that the boat on which they had travelled was first thought to have been the fishing boat *North Star*. However, MI5 thought this unlikely, in part because the rubber dinghy in which they had landed was of the type carried by a seaplane or submarine. They also noted that, 'De DEEKER and ERIKSON were partners in an enterprise, the exact nature of which is still uncertain.' The report noted that Vera already had contacts in London, namely the Duchesse and 'Wilkinson', etc, and that possibly Drueke 'who has every appearance of being an important man in the German S.S. organization' was to establish contacts of his own, albeit with Vera's help, since he could not speak English. MI5's report also noted that Walti, 'who is as stubborn as de DEEKER in his refusal to supply details of his mission, appears to be an agent of the type of CAROLI and Wulf SCHMIDT', having in his possession the same type of wireless transmitter, as well as Ordnance Survey maps of:

an area stretching from the extreme North of Scotland to Edinburgh, mostly the Eastern counties. In addition, he had maps of Norwich and the greater part of Norfolk, Wisbeach [sic], King's Lynn, Peterborough and the surrounding country, Bedford and surrounding country, Cambridge and surrounding country, Bury St. Edmunds and the greater part of Suffolk.[19]

The 7 October report concluded, 'As he [Drueke] also gives the impression of being a bigger man than any of the other agents recently captured, it is possible that he was fulfilling the role of an inspector of Abwehrstellen.'

An earlier report on 2 October had mentioned that the areas of Scotland covered in the maps were the Eastern Highlands, Elgin, Aberdeen, Sutherland, Caithness, Ross and Cromarty; more specifically, taken from a statement by Superintendent William Merrilees of Edinburgh City Police (no date) they were: Aberdeenshire and Eastern Highlands; Elginshire and part of Banffshire; Aberdeenshire; Sutherland and Caithness-shire; as well as two maps of Norfolk, and one each of Peterborough; Bedfordshire; Cambridgeshire; and Bury St Edmunds.

The *Boreas* would again be used on 25 October 1940 when three men – Norwegians Gunnar Edvardsen, a journalist, and Ligwald Lund, a merchant sea captain, and a German from the Saarland named Otto Joost, a 'political adventurer' – landed near Nairn in Scotland from Åalesund, Norway. It was skippered by Ingwald Furre, with a crew of Georg Furre (his brother) and Georg Gerstrom, the engineer. Their *modus operandi* was the same: landed by seaplane, then rubber dinghy.

In the transcript of his interrogation by Lieutenant George Sampson at Camp 020 on 10 October 1940, Walti referred to the captain of the ship as being called Andersen, whom he had met in Antwerp. This was most likely Georg Andersen who Gunnar Edvardsen had met in 1934 and with whom he had worked on *The Sporting Life* as advertising manager, according to an extract of an SIS report, 'German Espionage Centres in Norway', dated 1 April 1941.[20] During his interrogation at Camp 020 Edvardsen had also mentioned to Stephens a certain Carl (or Karl) Andersen @ Fritz Engelmeyer who had planned his operation.[21] He also said that the captain was again Ingwald Furre, with Georg Furre as mate and Halfdan Olsen @ Harry Hagemann. Unfortunately, photographs of the Furre brothers provided by SIS in Edvardsen's MI5 file have been destroyed. Other than Oslo, where he stayed for about a week, Walti was unable to tell Sampson the names of any other Norwegian towns he visited – 'It was a big town, and it means a big town in Norway, there are no big towns.' He also said that the first time he had seen Drueke and Vera was when they were boarding the aircraft that was to take them to Scotland. It appears that Walti had been blackmailed into spying because of his smuggling activities.

Drueke had been travelling regularly to Berlin and Hamburg, during which it is supposed that he had been receiving instructions about the mission. Vera, on the other hand, had received no instructions until a few days before the mission when she met Rantzau in Hamburg. Rantzau had said that it was becoming increasingly difficult to send agents to the south of England. What MI5 found curious was why the two had intended to travel to London. Vera had said that the defences in the south of England were too strong for them to get too close, which was why they had landed in Scotland. This, MI5 found an unacceptable explanation, 'unless the Germans had been warned by the fate of the four Dutchmen landed at Dungeness'.

The four Dutchmen to whom he was referring were the so-called 'Invasion Spies' – Jose Waldberg, aged 27, born in Mainz; Carl Heinz Meier, aged 25, a Dutch subject of German origin born in Coblenz; Charles Albert Van den Kieboom, aged 27, a Dutch 'half-caste from the Far East' born in Takaramuka, Japan; and Sjoerd Pons, aged 27, born in Amsterdam, who had landed on 3 September 1940 between Dungeness lighthouse and Lydd coastguard station. Their arrival coincided with the planned German invasion of Britain, *Unternehmen Seelöwe* (Operation *Sea Lion*) on 15 September. All but Pons, who was acquitted then interned under Defence Regulation 18B, were found guilty under the Treachery Act (1940) and hanged.[22] Since the outcome of the trial was carefully stage-managed by the Home Office, and a cover-up about Pons' acquittal initiated, a leak must have come from another source.

The original plan had been for the three to travel to the Shetland Isles and hire a boat that would take them to England, or wait for a regular passenger steamer. Vera thought that by sending her it would add verisimilitude to their claim of being refugees, and that it was an experiment since no other woman had been sent to England as a spy.

Their journey began in the first week in September, travelling first by train from Hamburg to Stralsund, then by ferry to Trelleborg, train to Oslo, and car to Stavanger. A diagram of their journey in Appendix 8 also shows the proposed ferry to the Shetlands, which was abandoned. The itinerary and timetable for Vera's journey are summarised in a report by Captain McAfee on 3 October 1940:

8.9.40	Departure from Hamburg
9.9.40 p.m.	Arrival in Bergen
14.9.40	Left Bergen on motor boat with Captain ANDERSEN. Cruised up and down Norwegian coast.
21.9.40	Disembarked at Aalesund.
23.9.40 p.m.	Left for Oslo by train, motor-car and steamer.
24.9.40 a.m.	Arrived Oslo.
26.9.40	Left by motor-car for Stavanger.
27.9.40	Arrived Stavanger.
29.9.40 p.m.	Left Stavanger by seaplane.
30.9.40	Landed on Scottish coast near Port Gordon.[23]

A few days before the trip Vera was told that the name she would use would be Erikson. The account of the journey is worth including in full:

Hamburg. Hauptmann of Luftwaffe Bruhms sees Vera, Drucker and Waelti off on day in first week of September 1940. Dr. Krueger brings passports, identity cards and rationbooks [sic] to Station. Vera sees these papers for first time and signs them then and there. Drucker and Waelti receive their wireless sets. Vera, Drucker and Waelti are in the charge of Hauptmann Ahlers, who is to take them to Oslo. Ahlers is in the Reichwehr uniform of a Cavallery [sic] regiment.

Stralsund. Voyage from Stralsund to Trelleborg by ferry. Vera, Drucker and Waelti being civilians are not admitted to ferry, which is filled with German soldiers on way to Norway through Sweden. Captain Ahlers hurries off on a bycicle [sic] and secures permission for his charge to travel by ferry. On journey to Oslo Ahlers treats his three companions 'like dirt' and has his meals separately. There is a scene between Drucker and Captain Ahlers, in the course of which Drucker says to the captain: 'We are like beasts being taken to the slaughterhouse.'

Oslo. Dr. Mueller takes over from Captain Ahlers. A man from the 'Dienststelle' helps to buy clothes. Three bycicles [sic] for the trip to England are provided. Dr. Mueller accompanies Vera, Drucker and Waelti to Bergen.

Bergen. The party is met by 'Little Anderson', a German with knowledge of Norway. This man takes charge. Dr. Mueller stays on. They start by boat, provided by 'Little Anderson' for Shetland. The Norwegian captain of the boat also called Anderson and his brother are always drunk on the voyage and so are the Norwegian cook and the Norwegian, Edwardson, who has joined the party with the others.

Captain Anderson makes for the Shetland Islands, where the party is to b[e] landed but shows so little enthusiasm for this project, that the boat, at the slightest suggestion of proximity of British aircraft, constantly seeks shelter in Norwegian fiords [sic], where the native population is duly informed by the captain of the character and object of his passengers.

Aalesund. Captain Anderson brings his ship safely to port and temporarily renounces every idea of landing the party on the Shetland Islands. Two to three days later, Drucker, after 'Little Anderson' had phoned, leaves alone for Oslo. Vera and Waelti follow him after a couple of [days]. Edwardson remains in Aalesund.

Stavanger. Vera, Drucker and Waelti are brought from Oslo in a Rolls Royce car by 'Fat Anderson' and 'Little Anderson'. A German Air Force major tells the three would-be spies that the whole enterprise is 'sheer lunacy'. He says that no plane is immediately available, but that he is trying to provide one. Parachutes, he adds, are out of the question. Then Hauptmann Bruhms arrives by plane from Hamburg. Bruhms is visibly worried, that the party has not left yet. After everybody had already hoped, that the journey was abandoned and that the return journey home could begin, Bruhms provides a plane. 'Fat Anderson' and 'Little Anderson' depart. Bruhms sees Vera, Drucker and Waelti off in the night of 29/30 Sept.40 from Stavanger aerodrome. On board a pilot, observer and possibly a mechanic.

Scotland. After having been transferred from the aeroplane to a rubber boat near the Scottish coast, Vera, Drucker and Waelti row for 3½ hours, till they reach the Scottish coast. All three bycicles [sic] are dumped overboard to prevent the rubber boat filling with water. They land. Vera and Drucker turn left, Waelti turns right. Vera and Drucker are arrested on a station platform, where they are waiting to board a train.[24]

Vera described Hauptmann Ahlers as 'Very smart and exclusive' and was the first at *Ast* Hamburg to call her 'Frau Erikson'.[25] Hauptmann Bruhms of the Luftwaffe had been temporarily attached to *Ast* Hamburg; in August 1943 a Hauptmann Bruhm (or Bruhn) was commander of I/Flak-Regt.29.[26] 'Fat Anderson', who was connected with the circus and theatre in Oslo, was said by Vera to be a 'simple man', while 'Little Anderson' was a German who spoke Norwegian. Captain Anderson was likely the Carl (Karl) Anderson mentioned by Edvardsen. Dr Mueller, according to 'Little Anderson' worked only semi-officially for the Abwehr. The Mueller referred to here was Oberleutnant Dr Herman Muller [*sic*], described as an 'important official of the Oslo Stelle' who 'constantly travels between Hamburg and Oslo'.[27] The report concludes that since Drueke could not leave Germany at the beginning of 1940 because his passport had been withdrawn he could not have been a member of Canaris's Abwehr and calls him 'a man of no consequence'. It posed the question:

And what sort of people were the spies, whom these men, whose incompetence was only equalled by their callousness employed? A sullen dispirited group, destined to failure, and conscious of it. Small fry. People under fear and obligation. People whom one treats like 'dirt' as Captain Ahlers did, who refused to share his meals with them on the way to Oslo.[28]

Vera was dismissed as 'not a spy or an agent proper' but 'a "lounge lizard" of the German Intelligence Service'. This sounds like Stephens!

Mrs W. Gladstone's (of B2) interview with Vera on 4 February 1942 at Holloway Prison shed some light on the failed operation as well as the death of von Wedel:

The only real discussion which took place was when I queried why Vera, an intelligent woman, should be willing to sacrifice herself without demur in a plan which was so incredibly clumsy in its conception as to be doomed from the start. When, as she had said, she spied not for her love of the Nazi regime or for Germany but for a man whom she respected, and he was dead, I could not understand why she did not then refuse to carry out RANZAU's orders [*sic*]. It was at this point that she said that she was in love with one of the men who was being sent and that RANZAU knew this and knew that as he could not talk English she would not let him go alone. I asked the name of the man and she said DRUECKE.

She would not hear of the suggestion that it was DRUECKE who had engineered the 'accident' in which von WEDEL was killed, maintaining that they were good friends in spite of the triangle, and that it was RANZAU who was responsible for it. She thought it quite likely that RANZAU had ordered her to accompany DRUECKE, that he knew that for psychological reasons she would not refuse, and that this was the easiest way to be rid of her.[29]

When Mrs Gladstone appeared sceptical about Vera's story and how she had hardly been given any instructions, Vera told her that that was how Rantzau worked. She thought that Drueke had been given all the instructions, but that WELDY [*sic*] might also have been privy to at least some of them. Mrs Gladstone was left with the impression that Vera was 'a very intelligent woman, by nature extremely reserved, and although not beautiful, possessed of great physical charm'.[30]

In the MI5 file on Edvardsen[31] all the agents landed from Norway, with the exception of Drueke, agreed that their cover story, given to them by the Germans, was that they were refugees of Nazi oppression, and had travelled by boat and seaplane. In both cases, the pilot was the same, Leutnant Hoelbaum.[32] Edvardsen also said that Vera, Drueke and Walti had earlier been working for the German Secret Service in Paris, referring to them as 'real German spies'. He had seen them for the first time when they came to Bergen with Doctor Muller of the Hamburg *Abstelle*. On the voyage Vera and Drueke stayed together, although she slept in an upper cabin while Walti and Drueke slept aft (at the rear, to all you non-nautical types!).

Vera had in her possession a total of six passports, three legal – in the names of Vera Ignatieff (Nansen passport); Vera de Schalbourg (Danish passport); Vera von Wedel (German passport) deposited with the rest of her things at [*illegible*] in Hamburg – and three illegal, in the names of Vera Staritzky (Nansen passport) provided by her late husband Ignatieff; Vera de Cottani (Austrian or Hungarian passport) also provided by her late husband Ignatieff; and Vera Erikson (Danish passport) provided by the German Intelligence Service and thrown into the sea on the way to Scotland.

One story about Vera that has been around since at least 1984, perhaps earlier, suggests that she was one of Maxwell Knight's agents. In various statements in Anthony Masters' biography of Knight he claims that Vera had:

> worked for him from 1937 until the outbreak of war, based in a fashionable Mayfair salon and passing on scraps of information concerning potential Fascist sympathizers. Vera did not produce information of any great importance, but she was both intelligent and useful. Her value apparently came to an end at the outbreak of hostilities and she disappeared.[33]

Masters' account continues when Vera was arrested and she revealed to Major Peter Perfect, the RSLO in Edinburgh, that she was Vera de Cottani-Chalbur and that 'Captain King' (Knight) of the War Office would vouch for her:

Knight admitted knowledge of Vera but merely stated that she had worked as an informer for M.I.5 before the war. He did not say that he had carefully prepared her as a double agent so that she would be able to trap Abwehr agents, just as she had now done …Vera continued to give more details about the Abwehr, all of which were of vital importance to British security, and she was still passing information to Knight when she was later interned in Holloway.[34]

In mentioning the trial of Drueke and Walti, 'there was no mention of the part Knight's double agent, Vera de Cottani-Chalbur, had played'; and, 'German espionage was not normally Knight's responsibility, but his previous use of Cottani-Chalbur, and his idea of using her as a double agent was the reason for his involvement on this occasion.'[35]

The problem with all of these statements is that when Masters wrote his biography of Knight the files on Vera and her associates had not yet been released into the public domain by MI5 or the Public Records Office, as it was then known. Consequently, Masters offers no references as to how she had been recruited by Knight, if indeed she had, and all the evidence uncovered about her so far shows that she was not even in Britain at that time. Nor is there any reference to her in a new biography of Knight written by Henry Hemming,[36] 'only because I could not find any good evidence to show that she ever worked for Knight'.[37] As we have seen, Vera seemed reluctant to reveal too many details to her MI5 interrogators, although she did provide a list of various people known to her as either working for, or being associated with, the German Intelligence Service, many of whom were already known to MI5, and had already been interned. While it is true her files have been heavily redacted, there is nothing in them to suggest that Knight had ever recruited her. This, of course, may be because MI5 could not disclose the fact that she was a double agent, if that was indeed the case, and the reason why she was not brought to trial or appeared as a witness at the trial of Walti and Drueke. As Hemming notes to the author, 'In the years that followed [1940] she was certainly used by MI5 as an informant in an internment camp on the Isle of Man, which may have brought her into contact with Knight – possibly – but I have been unable to find any concrete evidence.'[38]

The other questions to be asked are, given that Knight's area of expertise was with infiltrating the Communists in Britain and the British Union of Fascists, why would he have recruited a so-called German spy such as Vera in the first place? And what was meant by 'a fashionable Mayfair salon'? It could not have been referring to the Duchesse's so-called 'salon', or circle of friends, because

Vera only stayed with her for a short while, and technically, the Duchesse did not live in Mayfair. Nor could it have been the salon or fashion house of Anna Wolkoff, which geographically was in South Kensington. None of the information about Knight's penetration of the Right Club and Wolkoff's circle suggests that Vera was ever involved; and the mysterious 'Miss X' often referred to at Wolfkoff's trial, turned out to be Olga Gray, one of Knight's agents.

Knight's pseudonym 'Captain King' appears in Bryan Clough's book about the Kent-Wolkoff Affair, in which Clough erroneously assumes that Wolkoff's letter to 'Captain King' actually refers to Vernon Kell, then Director of MI5.[39] Knight is also referred to as 'Captain King' in a recent biography of John Bingham when he was recruited by MI5.[40] However, there appears to be no references to this alias in any of Vera's files or in those associated with her.

15

AT HIS MAJESTY'S
PLEASURE

After the trio's arrest, the question now was what to do with them? On 1 October 1940 Vera was refused entry to land under Article 1(1) (a) of the Aliens Order, 1920 by G.A. Hawthorn, Immigration Officer, London, and taken first to Camp 020 at Latchmere House, then on 5 October to Holloway Prison.

Stephens prepared a report of an interview he had conducted with Drueke on 12 November 1940 in which Drueke (referred to in the report as De Deeker) admitted to being the father of Vera's child. As Stephens observed, 'De DEEKER is no doubt aware of the English law that a wife is not a compellable witness against a husband.' However, the couple were not married. This relationship was explored by Meurig Evans in his report of 7 October:

RELATIONSHIP BETWEEN VERA ERIKSON AND DE DEEKER
That there is some close link between Vera and De DEEKER is obvious because:-
Vera is plainly most anxious to save his life, even at the expense of her own.
They 'se Tutoient'. [They are on first-name terms]
This may be accounted for by:-
Blood relationship.
Marital relationship, legal or otherwise.
In support of (a) may be mentioned the distinct similarity of facial type, shown by Dr. Dearden's photographs. Against this may be mentioned the fact that Vera's accent when she speaks French is Russian, and that DEEKER's though probably foreign is certainly not Russian. If, however, DEEKER is really illegitimate, Vera might be only his half-sister and might have had a different upbringing.
As to (b), Vera might be DEEKER's wife or mistress and, indeed, has said as much: she has also described him as the father of the baby she professes to be

expecting. Furthermore, when enquiring as to Vera's fate, DEEKER several times referred to her as 'ma femme' [my wife].[1]

Evans went on to speculate that because of discrepancies in Vera's story – such as that Stuhrig (von Wedel/Dierks) was her legal husband, and that Drueke appeared not to know who he was – that the two might be one and the same. He also said that Wulf Schmidt had been told the story of the car accident twice, and that Vera had been injured in the face. But this was clearly not the case, unless any scars she bore were those from when she was attacked in Hyde Park; any from the car crash would have been fresher and barely healed. He also pondered whether Stuhrig was a fictitious person, or that Drueke was the Hungarian, de Cottani, with whom she had claimed to have had a 'mariage blanc' – an unconsummated marriage. Evans thought that there would have been no reason for Vera to have had such a marriage, but concluded that De Deeker's French accent was one 'compatible with Hungarian origin'.

A letter to Drueke (undated) written by Vera, who was in Holloway Prison, and handed to Dr Dearden on 21 December reveals more about the intimacy of their relationship:

My very dear Friend,

I have received you letter, and have so much to say, but it is so difficult to write.

I am in prison, and will not be freed, and I don't know what will happen. But it is a matter of complete indifference to me, because I am so worried about you, and can neither help, nor do anything. Terrible feeling to be so helpless.

I would only like to tell you that I love you as before, and perhaps still more. All my thoughts are with you, and will remain so until I die. God protect you.

Yours,

VERA

P.S. I do implore you to be clever enough to tell the truth. It is too stupid to die in this manner. I can't help you because I don't know enough. I cannot bear the thought that you should die like this. Everything can yet turn out well. Remember that I love you, and will bear everything if only things go better for you.[2]

Vera Eriksen. (© Crown Copyright, TNA KV2/16)

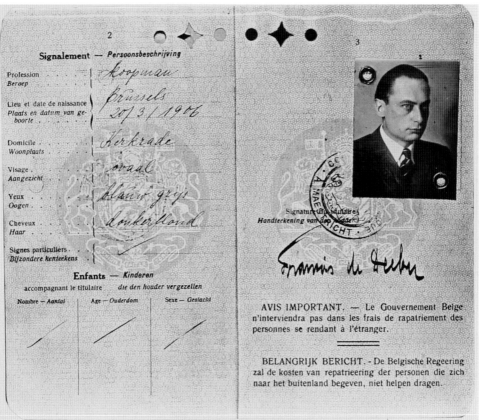

Walti. (© Crown Copyright, TNA KV2/17)

Hilmar Dierks. (familienarchiv: m. dierks)

Hilmar and his brother
Gerhard during the Second
World War. (familienarchiv:
m. dierks)

Nr. 1050   C

                    Hamburg , den 18.November   1940.

    D er Wehrmachtangestelte Hilmar Gustav Johannes
D i e r k s, Hauptmann zur Verwendung im stellvertretenden
Generalkommando X Armee-Korps, _____ evangelisch,
wohnhaft   in Hamburg, Papenhuderstrasse 1, _____ .

ist am   2. September1940 _____ um   24   Uhr   00   Minuten

in Hamburg, im Hafenkrankenhaus, _____ verstorben.

    D er Verstorbene war geboren am : 5. Januar 1889 _____

in   Leer / Ostfriesland. _____

(Standesamt   Leer _____ Nr.   9   ).

    Vater: Johannes Heinrich Hilmar Dierks, _____

    Mutter: Marie Louise Ida, geborene Lepin, beider

letzter Wohnort unbekannt. _____

    D er Verstorbene war — nicht — verheiratet geschieden. _____

    Eingetragen auf mündliche — schriftliche — Anzeige der Wehrmachtauskunft-
stelle für Kriegerverluste und Kriegsgefangene, Berlin W 30.

    D   Anzeigende _____

                Vorgelesen, genehmigt und _____ unterschrieben

                        Der Standesbeamte
                        In Vertretung

Todesursache: Unfall _____

Eheschließung d. Verstorbenen am _____ in _____

(Standesamt _____ Nr. _____).

Hilmar Dierks' death
registration, 1940.
(familienarchiv: m. dierks)

Passport of the Duchesse de Chateau-Thierry. (© Crown Copyright, TNA KV2/357)

Anne Valeska Uhlig, the Duchesse's daughter. (© Crown Copyright, TNA KV2/357)

Nicholas Ritter. (Private collection: Katherine Ritter Wallace)

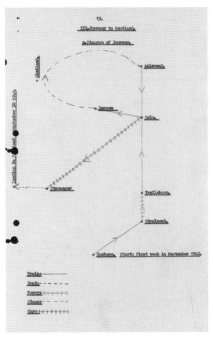

Nicholas Ritter and Irmgard von Klitzing, Ritter's second wife. (Private collection: Katherine Ritter Wallace)

Itinerary to Scotland. (© Crown Copyright, TNA KV2/15)

Heinkell He155a.

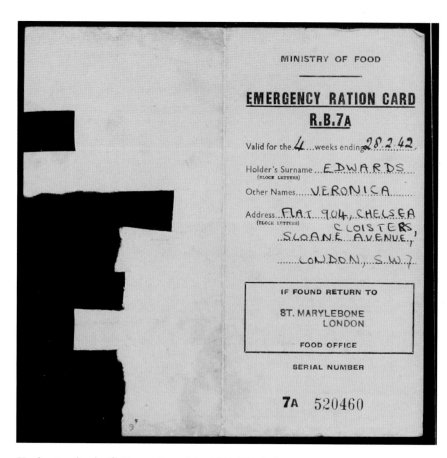

Vera's ration book. (© Crown Copyright, TNA KV2/16)

Klopstockstraße, Hamburg. (Giselle Jakobs)

Vera's death registration, 1946. (Giselle Jakobs)

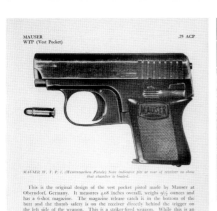

MAUSER
WTP (Vest Pocket)   .25 ACP

MAUSER W. T. P. I. (Westentaschen Pistole) Note indicator pin at rear of receiver to show that chamber is loaded.

This is the original design of the vest pocket pistol made by Mauser at Oberndorf, Germany. It measures 4.08 inches overall, weighs 9½ ounces and has a 6-shot magazine. The magazine release catch is in the bottom of the butt and the thumb safety is on the receiver directly behind the trigger on the left side of the weapon. This is a striker-fired weapon. While this is an excellent arm of its type, it is inferior to the Colt in design and safety. This model introduced in 1908, was replaced by the W.T.P. 2 in 1939 replaced the earlier Mauser type originally produced to compete with the Baby Browning.

Mauser pistol carried by Walti.

Theodore Mally @ Paul Hardt. (© Crown Copyright, TNA KV2/1008)

Alfred Kraus. (© Crown Copyright, TNA KV2/1729)

Walter Simon, Reichpass. (© Crown Copyright, TNA KV2/1293)

The original typed letter in German is dated 23 December 1940, so the translation must have been done either before Christmas or shortly thereafter. Another letter, also handed to Dearden on 22 December whose translation is also dated 23 December 1940, reads:

My dear Theo,

I want to ask you once again to tell the truth, it will do us both good. Hans [most likely Walti – his middle name was Heinrich] does not want you to die, and I ask you, if you love me, do try to save us both, it is so terrible to think of us dying in that manner and your mother and my parents will never get over it when they read about it in the papers, we mustn't do it.

Dear dear Karl-Theo, I am pregnant ~~and our unborn child is trying to help us~~ [added, handwritten - *and you must help us for our child's sake*]. Do speak to Dr. Dearden ~~often~~ [added, handwritten - *openly*], he is a wonderful person and a gentleman. I am writing to you just this once and think about after the war and when [illegible] free our friendship. But for goodness sake be sensible and speak as that will help us.

All the best,

Your

VERA[3]

Lieutenant MacIntosh of B8l had learned more about Drueke when he interviewed him on 2 October, although Stephens, when submitting his report, noted that 'a considerable amount of the information given by DE DEEKER is false'. MacIntosh agreed with Stephens that he also felt 'much of it is palpably untrue, and … that the remainder is also a concoction'. He reported that when De Deeker pronounced his name it was like it was spelled 'De Decker', but if he were truly Belgian, as he claimed, it would be pronounced 'Dayker'.

Karl Theodor Drueke @ François De Deeker was vague about his early life. He told MacIntosh that he was born on 25 March 1906 in the Ixelles district of Brussels on a street near the Place Communale. This is confirmed in his Belgian passport. Interestingly, a Personal Identification form in his file gives his nationality as German and his birthplace as Grebenstein, Germany, in the district of Kassel in the state of Hesse. Strangely, he said he could not remember the name of the street on which he lived, nor the name of the school he attended. He thought he left school in 1919 or 1920 and became an apprentice doing all sorts of odd jobs. In fact, the only address he could remember was 45, rue d'Edimbourg, a long, narrow street now filled with anonymous-looking offices. He did not know who his father was, but his mother was Françoise de Deeker, who died in about 1920. She did not work but lived on a small income, although he did not specify what this was or how she came by it. Vera's later statement in her letter (c. 23 December 1940) would seem to contradict this, implying that his mother was still alive. There were no other relatives that he knew of. In his file the hand drawn map he provided marks a 'Place de Sablons', actually the Place du Grand Sablon in part of the historic upper city of Brussels. The church nearby could either be the Église Nôtre-Dame de la Chapelle, or the Église Nôtre-Dame du Sablon.

He was turned down for military service in 1926 on account of a '*déformation des doigts de pieds*', which MacIntosh took to mean hammer toes.[4] When MacIntosh tried to elicit any concrete information about employment, Drueke feigned *amnésie* (amnesia) or an inability 'to recollect exactly', saying that he had bought and sold things to make a living. He claimed not to have any knowledge of German and that he had been brought up speaking French. The incident with which he had been involved in Brussels that he had not told Vera about was when he had struck a German soldier who had insulted the girlfriend of a Polish Jew who was his friend. The remainder of the interrogation was spent confirming the details of the trio's landing in Scotland. He said that it had been his intention as a refugee to approach the Belgian Consul and obtain work in Britain.

MacIntosh expressed doubt that Drueke's accent, while French, was 'not the accent one would expect to hear from a man who claims to have lived all his life in Brussels with the exception of a few odd days spent either on holiday or on short business trips outside of Belgium'. He suggested that:

> there is a possibility of this man having acquired his knowledge of French in the North of France or in a non-Flemish speaking part of Belgium. His slurred guttural 'r' is certainly not typical of either France or Brussels. He does not use many expressions that might be described as Belgian, in fact his fluent knowledge of French is consistent with a German having learnt French in Belgium or the North of France. His language cannot either be described as typical Walloon French. The handwriting which appears on the attached papers is emphatically not the sort of handwriting taught in Belgian State Schools, and I have no hesitation in stating that I consider it as typically German handwriting.[5]

There were also clues in what Drueke had said about his schooling that did not ring true: that he had not had to learn Flemish as well as French, which was compulsory in Belgian schools; and that the various half-holidays he mentioned were more consistent with the German school system. MacIntosh thought that he may have attended the German School, which was in Brussels until 1914. There *was* a school in the rue des Minimes, which Drueke said he attended, but it had in fact been a German school. What might have given him away as being German was when MacIntosh suggested that he should furnish him with the names of friends or places that could be checked out. The following dialogue has been invented, but it serves to illustrate Drueke's reaction; the words of Drueke are his own, those of MacIntosh were based on his narrative:

MacIntosh: 'What if I suggested to you that you *are* German, but that after investigating your story, and it checks out, we release you because we don't regard you as a security threat?'

MacIntosh watched him closely, then added, 'You know, there are presently maybe a hundred, perhaps even a thousand or so Germans free in this country, although they do have to report regularly to the Police.'

De Deeker jerked and sat up straight. 'Really?' he asked. 'I don't think there are many English at liberty in Berlin!'

'Why do you say Berlin?' MacIntosh enquired.

'You know what the Germans are,' De Deeker replied.

Was this a Freudian slip on Drueke's part? CX reports from Section VB3 of MI6 sent to Dick White on behalf of Felix Cowgill on 15 November and 14 December shed more light on Drueke's true nationality and his contacts:

CX/[redacted]/94 dated 15.11.40

V.B.3

Reference my CX/ [redacted] /94 of 14.12.40.[*sic*] here are some further particulars, all we have got:-

1. Karl Theodore DRUCKE, German, born on 20.3.06 at Grebenstein, about 20 km. north of Kassel.' He had resided in France since 1919. It seems that he offered his services to the Gestapo as he did not know which German authorities to approach. In view of this fact he must have started his espionage activities about 1933 at the earliest, although it is probable that he had only worked for a short time before he was caught.

2. DRUCKE knew two French officer brothers, one of whom he believed to be in want of money. When he contacted the man, however, the latter informed his own military authorities, who supplied DRUCKE with bogus military information and he was subsequently arrested with this in his possession.

3. He was sentenced on 12.5.36 by the 14th Chambre Correctionnelle in Paris to three years' imprisonment, 2000 francs fine and 10 years banishment from France for espionage. The sentence was upheld on 22.10.36 by the Cour d'Appel, Paris. It is not known when he was released.

4. It is probable therefore that his espionage activities in Belgium must have been before 1936 and it is unlikely that he could have been in charge of German espionage activities in that country. On the other hand DRUCKE is such an accomplished actor that he may have succeeded in misleading the French as to his importance.

5. As DRUCKE left Germany about 1919 it would account for the fact that he only knows a type of German shorthand which became obsolete about that date. His attempts to pass himself off as a Belgian refugee are also explained.

If we can establish the date on which he was released from prison, presumably before the war and perhaps sometime in early 1939, we will have a point from which we can start building up his career, activities, contacts and organization. Perhaps VERA could help us?[6]

CX/ [redacted] /94 dated 14.12.40
V.B.3

1. Reference your S.0269/T/PF.53990/B.2. of 13.12.40. we have the following information about Karl Theodor DRUCKER, born at Grebenstein, Germany, on 20.3.06, who resided at 5 rue Feder (1st floor), Brussels.

2. DRUCKER was condemned on 22.10.36 by the Cour d'Appel, Paris, to three years imprisonment as a German agent-provocateur. He was also expelled from Belgium. It was believed that he was head of German secret intelligence activities in Belgium. He was the owner of a Peugeot car with a French number plate.

DRUCKER was in contact with Carl SPITZBERG(EN), German, born at Eschwege on 16.7.05. He was domiciled at Hamburg but also resided at 5 rue Feder [*sic*], Brussels, where his telephone number was 377650. This house belongs to Frau Philip RINSBERGH.

DRUCKER was also in contact with Theodor BOLLWAHN, born at Dusseldorf on 22.7.01, who in turn was in contact with Henri PIPER, Belgian, born at Fraipont on 17.4.1900, and a German, Hugo ADLER, born at Essen on 24.3.86, domiciled at Anneessenstraat 24, Antwerp.

4. DRUCKER had contacts with Max CAAN, Jew, born at Gelsenkirchen on 5.10.82, arrived in Belgium in 1931. The son is also Max CAAN, born at Dusseldorf on 12.11.21., and both were resident at 9 rue de Flandre, Ostend. Papers containing military information were found in his flat, also parts of

a wireless transmitter. The son was a W/T expert and worked at the Palace Hotel. The father was arrested and shot by the French.

5. The CAANs were also in close contact with Sandor GORLINSKY, born at Sashaloon [Hungary] on 28.2.08. He resided at 14 Avenue Henri Sarrups, Ostend. His mistress was Margaret KONCENS, Hungarian, born at Riga, 1.3.05. GORLINSKY came to the U.K. during the invasion of Belgium and is now in prison here or in Canada. The younger CAAN was employed in BUTLIN's Camp, Ostend, with which GORLINSKY was also connected. BUTLIN's Camp has a London office.

6. DRUCKER was also in contact with Max BAUER, an ex-Colonel in the German Army, who was expelled from France as undesirable. Further contacts of DRUCKER were Victor FILIPEX and Ernst LEVY.

From this it appears that DRUCKER was in fact a very important agent of the German Service. I am having a further search made of our records and will write and let you know anything that comes to light. Meanwhile interrogation of GORLINSKY might give us very useful lines onto the DRUCKER/VERA/DIERKS show.[7]

A translation of a shorthand message written in French which Drueke had attempted to smuggle out of Latchmere House (Camp 020) by de Jaeger was sent to Dick White by VB of MI6 also on 15 November:

Would you be good enough to give 3000 francs to bearer of this letter, my dear KAIN (?) or KIN (?). On the other hand don't you pay a single farthing to that person to whom I made over 50000 francs in my last or last but one letter (written at (?) the Professor's (?) before my departure). She has always worked for England and (2 words) has given to the police ... and the ... during our stay in Norway, she has poisoned me and has put drugs and sleeping draughts in my drinks. She has chloroformed and hypnotised me. She has injected me by hypodermic needle a ... which since is working in my body. Destroy this letter as I fear I shall die of poisoning. She has also poisoned the 'doctor' but with another poison which works in the ... perhaps pieces of glass I suppose she has [two words illegible] prison Mrs [von Wedel(?)] her family at Bl...ille and her brother in Danemark are working likewise for the English. In the German Service in Norway there are several people working for the Intelligence Service [or 'In the Service going to Norway there are ...']

1) ENGELMEYER (or ENGELMAYER)

2) The fat ANDERSEN (or ANDERSON) (Director of a circus) and also
I suppose the man I knew as
3) ZIEGLER (? ZWEIGLER)
The Norwegian 4) EDWARDSON (?) (a Norwegian journalist) is likewise
very suspect. On his arrival in England he … immediately the police … with
another one from the German Service. Everybody was more or less aware
what the woman was doing to me. I had a jealous fear that I would have liked
to have seen her imprisoned at the given moment. If I were not detained
I would certainly take revenge at a certain moment. But now I am going to
die in 3 to 4 months or perhaps sooner.

Take revenge for me against that woman. She will assassinate the whole
German Service if she can. Will you remit … keys (nails) to the firm. I have
not much … to die of poisoning. The doctor does not believe me and thinks
me (a fool?)

   Take revenge on that woman. She works with the most disgusting aids.
Firstly, 'elle m'affaiblit son amour' … she gave me an injection, I don't know
what and she has given me drugs that have completely stupefied me and it
is possible that she has made me write something under hypnosis. … refuse
to think of after the two last letters. I have no reason to write and as to questions I only write in shorthand. I am using all my will power to keep my
neck. Let us hope that I return. I wish you all the best you and your wife,
and if for always … thoughts. For safety's sake I don't put my signature. All
the best to you.

   I am in an internment camp of the security police near London about 10
kilometres away. The treatment is very good.[8]

Clearly the ramblings of a deranged person, but not necessarily under the influence of drugs. Stephens noted in a letter to Dick White on 5 December that:

   The note from DE DEEKER appears to be in shorthand and although it
   might be possible for us, in due course, to decipher this document, I think
   it well to send it to you as you suggested for urgent action by the Code and
   Cipher School [the Government Code and Cipher School at Bletchley Park
   (GC&CS)].

Anderson and Edvardsen have been referred to earlier. Exactly who
Engelmeyer (Engelmayer) and Ziegler (Zweigler) are remains to be seen.
There is a Hauptsturmführer (Captain) Engelmeyer listed as belong-

ing to Referat VI C of the RHSA, as well as a Hauptsturmführer Eugen Engelmeier mentioned in an article regarding Latvian collaborationists in Belarus who may be one and the same. An annotation with the MI5 personnel file number PF 601,936 has been added next to Engelmeyer's name. Unfortunately that file does not appear to be publicly available.[9] Cain is obviously the younger Max Caan referred to in the CX of 14 December. De Jaeger was Albert de Jaeger, a member of the Sicherheitsdienst (SD) in Lisbon who had defected in 1940. He was turned as a double agent code-named HATCHET.[10] Gorlinsky came to England in 1940 and was questioned by MI5 as a suspected spy, but according to his file there was no evidence to suggest that he was.[11]

A note handed to de Jaeger by Drueke on 15 December reads:

Cher ami,

Je n'ai rien à part de ce qui est convenue. Mais il est fort possible que le Monsieur en question aura un emploi pour vous. Demandez le nom de la firme, dont le dit Monsieur est un des chefs, et vous connaitrez mon vrai nom, à moi. Si le Monsieur n'est pas present, vous aurez tous renseignments dans la firme. Dites lui de vous recommendez à l'autre firme, dans laquelle je suis intéressé. Cela dans le cas, ou il n'aurait pas d'emploi pour vous, lui-même. Je compte sur vous, et je vous souhaîte bonne chance!

Bien à vous[12]

[Dear friend,

I have nothing apart from what was agreed. But it is highly possible that the gentleman in question will have a job for you. Ask me the name of the company, in which he is one of the bosses, and you will know my real name. If the gentleman is not present, you will have all the information on the company. Tell him to recommend to you another company in which I am interested. That being the case, or if there isn't any job for you. I'm counting on you, and I wish you good luck!

Best wishes]

In keeping with Drueke's earlier comments, he had not signed it. Meurig Evans, who initialed and dated it, notes: 'Above note handed to de Jaeger by Drueke on December 15th 1940 for R.S.' (Robin Stephens)[13] It is unclear exactly what it means and there do not appear to be any comments offered by MI5 or GC&CS about its meaning. Whatever it was, it was a coded message, but to whom was it intended? Drueke could hardly have known that de Jaeger had been 'turned'. Who was the 'gentleman in question'? Was it Ritter? Was the name of the company the Abwehr?

There was more speculation about Drueke's role in a B8l report dated 4 October 1940, a copy of which appeared in the MI5 file on Werner Unversagt, containing an analysis of 'Whether De Deeker is an officer and if so whether he is important', and is worth reproducing in full:

1. Demeanour. Major Stephens, Mr White and Mr Short consider that he is an officer. Captain Stimson thinks he has been subject to discipline and would be equivalent to a British Temporary Officer. He might be an Intelligence Office [*sic*] with a military background. Dr Dearden thinks he has had a military training and is of the N.C.O. type. Captain Nunn regards him as a Naz[i] Officer, but not of the regular German Officer type. Mr. MacIntosh is of the opinion that DE DEEKER, who claims to have lived his whole life in Brussels, is lying when he makes this statement. His impression of him is that the man is undoubtedly a German and he consideres [*sic*] him to be either of the Officer or the senior[r] N.C.O. type and he suggests that DE DEEKER may be an officer on the reserve. Captain McAfee and Mr Sampson consider that he is inferior to the Officer type. Mr Evans thinks he is rather a party man than an army man.

2. Importance. Vera ERIKSEN sated [*sic*] that he was the right hand man of her husband, who was an Oberleutnant. That he had been an agent for two years. She suggested that he should be exchanged for an important British Agent. [Redacted] has seen him before, but cannot remember where. He thinks he met him in the office of Hauptmann BRUHNS, who called him 'Herr Doktor'. The man in question was supposed to be an official of the German Legation in London and was called in to indicate on the map the place in the North West of London suitable for hiding a wireless set and transmitting. [Redacted] qualifies his statement by observing that he cannot swear that this is the man he saw in Hamburg and is rather inclined to state that he is not the man.

3. Is De DEEKER identical with WERNER?

Description of WERNER (acc: to WALDBERG)

Age.   31 (looks 27).
Height.   6' athletic build.

Eyes.   Blue – no glasses.

Hair.   Dark blond – plastered back.

Special Marks. 2 gold teeth on right side.

Speaks French with sufficient fluency to pass a Belgian, also English, French, Italian and Malay.

Been to England during the war. According to WALDBERG due to return here on Spet: [*sic*] 25th. The object was to contact agents in London.

Description of DE DEEKER.

Age.   34.

Height.   6' athletic build.

Eyes.   Blue grey – no glasses.

Hair.   Dark blond plastered back.

Special Marks. Several teeth with gold edges on left side.

Speaks French extremely well without any special indication that he is a Belgian. Professes not to know English and to know very little German.

Professes never to have been in England before. Arrived end of September. ERIKSEN states that the first destination of DE DEEKER and herself was London.

As against these similarities there is the fact that WALDBERG, who alleges that he knows WERNER intimately, professed not to recognise DE DEEKER.

4. Connection with Air Force. There is no evidence that WERNER was in the Air Force. WALDBERG never saw him in uniform, but thought that he was in the 14th Artillery.

DE DEEKER had in his possession a list of places all concerned with R.A.F. grounds. He wore a blue trench coat bought in Oslo. [Redacted] states that this trench coat was not of the kind used by airmen and was not, in fact, a military garment.[14]

Hauptmann (Captain) Bruhns was actually Major Julius Böckel @ Beyer @ Dr Julius Werner. He was listed as being in either *Amt* I Luft (June 1942) or *Ast* Hamburg. In Hamburg he was responsible for the training of agents to be sent to the UK such as Gösta Caroli (SUMMER), Wulf Schmidt (TATE) and Karel

Richter. He is reported to have visited Vera in her Hamburg hotel in August 1940 to give her instructions about her impending mission to the UK. Later, in September 1940, he is listed in his MI5 file as having gone to Stavanger, Norway to dispatch agents Vera, Drueke and Walti to the UK.

So were Werner and De Deeker one and the same? Werner was seen in Brussels in the summer of 1940 (August to the end of September). Vera and Drueke were also there at the end of August. As noted earlier, there are a number of similarities between the two men, except that when their photographs are compared, Drueke has a beard, and the shape of their heads is different. Attention is drawn to the statement, 'WALDBERG, who alleges that he knows WERNER intimately, professed not to recognise DE DEEKER.' This is contradicted from a B8l report on 'Karl Theodor DRUCKE @ DEEKER, Francois, German Agent', dated 2 October 1940, extracted on 24 June 1944 and included in Werner Unversagt's MI5 file, which states:

> Both SCHMIDT and WALDBERG recognised DE DEEKER, but are unable, or unwilling, to identify him. SCHMIDT says he thinks he saw him in Hamberg [sic]; WALDBERG states that he saw him in Brussels, but neither will go into further detail.[15]

Waldberg had attended one of Werner's courses at the Le Touquet Training Centre at the end of August 1940 just prior to being sent to Britain in mid-September. If Werner and De Deeker were actually the same person, then the man claiming to be De Deeker (Drueke) must have been someone else. Interestingly, a letter dated 14 (or 19) April 1941 by Captain P.D. Parminter, B2 Division, Home Office Aliens Department documenting Gorlinsky, mentions that:

> On April 1, 1940 Gorlinski was reported to me as having been seen having tea in the Bon Marché, Bruxelles in the company of NEUMANN and Siegel…NEUMANN, Erick, a German, another Wagon Lit employee and a definite enemy agent, formerly living 93B rue de la Chappelle Ostende who was arrested by the Belgian authorities and deported but returned unknown to them and was living in Bruxelles, for a time certainly with SIEGEL [also worked for Wagons Lit].[16]

Was he any relation to the Neumann referred to earlier who lived in The Hague and had employed My Eriksson?

THE DOCTOR'S REPORT

By far the most successful interrogations of Vera and Drueke were obtained by Dr Harold Dearden where, perhaps due to his training as a psychiatrist, he managed to inculcate his way into her confidence. All the quotes here are taken from Vera's file (KV2/14). Dearden had first interviewed her on 3 October 1940 when she had requested to see him to make a 'confession', as Stephens had put it. Dearden had been unable to see her beforehand owing to some previous business with Osbert Peake, the Permanent Under-Secretary at the Home Office.

On that afternoon, in Dearden's sitting room, she told him that she was six weeks pregnant. She asked him to give her something to kill herself, or failing that, something that would cause a miscarriage, both of which Dearden refused. He urged her to tell the whole truth to Stephens, but she refused saying that she had 'never let anyone down in her life'. The father of her child, she said, was Stuhrig (von Wedel/Dierks), but now that he was dead and she had lost the only person she had ever cared about she didn't care what happened to her. Dearden pointed out that when the child was born 'it will undoubtedly suffer from the strain of the repeated interrogations and privations in prison and elsewhere, which she will impose upon herself and indirectly on it …' However, Vera's claim that the baby was her late husband's contradicts the letter she would send to Drueke on 22 December telling him it was his (referred to in the previous chapter), which seems more likely. Dearden advised that since he only had Vera's word for it that she was pregnant, she should see a gynaecologist, in case 'she seeks to make capital out of this'. He reported that she was also complaining of pain from her knife wound.

At the end of the interview Dearden concluded that she had softened, 'but I doubt very much she will remain acquiescent for long. She is undoubtedly a pathological liar and herself admitted to me that she finds it very difficult to tell the plain truth, even when there is no need to lie.' What she did tell him was that Eduardsen (Edvardsen), a tall, good-looking Norwegian, was to arrive in England imminently, and that he would be bringing over a supply of bombs. In fact, Gunnar Edvardsen arrived in Scotland on 25 October, together with Legwald Lund and Otto Joost, and were taken to Camp 020.

On 7 October the Governor and medical officer at Holloway, Dr John Matheson examined her and sent his report to MI5:

> She is in satisfactory general health, but complains of slight pain in the left chest and of pain in the abdomen and vaginal bleeding.
>
> On examination I found that she had a belladonna plaster on the left chest; she stated that it had been applied about five days ago to ease the pain in the chest. She attributed this pain to having been wounded with a knife by her first husband about seven years ago, and said that she has been subject to occasional pain in the chest during the last seven years. There were two scars of old incised wounds of the chest, one over the lower left ribs and the other over the lower part of the sternum; no signs of active disease were found.
>
> The abdominal pain and haemorrage she attributed to a recent early miscarriage occurring in the following circumstances. She stated that she believed herself to be about two months pregnant, and that three days ago she fell down some stairs. Yesterday she had abdominal pain and vaginal bleeding. She further stated that about a fortnight ago, before arriving in this country, she took quinine in an unsuccessful attempt to end the pregnancy, but denied that the present symptoms could be due to interference. She also said that she had an induced abortion in France about two years ago. On examination I found that she had a slightly enlarged retroverted uterus and a sanguine-purulent vaginal discharge; these signs are suggestive of early abortion but a[re] not conclusive. Germs of venereal disease were not identified on microscopical examination, but in view of the sanguinous nature of the material examined this result is also inconclusive.
>
> Mentally she was somewhat depressed and apathetic. She stated that her second husband had died about a month ago and that she did not care what happened to her. She further stated that she had been engaged in espionage in Russia, Norway and Denmark and that she had been sent to England by the German Secret Service. She said that she had no desire to act as a spy in England, but that she had nowehere else to go.[1]

Matheson summarised the main points of her health and stated that, 'At this early stage a definite opinion cannot be given on the question of pregnancy,

but there are signs suggestive of recent early abortion. A more definite opinion on this point could be given in three or four weeks time.' That Vera may
have attempted an abortion is interesting since her letter sent to Drueke on
22 December suggests that she wanted to keep the fetus. Perhaps at this stage
she had changed her mind, since her mental condition always seemed to be in
a state of flux.

When Dearden met Vera again on 20 October 1940, 'She made what should
have been a very moving entrance, approaching me from the door slowly,
timidly, and as though at the sight of me, something worth living for had at
last come into her life.' She told him that she was in a lot of pain in her lower
abdomen and was suffering from hallucinations, seeing her late husband (von
Wedel/Dierks) bleeding and standing beside her bed. Dearden reassured her
that since she realised that they were hallucinations there was nothing to be
afraid of. He added, 'In her present situation, with nothing to occupy her mind,
her thoughts would inevitably take on a morbid vividness, with results which,
though they were doubtless annoying, were of no significance whatever.'

Having got the state of her health out of the way, she asked about her
'friend', de Deeker (Drueke). Dearden told her quite bluntly that once
Stephens had finished with him at Latchmere House he would be taken away
and shot, which upset her immensely. She reminded him that he had promised
that if she told him everything she knew, Drueke would be exchanged for
one of their own agents in Germany. This cut no ice with Dearden, who told
her that Drueke was as good as dead from the moment he arrived, since he
had been equipped with a wireless transmitter, and that the penalty for spies
was death. The only thing now was to co-operate and tell MI5 all she knew
before it was too late. She protested that she had already done so, but Dearden
knew different: 'she had, as I knew well at the time, lied several times to me
that she had told me everything.' Then she started to cry and said, 'I thought
you trusted me.'

Dearden was obviously somewhat entranced by her, as can be seen in his
next statement:

> She was an experienced and attractive woman; de Deeker and she, on her
> own admission, were very fond of each other and had been so for two years.
> I could be reasonably reticent myself, I said, when I wished to be; but I had
> never spent much time with an attractive and experienced woman without
> later being astonished at the extent of her knowledge of my private affairs.
> I had too much admiration and respect for her to believe that she had done
> less with de Deeker than other ladies had done with me.[3]

Finally, at his urging, she agreed to try to record everything that she and Drueke had done together. But then she asked him to give her a revolver with which to shoot herself. Dearden wisely refused, saying that he was not in the business of helping people to commit suicide. She wanted him to reassure her that if he were to see Drueke before he was shot, to tell him that she had not betrayed him to the authorities. 'I am the only woman he has ever trusted,' she said, crying. 'It seems terrible that he should die, thinking that I had betrayed him.' This display of melodrama was yet another example of Vera's insecurities. Ever the mediator, Dearden avoided making any promises, but pointed out that if she was the only woman Drueke had ever trusted then her ignorance of his private affairs made it even harder to believe.

As the interview wound down, Dearden focused on more trivial matters, such as her health and comfort, and her former life as a dancer. During this time she confessed that she knew nothing about Walti, only that he was supposed to work in Scotland, that the radio was hers, and that she was supposed to have taken it to the Duchesse's house for collection by an unknown person. Wilkinson, perhaps?

She turned the conversation back to a possible exchange, but Dearden told her that he could see no reason why the Germans should want to exchange a British agent except to get one of their own back. She tried to convince him that the Germans would be prepared to do this to honour her late husband. Dearden replied: 'I admitted that I knew little of the German authorities; but from what I did know I gathered the impression that magnanimity was not really their most striking feature.' He summed up by saying that 'nothing of value will be got from this woman. She is in my view a pathological liar; her tendency to deceive is so ingrained as to be almost instinctive.' As was demonstrated with the Duchesse, MI5, MI6 and SOE were all reluctant to make any exchanges, even for such a valuable agent as Andrée de Jongh, so it was unlikely they would have swapped Drueke. Stephens described Dearden's report as a 'fascinating account', adding:

> As we surmised, the woman's request to see the doctor was merely dictated by her curiosity as to the fate of De DEEKER. The odds were 100 to 1 that she would refuse to give further information and now I have to confirm a telephone report from Holloway Prison that this woman is not prepared to add to the statements she has already made.[4]

Dearden visited her twice more unofficially, on 21 and 22 December, while he was on other business there, and had not told Stephens about them.[5]

He remarked that 'if my interview with her was unduly prolonged, Major Stephens might ask what had kept me so long and I might not be able to evade his probing and suspicious mind.'

During the first of these visits on the 21st:

> I represented myself as the surreptitious bearer of a letter from DE DEEKER, and I explained this along similar lines to those with which I had outlined to DE DEEKER the friction which existed between Major Stephens and myself in regard to his callous treatment of their situation.

He told Vera that De Deeker (Drueke) was in a state of depression over the fact that Vera was still in prison:

> Then came the execution of MEIER, WALDBERG and KIEBOOM [on 11 and 17 December], closely followed by the news that an Englishwoman [Dorothy O'Grady on 18 December] had actually been sentenced to death for precisely the crime of which she (ERICHSEN) herself stood proved guilty for all practical purposes.[6]

Dearden referred to the fact that this news about the other spies had had an impact on Drueke, first to save himself, and second a recognition of the peril in which she found herself, and to do what he could to save her. As Dearden pointed out to Vera:

> That he should think of himself first ... was entirely in keeping with what she had said about the respective strengths of the love each other bore to the other. She had always told me that that her love for him was greater than his for her. I had been prepared to believe this, since my experience was that women alone were capable of really unselfish love, and I had recognised her at once as uniquely endowed with the capacity to love to the exclusion of self; but it had interested me to have her words confirmed.[7]

He relayed to Vera what Drueke had told him – that he wished her to tell everything that she knew in order to avoid the serious consequences that undoubtedly awaited her. He had told Drueke that if this was what what he really wanted, then he should say so in a letter to Vera, so that she would not think it was a trap set to extract a confession from her. Her first question after reading the letter twice was to ask what Drueke had said about himself. Dearden managed to bluff his way out of that by saying that he probably found it less humiliating to tell him than to give in to those whose job it was to extract such information. He tried to assure her that by Drueke doing this he had gone some way to making Stephens feel somewhat more charitable towards him and 'at least less determined to see him pay the full penalty for being a spy'.

Dearden laid it on the line that now that Drueke was prepared to co-operate she must do the same, saying that he was prepared to listen. 'But I must warn you of this: if I catch you out in one lie I shall stop trying to help you.' He told her he was growing tired of spending time with both of them, 'literally dragging you back from the gallows', and expressed the fact that she couldn't help lying. In return, Vera promised she wouldn't lie to him, adding, 'Major Stephens makes me afraid.' Then he asked her about Drueke's spell in prison that had been documented in an SIS report, which she said had been terrible.

Walti, he said, was 'terribly stupid; he's almost certain to hang.' She confirmed what had been suspected, that Walti was not his real name, but was unable to add much else because they had all been given such little information before the operation. What she told him contradicted what Drueke had said: that the Duchesse was supposed to find them some accommodation while he operated his radio. According to Drueke, he was only a courier and had been instructed to hand over his radio to someone else. It appeared to Dearden that perhaps he had finally won Vera's confidence, as she had asked him when he would return. This, he said, would depend on Stephens. In summary, he said that her demeanour:

> suggested a change of mind ... due, I think, to the sentence on the woman O'Grady, the news of which she told me had reached her. I think it not unlikely that she will now come as near to telling the whole truth of what she knows as lies within her somewhat limited capacity to tell the truth about anything.[8]

Stephens was obviously not averse to Dearden visiting her again as he returned the following day with a series of more questions. He asked her to describe Spitzenburg and his connection with Drueke. According to Vera, Spitzenburg was a partner of De Deeker (as she called Drueke) and an old school friend, 'aged about 35 or 36, shortish, dark, with a plump face and a lively manner. He is an exporter and importer of various goods. He lives somewhere in Brussels near the Rue Faider.'[9] She had only seen him once while she was in a car with Drueke. Walti was a Swiss who had had a very unhappy childhood and as a result hated everyone, although she admitted that he had been a good and helpful comrade. Then she described how she had met him.

Before coming to Scotland she was supposed to go to Spain on a mission but Dierks had received orders from Berlin for her to proceed to England instead. She had met Walti at the Hotel Reichshof in Hamburg with Drueke, her husband Dierks, and Captain Brunes [*sic*], a subordinate of Rantzau, who, according to her was 'of no great importance in the German Secret Service', and only there to give them instructions. This must have been Hauptmann Bruhm (or Bruhn) of the Luftwaffe who was temporarily attached to *Ast* Hamburg, referred to earlier. Bruhm took Vera to one side to brief her about her mission, while her husband, Walti and Drueke discussed 'other matters'. It was only afterwards that Dierks spoke to Bruhm, 'presumably for the purpose of getting her out of the mission', but with no success.

On the day after the car accident in which Dierks was killed, she had first met Walti. Rantzau, who had arrived, played on her 'state of great distress' by telling her that she was now alone in the world, with no one to protect her. She was to obey his orders without question or he would make things bad for her and her parents, as well as her brother (Constantin) who had volunteered for Norway. His orders were that she should proceed to England; contact the Duchesse; and move into the accommodation that the Duchesse would provide for her and 'the man you will see', and look after him and help him in every way she could.

The information elicited about Drueke has already been discussed. She did not recall an incident related by Edvardsen when he had come into a room where Drueke and Walti were sending a wireless message, as she admitted to having taken heavy doses of morphine and opium at the time, so her memory was vague. This, Dearden noted, 'is entirely consistent with the behaviour of drug addicts'. The address in Brussels she had given her interrogators – 150 Avenue Roger – had been one she had lived in some time ago, but had told them of it 'to keep them quiet'. This must actually have been Avenue Rogier, in the Schaerbeek district of Brussels. At the end of the interview Dearden remarked to her, 'It is a great pity … that you had this miscarriage. If you were still pregnant it might be that DE DEEKER would do more to save your child and yourself than he is prepared at the moment to do to save you only.' 'Would it not be a good thing,' she said, 'to tell him that I am still pregnant?' to which Dearden replied, 'If you feel like that about it … of course you must use your own discretion …' and instructed her to write it all down so that Drueke would believe her.

Toby Pilcher interviewed Vera in Holloway Prison on 24 December 1940. In his report he summarised the main points of the events that occurred, many of which have already been discussed. Vera told him that she thought that the

Duchesse did not actually know Heine Tini, whom she was told to go and see, but that it was purely somewhere to go to obtain money. As reported earlier, Vera claimed to have met Drueke for the first time at Tini's boarding house. She formed the impression that he was not someone who had just come out of prison as he was well dressed and cheerful. She told Dearden that while Drueke had never been to England, he knew someone in Soho, the name of whom is not mentioned in the files. When asked about Drueke's business contacts – Bouchillon, Engelmeyer, Gorlinski and Max Caan – Vera said he never spoke about them.

Sandor Gorlinsky was referred to in his MI5 file as being Hungarian but, according to him, was actually born in Ilintzy near Kiev in the Ukraine on 28 March 1908 (the source cited below states 28 February 1908). As noted earlier, he had been working at Butlin's holiday camp in Belgium, had come to the UK in 1940 as a refugee, and was immediately detained on suspicion of being in contact with German Intelligence. He was released in 1943 and became a naturalised British citizen.[10] In 1945 he attempted, unsuccessfully, to partner with band leader Jack Hylton, but in 1946 went on to become an impressario, inviting tenor Beniamino Gigli and the San Carlo Opera Company to perform at the Royal Opera House, Covent Garden. In the late 1940s he promoted a series of Gigli's tours in Britain, as well as bringing the La Scala Opera to Britain in 1950. By 1947 he was promoting over 250 concerts with conductors Sir Thomas Beecham, Sir Malcolm Sargent and Sir John Barbirolli. Until the end of her career, he became the personal manager of Maria Callas, as well as managing soprano Montserrat Caballé, tenors Alfredo Kraus, Giuseppe di Stefano and Jose Carreras; bass-baritone Ruggero Raimondi; bass Nicolai Ghiaurov; and conductors Carlo Maria Guilini and Lorin Maazel. He was also a personal friend of baritone Tito Gobbi. Two of the ballet dancers he managed were the legendary Rudolf Nureyev (for thirty years) and prima ballerina Natalia Makarova, who defected in London in 1970 while on tour with the Kirov Ballet. In the context of managing Nureyev, *Dance* magazine described Gorlinski as a 'crackerjack Hungarian consultant'.[11] He died in London on 12 May 1990.[12]

Victor Rothschild, working for MI5's B1c, wrote to inform Stephens on 17 April 1941 about Gorlinsky and others. He quoted Major David Finlay, the former British Vice-Consul in Belgium, and now at the Home Office Aliens Department in Bournemouth, as saying that Finlay, 'Considers that GORLINSKY is a very dangerous type and is safer interned for the duration.' In fact, Finlay described him in a report to Rothschild as 'of very unpleasant appearance of the effeminate type, and very "oily" in his manners, giving the impression of being "foxy" and very "sly"'.[13] Finlay was equally disparaging about Vera: 'In appearance a very unattractive woman similating illness [*sic*], hysteria and stupidity, but in actuality as "sharp as a needle".' However, she may have been suffering the side effects of a car accident, as reported by E.R. Templer of the Home Office Aliens Department and the former Consul in Belgium, 1939–40.

Vera reported that amongst Drueke's other contacts were three Andersons (two of whom have already been mentioned); two Sieglers (also listed in MI5 files as Ziegler or Zweigler), one whose alias was Mueller; as well as Spitzbergen (or Spitzenburg or Spitzenberg); a German named Lehmann; and a Hungarian (actually a Russian former actress), Mademoiselle Marguerite Koncens, aged 34, Gorlinsky's mistress, but also said to be his wife, who Vera did not know. Marguerite Koncens was born in Riga on 1 March 1905. Spitzbergen and Koncens are referred to in the CX report of 14 December 1940 quoted in the previous chapter.

Rothschild described Max Caan as a German living in Ostend whose 18-year-old son, also named Max, worked at the Royal Palace Hotel who Gorlinsky collected daily to take him to work at Butlins. It was apparently Benno and Hilde Schwarz, Polish Jews who were associates of Gorlinsky, who persuaded him to employ Caan's son. The Camp 020 report of 27 February 1941 describes Caan senior as a 'good-for-nothing'. Felix Cowgill's SIS report states that he was born in Gelsenkirchen on 5 October 1882, and his son in Düsseldorf on 12 November 1921. They were forced to leave Germany because they were Jewish.

One of the Sieglers was probably Kurt Siegel, who was also known to SIS as Victor Hauer, and was involved with Count Almásy and Johannes Willi Eppler @ Husein Gafaar in Operation *Condor*.[14] Gorlinsky professed not to know the name and suggested it might have been a young sailing friend of Max Caan junior. In a report sent by Felix Cowgill to Richard Butler at MI5 on 18 February 1941,[15] Kurt or Karl Siegel had been employed as a concierge of the Hotel de Londres in Ostend in February 1940 but later became *chef de train* of the Ostend-Constantinople (Brussels-Berlin) train, until 31 March 1940 when the Belgian government revoked the 'permis de travail' (work permit) of all Germans working on the Wagon-Lits, Ostend. A close associate of Gorlinsky, he was at one time living at 47 rue Belliard, Brussels, but thought to actually be 147, rue Belliard, which was the German Passport Office and a known cover address for the German Secret Service. The SIS report observed that, 'It is interesting to note that Max CAAN was known to be in touch with Karl Theodore DRUCKE. GORLINSKI may possibly know something about the latter.' However, when shown a photograph of Drueke, Gorlinsky claimed not to recognise him.

The little piece of blue paper found in Vera's possession when she was arrested was a mascot *pour bonheur* (for happiness), given to her by a Madame Kal-Touholka, a clairvoyant living, she thought, on the Boulevard or rue or Avenue de Clichy in Paris. She confirmed that the only time she had met Wilkins/Wilkinson had been at the Duchesse's on the morning in July already discussed in Chapter 6, but she did not know any Lieutenant Peter Wilkinson in the Royal Navy. The man who had visited her and the Duchesse on 21 August was Freddy Ayre, although Dearden thought this was doubtful, given the age difference, since Ayre was older than the person described by Mrs Morrish.

Vera reaffirmed that their reasoning for landing in Scotland rather than on the south coast of England was that it was safer, and that the intention for her and Drueke was to first go to London where he would make contact with his friend in Soho. Stephens' report of 23 December pointed out that:

> From the psychological point of view it was necessary to take action with Vera ERICHSEN without delay, and it was not possible to contact B.2. I had to bear in mind at the same time considerations which might affect an interrogation of Vera ERICHSEN. I came to the conclusion that it would be a mistake if Dr. Dearden attempted an interrogation himself, and I was averse to sending an interrogating officer to Holloway in the absence of Mr. White. In the circumstances, a scheme was worked out whereby the Doctor would ask Vera ERICHSEN a certain number of 'test questions'. The fiction was that we knew the answers, and that the Doctor was merely being sent to test ERICHSEN's good faith to enable us to decide whether an interrogation was justified. In this way there was a good chance of obtaining certain information without compromising an interrogation. In any event, ERICHSEN was anxious to speak but her plea was that she could not speak 'unless the authorities asked her questions'.[16]

Stephens concluded that the evidence was now clear that the Duchesse de Château-Thierry was indeed a spy. Earlier, she had confused the issue by saying that Rheinhardt (Ritter) had been conducting land deals for her, but she had issued instructions to Vera prior to her departure from her household to contact Tini when she reached The Hague. There the Duchesse's contact, 'Kanfie Feine [*sic*]' (Heine Tini) had allegedly introduced Vera to Drueke, who had then paid and arranged for her trip to Germany on 10 September 1939. (This may have been the trip to Germany to which Regna Schalburg was referring in her letter to Michael Dierks.)

It is worth noting that when the Duchesse was examined by the Advisory Committee she admitted giving Vera's name to Tini, yet in the next breath denied any knowledge of her. When questioned further about it and whether Reinhardt had given her the address, she said she thought that it was her sister-in-law, Ellen Duwell, who had first given it to her.[17] She also contradicted herself by saying that she had told Vera to get in touch with an old family servant about 70 years old named Gerda Speyer who lived at Sweerts de Landestraat 30, in Arnhem because, 'I wanted her to get to know her, and I wanted news from my sister.' Vera, however, denied ever meeting Speyer, and the Duchesse had only met her once a few years before. The Duchesse claimed that at that time her sister was in Germany, although when Stephens, Evans and Sampson interrogated her in Holloway on 12 November 1940 she was informed that her sister was in the Netherlands the day Speyer sent her money. Speyer acted as an intermediary whenever Ellen Duwell sent any money to the Duchesse, the last time being a year beforehand, and that it was about £35. Her interrogators concluded that, 'The prisoner was unable to explain why she sent a professed spy to GERDA SPEYER.'

What would appear to back up the Duchesse's story, and was preferred by her interrogators, are two letters from Gerda Speyer dated 23 September 1939 that were found in the Duchesse's flat:

Miss von SCHALBURG brought me your letter, for which many thanks. What trouble and anxiety you seem to have had in these times. I am sorry that recently I have not been able to do very much. I send you herewith £30 …

Miss von SCHALBURG is always heartily welcome here. She has been particularly good and friendly towards me and her visit gave me much pleasure.[18]

And, from the same address, but from her sister-in-law Ellen Duwell:

Dear Sirs, [*sic*]
Many thanks for your nice letter … Your friend Vera, has she visited the grave of her grandfather at Nijmegen? When you go to The Hague I shall meet you there? …[19]

The Duchesse had tried to explain this by claiming that the 'Vera' referred to was a daughter of Ellen Duwell who had committed suicide, not Vera Schalburg, and that, 'We are in the habit – either of us to put flowers on the graves …' Her MI5 interrogators did not believe her story; nor does it make any sense. Why would Ellen Duwell refer to the Duchesse's late niece (or step niece) as 'your friend'? The Duchesse had tried to pass this off as her sister misunderstanding something: 'She's muddled something there. She's quite crazy when she speaks of her children, and the suicide of her daughter.'

There has been no mention anywhere of Vera having any grandparents in the Netherlands; indeed, as has been shown earlier, her family background is somewhat suspect and clouded in mystery. And if Vera had met Gerda Speyer in Arnhem and not Heine Tini in The Hague, when and where had she actually met Drueke, and who had introduced them? There appears to have been a Gerda Speyer, a German Jew born in Herford, North Rhine-Westphalia, who moved to Osnabrück in Lower Saxony on 2 May 1938, but no other information has come to light to make any connection.[20]

Stephens also reported that he considered Walti to be more important than first thought because of his close friendship with 'von Stuhrick [*sic*]' (Dierks), adding:

> There are cross currents of sex and jealousy in this case, a fact which has been patently obvious for some time. DE DEEKER was detailed for the English mission weeks before his actual departure. The selection of DE DEEKER was apparently engineered by VON STUHRICK to rid himself of a competitor for ERICHSEN's favours. Berlin, with a rare touch of humour, riposted neatly by detailing ERICHSEN to accompany DE DEEKER.[21]

WALTI'S ROLE

As if to have a clear out of unwanted prisoners, on 25 November 1940 Stephens wrote in a 'Yellow Peril' (from the colour of the paper):

> We discussed the other day the desirability of prosecutions under the Treachery Act as soon as prisoners had ceased to be of value from an Intelligence point of view. As you know, we have now a fairly full complement of spies, and, looking to the near future with optimism, I think it is essential to hand over a certain number of the prisoners to Colonel Hinchley-Cook.
>
> One such case is that of WALTI, Heinrich and I select him particularly because he has already been 'blown by the Press'. Furthermore he has been suspected by the Doctor [Dearden] of suicidal tendencies, and for this reason he has been under observation at Brixton Prison Hospital. I have little doubt, however, that in the near future he will be returned here, and I hope this procedure can be short-circuited.
>
> In order to be of assistance in these cases, I have deputed Captain Hancock-Nunn, a barrister, to state cases from the criminal prosecution point of view. His report is attached.[1]

Vivian Hancock-Nunn, whose identity as agent M/7 was revealed by Henry Hemming, and a 'dyed-in-the-wool Conservative', had worked pre-war for Maxwell Knight and had penetrated the Communist Party of Great Britain.[2] Stephens' report summarised the main points of the case, concluding:

> Bearing in mind the circumstances of WALTI's arrival in this country and the exhibits found on him, notably the wireless set, code, money and Mauser

revolver, together with the statement attached hereto, it is submitted that there is a clear prima facie case against this prisoner.[3]

At Camp 020 Walti had first been interrogated on 2 October. Two days later it was the turn of Meurig Evans and Mr Short, followed by Dr Dearden; Stephens spoke to him on the 6th. The report by Evans, Short and Dearden concluded that 'the interrogations were a complete failure' and highlighted the fact that he was vulnerable to the point of tears at any mention of his girlfriend, Betty, his aunt who had raised him, and his home town:

> The question arises of why WALTI ever became involved in such an adventure and why he so stubbornly refuses to give the least information concerning this.
>
> The most likely explanation would appear to be as follows:-
>
> The young woman with whom WALTI is plainly infatuated has apparently expensive tastes. Against his wishes she led him to get rid of 15,000 francs of his total capital of 55,000 francs in a very short time, and seems to have given him to understand that unless he is in a position to to provide her with plenty of money his chances of marriage were small. It may be therefore that the Germans have held out to him some sort of promise of future advancement such as was given to CAROLI and SCHMIDT. It is even possible that BETTY, about whom WALTI will furnish no particulars, was herself a German recruiting agent or acting in conjuction with the German S.S. The fear of compromising her seems to be the best explanation at the moment of WALTI's unreasonable attitude.
>
> He is almost certainly not a professional agent and is not at all of the same temper as DE DEEKER.[4]

The end of the report noted that:

> The interrogating officers consider it their duty to report that through a misunderstanding as to their own powers they made a formal offer to WALTI of his life in return for a full confession. As will appear from the above summary the offer was not accepted.

Walti was again interrogated by Lieutenant Sampson on 10 October 1940, who began by asking him about his journey to Norway and the house in which he first stayed outside of Oslo. Walti claimed that Anderson, whose name he did not actually know at that point, had locked him in, effectively making him a prisoner. When they reached Bergen, Anderson had taken him to a hotel for a meal. When asked how the Germans had first approached him about his smuggling, Walti explained that it was when he had applied for a permit for his car in Antwerp in June 1940. The Germans had refused to issue him with one, so he sold the car and then thought of getting away, first to England. He had hung around the cafés down at the harbour in Antwerp hoping to find someone willing to help him escape, in particular at the Café Stanley.[5] In July the Germans had searched his room, threatening that he would not be able to use any of his money (he had 45,000 francs, 5,000 from the sale of the car), and warning him not to try to escape. Later the Gestapo took him to Brussels, where they questioned him and asked him about what he was trying to do in England, and whether he was involved with the British Secret Service. They accused him of helping take the Jews and their money, gold and diamonds out of the country and told him that it was a serious offence, even though Walti claimed this was before the Germans had occupied the country. They then beat him up and threatened him with ten years' imprisonment.

When the Gestapo had finished with him they allowed him to go back to Antwerp. There he returned to the harbour and met a Norwegian at the Café Stanley who said he would help him for 2,000 crowns – he was sailing in a couple of days and he should meet him again if he still wanted to get away. The Germans returned, including one of the same men who had interrogated him before – a tall man with a long nose – who told him that he should come back to Brussels and join the German Army because he could speak several languages. The man also suggested that he should learn Morse code. When Walti said he could get into trouble with the Swiss authorities if he signed up in the German Army the German gave him an ultimatum: either join the German Army (but not in uniform) or get ten years' imprisonment. Eventually he agreed. He was told to take all his possessions to Brussels and request a room at the Royal Nord Hotel near the Gare du Nord, from the Quartieramt – the billeting office.

While in Brussels he was free to move around, but he decided not to see his girlfriend Betty, because he didn't want to implicate her in anything. After about a week of one-hour training sessions he was unable to master Morse, so instead the Germans told him that his case would be dismissed if he agreed to take a bag to London. He agreed and went back to Antwerp with the tall man. When he got off the bus he was met by the same Norwegian who he'd met before. It was at this point that Walti realised the Norwegian was a German agent. In spite of being made to hand over his money at the hotel in Brussels he did not receive any English money in exchange. He was allowed to retain his own passport, but did not receive his identity card and ration book until he landed in Norway.

On arriving in London he was told he would meet a man on Victoria Station who had a duelling scar, wore gold-rimmed glasses and a grey suit. Whether this was the same man who Drueke had been instructed to meet at the ABC restaurant is unclear as Drueke had not been given any physical description of his contact, only a recognition signal. Seeing him get out of a taxi, his contact would approach him and say, 'You have a good deal of luggage, can I help you?' having already seen him arrive earlier at King's Cross Station. Sampson queried the time frame of Walti arriving first at King's Cross, then making his way to Victoria. To make everything connect would depend on whether there was a train arriving at King's Cross at 2 p.m. in time for Walti to make his way to Victoria by 3 p.m. If for some reason the man did not show up, then Walti was to be there the day after or two days later at the same time. He was not instructed where to stay in London, but to use his discretion. There was also the question of taking a train from Edinburgh at 10 p.m., arriving the next day after a twelve-hour journey. However, it was not explained what he would do in Edinburgh all day until his train left for London.

Walti told Sampson that he was supposed to hand over the Mauser revolver to the same man to whom he was to give the bag. He claimed that the gun had been given to him just before boarding the plane but he had had no time to stow it in the bag Anderson had given him. That is how he came to have it in his left-hand pocket when he was challenged by the police on Waverley Station. He pulled the gun because:

A few men came from behind, and took me. At first I didn't know what had happened. I was turning around like this, and that was without any possibility to use it. The man was making a hero of himself ...'

He denied knowing anything about the squared paper with the name of the head of the Luftwaffe in Norway on it and thought it came from the bag.

It seems that Drueke had wanted him to throw the wireless set overboard when they were in the rubber dinghy because there was water in the boat and he fully expected it to overturn. In fact, Drueke had wanted to throw everything overboard. While the two men rowed for several hours, Vera sat there doing nothing. It was the first time he had met De Deeker (Drueke) and the two barely exchanged more than a few words.

18

THE TRIAL

On 26 April 1941 Detention Orders under paragraph 5(A) of Article 12 of the Aliens Order, 1920 As Amended were issued for Vera and Walti and signed by Herbert Morrison, the Home Secretary. They were sent to Dick White by Jennifer Williams of the Home Office and Secretary to the Advisory Committee. These were duly served to Camp 020 and Holloway Prison where Walti and Vera were being held.

The trial of Karl Theo Drueke and Werner Heinrich Walti began at the Old Bailey on Thursday, 12 June 1941 before Mr Justice Asquith. All quotes are from the transcripts of the trial in Drueke's file (KV2/1704) unless otherwise specified. (In these court documents Drucke was referred to as Drueke.) They were charged with two counts under the Treachery Act (1940), to which they both pleaded not guilty:

> That they on 29/30 September, 1940, with intent to help the enemy conspired together with other persons unknown, to do an act designed or likely to give assistance to the Naval, Military and Air operations of the enemy, or impede such operations of His Majesty's Forces, viz: landed in the United Kingdom, contrary to Section 1, Treachery Act, 1940.[1]

In contrast, in the transcript of the trial the wording is slightly different and contains both counts:

> Karl Theo Drueke and Werner Heinrich Walti, you are charged that between the 30th of June, 1940 and the 1st of October of that year with intent to help the enemy conspired together and with other persons unknown, to do an act designed or likely to give assistance to the naval, military or air operations of the enemy, or to impede such operations of His Majesty's Forces.

In a second count of the same indictment it is charged that you on the 30th September, 1940 did an act designed or likely to give assistance to the naval, military or air operations of the enemy, or to impede such operations of His Majesty's Forces; that is to say, landed in the United Kingdom.

The Solicitor General, Sir William Jowitt, and Mr L.A. (Lawrence) Byrne appeared for the Crown. Initially, there had been no one to represent the defendants, but after a short adjournment Mr H.B. Figg appeared for Drueke and Mr J.C. Whitebrook (barrister at Lincoln's Inn) appeared for Walti. After the trial Sir Ernley Blackwell, who had been Legal Assistant to the Under-Secretary of State at the Home Office, is quoted as saying that Whitebrook requested to see Sir Alexander Maxwell, Permanent Under-Secretary at the Home Office, to say that 'the Judge had said that it was unsatisfactory that the prisoners were not represented by counsel either at the beginning of the trial or when the depositions were taken'. Whitebrook complained to Blackwell on 4 August 1941 that, 'I had no opportunity to see the Depositions, save as they were passed to me whilst the witnesses were giving evidence at the trial.'[2] This contradicts the official transcript, where it quotes the judge as saying to Whitebrook and Figg that:

> You wish to consult with your clients. This case will not be taken until two o'clock. I think that the Solicitor General's opening will take most of the afternoon, and therefore you will have the evening and the night if necessary in which to fortify yourselves.

The judge's use of the word 'fortify' here implies not necessarily that they were to wine and dine, but to familiarise themselves with the case. Jowitt added, 'I think it would be better if I had five minutes with my learned friends and tell them about the documents and so on.' In the Home Office file on the case Whitebrook had argued that Walti be treated under the Hague Convention, which:

> imply [*sic*] that a spy is not to be treated as a felon. Walti is a spy within the meaning of the article in the Hague Convention, therefore, though he might have been sentenced to death by shooting by a Military Court for a war crime he ought not to have been convicted of felony and sentenced to be hanged under the Treachery Act.[3]

In keeping with all such trials involving national security, it was held in camera. In his introduction to the jury Jowitt explained that, 'because of this Treachery Act, we are enabled to try the offences in England, albeit the offences are committed in Scotland ...' and said that 'in popular language what these two accused men are accused of is being enemy spies'. He warned them that, 'The life of a human being is in your hands.' He added, enigmatically, 'The woman [Vera] is not being charged for reasons which you can perhaps imagine. Anyhow, she is not being charged.' Exactly what these reasons were that the jury was expected to imagine were not made clear. Neither was she required to appear in court either as a defendant or as a witness, and continued to be referred to as 'the woman' throughout the trial. Indeed, on 23 July 1941 an unnamed source (there is no signature on the document), but possibly Jowitt, wrote in the accused's Home Office file:

> It does not seem to me that, if questioned in the House of Commons, the Attorney General would be able to give any satisfactory explanation of why proceedings were not taken when there was clearly a very strong case against this woman.
>
> I think it is perfectly clear in a case of this kind that the proper course would have been to proceed against the woman and get a conviction. It would have then been open to M.I.5 to represent to the Secretary of State the desirability of the sentence not being carried out, and she could have been reprieved without any awkward questions being raised, and if questions are asked they need not be answered.[4]

Jowitt began by outlining the circumstances of how the trio came to be caught. What first gave them away, he said, was when Vera asked which railway station they were at; second, how the number '1' on Drueke's National Registration Identity card had a curl to it, typical of how it is written in Germany; there was also no immigration stamp on his Belgian passport. When Vera had first told Police Constable Grieve that Drueke was Belgian and she Danish, then said they had come from London, Grieve was not convinced. He asked where they had stayed overnight, to which she told him Banff; however, neither of them was able to remember the name of the hotel. They also claimed they had hired a taxi and then walked to Port Gordon, something which would have been easily checkable. When they were taken to the local police station and Grieve explained the situation on the telephone to his superior, Inspector John Simpson, Vera confessed that she had lied and that they had landed by boat a mile further up the coast. Jowitt suggested to the jury that, 'You will have no doubt that that is another lie.'

Jowitt elaborated on the evidence that their presence in Scotland was not as it should be: ammunition; the torch marked 'Made in Bohemia'; Drueke's ration book not filled in; a third-class ticket to Forres bought at Port Gordon station; the sum of £327 10s in English bank notes in Drueke's possession, and, by way of a comic aside, 'some foodstuffs, including – you might have guessed this might not you! – some german sausage [sic]'. As if that wasn't compromising enough, when Inspector Simpson had forced open the box carried by Drueke, he found the Mauser pistol and further ammunition; some cardboard discs that later turned out to be coding discs; and a list of RAF airfields and other installations (see Appendix 3), thirty-two out of the thirty-four of which were 'very important and very secret aerodromes', according to Jowitt. These and the wireless set – 'a mass of stuff which is suitable for transmitting messages to the enemy' – were what incriminated him, but Jowitt added, 'one can have a measure of sympathy with him, perhaps if he thought he were doing something in the interest of his country, as no doubt he was'.

Leaving aside Drueke, Jowitt turned to Walti, to whom 'one feels rather differently' and explained what had happened to him, how he had been confronted by Paterson, the porter at Buckie station, and how he eventually found himself in Edinburgh. The inflatable boat and its equipment (oars, air bottle, sea anchor, etc.) were all produced as evidence with the offer of inflating the boat in court, although, sensibly, the judge does not appear to have accepted it. When Walti was arrested another wireless set and the equipment for operating it were found in his suitcase. There were also some sheets of graph paper from an exercise book with the name 'Major Harlinghausen, Chief of the General Staff', and then 'Felf, 10th Air Force Corps', and 'Andersen, Bergen, Hotel Nord', as mentioned in Chapter 10. Jowitt referred to the code discs found with the transmitter as well as his British ration book and Swiss passport, German copies of Ordnance Survey maps, and a compass. Then he added wryly, 'I need hardly tell you that he had some sausage meat and bread.'

Referring to the statements made by Drueke and Walti, Jowitt began by reading them out to the jury, beginning with Drueke and how he had admitted that his real name was Karl Theo Drueke, and that his assumed name was François de Deeker. In his statement Drueke had admitted that he was a German citizen who had come over with 'Mme. Eriksen' (the first time her name was mentioned in court), but declined to reveal where and how he had obtained his Belgian passport, nor the identity of the third person to whom he was to give the transmitter. He also denied any knowledge of Walti and claimed that the address in London, 15 Sussex Gardens, W2, was 'some kind of boarding house'. The watch, he said, bearing the initials 'H.W.D.', was that of his dead brother, Hans Werner Drueke, and all the documents were given to him by the same person. He assumed that the discs were for some sort of code but claimed he did not know how to work it. Both he and Vera had intended to travel to London but he said he had no idea what she intended to do once there, nor would he reveal how long he had known her. In completing his reading of Drueke's statement, Jowitt discussed how his possession of the transmitter incriminated him:

> it is not the fact that he simply wanted to hand this wireless set to somebody else, even if that were the truth, in my submission to you that would not constitute any defence; because I can imagine nothing more likely to give assistance to the enemy than to bring to this country a morse transmitting set and hand it over in London to some unknown person. The difference would be that instead of himself being empowered, he would be giving the material to another person to have this power against us; and in my submission that would be no sort of case.[5]

In Walti's statement he said that he was a professional chauffeur who had been employed at various times to take Jews across the border from Belgium to France, for which he received 55,000 francs in one week. He told of his arrest by the Gestapo, how they had recruited him to take a case over to England, and how his subsequent training in wireless telegraphy was a failure. The rest of the statement was about how he had travelled by ship from Zeebrugge to Norway and his meeting up with a tall man and a woman – Drueke and Vera – whom he claimed he had never met before. His instructions were to hand over the case to a man in London whose description he had been given (referred to earlier). It is interesting to note that the address in London he had been given was 25 Sussex Gardens, W2. Both addresses are part of a series of Georgian terraced houses. Almost all the accommodation in Sussex Gardens form small hotels; numbers 26–28 are now the Four Stars Hotel. It is quite likely that both Walti and Drueke were given the same address and that one number was written down incorrectly.

Walti claimed that he wanted to get rid of the case and to leave it at Victoria station once he had got to London, but had not thought of going straight to the police. This, Jowitt found quite implausible:

If this man were really going to double-cross the Germans, it is quite obvious is it not, that having got to this country with all this luggage and the wireless and the rest of it, he would have gone straight up to the nearest policeman and told him the facts, or to any responsible authority; instead of which, as you know, he went from this place to Aberdeen, and from Aberdeen to Edinburgh; and it is not until nine o'clock at night that this man is arrested.[6]

He posed to the jury the question they must ask themselves:

that it is not just as plain as a pikestaff in this case that these two people were conspiring with each other, and apart altogether from conspiring, were doing an act designed or likely to give assistance to the enemy. The true view of the fact, I suggest to you, is that these men were obviously here to spy and as spies to transmit messages.

So far as Drueke is concerned, he is a German. Perhaps that is his trade; and perhaps he undertook that trade with honourable motives. But war is a merciless thing, and all of us, and every child, know the penalties which spying carries with it.[7]

Walti, although Swiss, was possibly attracted by the 'blood and lucre', and quite obviously a spy, doing an act likely to assist the enemy. He went on to describe how the coastguard had found the rubber dinghy and its contents.

Following Jowitt's opening statement, the first of the witnesses – John Donald, the stationmaster at Port Gordon – was called to give evidence. Byrne examined him on his encounter with Drueke and Vera. As noted earlier, Vera had asked him 'What station is this?' It was after Drueke had run his finger down the list of stations on the timetable to Elgin and Forres that Donald had called the police. He told the court that Vera had bought two tickets to Forres. He noticed that their trousers and shoes were wet, when it had been a dry day. Figg then cross-examined him about how to get to London from Port Gordon, to which Donald replied that it was necessary to take a train to Aberdeen, while admitting that it was possible to take a train to London direct from Forres.

When the court resumed the following day, Police Constable Robert Grieve was sworn in. He told Byrne that he had asked to see Drueke's National Registration Identity Card. Byrne drew attention to the tail on the numbers '141/1'. When Figg cross-examined him about this he admitted that this characteristic had 'excited his suspicion', as the judge had interjected. When he had enquired as to their nationality, Vera had told him that Drueke was

Belgian and she was Danish. Drueke had produced a Belgian passport in the name of De Deeker. Grieve observed that there was no immigration officer's stamp on it. He asked them where they had come from, to which Vera had eventually replied that they had come from London. She added that they had stayed overnight in Banff but could not remember the name of the hotel. She claimed that they had hired a taxi then walked the rest of the way to Port Gordon. Both PC Grieve and Donald had confirmed that Drueke had a blue suitcase in his possession.

At Port Gordon police station Grieve called Inspector John Simpson. Later Vera admitted that she had lied to him and that they had landed by a small boat a few miles up the coast. She also mentioned Anderson. When Inspector Simpson arrived, the pair were taken to Buckie police station. That afternoon the beach was searched and two oars in sections were found about a mile east of Port Gordon and three-quarters of a mile from Buckpool railway station. Grieve was questioned about whether he had addressed any of his questions to Drueke or just to Vera, to which he replied 'both' but could offer no opinion as to why it was always Vera who had answered. It was at that point that Jowitt rose to re-examine him about the handwriting and the tail on the '1'. Grieve admitted that there was no such tail on the address, '15, Sussex Gardens' or the date '11th June 1940', only on the date '1941'.

When it came to his turn, Inspector John Simpson of the Banffshire Constabulary was questioned by Byrne about the identity card, the blank ration book, torch, ticket to Forres, and ammunition, all found in Drueke's overcoat pocket. The suitcase contained a fully loaded Mauser pistol, cardboard code discs, a wireless set and all the accoutrements for operating it (valves, batteries, Morse key). Simpson described how he had forced open the lock on the case as he had not found any key in Drueke's possession. The gun, he said, which was referred to as either a pistol or revolver throughout the trial, was loaded with one in the breech and five in the chamber.

George James Smith, a porter at Buckpool station, was the next witness and first questioned about his encounter with Walti, who had asked him about the Aberdeen train. Smith informed him that he had missed the train and would have to go to Buckie by bus in order to get the next one. Walti had followed him back to the ticket office and asked for a ticket for Perth but was told that he would have to get it from Buckie, so he asked for a ticket to Aberdeen instead. That was the last he had seen of him.

Another porter, Alexander Paterson, was also questioned by Byrne about Walti. When he saw Walti looking at the timetable at Buckie station he asked,

'Have you lost your train, Sir?' but Walti did not reply, instead producing a ticket to Edinburgh. Whitebrook cross-examined him about it and focused on Paterson's northern accent, suggesting that perhaps Walti's lack of response was due to his not being used to hearing such an accent. He then pursued the matter of Walti's ticket, which Paterson said he had not seen issued (it was from Buckie to Edinburgh so obviously he couldn't have) and enquired about the price – 28*s* 1*d*. There being no further questions, it was the turn of Thomas Cameron, porter at Waverley Station, Edinburgh, who was asked about Walti's luggage and his leaving it at the left-luggage office.

Acting on Cameron's advice, Walti left his luggage and returned at nine o'clock that evening. Cameron stated that Walti never told him where he was coming from, only that he was going to London. He only knew that he had come from Aberdeen because of the label stuck to his suitcase. The case was placed in the guard's van of the train, the reason being because of what he called:

> a Scottish Command Order, or military order, that all suitcases going over the Forth and Tay Bridges must be handed over to a railway servant and deposited in the guard's van. You are not allowed to carry a large suitcase over the Forth or Tay Bridge in a compartment.

It is not clear what the logic of this was. If it was to prevent a bomb contained in the luggage from exploding, then no matter where it was stowed, if the bomb exploded while crossing either of these two bridges, then the bridge would almost certainly be damaged or destroyed. Cameron described the instructions he had been given and Walti's arrest by Superintendent Merrilees of the CID when he came to claim his suitcase.

Having pointed out Walti, 'Superintendent Merrilees gave a sign to his men, the detectives, and one pounced on each side of him, and got hold of him.' This was Inspector Sutherland and another man, according to Cameron. Whitebrook concentrated on how Walti had been restrained:

Q. You saw the detectives holding the arms of the Accused?
A. Oh yes.
Q. And they were holding him with much firmness?
A. Well, they jumped on him. The chap gave a jump, naturally, I should say with fright. Then they got him into the left luggage office. I was told the police inspector had dropped his gloves, and I ran out to get hold of his gloves. That practically finished it so far as I was concerned.

Q. Did you see the Prisoner do anything at the time the detectives seized him?

A. No; I did not.

Q. You were watching him carefully?

A. Yes; until I left the left luggage office to try to find the detective's gloves.

Q. You did not see him try to resist, or any threatening movements of his hands or arms?

A. Certainly not.

Inspector Alexander Sutherland of the Edinburgh City Police was first examined by Lawrence Byrne. He was questioned about how at ten past five on the evening of 30 September he had been called to Waverley Station, where he examined the suitcase left by Walti. He noted that the bottom part of it was wet. He had opened it with a key he had 'on my person', but was not asked to explain how he had come by it. Presumably, it was a fairly common lock that could be opened easily by a basic type of key. Apart from clothes, the suitcase contained a volt-meter; the smaller case a pair of headphones; a Morse key and lead; two wireless valves; six lengths of insulated wire; three bulbs; two loose insulators; a piece of yellow oilskin; a linen-covered graph book; two circular discs; a piece of graph paper; and a small note book with groups of letters 'in a foreign hand'. He was asked to describe the arrest, which is worth quoting in full:

A. I received a signal from Superintendent Merrilees, and on receiving this signal, both of us immediately closed with Walti. He was then at the counter handing over his ticket for the case. I saw at that time that the ticket that he had in his possession bore the same number as the corresponding one on the case.

Q. Did he do anything that attracted your attention?

A. I gripped his right arm and Superintendent Merrilees gripped his left one; and he appeared to make a motion to get at his left hand trouser pocket. He was prevented, of course. He was wearing a coat.

Q. What do you mean by that: an overcoat?

A. A shower coat. He was taken immediately into the left luggage office.

Q. Who prevented him putting his hand into his pocket?

A. Superintendent Merrilees had his left hand.

Q. Which pocket was he trying to put it into?

A. Left hand trouser, I should say.

Q. And did you see the Superintendent take something from him or from his pocket?

A. Yes, He took a revolver out of his left hand trouser pocket – a small automatic.

Q. Is that the revolver? (Handed witness)

A. That is the revolver.

Q. From where did the Superintendent take that?

A. Out of his left hand trouser pocket.

Although the model was never formally identified in court by a firearms expert, from photographs in the file the gun appears to be a Mauser WTP Mk2 .25 ACP-calibre pocket pistol, capable of carrying six rounds – not a revolver. There is no such thing as an automatic revolver. Its compactness – it can easily fit into the palm of one's hand – would certainly lend itself to a trouser pocket. Whitebrook cross-examined him about the incident, and whether he had been in a good position to see what was happening, which he said he was.

Q. And you will not put it higher than than that he appeared to try to to take a revolver out of the pocket?

A. That was my impression.

Q. You do not support that the trouser pocket would be a good place in which a person intending to fire a revolver would place it? If a person intended to fire a revolver, he would scarcely try to fire from the trouser pocket, would he?

A. He might – from the pocket, do you mean?

Q. Yes.

A. I do not know. He might.

Q. Have you ever heard of a person attempting to fire a revolver from a trouser pocket?

A. Not me, personally.

Byrne also questioned Superintendent William Merrilees about Walti's arrest. He told much the same story as Inspector Sutherland. On being asked about grabbing Walti after he had put his hand in his left trouser pocket, he said that, 'I grabbed his arm out of his pocket and held it back, put my hand into his left hand trouser pocket and brought out a pistol.' Merrilees was then shown, and identified the pistol. He said that at police headquarters he had examined it and found it to be loaded. The other questions related to the sums of money and the scrap of paper in Walti's possession, with the address of 23 Sussex Gardens on it [sic]; the contents of the case, and the maps.

During Whitebrook's cross-examination he took up the matter of the key and where it had come from. Merrilees said that the keys [sic] had been found in his office on Walti's person when he was further searched, although not by him. Whitebrook asked him about the circumstances of Walti's attempt to draw the gun – whether it was secured with a safety catch, and suggested that Walti might have wanted to throw away the gun. Walti had stated that he had gone to the hairdresser and the cinema between depositing the suitcase and returning later. However, when asked about Walti's statement of his whereabouts, Merrilees claimed not to have seen that statement; nor had the police checked to verify where Walti had been. This seems sloppy, considering that the police could have found witnesses to verify this. He was also asked about whether there was any connection to Walti and the address in London, or the address in Antwerp, the rue Van Dyke where Walti claimed to be living, as well as whether the police had followed up on this. Merrilees explained that that was not his duty but that of MI5 when Walti was handed over to them.

James Addison Anderson, the coastguard at Buckie, and the next called to give evidence, described the discovery of the bellows that were found floating a hundred yards off West Buckie pier, and the rubber boat that had been deflated and rolled up further away. In it, Anderson had found a brown blanket, a canvas cover, a puncture repair kit, a sea anchor, and an air bottle. Under cross-examination by Figg, Anderson was treated as a somewhat hostile witness when he was asked about how far the rubber dinghy would have drifted, given the tide at that time. Anderson was non-committal in his answers but, after Figg's third attempt to elicit a satisfactory answer, was finally pinned down to 2 miles. Whitebrook questioned him about whether an ordinary person would become sea-sick paddling a mile to the coast, to which Anderson replied, 'It all depends whether one is accustomed to the sea or not,' which seems like a reasonable answer.

Leonard William Humphreys of the Radio Branch of the Post Office Engineering Department was called upon to comment on the radios found in Drueke's and Walti's possession. Ronnie Reed of MI5 had previously examined Walti's radio and described it as:

1. Operating characteristics
Unknown.

2. Apparatus
A combined transmitter and receiver in brown imitation leather crocodile case, set number 21. Two crystal frequencies 6592kc and 4365kc. Receiving frequency unknown. A graph was supplied similar to those found in the other transmitters. The aerial supplied was again a dipole aerial tuned at the

centre with the usual small lamp and press-button. It has no unusual features
and one interesting point is that the H.T. Batteries which were in the transmitter were run down so that they only registered 10 volts each.

3. Codes
This was a circular code similar to the ones supplied with the set of
SUMMER, TATE, etc.

[A handwritten note below reads: 'For line drawing of this type of set see
SUMMER's folder, 4A.' 4A shows a circuit diagram.][8]

Humphreys told Byrne that the range of such radios could easily reach the
Continent. He explained that the use of the graph paper was for determining
the wavelength on which the radio was transmitting or receiving. It is clear
from Figg's line of questioning during his cross-examination that he did not
fully understand the complexities of radio transmissions or the settings of the
radio, but he nevertheless set out to disprove Humphreys' assertion that the
radio was capable of transmitting across the North Sea, by suggesting that 'you
can tell that that set, when you have tested it over a few yards can transmit across
the North Sea?'; and that a 'superficial examination which you have carried out,
or which you are suggesting you carried out, you can tell the distance it would
send?' Humphreys refuted the allegation by saying that, 'I would never say I can
tell any distance. I would only say that it would work efficiently.'

From Humphreys' testimony it can be inferred that his reasoning for not
wanting to test the radio any further than a few yards was because the signal
was capable of being heard across the North Sea, thus alerting the Abwehr listening station outside of Hamburg that someone was transmitting, and giving
them the opportunity to triangulate in on the transmitter. There were further
questions about the type of aerial used and how it was erected. Figg, who was
clearly on a roll, posed his final question, which is worth quoting in full:

Q. I just want to ask one final question, because this is a very serious thing
for this man. As an expert, would you like to say definitely on your oath that
that set, or that set (indicating) would transmit from this country and be
received on the continent?
A. I would definitely say so.

When it came to MI5's turn, Lieutenant Colonel William Edward Hinchley
Cooke, described as being on the General Staff of the 'Directorate of Military

Intelligence, War Office' (a euphemism or cover name for MI5), was asked about the notations on Walti's National Registration Card and the rubber boat. He said that the code on the discs carried by Drueke and Walti was a simple transposition code. Byrne asked him to explain and translate from German the meaning of the notes on the back of the discs. He said that upon examination when the boat was inflated there was a slight leak, and that the markings on the paddles were German. He said '[T]he whole outfit' was like those carried by German pilots in case they had to bale out, thus confirming that the trio had arrived by plane.

The meaning of the list of names on the piece of paper carried by Drueke was said to be 'rather a secret matter'. The full list and function of these bases is explained in Appendix 4, but suffice it to say, they were mainly bomber or fighter stations, as well as a couple of balloon stations. Byrne turned to the matter of the inscriptions in Drueke's graph note book:

Q. Now, the first thing is Carl Anderson, Munkedainsveien, 21 III, Oslow [*sic; actually Munkedamsveien*]; and then under that comes what?
A. 'Major Harlinghausen', then 'Chief of Staff, 10th Air Force Corps'.
Q. What is the German of 'Air Force Corps'?
A. 'Flieger Korps'.
Q. And then under that there is what?
A. 'Felf', and again 'X Flieger Korps' – Air Force Corps – and in brackets behind it, 'Kommando'.
Q. And then there is 'Anderson, Bergen, Hotel Norge'?
A. Yes.
Q. And then under that the word 'Verwaltung'?
A. That means Administration.
Q. What is the next word?
A. 'Unterkunft Inspektor Hanke', best translated here as 'Billeting Inspector Hanke'.
Q. Then underneath that there is 'Carl Anderson' and 'Kaffe Stanley'?
A. Yes; 'Carl Anderson' and 'Kaffe Stanley' (Café Stanley).

When asked about the gun in Walti's pocket, Hinchley Cooke explained that it had been in full working order and that he had fired all the rounds from it and replaced them in the pistol.

The maps in Walti's briefcase were German versions of Ordnance Survey maps and were of the type used by the Luftwaffe (see Appendix 4). Byrne returned to the contents of Walti's notebook and an explanation of what the terms meant. Some of the notes appeared to be in Drueke's handwriting, specifically the capital 'F' in François de Deeker, 'Bitte Frequenz Wechseln' (please change frequency) and 'Fragezeichen' (question mark). Byrne remarked that there were no stamps in Walti's passport. Hinchley Cooke countered that there was no indication that the passport had ever been used within Belgium even though, as Byrne pointed out, Walti had entered Germany on 5 September 1937 at Friederichshafen and left from there on 9 September 1937, as well as another occasion in May 1939 when he had been on the borders of France and Switzerland for a day. He asked Hinchley Cooke whether he thought both Drueke and Walti could understand English sufficiently well, to which he replied, 'I think so, yes' (Drueke) and 'Oh, undoubtedly' (Walti).

Jowitt read out to the court Drueke's statement in which Vera's name was again mentioned – 'I came together with a lady, Mme. Erikson,' and 'I do not know what Mme. Erikson intended to do on her arrival in London nor do I wish to disclose how long I have known her.' Drueke also claimed not to know the purpose of the names of English towns written in someone else's handwriting on the piece of paper. Walti's statement was also read out in which he claimed not to have seen either Drueke or Vera before, although he did not mention her by name.

When Figg cross-examined Hinchley Cooke he took him to task over the handwriting and the letter 'F'. Hinchley Cooke admitted that he had given it only a cursory examination so could not swear to it, but if given the opportunity to examine it more closely he would be able to give a better opinion. Figg rejected the offer, stating that he could only ask him about what was in his statement. The subject of the handwriting was examined in some detail, with Figg querying everything that Hinchley Cooke had stated. It suggests that the prosecution and defence would have benefitted from a qualified graphologist, rather than simply relying on Hinchley Cooke's evidence, for while he had experience with the German language (being half-German himself), his pronouncements about the way the 'F' had been written were considered suspect by Figg. When Figg asked him whether he considered Walti 'a good English linguist, or someone who had learned his English at school', Hinchley Cooke relied, 'He had a reasonable knowledge of English.' He drew Figg's attention to the fact that the 'S' in Sussex Gardens had also been written by the same hand.

Whitebrook also cross-examined him about whether he had attempted to identify the address in Antwerp, the rue Van Dyke, or obtain a map of the city. As with Superintendent Merrilees, Hinchley Cooke had not seen the need to do so, 'as I do not know the neighborhood of the Rue Van Dyke myself, there would not have been much point in my questioning him about it. I would not have known whether he was telling the truth or otherwise.' When Whitebrook took him to task over whether it would not have been prudent to question Walti about the topography of Antwerp, Hinchley Cook refuted the suggestion saying, 'No. He could have learned that by heart. Some agents are instructed to learn some topography by map, so that would not have been a proper test.' Whitebrook persisted with his line of questioning, with the exchange becoming somewhat argumentative and a trifle acrimonious:

Q. So that you say, that anybody who had learned the map of Antwerp by heart, would have been so careless to miss the mark on the passport?
A. Yes; but I am afraid the Germans are very careless in the way they send these agents over. Considering that they make a German '1' on an English Registration Card, one must admit that they are very careless; and that would be, happily, very consistent with their usual practice of being careless! They are also careless from the point of view of forgetting to put on a landing stamp of an immigration officer. That would be equally careless.
Q. Is it so careless for a foreign passport to have a foreign '1' on it?
A. To put a German '1' on an English National Registration Card issued by the English Authorities is distinctly careless to say the least – almost criminally careless!
Q. That scarcely answers my original question, as to why he was not questioned upon the topography of Antwerp at an early period so as to have tested his statement then?
A. Because I did not think it was worth while, to be quite honest.
Q. Did you test the remainder of his statement in any way?
A. No. I came to the conclusion that it was a pack of lies, frankly.

Whitebrook criticised Hinchley Cook on the amount of currency in Walti's possession, compared with the cost of train fares, and for not checking about the instructions for putting the suitcase in the luggage van. Hinchley Cook appeared to be on the defensive when Whitebrook tenaciously contested his argument and suggested that:

Q. In fact, the assumption that the statement was a pack of lies – which is a matter for the jury ultimately – was formed without consideration of many of the points in his statement?
A. When I suggest that it was a pack of lies I am thinking particularly of his mode of alleged transportation from Brussels or Antwerp to Norway. That

was checked in another way, and that I found out was wrong. Therefore I did not bother any more.

Q. Do you suggest that he did not come by seaplane and by rubber boat?

A. He didnot [*sic*] come, as he said in that statement, by boat from Zeebrugge via Norway. He did not make the journey from Zeebrugge via Norway by boat.

Q. That is a statement made upon the grounds of hearsay, made to you?

A. Departmental knowledge.

Q. Can you suggest any possible advantage to him of the statement that he made that he came from Zeebrugge to Norway, in altering his position here? Can you suggest any reason for a falsehood of that sort, being the one falsehood in the statement on which you can pick?

A. Yes. That would bear out his alleged statement that he is a refugee from Nazi oppression.

Q. And is that not the case with persons in Norway: That they are refugees from coercion and pressure? I cannot quite follow the reason.

A. Well, it is within my knowledge that German agents who come over here are instructed that when they are caught they are to make out that they are refugees from Nazi oppression.

Q. Are not persons coming from Norway refugees from Nazi oppression?

A. There are some, yes; and there are some from Belgium.

Q. Then I cannot see your reason.

A. That is his excuse; and he was to say tht [*sic*] as instructed by the German Intelligence Service.

Q. Whether he came from Norway, or whether he came from Belgium, he would still be in the same position, would he not? He would still be in the position of a refugee, if he chose to represent himself as a refugee from oppression? A. Yes.

Q. So that I do not yet see what purpose you are assigning to that, and why you should consider particularly that portion of the statement a falsehood.

A. Because would it not be rather difficult to picture him in Norway? He came from Norway; and it is easier to picture him saying he came from Belgium.

The argument then moved on as to whether Walti had actually used the radio. At first Hinchley Cooke stated that he 'could not use it', but when Whitebrook queried this assertion, Hinchley Cooke was forced to admit that, 'Well, he might have used it.' Whether he had or not had the opportunity to use it was examined in fine detail, down to the precise times when it was in Walti's possession and when it was in the guard's van or the left-luggage office. Whitebrook stated that he had had it on Edinburgh station for three or four minutes. This prompted Jowitt, the Solicitor General, to intercede with a re-examination and pose the question, 'Can you imagine a man sending wireless messages to Germany from the station platform at Edinburgh?' to which Hinchley Cooke had to agree he could not. Jowitt then questioned Hinchley Cooke again about the numbers and letters appearing in Walti's documents. The explanation for the Germans' carelessness was, according to Hinchley Cooke:

> … an intelligent explanation for these various mistakes … That was at the time when an invasion was considered very possible, and the German Intelligence Service were in a great hurry to send over certain agents quickly to get certain information; and if I may so put it, my opposite numbers were very hard pushed for time and therefore they made these mistakes.

Not exactly a stellar performance from Hinchley Cooke, whose testimony was successfully broken down by the defence finding holes in it. Clearly, MI5 had also made a few mistakes in not investigating thoroughly all possible information in their possession. Whether they were also 'very hard pushed for time' or simply anxious to pursue another prosecution remains to be seen.

When the next witness, Detective Inspector Frank Bridges of Scotland Yard's Special Branch, was called, he was first asked to produce the Attorney General's fiat, required for some offences, such as treachery, that require the Attorney General's permission to proceed. Therefore, a group, such as MI5 must apply for the Attorney General to institute legal proceedings on their behalf.

Byrne asked him about the process by which the accused appeared before Sir Robert Dummett, Chief Magistrate, at Bow Street Magistrates Court on the morning of 10 April to be charged under the Treachery Act (1940). At that time Drueke made no reply when he was cautioned, but Walti said, 'I do not agree with these charges.' In the 'Statement of the Accused' at Bow Street Drueke said, 'I do not wish to say anything,' while Walti said, 'I don't quite understand the charge of conspiracy. I have nothing more to say.' The final question to Bridges was about the state of Walti's right hand, in particular his right 'trigger finger', and the fact that, according to Bridges he had noticed that 'it appears to be crushed – It looks as if it is the result of an accident – and he cannot outstretch it.' Had this been injured in the car crash that killed Dierks, given that he admitted, 'That was done by a car'?

That concluded the case for the prosecution. There would be no witnesses called for Drueke, and he did not wish to go into the witness box.

Whitebrook then called on Walti to give evidence. When asked if he wished to add anything to his statement, Walti said he wanted to clarify the circumstances of his arrest on Waverley Station:

> ... the arresting in Edinburgh I would explain a little bit more clearly. I was arrested by two gentlemen who came from behind. I was wearing an overcoat and this overcoat was even-closed [*sic*]; and if a man will get his left hand in his trousers pocket, he has to open his coat; and if the overcoat were open, he would still have to get his hand round to get to his pocket. This policeman was not a man who might easily be thrown round. I do not understand how any man could get the opinion that I would start to get a pistol out of this pocket. In addition, this pistol was taken out of the pocket when I was taken in a room, and not before the booking office – the luggage office, or luggage room.[9]

He went on to explain about when he was in the rue Van Dyke in Antwerp in 1938, first at number 80, then at number 29. Whitebrook questioned him about his travels and how he had arrived in Belgium from Zurich. Walti reported that he had been there twice, once by car and once by train. He stated that as a Swiss he did not need any visa for going to France or to Belgium, which explained the absence of stamps on his passport:

> I need a passport, but not a special permit to go in one of those countries; and in addition, a stamp is very seldom made. A traveler can go through the whole of Europe by train or even more by car, without receiving a stamp in his passport [this was prior to the Schengen Agreement].[10]

He said he had arrived in Friederichshafen from Zurich on holiday via (Redacted) – 'that is a lake between Germany and Switzerland; that is on the border of this lake'. Therefore, the redacted place name must have been Lake Constance, known in German as Bodensee, although there seems no logical reason for it to have been redacted. The questioning then continued with Walti in Belgium and how he had helped Jews leave the country and relieve them of a total of about 50,000 francs, which equated then to £4,000 (in today's money approximately £55,560 or roughly $67,580). He said that he received about half of it back from the Germans after they had recruited him.

Walti had been seasick on the three-hour voyage in the rubber boat. After his experience with the Germans he had no desire to come clean to the police in Edinburgh. He thought that having just arrived by boat this would have appeared suspicious so he had intended to go to 'a quiet place' before going to the police. His plan was to dispose of his wireless set and look for work once he got to London. Whitebrook informed him that it would have been impossible to obtain work without the right papers. Walti countered that by saying that he had been told in Norway that, 'I would get every paper I needed to live in England for the beginning, and later on I could go to the police and it would be all right; and I would get regular papers here.' He claimed that he had never intended to spy for Germany. Whitebrook sought to establish just how sincere he was in making that statement:

Q. Did you intend at any time to serve German interests by the use of the wireless or in any other fashion?
A. I never did.
Q. You never did in fact?
A. Never.
Q. And did not do so?
A. Never from the beginning.
Q. And you did not intend to serve them at any time?
A. Never from the beginning have I had relations with Germans.
Q. You have never been a British subject or resided in England, have you?
A. No.

Whether Walti was lying and committing perjury, or whether he was telling the truth was dependent upon whether the Crown could prove intent and convince the jury. The Treachery Act, under which he was charged, stated in Clause 1:

It is an offence for any person, with intent to help the enemy, to do or attempt or conspire with any other person to do any act which is designed or likely to give assistance to the naval, military or air operations of the enemy, to impede such operations of His Majesty, or to endanger life … In each case, be it noted, the act must have been done with intent to help the enemy.

The Solicitor General cross-examined him about what he was supposed to do with the case and the pistol. Anderson's instructions, he told the court, were that he was to hand them over to a man at Victoria Station. Jowitt tried to establish why Walti had not decied to throw away the pistol instead of carrying it around all day, since by his own admission he had no use for it and had

not intended to use it. Walti used the excuse that he was rowing at the time
so had had no chance to dispose of it. He even claimed that he did not know
that the gun was loaded, which beggars belief. Normally, when someone is
handed a gun they tend to ask whether it is loaded; anyone having experience with guns, which Walti may not have had, would be able to tell whether
it was loaded simply by the weight, and would certainly check. They would
also check whether the safety catch was on or off. Even more incredible is
the fact that he claimed he had forgotten the pistol, otherwise he would have
thrown it away. How, one wonders, does someone forget they are carrying a
pistol, loaded or otherwise, in their trouser pocket? He claimed that the police
accounts of his putting his hand in his pocket, ostensibly to draw the gun, were
a complete invention. In an extraordinary piece of pure fiction about the gun
incident, invented in Farago's book for melodramatic effect, he quotes Ritter
as recording in his diary that:

> Theo had succeeded in reaching Birmingham. There as he was boarding
> a train for London, he was challenged by security agents. Crying, 'They'll
> never get me alive!' Druecke drew his Mauser, killed one of the agents,
> wounded the other, then tried to commit suicide with the last bullet in the
> magazine. But he merely wounded himself.[11]

Nowhere in any of Drueke's or Walti's MI5 files is there mention of any of this.

Jowitt continued by pursuing the matter of Walti's possession of the wireless
set, which he said he had first discovered when he had come from the rubber
boat and was on the road and had opened the case. Their exchange is worth
repeating in its entirety:

Q. Now, do you tell the jury that that was the first time that you realised that
there was a wireless set in there?
A. I had not seen the small case before. It was the first moment, I saw that
there was a small case in it, and what it looked like; and out of pure curiosity
I opened the small case too.
Q. And you saw the small case and a wireless set?
A. Yes. I felt that there was some machinery in it.
Q. If this be true, you did not intend to spy for Germany at all?
A. No.
Q. This case had been planted on you by the Germans?
A. Yes.
Q. What did you think was in that case?

A. I had no idea.

Q. When you found that the Germans had planted this wireless and case on you, were you very annoyed?

A. Indeed I was.

Q. Indeed you were?

A. Yes.

Q. Why didnot [*sic*] you take the first opportunity to go up to a railway porter or a policeman or anybody else, and tell him the truth?

A. I had the idea to get this case to Victoria Station, that it should stay there, and if, however, I should be asked what happened to me and why my case was not handed over, that was the reason I could give to prove that the case could have been found there.

Q. Then you did intend to carry the case, which you knew contained a wireless set, to Victoria Station?

A. To Victoria Station and leave it for ever there, but not to hand it over.

Q. Why did you make up your mind to carry through from Scotland to London a wireless set? Why did not you, if your story now is true, go to the nearest policeman or the nearest railway official, and say: 'Look here, I am an innocent man, and the Germans have put a wireless set in my bag'?

A. Well, one day the Germans might have heard that I did so, and I would exclude that possibility.

Q. You thought the Germans were going to come over here, did you?

A. No; but I thought that even after the war they might hear of that.

Q. You were frightened of what the Germans would hear?

A. And I should still get ten years in Germany.

Q. Just follow. Were you frightened of what the Germans would do to you after the war?

A. Yes.

Q. Then if that be true, the Germans might have done things to you if you had not handed over the wireless set to the right man at Victoria?

A. Yes – but I could easily have found an excuse for that.

Q. What would the excuse have been?

A. Oh, it may be that my watch was not all right.

Q. Do you think that that would have satisfied the Germans?

A. I do not know.

Q. Do you really ask the jury to believe that?

A. That was my intention, to leave the case there.

When it came to remembering the details of the man to whom he was supposed to have handed everything over at Victoria Station, Walti now suddenly
had a lapse of memory, even though he had been given a full description of
him beforehand, and been shown a photograph of him. This Jowitt found
impossible to believe. A password had been arranged, with the man saying he
was coming from Glasgow. Walti was then supposed to hand over the case,
complete with all his clothes, which the man would have returned once he
had the wireless set. Again, Jowitt questioned the plausibility of that statement, and asked where they would have gone to unpack the case. Walti had
no satisfactory answer, feebly suggesting that maybe they would have gone to
a restaurant. He insisted, in spite of Jowitt's persistent questioning, that he had
never intended to do anything with the case other than to leave it at Victoria
Station. There was clearly a misunderstanding by both Walti or Jowitt, but as
the court interpreter put it, 'His meaning was that it would be perfectly clear
to them [presumably the Germans] from the circumstances of this case that
he had done his duty by taking the trunk to London.' Walti had been under
the distinct impression, one originally created by the Germans, that he would
have been acquitted for his actions, 'For always afterwards – for ever afterwards.'

Each time Jowitt asked him about something Walti either denied all knowledge of it or pleaded ignorance to it, the maps being another case in point.
He claimed that the first time he had seen them was when they were shown
to him, although it is unclear whether this was by the police or later by MI5.
When asked what he was to do with them he said that his orders were simply
to hand over the luggage, not the maps: 'I had nothing to do with the maps.'
It turned into a somewhat circular argument since in spite of receiving no
instructions to hand over the maps, only the luggage, since the maps were
inside the luggage they were de facto part of what he would have handed over.
This was finally cleared up when the judge interceded on the jury's behalf, and
initiated a second round of questioning about exactly what he was to hand
over and exactly what was in each item of luggage. Justice Asquith also succeeded in prising out of Walti that it was only after he arrived in Scotland that
he discovered the small case inside the suitcase.

Another sticking point was the circular disc, which he claimed not to know
how to use – he had learned about the code disc and how it worked while
in Camp 020. Likewise the Morse key and receiver, which he said he had
been shown but not instructed how to use. He admitted that his sole reason
for coming to England was to escape from the Germans and to double-cross
them. He also admitted to carrying a scrap of paper in his wallet, but again
claimed not to know its contents or meaning – he knew nothing about Major

Harlinghausen and maintained that he did not know who Anderson was. However, he managed to contradict himself by admitting that he had deduced that that was his name and had been given his instructions by him in Norway.

Before the judge adjourned the case for the day Whitebrook re-examined Walti about his own personal property that had been in the case, property he had been required to remove from his own suitcase on the ship before getting the case back later. What had been returned to him was only part of it, which he hadn't seen again until he was at Camp 020.

During his summing up on Monday, 16 June Mr Justice Asquith clarified various points of law for the benefit of the jury: the meaning of 'beyond reasonable doubt', and the matter of the two charges against Walti and Drueke, that of conspiracy, and 'intent to help the enemy'. Unlike some judges in earlier and later cases, he warned that:

> if in the course of what I say I should unfortunately convey to you my opinion upon any question of fact in this case, dismiss it from your minds. I must not infringe upon your province, or attempt to relieve you of the responsibility which belongs to you alone; but on questions of law I am bound to direct you, and you are bound to accept my directions.

'Beyond reasonable doubt', he said:

> does not mean beyond all doubt whatever. If it meant that, no one would ever be convicted of anything. What it does mean is that you are not entitled to return a verdict of guilty unless you can honestly say to yourselves: 'Applying our common sense to the evidence, we are left in no real doubt about the guilt of the Accused. It would be strange, it would be artificial, it would be perverse, to feel any such doubt.' If you feel that, you must not shrink from the logical consequence, painful as it may be.

He dealt with the indictment in reverse, starting with count two, that of 'intent to help the enemy', specifically with regard to Drueke and what he had admitted to: 'the question for you is whether the intention and the design which are charged against the accused have been proved; the intention, namely, to help the enemy, and the design, to assist his military and other war operations.'

As he went on to explain:

> Intention and design are not matters of direct observation. You cannot look into a man's mind as you can look into a glass beehive and see what is

going on inside. Intention and design are to be inferred, and they have to be inferred <u>inter alia</u> from the acts and statements of the persons charged.

He outlined the various facts to which Drueke had already admitted in his statement, adding that:

> it is no use his saying that he did not know the contents of that suitcase, because in his statement to the police he says he did … If you feel any reasonable doubt under those conditions that he landed here with intent to help the enemy, and that his landing was designed to help the enemy's war operations or to hinder ours, then of course you must give him the benefit of that doubt. If you feel no doubt that about those matters, you would be false to your oaths as jurors if you shrunk from pronouncing him guilty.

The judge posed the question as to whether the defence's assertion that Drueke had intended to hand over the suitcase and its contents to a third party would have made any difference. Turning to Walti, he summarised what he had admitted to, saying:

> The only question for you under this count is whether he landed with intent to help the enemy, and whether his landing was designed to help the enemy's war operations or hinder ours. In many respects his landing is attended by the same circumstances and incidents as that of Drueke's … [but there] are differences.

Walti was Swiss, not German. He also claimed to have acted under duress. The judge stressed the difference between coercion that was physical, and that which was moral. That the coercion exerted on Walti was moral was, as a point of law, no defence:

> But when a man commits a crime under the influence of moral coercion, for instance, threatened imprisonment, that in law is strictly speaking no defence at all … as a matter of strict law, coercion in the form of a threat, threat of imprisonment, for instance is no excuse.

It was also the fact that there was no evidence to suggest that he had ever been in Belgium, based on the lack of stamps on his passport, in spite of his claim to the contrary. Why also, since he claimed that he had never intended to carry out the mission and had wanted to avoid Nazi vengeance, did he think that by depositing the suitcase at the left luggage office at Victoria he could avoid such retribution once the 'third man' did not receive it?

The judge said that the first count of conspiracy contained similar elements to the first charge. It was necessary, however, for the prosecution to establish whether there had been an agreement between Walti and Drueke 'to transmit to the enemy information with regard to the naval, military or air operations of His Majesty's Forces'. The judge reviewed the evidence supporting the charge of conspiracy:

> They landed in Scotland at the same or almost the same place ... They had wireless receiving and transmitting sets ... with a pistol each ... a fake registration Card, and so on; each had a code disc ... and other minor facts which have been brought to your notice which might point to co-operation.

These 'minor facts' were the letters and numbers on Drueke's Registration Card. 'Many of these facts suggest these two men were sent out from a common source.' The jury retired at 12.53 and returned at 1.05 with a unanimous verdict – they found the defendants guilty on both counts. This seems an impossibly short amount of time to reach a verdict, without any real discussion, but clearly they had decided that the intent and the conspiracy existed. The judge pronounced the death sentence on each one in turn, beginning with Drueke.

Both Walti and Drueke were granted leave to appeal on 21 July 1941 under the Criminal Appeal Act, 1907, but their appeals were rejected. The Attorney General also refused to grant a certificate for an appeal to the House of Lords, under section 1(6) of the Criminal Appeal Act, 1907; nor was there any Royal Pardon. Sir Frank Newsam, Deputy Under-Secretary at the Home Office, wrote to the Secretary of the Prison Commission, 'The Secretary of State ... failed to discover any sufficient ground to justify him in advising His Majesty to interfere with the due course of the law.' Instructions issued by the Secretary of the Prison Commission regarding a double execution were as follows:

> Three assistant executioners should be employed. The executioner should put the cap on and arrange the noose of one man, and an assistant should carry this out simultaneously with the other man. The other assistants can in the meantime carry out the strapping of the legs simultaneously. By this means one culprit does not stand by while the other is being attended to.

Walti and Drueke were hanged at 9.00 a.m. on 6 August 1941 at Wandsworth Prison by Thomas William Pierrepoint, with Assistant, his nephew Albert Pierrepoint and Second Assistant Harry Kirk.[12] The inquests were held in camera by Raymond Benedict Hervey Wyatt, Coroner for the South-Western District. Evidence at the inquest was given by Sir Bernard Spillsbury. Death was instantaneous caused by 'injury to brain and spinal cord consequent upon judicial hanging'.[13] The following day the executions were reported in all the major Scottish newspapers.

A BREATH OF
FRESH AIR

By October 1941 the Director of Public Prosecutions had decided not to
bring proceedings against Vera under the Treachery Act (1940). Exactly why is
unclear, and there appears to be no documentation outlining this decision in
any of Vera's MI5 files. If there was any to begin with, it has now been redacted
or removed. Helenus 'Buster' Milmo wrote to Miss K.G. Davies at the Home
Office on 18 October in response to her letter of 11 October explaining this
and voicing the opinion that, 'So far as her continued sojourn in Holloway
is concerned it is felt that since this woman is an experienced and dangerous
spy there is no more suitable place for her to be lodged.' Edward Cussen in
the Legal Section agreed. There were those at MI5 who thought that a change
of scenery might help to loosen her tongue. On 5 January 1942 Dick White
wrote to the Director-General, Sir David Petrie, informing him that he had
discussed with Klop Ustinov the idea of Vera being released into his custody
for a short period of time:

> Vera ERIKSON would be taken to Aylesbury [prison from Holloway]
> where she would be seen by Colonel Hinchley-Cook [sic] and told that she
> was to be given a short holiday in the country with people who had agreed
> to take her as a paying guest, and that after this special privilege had been
> granted she would be further interrogated. U.35 and his wife [Nadia Benoit]
> would not pretend to know anything but the very barest particulars about
> her past, but they hope that in the course of time she will open up. U.35 feels,
> therefore, that if he or his wife see her beforehand they will appear to be too
> closely connected with Government authorities.[1]

White explained that the Regional Security Liaison Officers (RSLOs) would
be notified,[2] as well as the Chief Constable, and a Field Security Police (FSP)

representative from B1a would be sent to stay at the Ustinovs' house at Barrow Elm House, a Victorian farmhouse north of Fairford in Gloucestershire. Furthermore, he felt it unwise for Vera to be returned to Holloway unless others with whom she was associated, such as My Eriksson and Jessie Jordan, were removed by the Home Office to somewhere else as there was concern that she might speak to them about her sojourn on the outside. Nor did he think it suitable for Vera to be sent to the Isle of Man. A physical description of Vera was duly sent out to Major McIver of F1 and the RSLOs, together with photographs:

Height: 5'5"
Weight: 9 stone 9½ lbs
Complexion: pale
Eyes: dark brown
Hair: dark brown turning grey
Build: proportionate
Shape of face: oval[3]

The provisional date for her arrival at the Ustinovs' home in Gloucestershire was scheduled for Tuesday, 3 February. In writing to Major E.A. Airy, the RSLO based in Bristol,[4] White stressed that, while Airy would have to inform the Chief Constable of Gloucestershire, 'it is essential that the whole matter should be treated as highly secret'. He also informed Airy that:

There are good reasons for believing that Vera must be in possession of a mass of information about the German Secret Service and its personnel which would be of great interest and assistance to us in the organisation and direction of counter-espionage measures. So far it must be admitted that we have obtained singularly little information from this bunch of spies and it is now thought that we have nothing to lose and perhaps a lot to gain by adopting a different technique with Vera, in the hope that she may be induced to become more communicative. The scheme is that the Order [Home Office Detention Order under 12(5A)] under which she is detained will be revoked and that she will be given a holiday in pleasant surroundings, during which she will be encouraged to to talk and at the end of which she will be fully interrogated once more.[5]

Dick White's note to Milmo on 5 January suggested that John Marriott should organise a ration card for her. He observed that, 'We have to decide, however, whether it would be better to have the card issued in Vera ERIKSON's name or in a false name.' As part of the plan, Milmo requested from a Miss Verel in B1a an Emergency Food Ration card valid for one month and 'issued in any bogus name you like', as well as sufficient clothing coupons. He added that, 'It is desired to draw the rations on the card in the Chelsea area,' as Klop had suggested. Most likely this was because the Ustinovs had a ninth-floor London flat at 904 Chelsea Cloisters, Sloane Avenue, SW7, and a ration card issued in a small village in Gloucestershire might have raised a few eyebrows. The ration card was issued under the name of 'Veronica Edwards', serial number 520460 and valid until 28 February.

On 30 January 1942 Dick White wrote to Hinchley Cooke outlining the instructions he suggested should be issued to Vera about how she should behave whilst staying with the Ustinovs:

> You are to be granted the unusual privilege of a brief change from your prison surroundings, or, to put it in another way, you are to be allowed a short holiday in the country. You must realise, however, that although you are to be released temporarily from the custody of the Prison Authorities you must regard yourself as remaining under the direction of the people to whose care you are being consigned and who are to be responsible for you.
>
> The following conditions must be implicitly observed:
>
> You must obey without question all instructions which you receive from the people to whose care you are committed.
> You must not proceed further than 50 yds. from the house where you are going to live, unless you are accompanied by or have previously obtained the express permission of, your host or hostess.
> You must not be out of doors between the hours of sunset and sunrise.
> You must not use the telephone or send or receive any written communications to anyone.
> You must not converse with any persons except with the permission of your host or hostess.
> As long as you understand these conditions you will be treated with consideration and you will find yourself among persons who are prepared to treat you kindly and who speak your language.
>
> These privileges are being accorded to you in the hope and expectation that you will show your appreciation by reviving every memory you have of the past. If you choose to do this you need not fear that any further

consequences will befall you. You need have nothing to fear and it is up to you to make the most of you unusual opportunity.[6]

The note concluded that clothing would be obtained for her by Mrs W. Gladstone, whose primary role at MI5 was to use the Ellen Hunt employment agency based in Marylebone as a front so that they could place staff in foreign embassies. According to a website, the agency had been originally established in Manchester in 1898 to provide 'domestic staff of all kinds to middle and upper-class families around London, including butlers, housekeepers, parlour-maids, footmen and cooks'. In 1901 it was listed as 'Mrs Ellen Hunt's Servants' Agency' located at 86 High Street, Marylebone [7]. However, there is no mention of their later involvement with MI5.

Vera's file contains a series of receipts for various items of clothing purchased to the tune of just over £23 (see Appendix 6) from shops in Oxford Street and Piccadilly. On 3 February Mrs Gladstone collected Vera at Aylesbury and took her to her flat at 120 Wigmore Street, where she changed into the clothes purchased for her. Later that afternoon she was taken to a hairdresser to have her hair done. On 4 February the Home Secretary duly revoked the Detention Order. After Vera and Mrs Gladstone had been shopping she was collected by 'Jock' Horsfall and Klop and driven to the Ustinovs, where she took up residence the same day.

St John Ratcliffe Stewart 'Jock' Horsfall (1910–49) was the MI5 A3 Division, transport officer who had been a pre-war racing driver. Milmo informed Airy in Bristol and Major M. Ryde in Reading, the two RSLOs who needed to know, on 6 February. The removal of Vera to Aylesbury caused the inmates in Holloway – which included My Eriksson; the Duchesse de Château-Thierry; Countess (or Baroness) Lillian Huszar; a Mrs Wertheim; a French woman named Nicolle, and Jessie Jordan [8] – to speculate whether Vera had been taken away to be hanged. It should be noted that Mrs Wertheim is not the same Louise Wertheim who had been recruited by Dierks during the First World War as she had died in Broadmoor hospital for the criminally insane in 1920. Ironically, Louise Wertheim had first been sent to Aylesbury prison before being transferred to Broadmoor.

A list of names of persons connected with Vera appeared in a report from Klop on 24 February 1942, presumably compiled during the 'experiment', and included the names of Colonel From (died 1940); Tibor Weber; Wilkinson (who it was acknowledged was impossible to identify); Paul de Hevessy [*sic*] (c.1892–?), a Hungarian diplomat and friend of Weber; Captain Vivien de Chateaubrun; Hubrich, Schultze or Schmitz; a Hungarian woman painter (who MI5 concluded was also impossible to identify); the Earl of Mayo, and Mrs Stern.

In a long letter Paul de Hevesy wrote to Allen Dulles, then head of the CIA, at Christmas 1960 he stated that the last time they had met was at the Bellevue Palace when he was an Austro-Hungarian Secretary of Legation in Bern some forty-three years before.[9] That would have made it around 1917 when Dulles had been posted there from Vienna after the US declared war on Germany on 6 April. The rest of the letter was about current world affairs. Also known as Pal de Hevesey, he became a naturalised British citizen on 12 March 1952. It appears that he was also involved with SOE as there is a file at the National Archives at Kew with his name on it.[10] Captain Vivien de Chateaubrun was Victor Vivien, Marquis de Chateaubrun (1896–1975), described in one book about the Romanovs as 'the dashing young ensign of Grenadiers'[11] (actually the Imperial Russian Grenadier Guards). In 1940 he is listed as a second lieutenant in the Rifle Brigade. A miniature set of his medals that came up for auction in October 2010 included a Military Cross and a Croix de Guerre, as well as various Imperial Russian medals.[12]

The 'Vera ERIKSON experiment', as it was referred to by Milmo, would be concluded by 16 February, whereupon Vera would be returned to Aylesbury Prison. On 14 March Petrie wrote to Sir Alexander Maxwell at the Home Office summarising the experiment:

> I understand from Miss Davies' letter W16616 of 4th February that the Home Secretary has asked to be supplied with a report upon Vera ERIKSEN's recent stay in the country, and I now attach a summary of the information which was obtained from her by her host on the occasion of her visit. I would suggest that, when no longer required, it should be burnt.
>
> We feel that we have reason to be satisfied with the experiment, which has yielded a great deal of fresh information, and has removed our uneasiness that VERA and her companions were sent here on a much more important mission than any of the other spies who fell into our hands at or about the same time.
>
> I would like to take this opportunity of expressing our appreciation of the manner in which you have co-operated with us in the planning and execution of this somewhat unorthodox course of action, which has been fully justified by the results which have been obtained.[13]

As if to corroborate the lack of importance the Germans had attached to Vera's mission, a report on that mission has this to say in conclusion:

It is now considered that we have been told substantially the whole truth by Vera, and it would seem that she and her companions were not more important than any of the other operational spies who arrived roughly at the same time. They were obviously thrown to the wolves. Doubtless the satisfaction which the directors of the German Intelligence responsible received from the venture was their ability to report to the High Command that they were dispatching spies to the United Kingdom in preparation for the invasion, which was then the practical intention of the enemy.

The unhappy feeling that Vera, DRUCKE, and WALTI arrived in this country with some particular mission, the nature of which would always remain a mystery to us, has now been removed.[14]

Milmo wrote to Miss K.G. Davies at the Home Office in reference to a new Detention Order being issued for Vera. He emphasised that MI5 was strongly opposed to sending her back to Holloway to avoid her associating with 'the very people we least desire to know anything of what has taken place' (mentioned above), but they were considering sending her to Birch Holme, Camp W on the Isle of Man.

According to Klop's biographer Peter Day, Vera had much in common with Klop's wife, Nadia, whose uncle, Alexandre Benoit, had been the artistic mentor of the World Art Movement, of which the Ballet Russes with which Vera had danced, was a part. During the time that she stayed with the Ustinovs, Klop learned more about her background, which has already been elaborated on in earlier chapters. At the end of the stay Vera was returned initially to Aylesbury. She wrote him a thank you note, which read:

Dear Klop!
I have been very happy staying with you both and I hope the time will come when we shall meet again under more normal circumstances.
Vera.[15]

It seems that a flap had blown up about an apparent immunity from prosecution offered to Vera. On 25 February, Stephens wrote a letter to Dick White informing him of a telephone conversation he had had with Hinchley Cooke in which he stated that:

Colonel Hinchley-Cooke's contention is that a jury would be affected by the statement of a prisoner that an inducement has been held out to her, notwithstanding the fact that the statement might be false. From the point of view of a prosecution the normal procedure would be to call Dr. Dearden as a witness for the Crown to give the lie direct to Vera ERICHSEN. This procedure is open to extreme objection in view of the character of Latchmere House.

Colonel Hinchley-Cooke's solution is that he should be permitted to question a prisoner magisterially between the time of apprehension by the local police and admission to Latchmere House. From his point of view there are advantages but from our point of view there are considerable disadvantages and in view of our recent arrangement that we should have a Black Maria [prison van] to fetch prisoners from the R.S.L.O.'s direct I think the whole issue should be discussed between us?[16]

The most likely explanation is that she had been offered immunity from prosecution if she became a double agent. If documents existed shedding light on this, then they have been expunged from her files before handing them over to the National Archives at Kew. Stephens also wrote to Harold Dearden the same day informing him that Hinchley Cooke had examined Vera magisterially with a view to obtaining a statement for trial at the Old Bailey. He outlined the questions put to her and her answers:

Q. Where did you get the idea to come to this country?
A. You see I would rather not answer at all really. I would rather speak with the people from the Military Internment Camp and they told me I did not need to answer any more because I told them everything.
Q. Who told you that?
A. Dr. Dearden. I do not know the other people. There was six gentlemen there. Dr. Dearden came here (Holloway Prison). He told me I would off trial [*sic*] if I told everything and that I would not be shot or hanged.
Q. I know nothing about that. Do you remember when you left Stavanger?
A. Not exactly. Sunday. It was just at night. The morning we were arrested. I was told by Dr. Dearden I would be here for the duration of the war.[17]

Stephens stressed that he did not believe that Dearden had offered Vera such an inducement, but needed him to confirm it, 'knowing Vera ERICHSEN to be a prize liar'. He went on to say that Hinchley Cooke was worried that 'the impression which would be caused by her statement true or untrue might vitiate the trial not only of ERICHSEN but of DRUEKE and WAELTI also'. He therefore suggested that Dearden should appear as a witness for the prosecution. Dearden responded immediately, refuting Stephens' allegation that he had made a deal with her:

At no time have I held out any promise to this prisoner that she would not be sent for trial, nor have I at any time promised her that she would not be shot or hanged if she were sent for trial. I have advised her on many occasions to be frank and to tell the whole truth about herself and others, on the grounds that by so doing she was doing that which was wisest in her own interests.

I give this advice as a routine practice to every prisoner but I am invariably careful to make it clear that I have no connection with the Intelligence Branch of the Service and therefore no power to do other than give friendly and disinterested advice.[18]

This was not the end of the story, however. On 10 March 1942 Klop followed up with another visit to Vera, now back in Aylesbury. The following day he wrote in his report:

You know that I had grave doubts if statements made by VERA on her private affairs were true. I even thought the name of De SCHALBURG might also be an invention. At the same time I could not rid myself of the suspicion, expressed to you before, that VERA has relatives in England. [A note adds, 'PF64884 Ernst SCHALBURG'][19]

Before, when chatting about her life in Copenhagen, VERA had narrated how she took riding lessons there at a riding school which was run by a Russian. No names were mentioned. I asked a contact of mine in London for the name of the Russian who runs the riding school in Copenhagen, and was told that it was Colonel KULI-KOOSKY (married to a Russian Grand Duchess). I also asked for the name of the Russian Minister in Copenhagen and was told that he was called Van der VLIET.

… I stressed that VERA had now 'made her peace with us' and noticed unfeigned happiness descending over VERA's anxious features. I also emphasised that she had now a chance to live up to the trust put in her by showing that she wants to collaborate loyally with the people who have shown her consideration. This really moved VERA and she was quite sincere (I believe) when she said: 'Life is not worth living for me, if it starts again with distrust. The Russians did not trust me, the Germans distrusted me the whole time and if you now start with distrusting me, then it would be much better for me to make an end of it.'

After remarking 'Let us not become melodramatic' (VERA protested against this interpretation of her thoughts and said that she was dead serious) I continued in a sterner mood …[20]

What Klop focused on next was why she was calling herself Schalburg, when Kulikowsky and Van der Vliet had never heard of it.

Nikolai Alexandrovich Kulikowsky (1881–1958) was the second husband of Grand Duchess Olga Alexandrovna Romanova of Russia (1882–1960), sister of Tsar Nicholas II, and as mentioned earlier, Vera's godmother and provider of the reference to the Duchesse de Château-Thierry. He was also a former colonel in the Blue Cuirassier Regiment of the Imperial Russian cavalry. The riding school referred to must have been when the Kulikowskys moved from the Amalienborg Palace to Holte, near Klampenburg, where he managed the stables of Gorm Rasmussen, a Danish millionaire. After the invasion of Denmark by Germany on 9 April 1940, Grand Duchess Olga was implicated in the Danes' collusion with the Germans. After the war the couple fled first to London in May 1948, where they stayed in a grace-and-favour apartment at Hampton Court Palace; a month later they travelled to Canada on the Canadian Pacific liner *Empress of Canada* and moved to Toronto. They finally settled on a 200-acre farm near Campbellville in Halton County. They both died in a five-room house at 2130 Camilla Road, in Cooksville, Ontario, now part of Mississauga, he on 11 August 1958 and she on 24 November 1960. Van der Vliet was probably Peter Van der Vliet, alias Pierre Van der Vliet, a Russian resident in Kenya who received his British Naturalisation Certificate on 23 November 1935.[21]

Vera expressed her exasperation at the suggestion that Kulikowsky claimed not to know her when he 'knows me well both as Vera de SCHALBURG and as Vera von WEDEL …' She came to the conclusion that her brother, who she referred to as Konstantin de SCHALBURG, had told Kulikowsky that something had happened to her, and that Van der Vliet had heard the same. It is curious that this entire section of Klop's report (Page 2) has the annotation 'PF64884', which is the MI5 file on Ernst Schalburg (KV2/1307), implying that there might be information within it either about Kulikowsky or Van der Vliet. Unfortunately, there is no mention of either, and some pages have been redacted or removed from the file. Klop's next question to Vera was also about why she had not told anyone that she had relatives in England, to which she replied that she had only seen Ernst two or three times before the war and he hardly knew her.

When she was finally transferred from Aylesbury she continued to keep in touch with the Ustinovs from Camp W on the Isle of Man. Clearly being able to stay with them briefly had struck the right chord. Writing as Vera von Wedel, on 14 December 1943 she wrote to Klop in Russian a somewhat plaintive letter:

Dear friend,

I have been always waiting for a letter from you, but you seem to have forgotten me that hurts me as I have grown very fond of you and [Redacted – Nadia] and as you know I have full confidence in you. I would so much like to know how you are. I have (it was some time ago) sent you greetings through Mrs Skeene, she has been working here for a time for the Home Office. But from you there is always no sign of life. Write me at least a few words, how is everything; are you still polishing your bronzes and can you still *faire la cuisine* as well as before? Did you get back the Russian books that I had asked to return to you?

I think that I have been a good girl as I had promised to you to be. Baroness Lilian Huszar with whom I had become very friendly while still at Holloway, has been recently released. I am now very lonely, she was the only woman who inspired my confidence and of whom I had grown very fond. She is now in 'Manchester', she is a very charming and a very clever girl. You may perhaps have the chance of meeting her one day. She is a Hungarian [several words illegible or missing] Write to me at [words missing] little. If possible send me some Russian and French books. As soon as I have read them I'll send them back to you. I will be very grateful to you. While my friend was still here we used to work a great deal. We have learnt how to make bags, cigarette boxes, blotters etc. We worked together with yet [?] another girl. The camp was proud of our work. There, I have boasted a little bit. The females here are awful, they gossip and they knit and sometimes, presumably out of boredom, they fight. Many of them at the moment do not want to go back to Germany and write assiduously to the Home Office requests to be set free. It is fun and it is sin all in one (a Russian expression).

Happy Christmas to you, [Redacted – Nadia] and to all who remember me, and do not think badly of me.

Your devoted,

Vera[22]

Hungarian Baroness Lilian Huszár led a very chequered life. On 11 September 1993, in an article about the escapologist and illusionist David Blaine, *The Argus* reported that in the autumn of 1952 a New Yorker named Jack Wafer, also an illusionist, actually outdid Blaine by completing a seventy-six-day fast in a Perspex box in Brighton for which Lilian Huszár had put up a £2,000 wager. Her name is also given as Lillian Maria Adler. On 17 November 1950 she became a naturalised British citizen.[23] At one time she was married to Commander Harry Pursey (1891–1980), the Labour MP for Kingston-upon-

Hull East – they were married in Trenton, New Jersey, on 11 September 1954. The *Ottawa Journal* for 22 September 1954 reported that while on honeymoon in Canada she was arrested in Montreal for trying to buy a fur coat worth £430 with counterfeit US dollar bills, and possession of $1,700 in fake bills. An article in *Der Spiegel* dated 19 January 1955 also reported the charge, claiming that she was already divorced.[24] According to the *Ottawa Journal*'s report she was forced to put up her jewellery as bail. Later she was rearrested on a charge of possession of narcotics and received a six-month sentence. The couple divorced in 1959. The *London Gazette* of 22 April 1969 listed her as deceased in the names of Lilian Huszár, Livia Huszár, and Baroness Huszár.[25] Extracts from Vera's MI5 file provide some tidbits of information about her:[26]

Report forwarded [*sic*] from S.L.O. I.O.M. re interview with HUSZAR,[27] Lilian, Hungarian, who may have been connected with espionage in this country, and who is about to make a fresh petition to the H.O. for release.

…

HUSZAR is an inseparable friend of Vera von WEDEL @ ERIKSON, who I am persuaded is not pro-German.

…

Minute to H.O. [Home Office] in connection with their file for HUSZAR, Livia Maria Kovesdy, who was at one time a drug addict, and who may have been connected with espionage in this country. She is now applying for release from internment.

A report on Vera by Mrs Gladstone of B2 gives a brief description of Huszar:

This woman is a Hungarian, and was only in Holloway a fortnight with Vera before being transferred to the Isle of Man. She was a drug addict and as she was getting no supplies was nearly crazy as a result. Vera said she was an extremely nice little thing and that she became quite friendly with her.[28]

When Lilian had been transferred to the Isle of Man she wrote Vera a letter from Birch Holm, Port Erin internment camp, on 21 January 1942:

My dearest Vera, after a long and tiring journey at last we are here. I must write to you and thank you for all your kindness. You have been so very good to me when I was ill. I feel very lonely here, and pretty miserable. Vera, my dear, you know in what a state I've been before leaving, and so I've left several things behind. My two gold combs, one blue suede shoe, etc. Could you please ask about it, or see in my cell what I have left there. There is also I think a small bottle of Eau de Cologne which I left in your room. Keep the things for the moment, and perhaps someone will come here, to whom you could give the things, or perhaps you yourself will come?

Take care of yourself, Vera, my dear, don't work too much, you know you are not very strong.

Please write to me, if you or the Officers found any of my things, and how you are, and all the others. Give my love to Olly Hirsch. With all my best wishes and thanks, Lilian.[29]

Olly Hirsch (b. 1896) is probably the son of Siegfried (*c.* 1832) and Betty Hirsch (1867-1942). Betty died at KZ Treblinka in October 1942, having been deported from Theresienstadt on 4 September 1942. Exactly what their connection was to Vera or Lilian is unclear.

★★★

When the war drew to a close there were a number of people wondering first, what to do with Vera, and second what had happened to her after she was released from prison, which still remains a mystery to this day. Vera had written several letters to Klop Ustinov and his wife Nadia in about July 1944 and various notes in her file indicate that these were being passed on to them. One note, written by J.A. Cole, dated 7 July 1944, regarding her letter at Camp WY on the Isle of Man, has a handwritten note added saying, 'This letter has been handed by me to ADDB Security [?] for forwarding to U.' It appears to have been initialed by Guy Liddell on the 12th. However, a letter from Cole dated 7 November 1944 explained:

Vera appears to be rather distressed that she has received no reply to her last two letters to Mr. [Redacted, but U added, indicating Ustinov] In writing this, I do not want it to be thought that Vera is making any complaint, as [th] is would be unfair to her. She calls to see me every fortnight, however, and I have noticed the lack of response to her communications seems to be preying on her mind. It is not my intention to suggest that she ought to receive a reply, but I thought it would be a kindness to her to mention it in case it had been overlooked.

While writing I might add that Vera does not seem to be particularly well lately. She has a rather distraught look and she complains of insomnia. The Camp clinic supplies her with a small quantity of sleeping tablets every month, but otherwise she makes no claims on the clinic's services. I gather from one of my sources that she eats very little and that she smokes incessantly. When I talked to her today her eyelids were quivering and she was obviously in a nervous condition. I do not say that there is any cause for alarm about her health but her condition does seem to me to be deteriorating.[30]

Unfortunately, none of these letters are currently in her files and appear to have been destroyed.

Milmo wrote a personal letter to Mr Noble in the War Room[31] on 20 December 1944 asking if he could 'draw the attention of our mutal friend to the attached communication which I received from the I.O. at the Isle of Man'. Their 'mutual friend' is obviously Ustinov. He added a note at the bottom saying that Noble had spoken to Ustinov, who was going to ask his wife to write back to Vera and 'will himself write after he has arrived at his destination'. At the beginning of January 1945 Milmo wrote to Major S.H. Woolf on the Isle of Man asking that he deliver to Vera 'the enclosed books and letter … from the wife of a friend'. On 25 January Vera wrote back to Nadia Benoit; her letter was passed to J.A.Cole, who sent it to Woolf. This letter must have been the one to which Milmo was referring in his note to Noble on 1 February. A handwritten note scrawled at the top indicates that the letter was sent on 2 February. A further exchange of notes between Milmo and Noble on 9 April indicates that Vera had sent another letter to the Ustinovs, and a note saying 'Done' at the top.

Cole wrote to Woolf on 20 August 1945 informing him that Vera had requested to be transferred to Holloway rather than the London Reception Centre at Canons Park because she had been told that internees had to share a room. This, she said, would make her go mad if she couldn't be alone. His report on her from Camp WY on the Isle of Man dated 22 August 1945 to B1a (only identified with the initials 'JAC' – John Alfred Cole) at the end makes interesting reading and reveals a lot about her physical and mental condition, and is worth quoting in full:

From my knowledge of Vera over the past two years, I make the following observations on her.

POLITICAL
I should not care to say that Vera had any political views in the academic sense. Her political feelings seem to arise from her experiences. She feels strongly about Russian communism and all Germans. She has the

conventional 1920ish view of Russian communism, which is understandable as she seems to live very much with her memories. When she talks of Germans it is usually with contempt. She makes against them the customary accusations of the Germanophobe – that they are cruel, that they have a slave mentality, that they have no sense of humour, and that they are immature. It must not be supposed from these remarks that she displays her prejudices frequently. It is only rarely that she mentions the world outside herself and, indeed, she seems to have very little knowledge of current events at all. Incidentally, she says she would like to stay in England, always adding 'But I don't know what they will decide to do with me.'

PHYSICAL

I am not quoting the camp medical department on this subject; Miss Pinching will understand why. In appearance Vera is often a somewhat alarming sight – an expression for which the over-worked term 'mask like' is appropriate, a white drawn face and dark lines under the eyes. When I ask her how she is she invariably replies: 'All right', adding that insomnia is her only trouble. Just now she looks as though she has not slept for a fortnight. She smokes incessantly; internees in her billet tell me that she lives on nothing but cigarettes and coffee. I am also told that she has on occasions collapsed. She is sometimes troubled by pain from the wound in her side.

EMOTIONAL

Emotionally, Vera seems to me to be nearly dead. She has a look of remoteness. She has had a few women friends in the camp, but they have told me that she hardly ever loses her reserve and they make no progress in getting to know her. I understand that she is religious and spends hours praying before a crucifix. She has kept herself fairly busy in camp occupations, and is at present – rathe[r] oddly – running the camp café. She goes regularly to camp social events, and even dances, but her face hardly ever loses its expression of remoteness.

I think all of us who have known Vera for any time feel sorry for her. She is as dead as any living person could well be. I should not like to hazard a guess as to whether she will ever recover. I think it highly improbable that she will ever have the zest for any of the colourful activities in which she has engaged in the past. Taking her as she is now, I do not think she is of any security interest to us. I make this last observation without knowing whether she is in possession of any information that might cause such an observation to be qualified.[32]

The symptoms described here suggest to this author that Vera was possibly suffering from post-traumatic stress disorder (PTSD).

On 27 August 1945 Milmo wrote to J.H. Street at the Home Office regarding the 'nationality and disposal of Vera ERIKSEN @ Vera Von WEDEL'. They suggested deporting her to Denmark 'with the five Danes for whom we are negotiating an air passage at the moment'. Based on the information about her that MI5 had on file, he added:

> There does not appear to be any good grounds for suggesting that she is Danish and I think it would obviously be rash to assert that any degree of confidence what her true nationality is. It would certainly seem more likely than not that she is German ... I would suggest that the only convenient or indeed possible disposal is to have her deported to Germany with the other German women who remain in detention at the Isle of Man. I am, however, enclosing a note on the question of Vera's nationality which you may care to consider before you make any decision on the point.[33]

That information about her nationality has already been summarised elsewhere in this book. However, the concluding paragraph notes:

> We are disposed to believe that Vera was in fact married to von WEDEL whom we know to have been a German citizen. We have no documentary proof, however, though Vera says that she once had a German passport which was subsequently deposited with the G.I.S. in Hamburg before she departed for England.[34]

20

THE MISSING SPY

So what happened to Vera, and where did she go? On 28 August 1945 Evelyn Pinching[1] in E1a/B wrote to a Miss [Redacted] in B1b informing her of Cole's note and saying that the Camp WY internees were scheduled to leave the Isle of Man on 5 September for Canons Park. With that in mind, she suggested that B1b should consider sending Vera to Holloway as she had herself requested earlier. A handwritten note at the bottom of the page from the Director-General, David Petrie, to Milmo adds, 'I understand that you have spoken to Miss Pinching and that no further action is called for. 30/8.' Milmo put on record his reasons for not taking action on the note:

1) Although all of us may feel sorry for Vera, we as an organization have no grounds for recommending to the Home Office that she should receive preferential treatment. We certainly cannot put forward any legitimate case for urging the Home Office to allow her to remain in this country.
2) If we were to recommend that Vera be permitted to stay here we could scarcely recommend that any other Alien should be deported.
3) The most we can do for Vera in my opinion is to inform the British authorities in Germany if and when she is deported, that in our view she is no longer a danger and that there is no necessity to keep her in detention.[2]

On 5 September Vera wrote to the Under-Secretary of State at the Home Office Aliens Department respectfully requesting that, since she was being transferred that day to the London Reception Centre, she be transferred instead to Holloway:

In Port Erin, as you know, we have had privacy, but I understand that there will be very little at Canons Park. While I have no wish to claim privileges not accorded to other internees, I am in a state in which I dread having to live in such close proximity to others and which I am sure will have a most detrimental effect on my health, both physical and mental. I would be grateful, therefore, if you order my removal to Holloway.[3]

On 14 September the Home Secretary in the new Attlee government, James Chuter Ede, revoked the Detention Order applying to Vera. She was one of thirteen on the Schedule for Deportation, listed as Home Office Number W16616 and the date of the original Order as 16 February 1942.

Among those wondering what had happened to her was Oberstleutnant Karl Friederich Praetorius. A preliminary CSDIC/WEA report on him dated 18 September 1945 and 1 October 1945 stated that the trio's operation was to spy on shipping, but it had not been a success on account of the almost immediate arrest of Walti and Drueke. This is strange, considering that the list found on Walti was of airfields and not ports (see Appendix 3). *Ast* Hamburg then heard nothing about Vera until the end of 1944, when they heard that she was 'ill on the ISLE OF WIGHT Internment Camp [*sic*]. I M sent her a parcel of food and nothing has been [heard of her] since.'[4] Another was Mary Huysmans, who must actually be Marie Constance Prosperine Huysman, born in Antwerp 1907 and listed on the Nominal Roll for Port Erin for 1943–44. A Postal & Telegraph Censorship form detailing the interception of two letters addressed to 'Baronne Vera von Wedel' on 12 October 1945 and 29 October 1945 from Mary Huysmans, living at 36 Avenue de la Fauche, Brussels, are summarised by the Censor as follows:

Letter (1) Dated 12.10.45. (Two letters attached)
Writer is disappointed not to have heard or had an answer to her Antwerp Card, from her friend, and reminds her of the pleasant time they had in their little canteen at Port Erin. She thinks of it, now that she herself is so forlorn and far away. What are the quarters like in the Center. Writer has heard from Jacques that he and Vera v. Wedel have the Refreshment Bar (French 'Bistro') together now, and that he is very busy, he must be, for he forgot writer's birthday, 15th Sept., the date of his letter.

The form notes that the addressee is on MI5's Watch List.[5] It is interesting that the spelling of centre is 'center', the American way. On Page 2 it goes on to say:

Reasons of health and the difficulty in getting provisions have caused writer to return to her own house in the country, from her mother's. Life in Belgium is not always easy, and she has had a lot of troubles.

Mary Huysmans' husband returned at the same time as herself. After 2½ years it was a great shock to meet again, thus, at Croydon Aerodrome. She is still separated from him, and the future alone can reveal her own fate, of which she takes no rosy view.

Letter No.2. Dated 29.10.45.

Her friend is vexed at Vera Von Wedels continued silence which can hardly be due to her being too busy. Writer would like to know her latest news and if her woman friend has been to see her. Should addressee ever come to Belgium, she hopes that she won't have forgotten her friend's address. She can hardly imagine the almost unbearable troubles she has had, for not only is everything in Belgium very expensive, but the unlucky business about her husband cuts her off from everything. She remembers the good times in Port Erin and often talks of her correspondent.

She has made some good and sympathetic friends but is so exhausted, that on some days she is incapable of seeing anyone.

Hoping she won't have to wait too long for a letter she closes with 'all the best' (in English) and signs 'Mary'.

(Exrs. Note: Vera Von Wedel alias Vera Erikssen is on the list of Repatriated Internees although still on M.I.5 Watch List A. Her name occurs once in a submission in the 1943-44 file under Carl Joachim Baroness and Baron Von Wedel. This is merely in connection with a possible contravention of Work Regulations.)[6]

On 28 November 1945 a note from BAOR gives the results of Gerhardt Dierks's interrogation about von Wedel and also a note to WRC1:

Re. the attached. I don't think that there is any doubt that they did marry and that was the root of the trouble afterwards with de Ducke [?] – but as they did not live together after their marriage Gerhard may [illegible] have been unaware of it. Incidentally, why is Gerhard called <u>Dierks</u>? I had always understood that this was von Wedel's cover name: it seems strange that it should have extended to his brother.[7]

On 9 March 1948 Joan Chenhalls in B1d at MI5 wrote to Ian Roy at the Home Office Aliens Department regarding a request sent from the War Office as to Vera's whereabouts:

… and as this woman was a civilian internee and was originally interrogated at Camp 020, we should prefer that the answer is sent through the Home Office. From our file it would seem that this woman was repatriated to Germany in

October 1945 and we made special arrangements for B.A.O.R. to keep an eye on her. Unfortunately, however, there was a muddle at the camp, and she, together with a large party of other repatriates, was given her freedom. Although search has been made for her no other trace of her has been found. We have not the details on record of the camp to which she was sent, but this most probably occurs in the Home Office papers.[8]

Ian Roy replied to Joan Chenhalls on 8 April 1948 enclosing copies of letters from Vera's uncle, Ernst Schalburg, and Lieutenant Colonel Williams and requesting more information about her whereabouts as '... her address was not given on the nominal roll of the party with whom she was repatriated'. On the same day, Roy wrote to Ernst Schalburg to say that 'the Secretary of State ... regrets he has no information other than that she left this country for Germany on 29th October, 1945.' Williams worked for the War Office, Demob.5 at 29 Chesham Place, London SW1. Roy also sent a letter to him from the Home Office enclosing a copy of Schalburg's letter and saying that, 'we know nothing about her movements after she left the United Kingdom'.

There have been many theories and assertions about what happened to Vera that have tended to muddy the waters because none of them appear to be based on any hard evidence that has been cited by the authors making them. Nor is there evidence in her heavily redacted files.

Theory 1: Vera worked for British Intelligence

Given her Russian background, it has been alleged that she may have been recruited by MI5 or MI6 to carry out Cold War spying for them. Adrian Searle suggests that because Vera had admitted to MI5 that she had worked for the GRU [*sic*] before the war in Paris, 'it is possible to construct a convincing case that, unlike Karl Drücke and Robert Petter [Walti], Vera *did* agree to work for Britain against her former employers'.[9] The trouble is, the case is *not* convincing, and there is no evidence to confirm it. Besides, Milmo of MI5 had already stated quite categorically, 'We certainly cannot put forward any legitimate case for urging the Home Office to allow her to remain in this country.' And it was *not* the GRU she may have worked for, but the GPU, two totally different entities – the GRU being Soviet (now Russian) military intelligence, the GPU a forerunner of the KGB. If Vera had agreed to work as a double agent for British Intelligence that would have meant that she could not be prosecuted, or appear in court; however, this remains unproven. In the unlikely event that Vera had been recruited by MI6, this may never become known as their archives are permanently inaccessible to researchers. The official history of MI6 written by Keith Jeffery does not mention her, and in any case, does not extend beyond 1945.

Could the following entry in Guy Liddell's post-war diaries for 30 October 1946 be a clue, and was it Vera?

> I went to see 'C' about the employment of [Redacted], who is of Russian origin. We want to take her on for Russian work. We had made every enquiry that we could and were satisfied, as far as it was possible to be so, that she was all right. I did not, however, wish it to get round that we were employing a Russian woman and were consequently insecure. If, therefore, 'C' did not like the position, on account of any opportunities which might give this woman access to his information, I would much prefer not to take her on. He said that he, in fact, had White Russians and Poles himself and that it was a risk he thought we both had to take.[10]

Intelligence historian Nigel West, however, believes that it was probably not Vera to whom Liddell was referring:

> I think it is unlikely to be either Vera or TREASURE who were of Russian origin, but not really very Russian. My impression from the context is that MI5 intended to employ full-time, as a member of the staff, a genuine Russian, rather than an occasional agent. That would certainly rule out TREASURE who had been very temperamental as a wartime agent.[11]

This would certainly make sense, as Vera had become depressed and vowed to 'get out of the racket'. Besides, MI5 would have already known whether 'she was all right', as they had run her case. TREASURE was Nathalie 'Lily' Sergueiew, born in St Petersburg in 1912 and died in 1950.[12] Exactly who it was to whom Liddell was referring is unknown. Another non-starter for Liddell's reference is Baroness Moura Budberg (1892–1974) who, although Russian, came under the suspicion of MI5 as being a possible Soviet agent.

Theory 2: Vera had a child who was adopted

Searle also claims that when Vera's files were made available by the National Archives in 2000 they revealed that she had given birth to a son in the summer of 1939, but that the child had been handed over to an orphanage in Essex.

This means during the time that she was living with the Duchesse de Château-Thierry (from March 1939 to four days after the outbreak of war). When the Duchesse was interrogated at Camp 020 on 2 November 1940 she told Maxwell Knight that Vera had given as her reason for wanting to go to Holland at the beginning of the war that she was in the 'family way', but there is nothing else in either the Duchesse's or Vera's files that elaborates on this. In fact, Vera stayed mainly with her parents at their home at 195, Avenue Paul Deschanel, Schaerbeek, a municipality in the Brussels-Capital Region of Belgium. Searle also says that the files 'revealed that Vera had asked to see her son following her arrest in 1940, and it seems the boy may have been brought from Essex to visit her'.[13] If this were true, was Dierks the father, or was it someone else? Another possible candidate could have been Major William Mackenzie, who dated Vera on a number of occasions during that time. I have been unable to find any mention of this so-called Essex orphanage in Vera's files, although it is conceivable that since Searle accessed the files they have been redacted further. Searle's own experience with O'Grady's files was that they suddenly went missing when he wished to consult them again. A search on the National Archives' website only reveals one Home Office and two Prison Commission files, but strangely, nothing from MI5.[14] No one has ever come forward claiming to be that so-called long-lost child who was sent to the orphanage in Essex, but if that child actually existed, perhaps he was never told who the parents were, a common situation in orphanage and adoption cases.

Theory 3: Vera was pregnant when she arrived in the UK

What she told M. Baker of B8l on 2 October 1940 was that 'she thought she was going to have a child and that she had been taking a lot of quinine to bring about a miscarriage'; the father of her child was Stuhreck (Dierks). Dearden reported later that afternoon that she thought she was 'to the best of her belief, six weeks pregnant' and that the father was 'her late friend STURIG' [*sic*]. He recommended that she see a gynaecologist. When Dr Matheson, the Governor of Holloway prison, but not a gynaecologist, examined her on 7 October at Holloway, he found that she had suffered a miscarriage after a pregnancy of only about six to eight weeks prior to her coming to Britain in September 1940. In direct contrast, at Dr Dearden's suggestion, in her letter to Drueke of 23 December Vera lied, telling Drueke that she was pregnant with *his* child.

Dearden had said to her, 'It is a great pity … that you had this miscarriage. If you were still pregnant it might be that DE DEEKER would do more to save your child and yourself than he is prepared at the moment to do to save you only.'

'Would it not be a good thing,' she said, 'to tell him that I am still pregnant?'

To which Dearden replied, 'If you feel like that about it … of course you must use your own discretion …'

Drueke neither confirmed nor denied that he was the father.

Theory 4: Vera had an illegitimate child by a member of the Establishment

Other speculation by Searle and Portgordon historian, the late Dr Peter Reid, states that Vera's 'complicated sex life may have been the reason she escaped prosecution and the gallows. The question was asked: had a prominent British establishment figure fathered the child born to Vera in 1939? And, if so, had this in itself been enough to save her life?' Reid adds, 'Being the mother of a British subject with perhaps an important father may have played a major part in the decision not to put her on trial.'[15] Again, where is the evidence to suggest that this was the case?

No evidence has yet emerged to prove that she was being protected from prosecution because she was carrying the baby of an important member of the Establishment. Whatever child she may or may not have been carrying at the time of her arrest was either that of her late husband von Wedel, or Drueke. No conjugal rights were provided while she was in prison, and there is no evidence that she was visited by any members of the Establishment. When members of MI5 came to interrogate her there was usually more than one person present, often two or three. The only time when this was not the case was when she met alone with Dr Harold Dearden several times. When she was examined medically by Dr Matheson it must be assumed that a woman prison warder was also present, although there is no evidence to prove it. To suggest that these meetings were anything other than for the purposes of trying to extract information from her stretches the bounds of credibility and seems highly unlikely. Therefore, this cannot be the reason.

Theory 5: Vera lived under an alias in Britain

As mentioned earlier, during her interviews with Dr Dearden, Vera was aware of O'Grady's death sentence. Searle cites letters (unreferenced) from Vera's sister-in-law Helga 'Helle' von Bülow, Christian's widow, saying that she had been in regular contact with Vera and that she had gone to live in southern England, remarried and become a grandmother, eventually dying in 1993.[16] This date is also mentioned on a website relating to Port Gordon, where it refers to, 'A number of websites indicate that she may have lived under the name de Witte and that she died in England, in 1993 but none provide clear unambiguous evidence to support this' – including the website on Port Gordon!'[17]

One suggestion that has been taken up almost as fact is that she had gone to live on the Isle of Wight. The allegation was started by Major General Arnhim Lahousen (Erwin von Lahousen, 1897–1955) when he was interviewed at Bad Nenndorf camp (No.74 CSDIC) after the war, possibly by Hinchley Cook or Stephens. Lahousen was head of *Abteiling* II and the Abwehr officer who masterminded Vera's ill-fated mission to England.

> You're wondering what happened to Vera, the beautiful spy, as we called her.
> Well, you're absolutely right. She came over to us. If you ever want to see her
> again, well I would have a look around the Isle of Wight. I think you might find
> her there – with another name of course – and nobody there has the slightest
> idea of her background.[18]

Unfortunately, there is nothing in Lahousen's MI5 file that adds to this.[19] And what did he mean when he said, 'She came over to us'? That she simply returned to Germany, or that she went to work for German intelligence after the war? The latter could not mean the Gehlen Organisation, forerunner of the BND, the *Bundesnachrichtendienst* under General Rheinhard Gehlen, as this was not established until 1946. Given her early connections with Russia, she may have been in a good position to help whoever may have recruited her, but as stated before, she didn't want to spy anymore. So was Lahousen just making mischief? His allegation is again taken up in Searle's book about the Dorothy O'Grady case when he attempts to make a tenuous connection between Vera and O'Grady because they had both been in Aylesbury Prison at one time. But there is no evidence in Vera's files that they had actually met or even shared a cell, only that Vera became aware of O'Grady's death sentence. Nor is O'Grady mentioned in any of the other inmates' files, such as the Duchesse de Château-Thierry, Mathilde Carré, Mathilde Krafft, Stella Lonsdale and My Eriksson, who were also in Aylesbury at the same time.

Another question that must be asked is, why wasn't Vera prosecuted under the Treachery Act (1940)? She had, after all, entered into an agreement with the Germans with the intent to carry out spying activities in Britain, even though she claimed that she wasn't a spy. As the Act states:

The main provision in this Bill is contained in Clause 1, which provides that the extreme penalty of death may be exacted in certain grave cases of espionage and sabotage. Under this Clause, it is an offence for any person, with intent to help the enemy, to do or attempt or conspire with any other person to do any act which is designed or likely to give assistance to the naval, military or air operations of the enemy, to impede such operations of His Majesty, or to endanger life … In each case, be it noted, the act must have been done with intent to help the enemy.[20]

Under the Treachery Act (1940) it was not necessary to prove treason, but only, as in Clause 1 of the Act, that the accused had either *committed or intended to commit* an act which would endanger life or endanger the forces of the Crown, or had *conspire[d] with any other person* [my italics]. By that definition proscribed in the Act, it would seem to prepare the way for a prosecution against Vera. Miss K.G. Davies at the Home Office wrote to Milmo on 11 October 1941 enquiring as to whether MI5 intended to prosecute Vera or whether she would remain in Holloway. Milmo wrote to Edward Cussen in B1b on 14 October for his advice, saying:

I think I know the correct answer to this one viz: (i) the lady is not being prosecuted (ii) also must remain in Holloway, but before replying I would be grateful for your observations.[21]

Cussen replied on the 16th:

I agree with you that the answers should be as you state.
The case of this woman was reported to D.P.P. and he decided not to take proceedings against her under the Treachery Act.
As to Holloway Prison, it seems much wiser to keep her there.[22]

Milmo's reply to Miss Davies on the 18th informed her of their decision not to prosecute Vera and concluded by saying, '… it is felt that since this woman is an experienced and dangerous spy there is no more suitable place [Holloway] for her to be lodged'. Frustratingly, neither MI5 nor the DPP give any reasons for their decision, nor is there any correspondence to that effect.

The only plausible reasons why Vera would not have been brought to trial are because (a) she had been 'turned' as a double agent, or (b) that there was insufficient evidence against her to guarantee a prosecution, which seems unlikely. If she had been 'turned', where is the evidence? Other double agents' files contain a plethora of information about their operations, so why not Vera's? Is there a more detailed, unredacted Masterman Report somewhere? The only possible reason why that information currently doesn't exist is because she did actually work, at least for a while, for MI5 or MI6 and that information has been redacted or destroyed from her MI5 files. If it was for MI6, then any information in their files will never come to light, at least not in our lifetimes. It would have been necessary for her to 'go off the grid', to use a modern-day expression, and disappear. Blind alleys and red herrings put about by people such as Lahousen (see above) would have helped to reinforce this deception. MI5 would have played along with this when she was apparently repatriated to Germany after the war, and conveniently information on her whereabouts was 'lost' due to the 'fog of war' or the confusion in the aftermath. Their obfuscation in the correspondence to her uncle Ernst, for example, is clearly an attempt to wash their hands of the problem. If there was any follow-up, the documentation is not there because it wasn't their problem anymore.

The Double-Cross System was established on 2 January 1941 and run by the Twenty Committee chaired by Oxford don John Cecil Masterman (later Sir John) of MI5, with 'Tar' Robertson of MI5's B1a in charge of running these double agents, and John Marriott as Secretary. The thorny issue of a spy maintaining his or her freedom in exchange for co-operation with the authorities had first arisen at a meeting at the Security Intelligence Centre (SIC)[23] on 10 September 1940. Lord Swinton,[24] Chairman of the Home Defence (Security) Executive, outlined to representatives from the Home Office, the Armed Services, GHQ Home Forces, MI5 and MI6, a procedure to which Sir Edward Tindal Atkinson, the Director of Public Prosecutions, had also agreed: an alleged spy could make a statement under caution to the police or be interrogated by MI5. If the spy chose the latter course of action, then at a later date he or she would be asked to make another statement, again under caution, which would then be used as evidence for the prosecution. MI5 would later learn on 7 October 1940 than no deals regarding a spy's life could be made without the explicit authority of Lord Swinton. A memorandum in March 1941 stated that, 'the Prime Minister has laid it down as a matter of policy that in all suitable cases spies should be brought to trial'.[25] On 17 June 1941, Swinton added:

> I have given my undertaking that any spy or enemy agent whom we no longer require … for intelligence purposes shall be brought to justice if the case against him will lie. The right man to decide any case can be brought is the DPP, and we should have the insurance of his opinion and advice in every case.[26]

In November 1941 agreement was reached after discussions between Lord Swinton, MI5, the Director of Public Prosecutions, and Sir Donald Somervell, the Attorney General, that there would be no prosecution if MI5 had already used a spy as a double agent or made any promises to him or her. The fact that such information could be revealed in open court could not be entertained under any circumstances. There were two conditions set: first, that MI5 could approach the DPP about whether it would be possible to offer some sort of inducement to the agent if prosecution would compromise security; second, MI5 would not consult the DPP if there was no prima facie case. The DPP also ruled that 'no action could be taken against non-British subjects in respect of acts committed outside the territorial jurisdiction of British courts ...'[27] A more in-depth examination of this information and how it relates to Vera's case reveals that:

1. *An alleged spy* could make a statement under caution to the police or be interrogated by MI5. If the spy chose the latter course of action, then at a later date he or she would be asked to make another statement, again under caution, which would then be used as evidence for the prosecution. Vera would have made a statement under caution to the police when she was first arrested. She was certainly interrogated by MI5 on many occasions, but was not always very co-operative. It also does not appear that she made any later statements under caution to provide evidence for either her prosecution or those of Walti and Drueke. Those statements, made by other accused spies, were usually made at New Scotland Yard. She was not even called as a witness at their trial, even though she was mentioned obliquely several times as 'the woman' by Sir William Jowitt, the Solicitor General, and also named at one point by Drueke. Her initial statement is not included in her MI5 files currently available.

2. *There would be no prosecution* if MI5 had already used a spy as a double agent or made any promises to him. There is no evidence currently available to suggest that either MI5 or MI6 had used Vera as a double agent, or that they had made some sort of deal with her. Indeed, Dr Harold Dearden had incurred the wrath of 'Tin Eye' Stephens when it appeared that he had made a deal with Vera for her freedom and then had to refute it. When Henry Hemming was researching his biography of Maxwell Knight he had not been able to find any evidence that this was so. But supposing MI5, in the form of Knight, had used Vera before the war? When she was arrested she claimed to know 'Captain King' (Knight) of the War Office, who would vouch for her. That would indeed rule out being able to charge her with anything or bringing her to trial. Could there be other MI5

files on her waiting to be released to the National Archives that would settle this claim once and for all?

3. *There were two conditions set:* first, that MI5 could approach the DPP about whether it would be possible to offer some sort of inducement to the agent if prosecution would compromise security; second, MI5 would not consult the DPP if there was no prima facie case. There is no evidence currently available to suggest that (a) MI5 had approached the DPP to offer Vera some sort of inducement instead of a prosecution. In fact, it had been vehemently denied by Dr Dearden. For security reasons, all trials under the Treachery Act were held in camera and the press were barred from reporting on the details of cases. Therefore, the reason cannot be that MI5 or the government were afraid of information leaking out; (b) There *was a prima facie case* against her: she had entered into an agreement with the Germans to act as a spy, arrived in Scotland clandestinely 'intending to commit an act which would endanger life or endanger the forces of the Crown', and had been caught almost red-handed. Admittedly, all the spy paraphernalia was in the possession of Walti and Drueke when they were arrested, and not her, although at one point she had tried to claim that a suitcase was hers, not Drueke's; (c) She had also been infiltrated into Britain prior to the war to collect intelligence. That in itself could not have resulted in a charge under the Treachery Act because it had been committed prior to its becoming law in 1940 and she had not entered the country illegally, but it should have resulted in something more than just internment under Defence Regulation 18B.

One document gives Vera's death as 'about 1993', although it does not clarify where or when this occurred; the website *NobleCircles* also gives her death as 1993 in England, but annoyingly does not give any specific details either.[28] Both of these references would make her age as 100 years old, which while not impossible, seems unlikely under the circumstances, and must be discounted as incorrect in light of a more recent development.[29]

In a final footnote to her story, a death certificate has emerged from *Ancestry* showing that Vera von Wedel (Eriksen) died on 8 February 1946 at Marien hospital (Marienkrankenhaus) in Hamburg of pneumonia and heart failure. Her address, given as the Klopstock Pension on Klopstockstraße 2 is, coincidently, where the Abwehr trained its spies destined for England between 1940 and 1941; the names of her parents and husband (deceased) are given as unknown.[30] But how did she come to have the Klopstockstraße address in Hamburg?

Vera's death allegedly from pneumonia and heart failure in itself seems plausible. When she was released from prison in 1945 her health was not good. She had been very depressed – caused initially one would imagine by post-partum depression from the miscarriage; then the knowledge that her lover Drueke had been executed; and finally the fact that her past life had been a mess and her future was uncertain. According to Dr Dearden she had been living 'on nothing but cigarettes and coffee'. That and the meagre diet that would have been available back in post-war Germany could have contributed to her heart failure. . In fact it has been confirmed by Danish journalist Kirstine Kloster Andersen that Vera did die in 1946 as stated on the death certificate:

> Ernst Bodo von Zitzewitz paid for her funeral and her grave, which actually existed in Hamburg until 1971. He also stayed at the Pension Klopstock at the time of her death. (8th February 1946). She was buried the 13th February at 8.30 in the morning. He paid in total 82,50 Reichsmark for her funeral including flowers, music, the grave. [31]

A case study in *History & Policy* published in 2014 reported that even though there were fears of a tuberculosis epidemic in post-war Germany, those fears were unwarranted; nor were there any cases of hunger oedema as a result of famine, even though food supplies were scarce and continued to be a major problem; in 1946 calorie levels in the British Zone were reduced to 1,000 a day. [32] A study by the University of Munich in *Review of Economics and Statistics*, also published in 2014, indicated that post-Second World War nearly 6 per cent of the population of a war-torn country had experienced depression. [33] But without a full picture of Vera's medical history it is impossible to say whether she had been genetically predisposed to a heart condition or how much of these criteria were a direct cause of her death. If this is indeed her death certificate, and there is no reason to suspect otherwise, all other assertions made about her future must be discounted. But if one were to play devil's advocate – by suggesting that the death certificate is a fake – then it would play into the deception that Vera had vanished forever, perhaps to reappear as someone else. [34]

In conclusion, we will probably never know who the real Vera was, who she became in later life, or if she even survived for very long after the war. As noted at the beginning of this story, her whole life was something of a mystery, the secret of which was best known only to herself. Perhaps she always wanted it that way. Certainly she never attempted to dissuade people from believing whatever they wanted to about her. It suited her to be enigmatic – and that is the way she will remain. She was, as stated at the beginning, '… a riddle, wrapped in a mystery, inside an enigma'.

COMPARISON NOTES TO UHLIG DOCUMENTS HO45/23787 REDACTED 7 PAGES

Redacted Uhlig documents (HO45/23787)		Chateau-Thierry files	
Redacted text	Page	Missing text	Page/File
Uhlig's ration book will be delivered to the St Marylebone Post Office. [redacted]	1	Uhlig's ration book will be delivered to the St Marylebone Post Office. Uhlig shares a flat with Miss Winifred Elwine Mary DAVIS, British, who was present when the premises were searched by virtue of a search warrant issued under Defence Regulation 88A. The warrant, in duplicate, duly endorsed, is submitted herewith. The flat is also used occasionally by Miss K.M. WALSHE, nurse in Middlesex Hospital and also LLEWELLYN, friends of Miss Davis, and they have a quantity of clothing etc. stored there.	p.4 KV2/357-3
'…into touch with Mrs. Eriksson and to show the letters to [redacted]	2	'…into touch with Mrs. Eriksson and to show the letters to BARBARA'	p.5 KV2/357-3
[redacted] 'Vera de SCHALLBURG who stayed with the Duchesse de Chateau Thierry before the war'	2	The persons mentioned by her are Noel WILSON, now Countess of MAYO [some words redacted] She has not seen the Countess for several months and believes she is now in Scotland.	p.5 KV2/357-3
[redacted]	2	A man named HUBBARD, believed to be American, age about 20, who is connected with the U.S.A. Woolworths.	p.5 KV2/357-3
[Approx. 14 lines redacted]	3	See below ★	p.6 KV2/357-3

██████████ will move to the Mont Blanc'	4	'Captain DIXON will move to the Mont Blanc'	p.59 KV2/357-2
'If you phone ████ I suppose he would not be able to meet ██████ ,'	4	'If you phone Wolffie I suppose he would not be able to meet DUWELL'	p.60 KV2/357-2
'████████ suggested meeting him …'	4	'DUWELL suggested meeting him …'	p.60 KV2/357-2
'Ask ████ to write me dear.'	4	'Ask Wolffie to write me dear.'	p.60 KV2/357-2
████████████████	4	'His phone is in the mornings or evenings Molesey 2272 after 12 ocl. Mansion House 1316 (Netherland Chamber of Commerce) but Molesey is the best for private conversation.'	p.60 KV2/357-2
'I am terribly busy with correspond-ence re ████ '	4	'I am terribly busy with correspond-ence re DUWELL'	p.60 KV2/357-2
'It can either be ██████ (ask her whether she knows him) or Mrs ██████ or Mrs. ERIKSSON …'	5	'It can either be BARBARA (ask her whether she knows him) or Mrs HO[OD] or Mrs. ERIKSSON …'	p.60 KV2/357-2
'Dick is very agitated and fears it be a trap laid by ██████ '	5	'Dick is very agitated and fears it be a trap laid by DUWELL'	p.60 KV2/357-2
'You could ask Mrs. Eriksson to tea at ██████ if she is <u>interested</u>.'	5	'You could ask Mrs. Eriksson to tea at Barbara's if she is <u>interested</u>.'	p.60 KV2/357-2
'If you have cashed ██████ cheque dear you better send it.'	5	'If you have cashed Barbara's cheque dear you better send it.'	p.61 KV2/357-2
'I am not sure whether ██████ naturalised Dutch.'	5	'I am not sure whether DUWELL naturalised Dutch.'	p.61 KV2/357-2
'Had a nice letter from de ██████ '	6	'Had a nice letter from de BOURG'	p.61 KV2/357-2
'… and that liar ██████ will meet me …'	6	'… and that liar DUWELL will meet me …'	p.61 KV2/357-2
'P.S. Let ████ send this letter. Tell ████ all about it! Had a letter from ██████ wishing to make me <u>interesting</u>! proposition …'	6	'P.S. Let Barbara read this letter. Tell Barbara all about it! Had a letter from Dr. HENRY wishing to make me <u>interesting</u>! proposition …'	p.61 KV2/357-2
'██████ will put it in a bank …'	6	'DUWELL will put it in a bank …'	p.62 KV2/357-2
'What does ██████ think of ██ ██████ idea? No use at all I think, and I have not heard either. ██████ sent £5.'	7	'What does Barbara think of Dr. HENRY's idea? No use at all I think, and I have not heard either. Mrs. CHARRINGTON sent £5.'	p.62 KV2/357-2
'P.S.S. (Page 1) Show this to ██████ '	7	'P.S.S. (Page 1) Show this to Barbara'	p.62 KV2/357-2
'SAMSTAG 16 UHR FRANKFURT – ██████ '	7	'SAMSTAG 16 UHR FRANKFURT – DUWELL'	p.62 KV2/357-2

'Sorry you don't understand the affairs of ██████ Reinhardt etc. To put it briefly – a very small amount will come to me – ██████ sold his wife's house …'	7	'Sorry you don't understand the affairs of DUWELL Reinhardt etc. To put it briefly – a very small amount will come to me – DUWELL sold his wife's house …'	p.63 KV2/357-2
'… when this money is deposited by ██████ for me'	7	'… when this money is deposited by DUWELL for me'	p.63 KV2/357-2
'I thought ██████ could arrange …'	7	'I thought Dr. HENRY could arrange …'	p.63 KV2/357-2
'… for the sister-in-law ██████ ██████ but she is away now for six weeks and ██████ never saw her.'	7	'… for the sister-in-law DR. KASTELLAU but she is away now for six weeks and Barbara never saw her.'	p.63 KV2/357-2
'Now read the enclosed letter dear and see ██████ '	7	'Now read the enclosed letter dear and see Dr. HENRY'	p.63 KV2/357-2
'I wrote ██████ with this post …'	8	'I wrote Henry with this post …'	p.63 KV2/357-2
'I have intimated to ██████'	8	'I have intimated to Henry'	p.63 KV2/357-2
'(where Gamages used to be) about ██████ address …'	8	'(where Gamages used to be) about Arnold CHEVALLIER's address …'	p.64 KV2/357-2
'… country address of his ██████ ██████ Maidenhead	8	'… country address of his "Ripley", Woodlands Park, Maidenhead	pp.11,64 KV2/357-2
'Why I want ██████ address …'	8	'Why I want Chevallier's address …'	p.64 KV2/357-2
'… in London and ██████ told me'	8	'… in London and Chevallier told me'	p.64 KV2/357-2
'██████ did ask me …'	8	'Chevallier did ask me …'	p.64 KV2/357-2
'… those Jew people of ██████ '	8	'… those Jew people of Dr. Henry's'	p.64 KV2/357-2
'If I tell ██████ or anybody …'	8	'If I tell Henry or anybody …'	p.64 KV2/357-2
'██████ ██████ ██████ ██████ whom he wishes to introduce into London society'	9	from Dr. F. Henry which states that Henry is going to visit Mme de Froberville in the near future. The letter chiefly concerns a friend of Mr. Henrys' whom he wishes to introduce into London society'	p.12 KV2/357-3
'he is a friend of ██████ ██████ and various government officials at the Board of Trade. ██████ concludes the letter by suggesting that UHLIG or ██████ ██████ meet him informally'	9	'he is a friend of Mr. Hore-Belisha, Mr. Herbert Samuel and various government officials at the Board of Trade. Dr. Henry concludes the letter by suggesting that UHLIG or Mme de Froberville meet him informally'	p.12 KV2/357-3
'I had a good letter from ██████ '	9	'I had a good letter from Duwell'	p.64 KV2/357-2

'… do this bit of work re ███ '	9	'… do this bit of work re Henry'	p.64 KV2/357-2
'with that clever lunatic ███ '	9	'with that clever lunatic Chevallier'	p.64 KV2/357-2
'Just a line dear to say that I heard today from ███	9	'Just a line dear to say that I heard today from Chevallier'	p.65 KV2/357-2
'… and trust that I have ███ address'	9	'… and trust that I have Chevallier's address'	p.65 KV2/357-2
'Enclosed letter from ███ '	9	'Enclosed letter from Dr. Henry'	p.65 KV2/357-2
'… and ask for ███ as I believe …'	9	'… and ask for Dr. F. Henry as I believe …'	p.65 KV2/357-2
'The letter from ███ '	9	'The letter from Dr. Henry'	p.12 KV2/357-3
'A weird letter from ███ '	10	'A weird letter from Henry'	p.65 KV2/357-2
'███ or what not and I will take the commission.'	10	'Lady Cl or Lady T or what not and I will take the commission.'	p.65 KV2/357-2
'… so I am speaking to ███ ███ […]'	10	'… so I am speaking to Henry'	p.65 KV2/357-2
'The 2,000 marks should be in the Bank at Cologne soon after Sept. 1st ███ tells me'	10	'The 2,000 marks should be in the Bank at Cologne soon after Sept. 1st Duwell tells me'	p.13 KV2/357-3
'and letters from ███ are opened by State'	10	'and letters from Duwell are opened by State'	p.13 KV2/357-3
'that rotten humbug ███ ███ '	10	'that rotten humbug Frank BUCHMANN'	p.65 KV2/357-2
Did you read in the Sunday Express some time ago – ███ ███ ███ '	10	Did you read in the Sunday Express some time ago – how <u>Oxford</u> absolutely objects to F.B. calling his rotten show the "Oxford Group"?	p.65 KV2/357-2
'I had a weird letter today from ███ ███ '	10	'I had a weird letter today from Mrs. Henry'	p.65 KV2/357-2
Page 11 OK			
'How lovely of ███ '	12	'How lovely of Mary'	p.67 KV2/357-2
No.26. c/o ███ ███ Jan 18th 1939 Contains nothing of interest beyond the address.	12	c/o Mrs Duwell, 1c, Wilhelminenstrasse, Wiesbaden Jan 18th 1939. Contains nothing of interest beyond the address.	p.13 KV2/357-3
No.27. ███ ███ Jan 29th Back of Page 1…	12	No.27. c/o Mrs. de Froberville, 46, Chiltern Court, N.W.1. Jan 29th Back of Page 1 …	p.13 KV2/357-3

	12	'Winifred E.M. DAVIS, with whom	p.15
		UHLIG shared the flat, is employed	KV2/357-3
		as a clerk by the A.R.P., Middlesex	
		Hospital Annex, Cleveland Street W.1.	
		The telephone number is Welbeck	
		7100. Miss Davis was very helpful	
		and is prepared to give all possible	
▓▓▓▓▓▓She says she		assistance in this matter. She says she	
knows Uhlig very intimately and in		knows Uhlig very intimately and in	
her opinion Uhlig had nothing to do		her opinion Uhlig had nothing to do	
with her mother's affairs.'		with her mother's affairs.'	
'There is no trace of UHLIG @	13	'There is no trace of UHLIG @	p.16
CURTIS and ▓▓▓▓▓▓ in		CURTIS and Miss (?) DAVIS in	KV2/357-3
Special Branch Registry'		Special Branch Registry'	

★14 lines redacted from p.3 of Uhlig (HO45/23787) but included in Chateau-Thierry (KV2/357-3):

'That's Major AYERS' and after a little thought qualified it by saying 'No it couldn't be him because he must be 36 at least.'

She met or had heard of a man named HENRY, 'some kind of foreigner who was called "Doctor"'.

Philip de FROBERVILLE and wife Barbara. She has known them for many years and last met Barbara de Froberville in Paris. They reside in Chilton Court and he is now an officer in the R.A.F. The Duchesse 'looked after' Barbara until her marriage and Uhlig believes her mother 'arranged it' as she had several matrimonial schemes on hand at that time.

She had heard of Madame ALIVENTI. Later, on the way to Holloway Prison, Uhlig said she had just recalled the fact that some two years ago she had been hired to drive a Madame ALIVENTI or TALIVENTI to Sandown Races. She was a peculiar woman, very mean, and she (Uhlig) had heard she had disappeared. This was the only occasion she had met her.

She met Herr von RINTELIN, a former German agent, in the U.S.A. at one of her mother's parties.

Identification of names mentioned

Name	Identity	Reference(s): Vera Eriksen MS
BARBARA	Mrs Barbara de Froberville	pp. 64, 76, 86
Miss Winifred Elwina Mary DAVIS	Miss Winifred Elwina Mary Davis	p. 74
Miss K.M. WALSHE	Unidentified	
Mrs HOOD	Unidentified	
Capt. DIXON	Unidentified. Possibly Tom Dixon, BUF interned under DR18b	
DUWELL	William Duwell, brother-in-law of Countess de C–T	pp. 75, 76, 86, 87,
Mrs DUWELL	Ellen Duwell, stepsister of C–T	pp. 134, 135
Frank BUCHMANN	Dr or Rev Franklin Nathaniel Daniel Buchman (1878–1961)	Christian evangelist and founder of Oxford Group
Mrs de Froberville	Mrs Barbara de Froberville	pp. 64, 76,
Dr. KASTELLAU	Sister-in-law of Dr Henry	p. 26, KV2/357-2
Dr HENRY/HENRY	Dr Frederick Henry	pp. 64, 76, 86, 89
MARY	Most likely Mary Huysmans (Marie Constance Prosperine Huysman)	pp. 166, 167
CHEVALLIER	Arnold Louis Chevallier	pp. 63, 64, 65, 66, 77, 90
Lady Cl	Lady Clancarty – Diana Le Poer Trench *née* Younger (1919–1999) m. to William Francis Brinsley Le Poer Trench, 8th Earl of Clancarty	

Lady T	Lady Townshend – possibly Elizabeth Pamela Audrey Luby (d.1989), m. to Lord Townshend, later Marquess of Townshend, or Gwladys Ethel Gwendolen Eugénie Sutherst (1884–1959), Marchioness of Townshend m. to 6th Marquess of Townshend	
de BOURG	Unidentified	
Noël WILSON, Countess of Mayo	Noël Jessie Bourke Haliburton *née* Wilson	p. 64
HUBBARD	Possibly Anthony Hubbard, Woolworths heir. Unconfirmed	
Mrs CHARRINGTON	Possibly Elinor Mary Charrington OBE, *née* Baggalay, V-P Burton Divn. British Red Cross Society, b.1865, m.1886 Maj. Hugh Spencer Charrington, of Dovecliff Hall, Burton-upon-Trent. Unconfirmed	
Wolffie	'WOLFFIE is the man who used to be the honorary secretary of the Netherland Chamber of Commerce. He died last year.'[1939]	KV2/85, p. 23

APPENDIX 2

ANALYSIS OF VERA'S HANDWRITING

(TNA KV2/15)

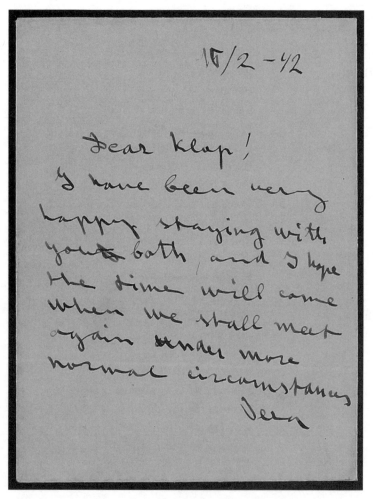

I have an <u>unpleasant feeling</u> with this handwriting.

The writer (woman) is a cold and calculating person.

Easy youth, good upbringing, education (culture) medium.

Certain doubtless existing talents were never developed because of <u>too little energy</u> and diligence.

Very selfish, a hard person, who feels <u>lost (lonely)</u> and <u>not happy</u> in her present situation.

She has great worries about a person close to her.

A great many social lies, even during the writing of the material in front of me there was some mental reservations. Has a great deal of interest, perhaps too much, in other people's affairs and often judges strangers too harshly.

Very easily offended pride, sufficient vanity.

Has had a great erotic disappointment.

On the whole very indolent, and lazy, in spite of occasional flickering of energy.

Cool, calculating, as mentioned above.

APPENDIX 3

ANNOTATED LIST OF AIRFIELDS FOUND IN THE POSSESSION OF WERNER WALTI

Author's italics. Information applies to units stationed there listed in order at that time, 1939–41. All bases are in Lincolnshire, Norfolk, Suffolk and Essex on the east coast of England.

Most Secret

1. GRIMSBY Bomber satellite aerodrome under construction (Previously civil airport) *(Established as Bomber Command 5 Group (RAFVR 25 Elementary and Reserve Flying Training School); satellite for RAF Binbrook; as of 1941 under 1 Group.)*

2. MANLEY [sic] Air Armament School *(should be Manby; No. 1 Air Armament School, 1AAS)*

3. LOUTH Nearest town to Manley

4. HEMSWELL Bomber Station *(61 Squadron)*

5. SCAMPTON Bomber Station *(5 Group:, 49; 83 Squadrons)*

6. WADDINGTON Bomber Station *(44; 50 Squadrons)*

7. DIGBY Fighter Station *(46; 611; 229 Squadrons; 29 Squadron; 222 Squadron)*

8. CRANWELL Training Station *(RAF College)*

9. SUTTON BRIDGE Fighter Station *(266; 19 Squadrons; 6 OTU)*

10. BIRCHAM NEWTON Coastal Command Station *(206; 220; 221; 229 Squadrons)*

11. WEST RAYNHAM Bomber Station *(101 Squadron)*

12. MARHAM Bomber Station *(115 Squadron)*

13. NORWICH Bomber Group H.Q.? *no group HQ; could refer to Horsham St. Faith 2 miles from Norwich*

14. WATTON Bomber Station *(82 Squadron)*

15. FELTWELL Bomber Station *(37; 57; 75; 214 Squadrons)*

16. IPSWICH Bomber Station *(known as RAF Nacton; could also be RAF Raydon)*

17. MARTLESHAM HEATH Fighter Station *(part of 11 Group, Fighter Command: 242; 71(Eagle) Squadron)*

18. NEWMARKET Bomber Station *(99; 107; 138 Squadrons)*

19. MILDENHALL Bomber Station

20. /24 CAMBRIDGE Training Station

21. HONINGTON Bomber Station *(IX; 311 (Czech) Squadrons)*

22. BURY ST. EDMONDS [sic] Army Co-operation Command aerodrome *(not listed as such; in use by USAAF 8th Air Force 1942–)*

23. STRADISHALL Bomber Station *(Many squadrons including 214 Squadron)*

24. HALSTEAD not identified *(could be RAF Ridgewell; unlikely to be Fort Halstead, a 'Y' Station)*★

25. BASSINGBOURN Bomber Station *(11 OTU; 215 Squadron)*

26. ELMDON Training Station *(RAF Training Command)*

27. /29 COLCHESTER no R.A.F. significance *(Army: 4th Infantry Division)*

28. HENLOW Depot *(assembly plant for Hurricanes)*

29. CHIGWELL Balloon Centre *(No.4 Balloon Centre)*

30. STAG LANE Factory aerodrome

31. FELIXSTOWE Flying boat base – also Naval motor boats

32. HARWICH Balloons

★Fort Halstead was in Kent and therefore out of the range of the other bases covered.

For more information see also: http://www.rafweb.org/Stations/Stations-H. htm; https://en.wikipedia.org/wiki/List_of_former_Royal_Air_Force_stations

APPENDIX 4

MAPS FOUND IN THE POSSESSION OF WERNER WALTI

1. German Map of Eastern Highlands of Scotland, Sheet no.5. 'Aviation Edition'. Scale 1 to 250,000. Numbered in pencil on back 24126.
2. Elgin in two parts. Sheet No.14. Map marks in coloured chalk. Scale, 1 to 100,000.
3. Aberdeen. Sheet No.15. (Aberdeen via Kinnaird's Head to Banff). Scale, 1 to 100,000. Marks in coloured chalk.
4. Map of Sutherland, Caithness, Ross & Cromarty, as far south as Loch Maree. Scale, 1 to 253,440 (4 miles to inch).
5. German map of Norwich and greater part of Norfolk. Sheet No.19. Scale 1 to 100,000.
6. Wisbech, King's Lynn. No.65.
7. Peterboro and surrounding country. No.64.
8. Bedford and surrounding country. No.84.
9. Cambridge and surrounding country. No.85.
10. Bury St Edmunds and greater part of Suffolk. No.86.

Note: Other documentation states it was eleven maps.

APPENDIX 5

AGENTS DESPATCHED TO OR CONTROLLED IN THE UK, BY RITTER

Number	Name	Details	TNA Reference
1.	SIMON	@ 3505 Herman Walter Christian Simon @ Carl Petter Wilhelm Andersson	KV2/1293
2.	ESCHBORN	'Charlie case'	KV2/454; HO396/19/259
3.	BELGIAN HOMOSEXUAL		
4.	WHEELER-HILL		
5.	My ERIKSSON		KV2/535-539
6.	Duchesse de CHATEAU-THIERRY		KV2/357-358
7.	Vera von SCHALBURG	@ Vera ERICHSEN	KV2/14-16
8.	Mrs DARGEL	Editha Ilsa Hilda Dargel	KV2/916
9.	JAKOBS	Josef Jakobs	KV2/24-27; WO32/18144
10.	[Redacted]	SUMMER. Identified by PF 53123. Goësta Caroli	KV2/60
11.	DRÜCKE		KV2/18-19; KV2/1701-06
12	KELLER @ WAELTI		KV2/17
13.	KRÖPFE		
14.	ROSE	See Chapter 11	KV2/532

EXPENSES FOR VERA ERIKSON

Item	Coupons	Cost		
		£	s.	d.
Coat	18	4	14	6
Dress	7	1	0	0
Etam	35	4	9	7
Slippers	5		6	11
Cardigan	5]	1	19	6
Jumper	5]			
2 pairs of shoes	10	3	0	0
Skirt	6		18	11
Camiknickers	3		11	9
Scarf	1		4	11
12 Handkerchiefs		3	10	4
Suitcase			18	9
Bag			15	11
Miscellaneous		2	17	2½
	98	22	8	3½
Expenses		1	0	0
		23	8	3½

Coupons advanced, 200   102 returned herewith
Cash advanced, £35   £11.11.8½. returned herewith

B.2. (London)
W. Gladstone

4.2.42

Specifically,

2 pairs of shoes from *Dolcis*, 350 Oxford Street (size 4½) at £1.7s.6d and £1.12s.6d.

1 cardigan and 1 jumper from *Herd & Walker*, 173-174-196 Piccadilly at £1.1s.0d and 18s.6d.

1 dress from *Selfridges*, Oxford Street at £1.

1 cardigan from *Selfridges*, Oxford Street at 6s.11d

1 pair slippers at 6s.11d

1 coat from *Penberthys*, Oxford Street at £4.14s.6d.

Lingerie from *Etam*, 488 Oxford Street to a total of £4.9s.7d

1 skirt from *Selfridges*, Oxford Street at 18s.11d

1 bag from *Penberthys*, Oxford Street at 15s.11d

1 pair cami knickers from *Selfridges*, Oxford Street at 11s.9d

1 scarf at 4s.11d

12 handkerchiefs at 10s.4d

1 suitcase at 18s.9d

LISTS OF PERSONS KNOWN TO VERA ERIKSON OR NAMED BY HER (FROM KV2/15)

k = known; n = named.
Author's italics.

A. Persons known to be members of German Intelligence Service

1. Ahlers, Captain (Hauptman) (k)
    Hamburg
    Very smart and exclusive. Was first, at Hamburg Station, to call Vera 'Frau Erikson'.
2. Braun, Captain (Hauptman) (k)
3. Bruhms, Captain (Hauptman) (k)
    Temporarily attached to Service. In Luftwaffe.
4. Buerkner, Captain (Hauptman) (n)
    High up in Service, works close to Admiral Canaris in Berlin.
5. Canaris, Admiral (n)
    Berlin, Chief of the Service.
    Of Greek origin, according to Frau Lieder (IVg). Small, dark, very clever
6. Fischer, Dr. Egon (k)
    His real name:.......mann (Vera cannot remember, says You have got name)
    Works mostly in Holland. Also connections with Belgium and Switzerland. Less important that Rantzau.
7. Fritsch or Fritsche, Dr. (k)
    Vera met him with Dr. Egon Fischer in Hamburg.
8. Hoffmann, Captain (Hauptman) (k)
    Stationed in Cherbourg. Vera met him in Brussels. 'Fat Idiot'.
9. Kayser, Dr. (k)

Vera met him in Hamburg with Rantzau. He spoke Swedish. Maintained contact with Sweden and Swedes.

10. Krause, Dr. (k)

An Austro-Italian, probably from Trieste. Small. Southern appearance. Vera met him in Brussels with Vladimir Orloff, when Krause was on his way to London.

11. Krueger, Dr. (k)

Hamburg.

Temporarily attached. Said of himself, that he had no relation with 'Nachrichtendienst'. Said further, that he was formerly at German Embassy in London and that he left England with personal [*sic*] of German Embassy when war started. He spoke of Tibor Weber (IVc) as 'Damned little double-crosser'. Very tall, thin, spectacles, several gold front teeth, long face, hollow cheeks. Dark hair. Spoke good English. Drunk a great deal but never drunk.

12. Krueger the photographer. (k)

In Rantzau's office at 'Oberkommando' in Hamburg where he taught Vera photography before she left for England in 1939.

13. Lueders, Dr. (n)

Nazi agent and spy in Denmark. Friend of Danish Nazi, Wending Christensen [*sic*], who fled from Denmark when his contact with Lueders became known. Friend and collaborator of Rantzau.

14. Mueller, Dr. (k)

'Little Anderson' (IVb), who worked under him, said that Mueller works only 'semi-officially'.

15. Rantzau (k)

Oberkommando, Hamburg.

Other name: Dr. Rencken, Hansen, Dr. Reinhardt. One of his addresses in Hamburg: Rotenbaumchaussee 83. Duchesse de Chateu Thierry knew him as Dr. Reinhardt. Vera knew him as Hansen or Dr. Rencken. Married to a German Baroness. Travelled extensively between Berlin, Hamburg, Brussels, Spain. When Vera departed in September 1940, was supposed to proceed to Spain.

16. 'Russian' in Oberkommando (n)

Vera does not know him, but has heard of him.

17. Schneider (k)

Worked in Hamburg with Rantzau. Unimportant, middle aged, short, square.

18. <u>Sommer</u> (k)
    In office of Oberkommando in Hamburg.
19. <u>Wedel</u>, Hans Friederich von. (k) Vera's husband
    Other names: Dr. zum Stuhreck, Oberleutnant Dierks
    Addresses:
    Hamburg: Pappenhutenstrasse 1 [*sic*]
    Amsterdam: Mej. Sophie Kruse, Prinsengracht No.?
    Antwerp: Rue de l'Etoile 26
    Brussels: 193 Avenue Paul Dechamel, Schaerbeck
    Died September 1940 in motor car smash
    For rest see IIc 1.

b. Persons working for German Intelligence Service

1. <u>Anderson</u>, Captain. (k) Norwegian captain of boat which made vain
    attempt to reach Shetland from Bergen.
2. <u>Anderson</u>, (k)
    Brother of above named.
3. <u>Anderson</u>, (k) ('Fat Anderson')
    Connected with a circus and theatres in Oslo. Simple man.
4. <u>Anderson</u>, (k) ('Little Anderson')
    A German who spoke Norwegian.
5. <u>Beck-Hansen</u>, Hans (k)
    Vera met him in German Legation in Kopenhagen December 1938 or
    January 1939, when she applied for extension of her visa. A German
    Legation secretary, who had been en poste in Russia, was married to a
    Russian woman and spoke Russian, introduced Beck-Hansen to Vera.
    Vera suspects that the purpose was to keep her under observation. Beck-
    Hansen got on well with Vera and even 'fell in love'. The two dined several
    times together and confided in each other. Beck-Hansen said that he was a
    naval officer and that his mother was Spanish. He spoke Spanish and went
    often to Spain. He knew Canaris and disliked the Germans. Vera suggests
    Beck-Hansen as a man to establish contact with. If he should be in Spain
    at present, a word from her might pave the way.

c. Persons belonging to circle of Duchesse de Chateau Thierry suspected of working for German Intelligence Service

1. Chateau Thierry, Duchesse de (k)
   Dorset House, London (See IIc 2)
   Duchess [*sic*], according to Vera kept a note book in which she meticulously entered all her contacts and addresses. Vera assumes that this notebook is in the hands of British.

2. Erikson, Mia [*sic*] (k)
   Vera saw her only once at Duchess when Mia Erikson bought a fur coat from the Duchess. Next meeting at Holloway.

3. From, Colonel (n)
   A Russian in London whose name was given to Vera by Rantzau as a person who 'may be useful' to her. On arrival in London Vera found that From had died.

4. Wilkinson (k)
   A fairhaired [*sic*] young Englishman who turned up one day in 1939 at the flat of the Duchesse de Chateau Thierry without leaving his address. Rantzau said of him that he gets a great deal from him for the £25 he pays him monthly. This remark was made in a fit of anger, because of the poor crop of information the Duchess was yielding, to whom Rantzau claimed to have paid £600.

5. Weber, Tibor (k)
   Hungarian, connected with Press matters at Hungarian Legation, London. Described by Dr. Krueger as 'a damned little double crosser'.

6. Wood, John (?) (n)
   'Inventor' in London. Vera assumes that Rantzau gave the Duchess this man's name, as Duchess spoke about Wood after her return from Holland, where she had met Rantzau. Duchess wrote to Wood. Vera does not know if Wood called at Dorset House. Duchess expected his visit. Vera never saw Wood.

d. Persons in touch with individuals mentioned under IV c

1. Chateaubrun, Captain Vivien de (k)
   Russian in London. Interested in commission on the sale of inventions.

2. Hevessy, Paul de (k)
   Hungarian ex-diplomat. Old friend of Tibor Weber.

3. Hubrich (k)

Hungarian in London. Vera met him at exhibition of Hungarian woman painter called Schultz or Schmitz. (hunchback) Hubrich was introduced to Vera by Tibor Weber. Vera met Hubrich several times after.

4. 'Hungarian' (k)

A little man in London who was connected with the 'Polish Count's' invention, which the Duchess tried to sell.

5. 'Jones' (k)

A Chinaman in London. Friend of the Polish Count and his wife. Wanted to sell 'Polish Count's' invention to War Office. Tried to do it through Earl of Mayo.

6. Mayo, Earl of (k)

Peverted Peer in London. See Chinaman 'Jones' above.

7. 'Polish Count' and wife (k)

Couple was brought to Duchess by From's widow, who later committed suicide. Polish Countess ran Beauty Salon in Jermyn Street. Speciality: Turtle Oil.

8. Schultz or Schmitz (k)

See: IV3.

9. Stern, Mrs (k)

American woman living in Chiltern Court who knew Tibor Weber and Hubrich.

e. Persons mentioned by members of the German Intelligence Service

1. Makaroff, widow of Admiral (n)

Paris. Dr. Egon Fischer was interested in her.

2. Petersen, Natasha (n)

Russian wife of Mr. Cayzer of British Legation in Brussels.
Dr. Egon Fischer was interested if Vladimir Orloff knew her. Natasha de Petersen's father lived in Amsterdam.

3. Rueter, Dr.

Vera heard his name in Rantzau's circle.

f. Persons belonging to circle of Duchesse de Chateau Thierry not associated by Vera with German Intelligence Service

1. Ayre, Captain Freddy and wife (k)

2. Bansky, Dr. (k)

Vera consulted him for a minor complaint. Went to dinner with him at the Ivy.

3. Chevalier. (k) Inventor
4. Froberville, Barbara de and husband (k)
5. Mackenzie, Major (k) 39 Bruton Place.
    A 'flirt' of Vera's 1939 in London. No affair.
6. Martin, Jane (k)
    American woman in love with Major Mackenzie.

g. Relatives, friends and acquaintances of Vera Erikson, not connected by her with Intelligence work.

1. Bergmann, von (k)
    A friend of von Wedel.
2. Buelow, von
    A Danish woman of this name is married to Vera's brother Constantine de Schalbourg. A sister of Constantin's [*sic*] wife is Frau Lieder, Kaiserallee Berlin, a great friend of Canaris and Buerkner.
3. Chervachnidze, Prince (k)
    Paris. Vera danced with him. Probably the Montecarlo [*sic*] gigolo. Vera showed some interest in his and his wife's whereabouts.
4. Guehl, Richard (k)
    Hamburg. A friend of von Wedel. Businessman, age 60, big white moustache.
5. Heyden, Doric (k) [*Count Doric Heyden*]
    Balt, connected with motor racing, possibly for Benz or Mercedes. His wife, a Danish woman had a dress shop in South Audley (?) Street, London called 'Irene'. Heyden came several times to London. Travelled all over Continent.
6. Lieder, Frau (k)
    (see IV g 2)
7. Najivin (k)
    A Russian writer, friend of Valdimir Orloff. [*possibly Ivan Fedorovich Najivin, 1874–1940*]

APPENDIX 8

JOURNEY TO SCOTLAND

(KV2/15)

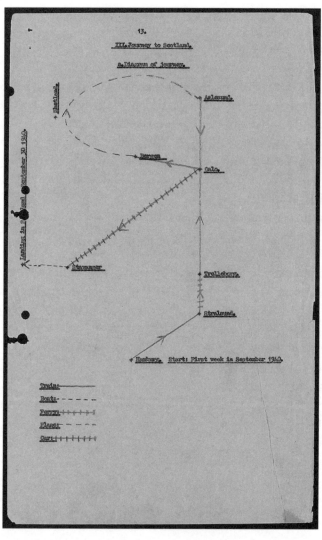

NOTES

Introduction

1. Shakespeare, William, *Two Gentlemen of Verona*, Act 4, Scene 2: Who is Silvia, what is she?
2. Searle, Adrian. *The Spy Beside the Sea* (Stroud: The History Press, 2012), p.143.
3. Ritter, Nikolaus, *Deckname Dr. Rantzau* (Hamburg: Hoffman und Campe, 1972).

Chapter 1. A Mystery Unfolds

1. Day, Peter. *Klop: Britain's Most Ingenious Secret Agent* (London: Biteback, 2014), p.142.
2. See: Kluiters, F.A.C. & E. Verkoeyen, *Abwehr Officer Hilmar Dierks (1889–1940) and His Agents*; http://www.nisa-intelligence.nl/PDF-bestanden/Dierks.pdf; http://www.westervoort1940.nl/AST_Hamburg.html
3. TNA KV2/15: In the Minute Sheet Register for PF53988, vol.2 (her personal file), the relevant page listing the date and author of the report are blank, having been redacted in November 1998. At the top of the page are the initials MK 93–96, for serials (documents) of those numbers. MK probably stands for Maxwell Knight who had interrogated her on a number of occasions. Part of the actual report also appears to be missing.
4. TNA KV2/15.
5. https://www.abendblatt.de/politik/deutschland/article107315818/Wohin-fuehren-Vera-Schalburgs-Spuren.html
6. Farago, Ladislas, *The Game of Foxes* (New York: David McKay Company Inc., 1971), p.248.
7. Moon, Tom, *Loyal and Lethal Ladies of Espionage* (San José: iUnverse.com, Inc, 2000) p.129.
8. Kahn, David, *Hitler's Spies. German Military Intelligence in World War II* (London: Hodder & Stoughton, 1978), p.353.
9. TNA KV2/15.
10. See: Københavns Stadsarkiv (Copenhagen State Archives): http://www.politi-etsregisterblade.dk/component/sfup/index.php?option=com_sfup&controller=politregisterblade&task=viewRegisterbladImage&id=2474147&backside=1&tmpl=component
11. http://www.myerichsen.net/p258.html

12. ibid.

13. TNA KV2/15.

14. This may have been Dr Ivan Joseph Martin Osiier (1888–1965), the Danish Olympic fencer, who had boycotted the 1936 Berlin Olympics.

15. TNA KV2/15. From 1944 to 45 Vagn Holm (1914–2005) was attached to Danforce, the Danish Brigade in Sweden. In May 1945 he was attached to 4 Squadron, 8403 Disarmament Wing, as liaison officer at Beldringe Airfield an Funen. In 1952 he was appointed Oberstleujtnant (Lieutenant Colonel).

16. Hume, Lucy (ed), *Debrett's People of Today 2017* (London: Debrett's Ltd, 2017), p.2036.

17. https://www.geni.com/people/Helga-Helle/6000000037306933984

18. 'Gestapo Agents in Copenhagen' in: *X-2 Manual. Denmark. March 15, 1944*, p.43: Declassified by the CIA 2001, 2007. https://ia801307.us.archive.org/33/items/GERMANINTELLIGENCESERVICEWWIIVOL1-0002/GERMAN%20INTELLIGENCE%20SERVICE%20(WWII),%20%20VOL.%201_0002.pdf

19. http://www.myerichsen.net/p258.html

20. These crosses are extremely rare and fetch around US$2,500 at auction.

21. Founded in Paris in 1917 by Vera Trefilova (1875–1945).

22. TNA KV2/15.

23. http://www.suche-im-dunkeln.de/_die_Story/_die_story.html and follow link to letter: Ein aktueller Brief aus 2001, der 84 jährigen Schwägerin Veras, der dem Verfasser vorliegt, beschriebt diese Zeit: mehr Infos

24. James, Clive, *Cultural Amnesia. Necessary Memories from History and the Arts* (London: Macmillan; New York: W.W. Norton & Sons, 2007), p.169.

25. TNA KV2/282.

26. Farago, op.cit., p.249.

27. ibid., p.249.

28. Simpson, A.W. Brian, *In the Highest Degree Odious: Detention without Trial in Wartime Britain* (Oxford: Oxford University Press, 1984), p.57, n.45.

29. TNA KV2/15.

30. Farago, op.cit., p.243.

31. TNA KV2/357.

32. According to his entry in the National Archives at Kew, Horst Gustav Friederich Pflugk-Hartnung (1889–1967) was a former German intelligence chief in Denmark. In 1938 he was captured after involvement in illicit activity. This time he was found to be running an espionage network spying on British shipping movements into and out of the Baltic. The Danes rolled up the entire organisation. Secret Intelligence Service reports of the time, on file KV 2/2643, 1931–1946, complain at the inadequacy of their information on the case, as they had to rely on newspaper reports. Pflug-Hartnung's history is summarised at serial 59a. Pflug-Hartnung was released in Germany in November 1947. See: TNA KV2/2643; KV2/2644; and GFM 33/2111/4764.

33. TNA KV2/14. Millicent Jessie Eleanor Bagot, CBE (1907–2006), who worked for MI5 and MI6.

34. http://website.lineone.net/~stephaniebidmead/russian_refugees.htm

35. TNA KV2/14.

Chapter 2. The Red Menace

1. West, Nigel & Oleg Tsarev, *The Crown Jewels: The British Secrets at the Heart of the KGB Archives* (London: Harper Collins, 1999), p.115.
2. Glading was involved in the Woolwich Arsenal spy ring case in 1938.
3. TNA KV2/1242.
4. TNA KV2/1009.
5. Duff, William E., *A Time for Spies. Theodore Stephanovich Maly and the Era of the Great Illegals* (Nashville & London: Vanderbilt University Press, 1999), p.46.
6. TNA KV2/1242.
7. TNA KV2/1241.
8. TNA KV2/1241.
9. TNA KV2/1241.
10. TNA FO371/94904.
11. Volodarsky, Boris, *Stalin's Agent. The Life and Death of Alexander Orlov* (Oxford: OUP, 2015), p.695, note 73.
12. Burke, David, *The Spy Who Came in from the Co-op* (Woodbridge: Boydell Press, 2008), p.74. See also Burke, David, *The Lawn Road Flats* (Woodbridge: Boydell Press, 2014), pp.96–8; 224.
13. TNA KV2/1241.
14. TNA KV2/14.
15. Macintyre, Ben, *For Your Eyes Only: Ian Fleming & James Bond* (London: Bloomsbury, 2009), pp.58; 142. Fleming had met Dunderdale in 1940. See also: Harling, Robert, *Ian Fleming. A Personal Memoir* (London: Robson Press/ Biteback, 2015), p.323.
16. TNA KV2/1008; KV2/809.
17. TNA KV2/815 and KV2/816.
18. TNA KV2/810-813, KV2/1388.
19. TNA KV2/1008.
20. TNA KV2/1008.
21. Yakov Isaakovitch Serebyansky (1892–1956) was head of the international department (INO) of the OGPU in 1929.
22. Andrew, Christopher & Vasili Mitrokin, *The Sword and the Shield. The Mitrokin Archive and the Secret History of the KGB* (New York: Basic Books, 1999), p.79.
23. TNA KV2/2389.
24. West, Nigel, *Mortal Crimes* (New York: Enigma Books, 2004), p.215.
25. TNA KV2/2389.
26. Trenear-Harvey, Glenmore S., *Historical Dictionary of Atomic Espionage* (Lanham, MD: Scarecrow Press, 2011), p.7.
27. TNA KV2/2389.
28. West, *Mortal Crimes*, p.214.
29. Duff, op.cit., p.164.
30. Krivitsky, W.G., *In Stalin's Secret Service* (New York: Harper & Brothers, 1939), 3rd edition, p.262.
31. West, *Mortal Crimes*, p.214–215.
32. Weissman, Susan, *Victor Serge. A Biography* (New York: Verso, 2013).
33. TNA KV2/1008.

34. TNA KV2/2389.
35. TNA KV2/2389.
36. Benson, Robert Louis & Michael Warner (eds), *VENONA. Soviet Espionage and the American Response 1939–1957* (Washington DC: National Security Agency & Central Intelligence Agency, 1996), No.41, New York 847B-848 to Moscow, 15 June 1944, p.295.
37. Sudoplatov, Pavel & Anatoli Sudoplatov, with Jerrold L. & Leona P. Schecter, *Special Tasks* (London: Little, Brown & Company, 1994), p.47. See also: Trenear-Harvey, Glenmore, *Historical Dictionary of Atomic Espionage* (Lanham, MD: Scarecrow Press, 2011), pp.7–8.
38. David Ainslie, the agent for the flat in Marylebone Road.
39. TNA KV2/1008.
40. TNA KV2/1008.
41. The Brandes were Romanian/Canadian working for the Soviets and involved with the Percy Glading case. See: TNA KV2/1004, KV2/1005, KV2/1006, and KV2/1007.
42. Kern, Gary, *A Death in Washington; Walter G. Krivitsky and the Stalin Terror* (New York: Enigma Books, 2004), p.282, and TNA KV2/802.
43. Robinson, Curtis B., *Caught Red Starred: The Woolwich Spy-Ring and Stalin's Naval Rearmament on the Eve of War* (Bloomington, IN: Xlibris Corporation, 2011), p.66.
44. West & Tsarev, op.cit., p.121.
45. KGB Archives, File MANN, No.9705, Vol.1, pp.239–40.
46. Costello, John & Oleg Tsarev, *Deadly Illusions* (London: Century, 1993), p.207.
47. Nikolai Ivanovich Yezhov or Ezhov (1895–1940), head of the NKVD from 1936–38; executed in 1940.
48. Genrikh Grigoreyvich Yagoda (1891–1938), head of the NKVD from 1934–36; executed in 1938.
49. TNA KV2/804.
50. http://spartacus-educational.com/Theodore_Mally.htm
51. TNA KV2/2887.
52. TNA KV2/1009. Konstantin Mikhail Basov born as Jan Ābeltiņš in Latvia on 25 September 1896 (some sources say 1897) and died 1 June 1964. He became a naturalised American citizen in 1931: Volodarsky, Boris. *Stalin's Agent: The Life and Death of Alexander Orlov* (Oxford: Oxford University Press, 2015), p.528. For more on Bassoff see: TNA KV2/2888 and KV2/2889, and https://www.myheritage.com/research/collection-10024/us-naturalization-records?itemId=547187-&action=showRecord
53. TNA KV2/1009.
54. For more information on Krivitsky see: Quinlan, Kevin, *The Secret War Between the Wars. MI5 in the 1920s and 1930s* (Woodbridge: Boydell Press, 2014), Ch.6, pp.139 –78; West, Nigel, *Mask. MI5's Penetration of the Communist Party of Great Britain* (Abingdon: Routledge, 2005), Ch.5, pp. 200–14; and: KV2/802, KV2/803, KV2/803 and KV2/804.
55. Goulden, Joseph C., A Washington Suicide?': *Washington Times*, Saturday August 9, 2003, http://www.washingtontimes.com/news/2003/aug/9/20030809-

110425-9559r/ reviewing Kern, Gary, *A Death in Washington. Walter Krivitsky and the Stalin Terror* (New York: Enigma Books, 2008).

56. TNA KV2/805.
57. As yet, the exact details of her family have not been determined. There was a Count Nikolai Osten-Sacken Dimitrievitch, Russian Ambassador in Berlin 1895–1912, who may be connected.
58. TNA KV2/14.
59. TNA KV2/14.
60. Smith, Douglas, *Rasputin* (London: Pan, 2017), paperback edition, p.631.
61. Milton, Giles, *Russian Roulette. How British Spies Defeated Lenin* (London: Sceptre, 2014), paperback edition, pp.100–1.
62. TNA KV2/14.
63. TNA KV2/14.
64. TNA KV2/15.
65. TNA KV2/15.
66. TNA KV2/15.
67. TNA KV2/15.
68. TNA KV2/15.
69. http://www.suche-im-dunkeln.de/_Familie/_familie.html
70. http://www.suche-im-dunkeln.de/_Familie/_familie.html
71. TNA KV2/802.
72. TNA KV2/16.
73. TNA KV2/357.
74. TNA KV2/357.
75. Alltools was responsible for making some parts for the De Havilland Mosquito. The other directors were Francis S. Gentle and Captain Victor Ramsden. See: http://www.gracesguide.co.uk/Alltools; *Flight* magazine, 17 November 1938, p.465.
76. A William Herbert Mackenzie is listed as being in the Royal Flying Corps: http://www.airhistory.org.uk/rfc/people_indexM.html
The National Archives at Kew also lists a William Herbert Mackenzie as being in the Royal Naval Air Service (RNAS) on p. 58 of the *Royal Naval Air Service, Register of Officers' Services*: ADM/273/8/58; his service number was 37671-37967. It is possible that when the RFC and RNAS amalgamated in 1918 to form the RAF that he transferred and thus held an Army rank. Further source appear to confirm his identity – see http://rcafassociation.ca/uploads/airforce/2009/07/gong-6m-n.html; *London Gazette*, 3 June 1919;
London Gazette, 24 October 1919; http://nauticapedia.ca/dbase/Query/Biolist3.php?&name=Mackenzie%2C%20William%20Herbert&id=29319&Page=26&input=1

Chapter 3. The Importance of Being Ernst

1. As well as TNA KV2/1307 see also: Calder, Angus, *The People's War. Britain 1939–1945* (London: Pimlico, 1969), p.381, reprinted 2008.
2. TNA KV2/1307. Entries dated 20.10.41, 21.10.41
3. 1897–1976. TNA KV2/3329, KV2/3330 and ADM340/136/22. A Devon hotel proprietor, he masqueraded as a naval officer (Temporary Sub Lieutenant).

1915–18 he is listed as a Midshipman, RNR on the crew list of the RMS *Arlanza* listed then as HMS *Arlanza* assigned to 10th Cruiser Squadron Northern Patrol, North Russia, North Atlantic Convoys which sailed from Liverpool mainly to the coast of Iceland: http://www.naval-history.net/OWShips-WW1-08-HMS_Arlanza.htm; he had formerly served on HMS *Excellent*. He was a member of the BUF and came to the attention of MI5 in 1938. He is listed as being one of the BUF detainees on the Isle of Man, based on a Home Office Suspect File (SF), under Defence Regulation 18B: https://www.oswaldmosley.com/downloads/18b%20Detainees%20List.pdf; See also: *London Gazette*, 27 August 1940, p.5256.

4. TNA KV2/1307.
5. TNA KV2/1307.
6. TNA KV2/1307.
7. See: West, Nigel, *MI6. British Secret Intelligence Service Operations 1909–45* (London: Weidenfeld & Nicolson, 1983), p.ix.

Chapter 4. Recruitment

1. Hart, Derek, *The Secret of the Dragon's Claw, Book Three*, (New York and Bloomington: iUniverse Inc., 2010), p.27.
2. http://www.undiscoveredscotland.co.uk/usbiography/e/veraeriksen.html
3. TNA KV2/14. A declassified CIA file, *Denmark. X-2 Handbook, March 15, 1944*, p.12, lists an Ove Børresen as being an Abwehr agent. Jørgen Børresen was mentioned by Guy Liddell in his wartime diaries as having been 'broken' by MI5 and as having been captured and brought to England on 18 September 1940: West, Nigel (ed), *The Guy Liddell Diaries, Vol.1, 1939–1942* (London: Routledge, 2005), p.109.
4. In TNA KV2/14.
5. TNA KV2/3306.
6. TNA KV2/14.
7. Counterintelligence War Room London. War Room Publication. Bibliography of the G.I.S. Central Intelligence Agency, declassified 2001 and 2007, p.7.
8. 'Gruppe VI F was the technical section of Amt VI and was broadly responsible for the provision of technical material for the use of Laendergruppen, and also for the supervision of W/T for the Amt.' Secret report from the Counterintelligence War Room London. Amt VI of the RSHA. Gruppe VI F. CIA document declassified in 2001 and 2007, p.2.
9. An article about Värnet's work appears in: http://www.petertatchell.net/international/denmark/vaernetbook.htm
10. TNA KV2/3306.
11. TNA KV2/3306.
12. TNA KV2/3306.
13. TNA KV2/3306.
14. TNA KV2/15.
15. West, Nigel & Madoc Roberts, *SNOW. The Double Life of a World War II Spy* (London: Biteback, 2011), p.186. There is also an Ove Borresen listed in Denmark X-2 Handbook, March 15, 1944, p.11, declassified CIA file

(2001;2007). See also: West, Nigel (ed), *The Guy Liddell Diaries, Vol. 1, 1939–1942* (London: Routledge, 2005), p.109.

16. TNA KV2/281.

17. TNA KV2/282.

18. http://numbers-stations.com/cia/German%20Intelligence%20Service%20 %28wwii%29%2C%20%20Vol.%203/GERMAN%20INTELLIGENCE%20 SERVICE%20%28WWII%29%2C%20%20VOL.%203_0001.pdf

19. Walter Arthur Speck, recruited by the Abwehr in 1939, worked mainly in Lyon. See: TNA KV2/2748. Listed in an OSS report: Headquarters 7707 Military Intelligence Service Center APO 757 US Army, CI Intermediate Interrogation Report (CI-IIR) No.57, pp.2; 8; 9; 11; 19; 22; 29; 31; 41; 42; 43; 49; 54: Speck, Dr. Walter @ Wallis, Lt, MK Rennes.

20. OSS/X2 decrypt. See *Counterintelligence in World War II*, Frank J. Rafalko (ed.), (National Counterintelligence Center),vol.2. Also referenced in: MacPherson, Nelson, *American Intelligence in Wartime London: The Story of the OSS* (London: Frank Cass, 2003).

21. TNA KV2/281.

22. https://www.cia.gov/library/readingroom/docs/OSS%20-%20SSU%20-%20 CIG%20EARLY%20CIA%20DOCUMENTS%20%20%20VOL.%201_0007.pdf

23. He is listed as head Abwehr official in Switzerland in: Petersen, Neal H. (ed), *From Hitler's Doorstep: The Wartime Intelligence Reports of Allen Dulles 1942–45* (Pennsylvania: Pennsylvania State University Press, 1996), p.558.

24. Gisevius, Hans Bernd, *Valkyrie: An Insider's Account of the Plot to Kill Hitler* (Boston: Da Capo Press, 2009), p.5.

25. Macintyre, Ben, *Agent Zigzag* (London: Bloomsbury, 2007), p. 251; Booth, Nicolas, *Zigzag* (New York: Arcade Publishing, 2007), pp.238–9; https://www. cia.gov/library/readingroom/docs/OSS%20-%20SSU%20-%20CIG%20 EARLY%20CIA%20DOCUMENTS%20%20%20VOL.%201_0007.pdf; The National Archives at Kew only lists an MI5 file on Udo Wilhelm Bogislav von Bonin (KV2/1973) and as being posted to Paris and Angers in 1940, and Oslo in 1942–43. An article in *Der Spiegel* on 21 November 1966 gives his name as Bagislaw von Bonin and his rank as colonel, so it must be a relative.

26. http://archivesnantes1941.blogspot.ca/2014/03/1941-12-08-abwehr-angers.html; http://secondbysecondworldwar.com/?p=4731; see also: http://www.nizkor. org/hweb/imt/tgmwc/tgmwc-05/tgmwc-05-42-05.shtml

27. http://www.executedtoday.com/2011/10/22/1941-forty-eight-french-hostages/

28. TNA KV2/14.

29. TNA KV2/756. Graham may be Graham Greene or Graham Maingot.

30. Verhoyen, Etienne, *Spionnen aan de achterdeur; der Duitse Abwehr in België 1936–1945* (Antwerp; Appeldoorn: Maklu, 2011), p.29. Lips and Moll were both in I H (Heer/Army) of *Ast* Hamburg.

31. TNA KV2/756.

32. PF 53998 [*sic*] – should be PF 53988/KV2/14.

33. TNA KV2/756.

34. TNA KV2/88.

35. Verhoyen, op.cit., p.30.

36. https://www.joodsmonument.nl/en/page/190047/leo-harry-abas

37. Listed as an agent for Hamburg Abwehr Stelle, 1939–40: www.westervoort1940. nl/AST_Hamburg.html&prev=search; See also: TNA KV2/14.

38. 'Leo Harry Abbas was geen slachtoffer' ('Leo Harry Abbas was no victim'): https://www.joodsmonument.nl/nl/page/548313/leo-harry-abas-was-geen-slachtoffer

See also: Kluiters, F.A.C & Verhoeyen, E. 'An International Man of Mystery. Abwehr Officer Hilmar G.J. Dierks (1889–1940) and His Agents'.

39. Translated from an entry in a duty report of the Amsterdam police for 25 September 1941, © Archief. Amsterdam Politierapporten 40-45/NL-SAA-19952875 EVOPR00110000191. I am grateful to Peter Miebies for providing me with this information and the translation.

40. Nachtrag sur Veränderungenaldung von.29 Januar 1944. Nameliche Aufstellung der 56 Neuzugänge (Addendum to charges. Roll List of 56 new arrivals). A Leopold Busch is listed in the Holocaust and Victims Database of the United States Holocaust Memorial Museum, Washington, DC; however his date of birth is given as 11 January 1891.

41. TNA KV2/3297.

42. TNA KV2/103.

43. TNA KV2/3297.

44. A Baron de Graevenitz is listed as an assistant secretary at the Fourth International Prison Congress, St Petersburg, held between 15 and 25 June 1890. There is also a Baron Graevenitz listed as a Counsellor of State, Russian Ministry of Foreign Affairs in 1900. This would be Georges Ludwig Alexandrovich Graeveniz, (1857–1939); Foreign Office files (FO 65/1653–54; FO 65/1635) on *M. de Stael, Baron de Graevenitz, M.Poklewski-Koziell. Diplomatic* dated 1901 are available from the National Archives; Another Baron Graevenitz is Peter Nicholas Alexander Charles (d.1943) listed in the England & Wales, National Probabte Calendar (Index of Wills and Administrations), 1858–1966, 1973–95.

45. There is an Arthur Emile Bay listed in *Allemands recherchés* JB (AA 1312) prepared by the Belgian Sûreté de l'État, 6 July 1996, although no details are given of his affiliation. An MI6 CX report states that Bay was a Swiss journalist, living in the Avenue Brugmann 39, Brussels.

46. Coudenys, Wim, 'A Life Between Fact and Fiction: The History of Vladimir G. Orlov', in: *Revolutionary Russia* (Abingdon: Taylor & Francis), Vol.21, No.2, December 2008, pp.179–202.

47. ibid., p.187.

48. See: *Who's Who in Nazi Germany*, London, c. 1944, p.54; CIA copy declassified in 2001 and 2007.

49. Lt Col Ulrich Fleischauer (1876–1960), influential publisher of anti-Semitic propaganda; also mentioned as 'an agent of the *Weltdienst*, an anti-Jewish press agency supported by the Nazi party in Erfurt [the HQ]' in Marrus, Michael Robert & Robert O. Paxton, *Vichy France and the Jews* (Stanford, CA: Stanford University Press, 1981), p.284.

50. Prince Anton Vasil'evich Turkul (1892–1957), an Army general in tsarist Russia, later in the White Russian Army. He was also an MI6 agent for Charles

Howard 'Dick' Ellis and formed with Claudius Voss the Narodnyi Trudovoy Suyuz (NTS), a Russian emigré group. During WW2 he was part of the Max-Klatt (Richard Kauder) spy network channeling Russian disinformation to the Germans. See: https://www.cia.gov/library/center-for-the-study-of-intelligence/kent-csi/vol37no4/html/v37i4a07p_0001.htm; https://www.cia.gov/library/center-for-the-study-of-intelligence/kent-csi/vol37no4/pdf/v37i4a07p.pdf; TNA KV2/1591–1593.

51. Bunyan, Tony, *The History and Practice of the Political Police in Britain* (London: Quartet, 1977), p.159: 'The two forgers in Berlin were Alexis Bellegarde and Alexander Gumansky who were both members of an exiled White Russian organization, the Brotherhood of St. George.' Strangely, in Gill Bennett's definitive study of the Zinoviev Letter, *'A most extraordinary and mysterious business. The Zinoviev Letter of 1924'*. Foreign & Commonwealth Office History Notes, No.14, January 1999, she makes no mention of Gumansky.

52. TNA KV2/14. Hubert Renfro Knickerbocker (1898–1949), American journalist and author who reported from Berlin 1923–33 but was deported when Hitler came to power.

53. West & Tsarev, *The Crown Jewels*, pp. 33–6; 38; 39–40; 41.

54. TNA KV2/14.

55. TNA KV2/14.

56. TNA KV2/15.

57. Booth, op.cit., p.262.

58. The Hotel Lutétia, the Paris headquarters of the Abwehr in the Second World War.

59. MacIntyre, *Agent Zigzag*, p.261.

60. TNA KV2/1729.

61. TNA KV2/1727.

62. TNA KV2/961.

63. Heino Hans Lips @ Dr Luders @ Dr Lorenz head of 1 H (1 Heer/Army) *Ast* Hamburg. See: TNA KV2/756.

64. http://www.myerichsen.net/p258.html

65. Boghardt, T, *Spies of the Kaiser. German Covert Operation in Great Britain during the First World War Era* (Basingstoke: Palgrave Macmillan, 2004); See also: West, Nigel (ed), *MI5 in the Great War* (London: Biteback, 2014), Ch.III, pp.189–360; Appendix I, pp.426–30. For information on Jannsen see: Hennessey, Thomas & Clair Thomas, *Spooks. The Unofficial History of MI5, From M to Miss X 1909–1939* (Stroud: Amberley, 2010), pp.78–80; Cook, Andrew, *M. MI5's First Spymaster* (Stroud: The History Press, eBook 2011); Sellers, Leonard, *Shot in the Tower* (Barnsley: Pen & Sword Military, 2015), paperback edition, pp.64–79; Morton, James, *Spies of the First World War* (Kew: The National Archives, 2010), pp.112–13; Northcott, Chris, *MI5 at War 1909–1918* (Ticehurst: Tattered Flag, 2015), pp.146–9, 234, 237. For information on Buschmann see: Hennessey & Thomas, op.cit., pp.84–6; Sellers, op.cit., pp.106–39; Morton, op.cit., p.114; Northcott, op.cit., pp.135,164; For information on Dierks see: Morton, op.cit., pp.112-15; Hennessey & Thomas, op.cit., pp.77–78; Northcott, op.cit., pp.134–5,146–8, 150, 159, 173, 176, 234; For information on Roos see: Sellers, op.cit., pp.66–79; Hennessey & Thomas, op.cit.,78–80; Northcott, op.cit.,146–9, 234, 237.

66. TNA KV2/14.
67. TNA KV2/756, Hans Lips. Report to Dick White from Felix Cowgill, signed by Rodney Dennys, MI6, section VB3, dated 22 November 1940.
68. TNA KV2/14.
69. TNA KV2/91.
70. TNA KV2/88.
71. TNA KV2/88.
72. Kluiters & Verhoyen, op.cit., p.6.
73. Abw 04-Vooroologse spionage in en vanuit Nederland I (Pre-war espionage in and from the Netherlands I), p.29, n.344.
74. TNA KV2/2133.
75. For more information see: Beeby, Dean, *Cargo of Lies. The True Story of a Nazi Double Agent in Canada* (Toronto: University of Toronto Press, 1996).
76.. TNA KV2/14.
77. TNA KV2/15.
78. TNA KV2/15.
79. TNA KV2/15.
80. TNA KV2/15.

Chapter 5. Vera and the Duchesse

1. HO45/23787. A seven-page letter and another one-page document (HO45/23787/1) cannot be accessed until 2023 under FOIA exemption sect.40. However, my FOIA request filed in January 2017 was approved; in July 2017 I received a heavily redacted version of the pages. I discovered that all the information on those pages was identical to that in KV2/357 regarding Anna Sonia, Duchesse de Château-Thierry in unredacted form; see Appendix 1 for comparison.
2. West, Nigel, *Historical Dictionary of Sexpionage* (Lanham, MD: Scarecrow Press, 2009) p.52.
3. TNA KV2/358.
4. *London Gazette*, 23 January, p.573.
5. For a contemporary account and discussion of DR18B see: Aldred, Guy & John Wynn, *It Might Have Happened to You* (London: Black House Publishing, 2012). Aldred (1886–1963) was an Anarchist Communist.
6. TNA KV2/357.
7. TNA KV2/15.
8. Stephens, Robin; Oliver Hoare (ed), *Camp 020. MI5 and the Nazi Spies* (London: Public Record Office, 2000), p.146.
9. TNA KV2/15.
10. TNA KV2/15.
11. This may have been Otto Krueger (Krüger) who had been recruited by SIS in 1919, who was betrayed by John William 'Jack' Hooper. Also described as a retired German naval officer. See: Richelson, Jeffery T., *A Century of Spies: Intelligence in the Twentieth Century* (New York: Oxford University Press, 1995), p.83.
12. TNA KV2/535.
13. TNA KV2/535.

14. TNA KV2/357.
15. Farago, op.cit., p.251.
16. TNA KV2/536.
17. The Hon. Mrs Frederick Cripps was Violet Mary Geraldine *née* Nelson (1891–1983), ex-wife of the Duke of Westminster, who married Col The Hon. Frederick Heyworth Cripps, DSO and bar (1885–1977), brother of Sir Stafford Cripps, on 8 October 1927, who became 3rd Baron Parmoor on 12 March 1977. They were divorced in 1951.
18. TNA KV2/1293.
19. TNA KV2/1293 and TNA/KV2/88. The final interrogation report on Oblt Nikolaus Fritz Adolf Ritter @ Dr. Norbert RANTZAU @ Dr. RENKEN @ Dr. Wolfgang JANSEN @ The DOCTOR @ REINHARDT, dated 16.1.46. forwarded by IB C.C.G. (B) E Bad Oeyenhausen, under reference IB/B3PF.539 dated 24.1.46, a copy of which is in Simon's MI5 file (TNA KV2/1293), states that he was first contacted by Ritter at the Seemannsheim (Seaman's home) in the autumn of 1937.
20. TNA KV2/1293.
21. PF 45152, unfortunately not available from the National Archives, Kew.
22. No.1 Balloon Centre, 901, 902, 903 (County of London), Squadrons, Royal Auxiliary Air Force (R.Aux.A.F.)
23. TNA KV2/1293.
24. TNA KV2/535.
25. TNA KV2/1293.
26. TNA KV2/1293.
27. Krafft had supplied Agent SNOW with funds in 1939. See: TNA KV2/701-706; HO144/3618 is closed until 2025. The file on SNOW is KV2/444.
28. TNA KV2/392.
29. For more information on Dargel see: TNA KV2/916.
30. TNA KV2/535.
31. TNA KV2/357.
32. TNA KV2/88.
33. TNA KV2/357.
34. TNA KV2/14.
35. TNA KV2/14.
36. TNA KV2/357.
37. Jessie Jordan (1887–1954) was a Scottish hairdresser arrested on 2 March 1938 and found guilty in 1939 of espionage; in May 1939 she was sentenced to four years' imprisonment. See: TNA KV2/193-194; KV2/3532-3534; KV2/3421 (Guenther Gustav Marie Rumrich @ Gustav Rumrich).
38. TNA KV2/358.

Chapter 6. A Taste of Freedom?

1. TNA KV2/539.
2. http://hansard.millbanksystems.com/commons/1941/nov/26/defence-regulations#S5CV0376P0_19411126_HOC_291
3. TNA KV2/539.
4. TNA KV2/539.

5. TNA KV2/539.
6. TNA KV2/539.
7. TNA KV2/539.
8. TNA KV2/930.
9. A.R. Ingrao, born in Italy and studied medicine in Naples, between 1915 and 1921 he served in the Italian army. Between 1924 and 1930 he practised medicine in Italy before immigrating to the USA. See: Fedorowich, Kent, 'The Mazzini Society and political warfare', in Wylie, Neville (ed), *The Politics and Strategy of Clandestine War: Special Operations Executive 1940–1946* (London; NY: Routledge, 2007), pp.163–4. The National Archives at Kew list an Andrew Ingrao, a psychologist (KV2/3172), Dr Andrew Richard Ingrao (FO371/34202), and Andrea Albertelli alias Ingrao Forlani (HS9/18/1), born *c.*1898, recruited by SOE in 1941 to persuade Italian POWs to work for the Allies. During training he was considered unsuitable for secret work and too knowledgeable about SOE operations, so he was interned until 1943 when he was repatriated to the USA.
10. Admiral Émile Muselier (1882–1965), was appointed commander of the Free French Naval Forces by De Gaulle on 1 July 1940. Sentenced to death *in absentia* by the Vichy forces in 1940 and losing his French citizenship in 1941, he led the attack on Saint-Pierre et Miquelon (off the east coast of Canada).
11. TNA KV2/930.
12. TNA KV2/539.
13. Hollingsworth, Mark & Nick Fielding, *Defending the Realm. MI5 and the Shayler Affair* (London: André Deutsch, 1999), pp.84–85; 269.
14. TNA KV2/539. Lt Col Maurice Buckmaster, Head of F Section, SOE; Commander (Sir) John Watt Senter, RNVR, Director of Security, Special Operations, SOE, August 1942.
15. TNA KV2/539.
16. TNA KV2/539.
17. Ethel K. Houghton is associated with *Holocaust Records from the Religious Society of Friends, 1933–1942* (USHMM – United States Holocaust Memorial Museum).
18. TNA KV2/539. Margaret Nolan was an IRA detainee under Defence Regulation 18B; See: Simpson, op.cit., p.79; her file at the National Archives (HO144/21989) is closed until 2045.
19. TNA KV2/539.
20. See: Neave, Airey, *Little Cyclone* (London: Coronet/Hodder & Stoughton, 1985); Stourton, Edward, *Cruel Crossing. Escaping Hitler Across the Pyrenees* (London: Transworld/Random House, 2014); Foot, M.R.D., *Six Faces of Courage* (Barnsley: Leo Cooper, 2003); Clutton-Brock, Oliver, *RAF Evaders* (London: Bounty Books, 2009).
21. TNA KV2/3009; KV2/3010.
22. TNA KV2/931.
23. See: Masterman, J.C., *The Double-Cross System* (London: Vintage Books, 2013), p.xxii; West, Nigel, *Historical Dictionary of World War II Intelligence* (Lanham, MD: Scarecrow Press, 2008), p.18; Holt, Thaddeus, *The Deceivers* (London: Weidenfeld & Nicolson, 2004), p.852.

24. TNA KV2/357.
25. TNA KV2/539.
26. Vicomte Théophile de Lantsheere, CVO, was Counsellor at the Belgian Embassy in London in 1939 and to the Belgian Government in Exile during WW2; in 1933 he was First Secretary and Chargé d'Affaires ad interim.
27. Jonkheer E. (Edwin Louis) Teixiera de Mattos (1898–1976). At the Dutch Embassy in London during the Second World War. See: FO371/45760/19; FO37122538; FO371/45759/6.
28. TNA KV2/539. Pay Commander Philip L. Johns, RN had been SIS Head of Station in Lisbon, now assigned to SOE's T Section (Belgium), then LC (Belgium & Holland). See: West, Nigel, *Secret War. The Story of SOE Britain's Wartime Sabotage Organization* (London: Hodder & Stoughton, 1992), pp.101–3; 250; 264; 280; West, Nigel, *MI6. British Secret Intelligence Service Operations 1909–45* (London: Weidenfeld & Nicolson, 1983), pp. xxii; 83; 99; 187; 188; 189; Mackenzie, William, *The Secret History of SOE. The Special Operations Executive 1940–1945* (London: St. Ermin's Press, 2000), p.637; Seaman, Mark (ed), *Special Operations Executive. A New Instrument of War* (London; NY: Routledge, 2006), p.89. Foot, M.R.R.D., *S.O.E. in the Low Countries* (London: St. Ermin's Press, 2001), pp.27–8; 86; 207–8; 215; 334; 348; 369; 406–7; 443; 520. For an account of Johns' career, see: Johns, Philip, *Within Two Cloaks: Missions with Secret Intelligence Service and Special Operations Executive* (London: William Kimber, 1979).

Chapter 7. A Stranger Calls

1. This is not Peter Wilkinson who worked for SOE.
2. TNA KV2/14.
3. TNA KV2/14.
4. TNA KV2/357.
5. TNA KV2/357.
6. 2nd Lt Albert Dan Meurig Evans (1902–?)
7. TNA KV2/357.
8. Listed in the *Navy List* for July 1939.
9. *The Navy List*, October 1940, p.123 lists Paymaster Lieutenant A.P. Wilkinson, as being Secretary to Captain W.H.G. Fallowfield as of 28 November 1939.
10. TNA KV2/357.
11. TNA KV2/90.
12. With the permission of the Commanding Officer. See: BR3, Part 6, Chapter 38; and BR 81, *Royal Navy and Royal Marines Uniform Regulations*, 2005, 0222 Male Personnel Paragraph 4, Beards and moustaches; www.rm-badges.com/images/Dress%20Regulations%202005.pdf
13. TNA KV2/85.
14. TNA KV2/15.
15. Listed in *London Gazette*, 23 November 1915, p.11602, in the Special Reserve of Officers as a Lieutenant in the Royal Field Artillery.
16. TNA WO373/149. See also: Second Supplement to *London Gazette*, 17 September 1948, p.5038.
17. The MI5 report frequently refers to a Personal File (PF54688) on A.P. Wilkinson; however, this is no longer available from the National Archives

at Kew; a note on the Duchesse de Château-Thierry's file (KV2/357) in the 'Yellow Peril' of Stephens 25 November 1940 states that it had been destroyed.

18. Maxwell Knight (2 November 1940), Major Stephens, Major George Sampson, Assistant Commandant of Camp 020, and Meurig Evans (12 November 1940) and Meurig Evans (19 November 1940).

19. I can find no record of such a play or film.

20. A jazz club opened in 1925, believed to have been destroyed in a bombing raid during the Second World War. The Embassy Club was in New Bond Street. For a description of the former see: http://www.vjm.biz/Reviews.html

21. TNA KV2/357.

22. TNA KV2/357.

23. TNA KV2/357.

24. TNA KV2/357.

25. TNA KV2/357.

26. TNA KV2/357.

27. TNA KV2/90 and KV2/91.

28. Walter Albert Lothar Sensburg. See: TNA KV2/977.

29. TNA KV2/91.

30. Her Home Office file, HO405/50232, is embargoed until 2056.

31. TNA KV2/357.

32 TNA KV2/357.

33 http://pockley.org/family/pockley03.html; http://www.bellsite.id.au/helen_ tree/HTMLFiles/HTMLFiles_04/P5588.html

34. TNA KV2/357.

Chapter 8. The Duchesse's Circle

1. A Personal File on him was opened by MI5; however, this does not appear to be accessible from the National Archives. Number is PF53785 or PF53985 or PF53185; the third number is unclear.

2. TNA KV2/357.

3. TNA KV2/357.

4. West, Nigel, *Sexspionage*, p.52. Guy Liddell had also noted this fact in his diary on 17 October 1940.

M.J.P.F.H. D'A. de Froberville, Equipment Branch. Promoted from Pilot Officer to Flying Officer, 26 January 1940, according to *Flight* magazine, 28 March 1940, p.295; Marie Joseph Philippe Fouquereaux Huet d'Arlon de Froberville (*London Gazette*, 22 August 1939, p.5760); *The Air Force List*, August 1940, listed as a Flying Officer under the Air Ministry's Directorate-General for Equipment, p.22a.

5. TNA KV2/357.

6. TNA KV2/357.

7. 28 June 1922–24 May 1923.

8. Stephens, op.cit., p.147.

9. West, *Sexspionage*, op. cit., p.253.

10. *Ottawa Journal*, Saturday 27 January 1940, p.19 and Saturday 2 February 1940, p.17.

Notes 341

11. Simpson, op.cit., paperback edition, p.79, citing her two Home Office files, HO45/25115 and HO45/25752.

12. TNA HO405/50232, embargoed until 1 January 2056.

13. *Ottawa Journal*, Saturday, 2 February 1940, p.17.

14. ibid., p.17.

15. Also shown as being in B1d, Special Examiners, at the London Reception Centre.

16. This is most likely Erich Walter Schmidt-Rex of Carshalton, Surrey. See: Barnes, James J. & Patience Barnes, *Nazis in Pre-War London, 1930–1939. The Fate and Role of German Party Members and British Sympathizers* (Brighton; Portland: Sussex Academic Press, 2010), p.268. He also wrote a letter to *Flight* magazine about fog landings, signing himself as W.E. Schmidt-Rex, London Manager of Deutsche Luft Hansa A.G., Croydon (*Flight*, 4 October, 1934, p.1042).

17. TNA KV2/357.

18. ROF, No.10, also known as 'Roften', Wirral, Cheshire; used to make anti-aircraft guns.

19. This was Captain Walter Rogers (1895–1976), one of the original sixteen pilots of Imperial Airways. A photograph of him online pictures him in 1917 as a sergeant in the Royal Flying Corps: http://afleetingpeace.org/index.php/ business-pleasure/14-business-and-pleasure/167-the-pilots-of-imperial-airways. Another photograph shows him in 1928 with singer Josephine Baker. A report in the *Argus* (Melbourne) for 2 June 1936 states that on a flight to Cairo, he and his three-man crew were 'brutally treated' by Italian soldiers in Mesylam, Libya.

20. Koen Dirk Parmentier (1904–48), KLM chief pilot, killed at Prestwick in an air crash in 1948 piloting a Lockheed Constellation, PH-TEN, *Nijmegen*.

21. 9 Carlton House Terrace, 'The Prussia House'.

22. Alexander Alexandrovich Postnikow of Russia; naturalization certificate no. BZ301, issued 14 February 1934; daughter Ludmilla Alexandrovna, see TNA HO 334/226/301 and HO 144/19151.

23. TNA KV2/357.

24. Married to Cecilia Elizabeth Gaetjens, d.23 July 1925. The *London Gazette* entry for 5 February 1935 (p.903) gives his address as 'Silver Birch Cottage' lately known as 'Verdun Cottage', Bacton, Norfolk, with an Adjudication hearing at Shire Hall court in Norwich scheduled for 13 February 1935 at 10.30 a.m.

25. Mentioned in the *London Gazette*, 17 March 1936 (p.1767) in a Special Resolution of the Franco-British Oil Trust Limited and gives his address as 69 Basinghall Street, London EC2 as being appointed the Liquidator.

26. Baxter cites the reference as 84/H8710/(MGO(A)b).

27. TNA KV2/357.

28. TNA KV2/357.

29. TNA KV2/15.

30. This is possibly Gaston Tiburce Joseph Marie Proot (b.1892 - ?), Naturalisation Certificate AZ48127 issued 28 October 1948; see: HO334/222/48127; his wife, Christiane Sonia Odile Dorothee was issued her Naturalisation Certificate, BNA384 on 21 January 1949; see: HO334/315/384; The *London Gazette* entry for 17 December 1948 (p.6557) gives him as Company Director (Cosmetic

Manufacturers) his address as 35, Manor Park Gardens, Edware, Middlesex; the date, 3 November 1948 may be when he actually became a British citizen. His wife is listed in the *London Gazette* entry for 22 March 1949 (p.1465) as a psychology student; her date of becoming a British citizen is 28 January 1949.

31. TNA KV2/357.

32. TNA KV2/735.

33. TNA KV2/358.

34. http://www.maxvandam.info/humo-gen/family.php?id=F12439

35. TNA HO405/18061.

36. TNA KV2/357.

37. TNA KV2/357: 'Summary of steps taken on the report on the case of the Duchesse de CHATEAU THIERRY, dated November 23rd and 25th, and the covering letter addressed to Major Stephens by Mr. Meurig Evans dated November 25th.'

38. http://hansard.millbanksystems.com/commons/1940/nov/07/detentions

39. *New York Evening Post*, Monday February 2, 1931, p.9: http://fultonhistory.com/newspaper%2011/New%20York%20Evening%20Post/New%20York%20NY%20Evening%20Post%201931%20Grayscale/New%20York%20NY%20Evening%20Post%201931%20Grayscale%20-%200852.pdf

40. *Kingston Daily Freeman*, No.172, 10 May 1909: https://news.hrvh.org/veridian/cgi-bin/senylrc?a=d&d=kingstondaily19090510.2.75&srpos=0&e=-------en-20--1--txt-txIN-------#

41. TNA KV2/358.

42. TNA KV2/358.

43. This is now Marsh Ferriman & Cheale, Solicitors, Worthing, Sussex.

44. TNA KV2/358.

45. TNA KV2/358.

46. TNA KV2/358.

47. TNA KV2/358.

48. See TNA KV2/839. Also: Willetts, Paul, *Rendezvous at the Russian Tea Rooms* (London: Constable, 2016), paperback edition; and Clough, Bryan, *State Secrets. The Kent-Wolkoff Affair* (Hove: Hideaway Publications Ltd, 2005). On 13 November 1942 Christopher Harmer of B1a had written to Major Whyte of B4a to inform him of letters being sent by Eriksson, of which one was from Enid Riddell in Holloway, 'because it contains a suggestion that CHATEAU-THIERRY might try and petition for removal on the grounds of ill health. I was at Aylesbury yesterday and they all seem to be making a tremendous fuss about their health.'

49. TNA KV2/928.

Chapter 9. What Her Daughter Knew

1. *The Times*, 21 April 1923. At that time she was living at 32 Lower Belgrave Street, SW1; Somerled Hamilton Watson (1899–1938); Elma Mary Walker (d.1983): http://www.thepeerage.com/p48436.htm#i484360

2. TNA KV2/357.

3. TNA KV2/357.

4. TNA KV2/357.
5. TNA KV2/357.
6. TNA KV2/357.
7. Chevallier, Arnold Louis, *A treatise on the true dynamic flight of projectiles: dealing with new factors in gunnery and the theoretical exposition of a fundamental system of a complete projectile control* (London: Syndicate Publishing, 1924).
8. https://www.thegazette.co.uk/London/issue/34067/page/4336/data.pdf
9. TNA KV2/357.
10. This is Serge Karlinski, who was issued with a Naturalisation Certificate (AZ4380) on 1 June 1934 and resident in London. His files (HO334/134/4380; HO144/20664; FO1004/229 and FO1004/250) are closed until 2038 and 2039 respectively; *London Committee of Deputies of the British Jews, Annual Report, 1938,* p.11: 1938 Karlinski, Serge (Philpot Street Sephardish) (Elected October) 1, 11a Belgrave Square, S.W.1. The address is now a Grade II Listed building.
11. 'Circle of the Duchesse de Chateau Thierry', TNA KV2/357, serial 47a (no date).
12. http://hansard.millbanksystems.com/commons/1939/jun/05/trade-and-commerce-china#S5CV0348P0_19390605_HOC_142
13. http://hansard.millbanksystems.com/commons/1939/jun/06/personal-explanation#S5CV0348P0_19390606_HOC_216
14. http://www.ordiecole.com/gen/cimetieres/veyrier_liste_cimetiere.pdf
15. TNA KV2/357.
16. TNA KV2/357.
17. TNA KV2/357.
18. Brentford, where Mackenzie's company was located is in the London Borough of Haringey.
19. TNA KV2/357.
20. TNA HO334/205/39816: Naturalisation Certificate AZ39816 issued 3 March 1948.
21. https://caltechcampuspubs.library.caltech.edu/422/1/1956_04_05_57_22.pdf
22. Carver, John Lewis, 'The Spy Queen was a Nympho!' in: *Top Secret* magazine, February 1958, pp.6–11.
23. TNA KV2/535.
24. TNA KV2/536.
25. Maria Nermi-Egounoff (1899–1997). Also known as Maria Amy Nermi-Ergounoff, Princess Alice Reuss-Eberdoft, Maria Nermi, and Maria Egounoff. Born in Budapest, she graduated from the Franz Liszt Academy. She was a member of the former Royal Opera House, Budapest; Volksoperhaus, Vienna, and Staaopersänger in Germany until 1933. In 1937 she came to London, and in December 1940 was married.
26. TNA KV2/538.
27. He should not be confused with Alfred Stern, born in Fargo, North Dakota on 29 November 1897 who married Martha Dodd on 16 June 1938. Dodd was responsible for his recruitment as a NKGB agent and later investigated by the House Committee on Un-American Actvities (HUAC). He and Dodd moved to Prague in 1956, where he died in 1986, having been charged in absentia with spying for the Soviet Union on 9 September 1957.

28. GR-3016.8457 and GR-3016.9905 respectively; http://search-collections. royalbcmuseum.bc.ca/Image/Genealogy/6b9e144a-e402-4566-b824-0037d7380405

29. Alias Eugen, Jeno. See: TNA KV2/3400 (vol.2); KV2/3401 (vol.3); KV2/3402 (vol.4). The notes indicate that vols. 1 & 2 were destroyed by fire in 1940 and vol.2 is a partial reconstruction from outgoing documents. Weiser came MI5's notice in 1940 as being pro-Nazi and also through his purchase of radio receivers. He was declared *persona non grata* and interned in 1943, but exchanged for the SOE agent Baroness Mary Miske-Gerstenberger. (Mary Alison Miske-Gerstenberger @ Walters, Mary Allison, Baron Mary Alison Miske, 'Miss May'; in 1947 she returned to Hungary to settle her husband's estate and disappeared into a Soviet prison camp in Siberia until 1955 forced to do hard labour. See: KV2/3324; HO382/108). Married to Baron Jenő Miske-Gerstenberger, the Hungarian Consul General in Istanbul and Munich. When she was released from Soviet prison she was employed by the Foreign Office to monitor the Russian and Hungarian press. See: Veress, Laura Louise; Dalma Takacs (ed), *Clear The Line. Hungary's Struggle to leave the Axis During the Second World War* (Cleveland: Propspero Publications, 1995), online version, pp.83–84, http://www.hungarianhistory.com/lib/clear/clear.pdf and Ogden, Alan, *Through Hitler's Back Door* (Barnsley: Pen & Sword Military, 2010), pp.11, 26. She was code-named FRUIT and was employed by Basil Davidson.

30. TNA KV2/15.

31. Rüter, a Counsellor at the German Embassy, c.1934, mentioned in: Urbach, Karina, *Go-Betweens for Hitler* (Oxford: Oxford University Press, 2015), p.187; Gesandtrat Ernst Rüter, mentioned in: Barnes, James J. & Patience P. Barnes, *Nazi Refugee Turned Gestapo Spy: The Life of Hans Wesemann, 1895–1971* (Westport, CT; London: Praeger, 2001), p.32: 'Rüter was a career diplomat with many years experience, the last two in his present job as First Secretary. However, in November 1933 he was alleged to be someone who could not be trusted to give unqualified support to Hitler and his new regime.'

32. TNA KV2/15.

33. In TNA KV2/15. The original is in PF 46614 which is not currently available from the National Archives, Kew.

34. *Hansard*, 18 May 1944: HC Deb 18 May 1944 vol 400 c348W. See also Hubrich's Home Office internment files: TNA HO214/81-82.

35. TNA KV2/357.

36. TNA KV2/357.

37. TNA KV2/357.

38. TNA KV2/357.

39. TNA KV2/357.

40. TNA KV2/357.

41. TNA KV2/357.

42. TNA KV2/357.

43. TNA HO45/23787 and KV2/357.

44. TNA HO45/23787.

45. TNA KV2/357.

46. TNA KV2/357.
47. TNA KV2/357.
48. TNA KV2/357.

Chapter 10. The Aliventi Group

1. The only SCO listed for Shoreham is B.C. Gee. See: Curry, John, *The Security Service 1908–1945. The Official History* (London: Public Record Office, 1999), p.323.
2. Macintyre, Ben, *A Spy Among Friends* (London: Bloomsbury, 2014), pp.19–20; 49.
3. Whole document extracted from TNA KV2/357.
4. According to his description in his MI5 files in the National Archives (KV2/347 and KV2/348): 'Andre ROSTIN, alias RUSTIN was a German who was based in London in the mid-1920s and late 1930s under cover as a journalist and businessman. He had some influential British contacts and also contacts with Comintern representatives in London. His brief was thought to be to obtain economic, military and political intelligence. He was flamboyant, extravagant and indiscreet.' See also: Day, Peter, *Klop: Britain's Most Ingenious Secret Agent* (London: Biteback, 2014), pp.59–60; 73. Many of the serials in Rostin's MI5 files appear to have been destroyed, and there is nothing to link him to Aliventi. However, he came to MI5's notice in the spring of 1925. It had kept him under surveillance since then as a suspected Soviet spy and intercepted his mail. He was at one time a friend of Jona 'Klop' Ustinov.
5. Dr Hans Wilhelm Thost, TNA KV2/952-954. Nazi Press representative in Britain (*Völkischer Beobachter*). Interestingly, when he came to London in 1933 his proposed address was 41 Swan Court, Chelsea, SW3; the Duchesse lived at 17 Swan Court in 1940 with a Mrs Osborne Smith. See also: *Headquarters Intelligence Center 6825 HQ & HQS Company Military Intelligence Service in Austria APO 777 US Army. First Detailed Interrogation Report THOST, Dr. Hans Wilhelm* Declassified by CIA 2000 and 2007; TICOM report 'I-190 Extracts from report on interrogation of Dr Hans Wilhelm Thost'.
6. Dr James Heyworth-Dunne, author of *An Introduction to The History of Education in Modern Egypt* (Frank Cass, 1968). First published by Luzac & Co., London, 1939, and dedicated to his wife Fatimah. See also *Preliminary Inventory to the James Heyworth-Dunne Papers 1860–1949*: http://www.oac.cdlib.org/findaid/ark:/13030/tf5g5003xq/; For more bilographical information see: http://trove.nla.gov.au/people/1309120?c=people
7. Sir Frank Hillyard Newnes, Bt., (1876–1955), publisher, business man and Liberal politician. He married his wife, Emmeline Augusta Louisa (Lena, but shown as Lana in the MI5 document) in 1913. She was a society hostess and philanthropist, and daughter of Sir Albert de Rutzen, the Chief Metropolitan Magistrate at Bow Street Court. She died in 1939.
8. Georgina (or Georgiana) Frances Isabella Blois (1888–1967) née Domvile; mother of John Dudley Blois (1915–54); married to Lt Col Dudley Blois, DSO (c.1875–1916). Archivist to Lady Mountbatten; employed at Broadlands after the Second World War to look after the Palmerston archive. Mentioned in MB1/P Mountbatten Papers: Papers of Edwina, Countess Mountbatten of Burma, 1923–47.

9. 'M' is likely Maxwell Knight of B5b.
10. Dudley Gordon Leacock was made a Knight Bachelor in the 1951 Birthday Honours List 'For public services in Barbados.' In 1915 he was Chairman of the Committee of Management of the Barbados Citizens' Contingent.
11. May be Alexandre Runge, mentioned in Thost's report. A report marked 'Secret' from the Sécurité Militaire, Direction des Services de Documentation Allemagne, No.1632, p.9 gives the following information on Runge (translated from the French): 'German, originally from Hamburg. Civil employee of Referat VI D 4 RHSA, Berlin. Lived in South America for a very long time. Returned to Germany when war was declared. Re-joined the RHSA in 1942. Former representative of the firm Hugo Stinnes in South America. Aged 48 years, approximately 1.75 m in height, 'thin corpulence' (?), sporty, brown curly hair, clear eyes, wears glasses, very energetic face. Intelligent, rarely speaks. Speaks perfect Spanish. Very rich. Lives in Hamburg where he is a businessman.'

Chapter 11. Dr Rantzau, I Presume

1. Duffy, Peter, *Double Agent* (New York: Scribner, 2014), paperback edition, p.14.
2. Shaw, Madelyn, 'American Silk from a Marketing Magician. H.R. Mallinson& Co.', in: Textile Society of America. Symposium Proceedings, 2002: http:// digitalcommons.unl.edu/cgi/viewcontent.cgi?article=1545&context=tsaconf
3. See: TNA KV2/87, Nikolaus Ritter. Mentions a report of September 1945 copied in the War Room on 10 October 1945.
4. TNA KV2/536.
5. TNA KV2/87.
6. TNA KV2/538. Knötel, Herbert, der Jüngere [the younger], "Uniformfibel" [Uniform Primer], von Geschichtsmaler". The pamphlet was produced in Berlin, 1933, Offene Worte. Copies are available from Abe Books.
7. IWM, Tirpitz Collection: catalogue number, HU50727.
8. West, Nigel (ed), *The Guy Liddell Diaries, Vol.1, 1939–1942* (London: Routledge, 2005), p.317, and http://www.warcovers.dk/greenland/wbs4_1.htm
9. For more information on von Boetticher see: Beck, Alfred M., *Hitler's Ambivalent Attaché. Lt. Gen. Friderich von Boetticher in America, 1933–1941* (Dulles, VA: Potomac Books, 2005), paperback edition.
10. TNA KV2/87.
11. Hayward, James, *Hitler's Spy. The True Story of Arthur Owens, Double Agent Snow* (London: Simon & Schuster, 2012), paperback edition, p.16.
12. AO, or Auslandorganization was the main Nazi agency for gathering foreign intelligence; also 'Abwehrofficizier'. The Ic/AO at army group was normally a Colonel or lieutenant Colonel. See: Kahn, David, *Hitler's Spies. German Military Intelligence in World War II* (London: Hodder & Stoughton, 1978), pp.98; 403.
13. See: O'Halpin, Eunan, *Spying on Ireland. British Intelligence and Irish Neutrality During the Second World War* (Oxford: Oxford University Press, 2008), pp.34–35; McMahon, Paul, *British Spies and Irish Rebels: British Intelligence and Ireland 1916–1945* (Woodbridge, Suffolk: Boydell Press, 2008), pp.258–59.
14. TNA KV2/756.
15. TNA KV2/87.

16. TNA KV2/87.
17. TNA KV2/87.
18. TNA KV2/756.
19. TNA KV2/1333.
20. TNA KV2/1333. A copy is also in KV2/88.
21. TNA KV2/88.
22. TNA KV2/88.
23. National Registration Card number BFAB 318-1; see: TNA KV2/114.
24. TNA KV2/114.
25. TNA KV2/534.
26. Bower, Tom, *Klaus Barbie: The Butcher of Lyons* (New York: Pantheon Books, 1984), p.126.
27. Farago, op.cit., p.266; Crowdy, Terry, *Deceiving Hitler* (Oxford: Osprey, 2008), p.77.
28. Joseph Jacob Johannes Starziczny @ Eduardo Rogada Quintinho @ Artur Viana dos Santos @ Oscar Liehr @ Nils Chritsensen. See: TNA FO1093/258, KV2/2844 and KV2/2845.
29. West, Nigel, *Seven Spies Who Changed the World* (London: Secker & Warburg, 1991), p.36; Jonason, Tommy & Simon Olsson, *Agent Tate. The Wartime Story of Harry Williamson* (Stroud: Amberley, 2011), pp.14–15.
30. TNA KV2/87.
31. Quoted in Walton, Calder, *Empire of Secrets* (New York: Overlook Press, 2013), p.49. The so-called 'English Patient' files from the National Archives at Kew are: KV2/1463 (Mohsen Fadl); KV2/1467-1468 (Johannes Eppler); and KV3/74 (German Espionage in North Africa).
32. Smith, Michael & Peter Day, 'English Patient was ugly, gay, Nazi Spy', in: *Daily Telegraph*, 21 May 2004, online edition: http://www.telegraph.co.uk/news/uknews/1462425/English-Patient-was-ugly-gay-Nazi-spy.html
33. Bierman, John, *The Secret Life of Laszlo Almasy: The Real English Patient* (London: Penguin, 2005).
34. TNA KV2/521. See also file on Herbert Wichmann, KV2/103.
35. Obergefreiter Walter Klein (2 September 1903–30 January 1945): http://www.deutsche-ehrenmale.de/ehren/sachsen/Namenslisten/D-S-TDO-Eilenburg.HTML
36. TNA KV2/88.
37. TNA KV2/87: Extract of Third Detailed Interrogation Report of: Eppler. S.F. 52/4/4 (15).Vol.1.2.8.42. Para 4 Major von Ritter.
38. See TNA KV2/1467 and KV2/1468. Eppler is also mentioned in interrogation reports of PoWs: TNA WO208/5520; Eppler, John, *Rommel's Spy. Operation Condor and the Desert War* (Barnsley: Frontline Books/Pen & Sword, 2013), paperback edition.
39. TNA KV2/103.
40. TNA KV2/87.
41. TNA KV2/87.
42. TNA KV2/88.
43. TNA KV2/86.

44. TNA KV2/86.

Chapter 12. The Mission. 'A Sullen and Dispirited Group'

1. According to Ritter's file (TNA KV2/88) and 'Agents Despatched to or Controlled in the UK'.
2. De Zeng IV, Henry L. and Douglas G. Stankey. *Luftwaffe Officer Career Summaries, G-K*, Version 01, April 2015: HARLINGHAUSEN, Martin.
3. TNA KV2/357.
4. TNA KV2/88.
5. TNA KV2/15.
6. TNA KV2/15.

Chapter 13. 'A Boyish Interest in Detectives'

1. http://www.josefjakobs.info/2014/12/the-mysterious-diary-of-kenneth-c-howard.html
2. TNA KV2/1701.
3. Cecil Charles Hudson Moriarty, CBE, OBE, CStJ, LLD (1877-1958), Chief Constable of Birmingham, 1935–41.
4. From a letter in Drueke's MI5 file (KV2/1702) from Philip Allen to Hinchley Cooke, Cornwall House was part of the Home Office, Stamford Street, London S.E.1.
5. TNA KV2/1701.
6. West, Nigel (ed), *The Guy Liddell Diaries, Vol.II: 1942–1945* (London; NY: Routledge, 2005), p.205.
7. The house at 56, Oakwood Avenue, technically in Beckenham, is now Jansondean, a nursing home. Shortlands House, at the far end of Scotts Lane, built in 1702 and named as such in the 19th century, was a hotel for the first half of the 20th century, then became Bishop Challoner School in 1950, a co-ed Catholic school, now at 228 Bromley Road, Shortlands. The name was changed in 1958.
8. http://www.poheritage.com/Upload/Mimsy/Media/factsheet/93969NIRVANA-1914pdf.pdf
9. Cassidy, Brian, *Flying Empires. Short 'C' class Empire flying boats* (Bath: Queen's Parade Press, 1996), pp.130–131: http://www.seawings.co.uk/images/EmpireProfilebookgal/Flying%20Empires%20Book.pdf
10. *The Western Mail*, 21 April 1936, p.1 and 23 April 1936, p.24.
11. Poem from: Hargreaves, James, *The Life and Memoir of the Late Rev. John Hirst Forty Two Years Pastor of the Baptist Church Bacup* (Printed and sold by Joseph Littlewood, 1816), p.399, used as Nuttall's epitaph on the Baptist burial ground in the Forest of Rossendale, Lancashire.
12. Allason, Rupert, *The Branch* (London: Secker & Warburg, 1983), p.92.
13. http://tenwatts.blogspot.ca/2009/10/8xk-8xs-w8xk.html
14. https://randsesotericotr.podbean.com/e/w2xad-and-w2xaf-sign-on-discs-circa-1938/
More about both shortwave stations appear in, Berg, Jerome S., *The Early Shortwave Stations: A Broadcasting History Through 1945* (Jefferson, NC & London:

McFarland & Company, 2013), pp.69, 72–73, 77–79, 83–85, 92–95, 104–106, 119–20, 129–31, 144–46, 177, 182–3; and Berg, Jerome S., *On the Shortwaves, 1923-1945: Broadcast Listening in the Pioneer Days of Radio* (Jefferson, NC & London: McFarland & Company, 1999), pp.50–51, 61, 96–7, 102, 104.

15. http://www.vintagepostcards.org/Northern-Ontario-Postcard-Photographers. htm; http://www.vintagepostcards.org/north-bay-ontario.htm; http://www. vintagepostcards.org/mattawa-ontario.htm

16. https://www.thefreelibrary.com/Passing+of+a+patriot%3A+Hilaire+du+ Berrier+--+daredevil+pilot,...-a094510547

17. A Count Hillaire du Berrier, an American, is mentioned in Pankhurst, Richard, *Sylvia Pankhurst: Counsel for Ethiopia: A Biographical Essay on Ethiopian Anti-Fascist and Anti-Colonialist History 1934–1960* (Hollywood, CA: Tsehai: 2003), p.23; also in Wasserstein, Bernard, *Secret War in Shanghai* (London: I.B. Tauris, 2017.

18. *London Gazette*, 6 September 1932, p.5703; 19 October 1945, p.5136.

Chapter 14. 'Something Particularly Odd'

1. TNA KV2/88. 'Final Report on Obstlt Nikolaus Fritz Adolf RITTER @ Dr Norbert RANTZAU @ Dr RENKEN @ Dr Wolfgang JANSEN @ The DOCTOR @ REINHARDT'. CSDIC (WEA), BAOR, 16 Jan 46.
2. MacKay, C.G. & Bengt Beckman, *Swedish Signals Intelligence, 1900–1945* (London; Portland, OR: Frank Cass, 2003), p.250, n15; TNA WO373/108/963.
3. He is mentioned in TNA KV3/413, *German Saboteurs Landed in the USA from U-Boats, in Boats in 1942. Report of Operations.*
4. Farago, op.cit., pp.244–5.
5. TNA KV2/14.
6. His file, a War Office interrogation report, is TNA WO204/12815.
7. TNA KV2/267.
8. TNA KV2/103.
9. TNA KV2/17.
10. TNA KV2/17.
11. There was an Air Force officer named Captain Dreyfus who had been taken to the Cherche-Midi prison in Paris while Meissner was stationed there. Dreyfus and a Captain Hirsch had been brought from the Drancy concentration camp and were to be shot as hostages because they were Jews. Whether there is any connection between this Dreyfus and the one with whom Walti travelled is unknown.
12. TNA KV2/1702.
13. TNA KV2/17.
14. TNA KV2/1701.
15. Vivian Wyntel Hancock Nunn, registered as a member of the Middle Temple; called to the Bar on 26 January 1922.
16. TNA KV2/17.
17. TNA KV2/17.
18. TNA KV2/17.
19. TNA KV2/17.
20. VB 1/1 in: KV2/21.
21. TNA KV2/21.

22. For a discussion of their case see: Tremain, David, *Rough Justice* (Stroud: Amberley, 2016), Ch.23 & Ch.24, pp.186–206

23. TNA KV2/14.

24. TNA KV2/15.

25. There are a number of Ahlers listed in the Luftwaffe: AHLERS, Bernhard. (DOB: 18.08.97). (W.B.K. Wesermunde). (n.d.) with Fl.Ers.Abt. 37. (n.d.) trf to Fl.H.Kdtr. Luneburg. 18.01.41 assigned to Lfl.Kdo. 2 became or assigned to Ic. 03.42 Hptm., in Ic Amt/Luftflotte 2 (and 11.43). 15.10.42 became Ic Lage in Oberbefehlshaber Sud due to unit renaming. 15.10.43 appt Ic 3 of Lfl.Kdo. 2. 01.12.43 RDA as Maj.d.R. 05.10.44 reassigned as Sachbearbeiter Ic of Stab Lw.Kdo. Sudost. 05.11.44 appt Sachbearbeiter Ic 5 Abwehr of Stab /Gen.Kdo. II. Fl.Korps. AHLERS, Conrad. (DOB: 05.11.42). (W.B.K. Hamburg IV). 44 assigned to Gen.Kdo. d. XI. Fl.Korps as a Fallschirm Lehrer. 01.03.44 promo to Lt 15.06.44 appt Ord. Offz. III./Fsch.Art.-Rgt. 1; AHLERS, Fritz. (DOB: 01.08.10). (W.B.K. Osnabruck). 1940 assigned to Lg.Kdo. IV. 15.08.40 appt Chef 4./Fl.Ausb.Rgt. 82 (still 15.02.42). 15.02.42 temporary duty with LKS 2 Berlin-Gatow (still 28.03.42). 10.01.43 appt Chef 3./ Feld-Ausb.Rgt. d.Lw. 5. 01.04.43 promo to Hptm. (Kr.O.)(RDA 01.02.42). 15.10.43 appt Fuhrer of Stabskp. Stab/Erdkampfschule d.Lw. 15.02.44 temporary duty with Stabskp./Fsch.-Waffenschule; AHLERS, Hermann. (DOB: 20.01.78). (W.B.K. Potsdam I). 01.09.33 RDA as Maj.d.R. 1939/40 appt Fu. of Lw.Bau-Kp. 1/III. 01.03.40 trf to Referent II B 1 in Abt. LC 7/RLM. 30.06.41 released from active service. See: De Zeng, IV, Henry & Douglas G. Stankey, *Luftwaffe Officer Career Summaries, A-F*, Version 01, April 2015. http://www.ww2.dk/Lw%20Offz%20-%20A-F%20-%20Apr%202016. pdf. It is unknown which if any of these four is the right one, but it is unlikely to have been number 2 as the rank is wrong for that time period.

26. De Zeng, IV *et al*, op.cit.

27. TNA KV2/21.

28. TNA KV2/15.

29. TNA KV2/15.

30. TNA KV2/15.

31. TNA KV2/21.

32. Probably Wolfgang Hohlbaum, b. 13 December 1914. 1 January 1942 promoted to Hauptmann (Captain); 01.08.43 in Fuhrerreserve RLM/Ob.d.L. (Sch.Etat), trf from the Kriegsmarine to the Luftwaffe in the rank of Hptm. (A 1/Fl.) (RDA 01.04.42).

33. Masters, Anthony, *The Man Who Was M: The Life of Charles Henry Maxwell Knight* (Oxford: Blackwell, 1984), p.121.

34. ibid., p.122.

35. ibid.

36. Hemming, Henry, *M: Maxwell Knight, MI5's Greatest Spymaster* (London: Preface Publishing, 2017).

37. Hemming. Personal communication to the author, 28 February 2017.

38. ibid.

39. Clough, Bryan, *State Secrets. The Kent–Wolkoff Affair* (Hove: Hideaway Publications Ltd, 2005), p.114.

40. Jago, Michael, *The Man Who Was George Smiley: The Life of John Bingham* (London: Biteback, 2013), p.83.

Chapter 15. At His Majesty's Pleasure

1. TNA KV2/18.
2. TNA KV2/19.
3. TNA KV2/19.
4. *Collins Robert French-English, English–French Dictionary* translates hammer toe as 'orteil en marteau', (pl. *orteils en Marteau*) (London: Collins, 1985), p.264.
5. TNA KV2/18.
6. TNA KV2/19.
7. TNA KV2/19.
8. TNA KV2/18.
9. A Hauptsturmführer Engelmeyer is listed as belonging to Referat VI C, with a note added, 'VI C representative with BdS Cracow' in *Counter Intelligence War Room London Situation Report No.8, Amt VI of the RSHA Gruppe VI C*, c.1946: There is also an SS-Hauptsturmführer Engelmeier listed in Dyukov, Alexander R., '"Destroy as much as possible", Latvian collaborationist formations on the territory of Belarus 1942–1944', Document Compendium, Helsinki, 2010, p.102.
10. West, Nigel, *A to Z of British Intelligence* (Lanham, MD: Scarecrow Press, 2005), p.138; *Historical Dictionary of British Intelligence* (Lanham: Rowan & Littlefield, 2014); *Historical Dictionary of World War II Intelligence* (Lanham: Scarecrow Pres, 2008), p.115; West, Nigel (ed), *The Guy Liddell Diaries, Volume I: 1939–42* (London: Routledge, 2005), p.102: 'Albert de Jaeger (code-named HATCHET) is now at Latchmere House …'
11. TNA KV2/1959.
12. TNA KV2/19.
13. TNA KV2/19.
14. TNA KV2/90.
15. TNA KV2/90.
16. TNA KV2/1959.

Chapter 16. The Doctor's Report

1. TNA KV2/14.
2. TNA KV2/14.
3. TNA KV2/14.
4. TNA KV2/14.
5. TNA KV2/19.
6. For discussions of the Meier, Waldberg, Kieboom and Pons case, see: Tremain, op.cit., Ch.23 & Ch.24, pp.186–206; for the Dorothy O'Grady case, see: Searle, Adrian. *The Spy Beside the Sea: The Extraordinary Wartime Story of Dorothy O'Grady* (Stroud: The History Press, 2012).
7. TNA KV2/19.
8. TNA KV2/19.
9. TNA KV2/19.
10. See TNA KV2/1958–1961, as well as naturalisation documents, HO334/207/40534 and HO405/17583.
11. Stuart, Otis, 'The merchant prince of ballet', in: *Dance* magazine, 1 February, 1995, cover story.

12. Gorlinsky Archive at the Victoria & Albert Museum: http://www.findmylibrary. co.uk/CollectionDetails/2750592.

Also referred to in: Kavanagh, Julie, *Nureyev. The Life* (New York: Pantheon Books, 2007), p.cdlvii; Flesch, Carl F., *Who's Not Who and Other Matters* (Cambridge: Vanguard Press, 2006), p.36; Panov, Valery & Terry Sivashinsky, *Scene from the Wings* (Xlibris Corporation, 2013), pp.48–9.

13. TNA KV2/1959.
14. 'Kurt Siegel' was also known as Victor Hauer, who was involved with Count Almásy, Johannes Willi Eppler @ Husein Gafaar and Operation CONDOR: '"Kurt Siegel" didn't exist, and the intelligence supplied by him actually came from one Victor Hauer. Employed by the Swedish consulate, Hauer was an Austrian by birth, but German by nationality …' in: Dear, Ian, *Spy and Counterspy: Secret Agents and Double Agents from the Second World War and the Cold War* (Stroud: Spellmount/History Press, 2013), p.37.
15. TNA KV2/1959.
16. TNA KV2/14.
17. TNA KV2/357.
18. TNA KV2/357.
19. TNA KV2/357.
20. https://stevemorse.org/germanjews/germanjews.php?=&offset=24901
21. TNA KV2/14.

Chapter 17. Walti's Role
1. TNA KV2/17.
2. Hemming, op.cit., pp.97–9.
3. TNA KV2/17.
4. TNA KV2/17.
5. There is a Café Stanley on Statiestraat 31, Berchem, Antwerp, also a Café Stanny on Stanleystraat 1, but neither is by the harbour.

Chapter 18. The Trial
1. TNA CRIM 1/1307.
2. TNA HO144/21636.
3. TNA HO144/21636. Whitebrook, quoting Article 29 of the *Hague Convention (IV) respecting the Laws and Customs of War on Land* and its annex: *Regulations concerning the Laws and Customs of War on Land*, defined a spy as: 'acting clandestinely or on false pretences … obtains or endeavours to obtain information in the zone of operations of a belligerent with the intention of communicating it to a hostile party.' Thus, soldiers not wearing a disguise who have penetrated into the zone of operations of the hostile army, for the purpose of obtaining information, are not considered spies. Similarly, the following are not considered spies: Soldiers and civilians, carrying out their mission openly, entrusted with the delivery of despatches intended either for their own army or for the enemy's army. To this class belong likewise persons sent in balloons for the purpose of carrying despatches and, generally, of maintaining communications between the different parts of an army or a territory.'

4. TNA HO144/21636.
5. TNA KV2/1704.
6. TNA KV2/1704.
7. TNA KV2/1704.
8. TNA KV2/17.
9. TNA KV2/1704.
10. Signed in 1985 it largely abolished borders between European countries who were signatories, and eliminated the need for border checkpoints, passport stamps or visas.
11. Farago, op.cit., p.247.
12. Thomas William Pierrepoint (1870–1954); Albert Pierrepoint, his son (1905–92); Henry 'Harry' Kirk (1893–1967).
13. TNA PCOM9/903; KV2/1701.

Chapter 19. *A Breath of Fresh Air*

1. TNA KV2/15.
2. All RSLOs, and SCOs for Liverpool, Glasgow, Holyhead, Manchester, Whitchurch and Poole, coordinated with Colonel John Adam in D4, Port Security.
3. TNA KV2/15.
4. This is most likely the same Lieutenant E.A. Airy who attended the Buffs Annual Dinner, as reported by the *Whitstable Times and Herne Bay Herald* on 20 June 1931. The Buffs was the name given to the Royal East Kent Regiment (3rd Regiment of Foot); later Colonel, Intelligence Division, South East Asia. Listed in the *Army List* for April 1941 as General Staff Officer, 2nd Grade in the Department of the Chief of Imperial General Staff (CIGS) at the War Office.
5. TNA KV2/15.
6. TNA KV2/15.
7. http://www.mrshunts.co.uk/about-us.html; http://a-backward-look.blogspot.ca/2014/10/edwardian-servants-agency.html
8. Jessie Jordan (1887–1954) was a Scottish hairdresser arrested on 2 March 1938 and found guilty in 1939 of espionage; in May 1939 she was sentenced to four years' imprisonment. See: TNA KV2/193–194; KV2/3532–3534; KV2/3421 (Guenther Gustav Marie Rumrich @ Gustav Rumrich).
9. https://www.cia.gov/library/readingroom/docs/CIA-RDP80B01676R003600070001-7.pdf
10. TNA HS9/702/2; HO334/359/22086. At the time of his naturalisation in Britain (1952) he was living at 5 Chesham Street, Belgrave Square, London, SW1. See: *London Gazette* 18 April 1952, p.2110: https://www.thegazette.co.uk/London/issue/39518/page/2110/data.pdf
11. Browne, John, *Hidden Account of the Romanovs* (Bloomington, IL: iUniverse Inc., 2013), p.681.
12. https://new.liveauctioneers.com/item/8015663
13. TNA KV2/15.
14. TNA KV2/15.
15. Day, Peter, *Klop. Britain's Most Ingenious Secret Agent* (London: Biteback, 2014), p.144.
16. TNA KV2/15.

17. TNA KV2/15.
18. TNA KV2/15.
19. See TNA KV2/1307.
20. TNA KV2/15.
21. TNA HO334/252/1539.
22. TNA KV2/15.
23. TNA HO 334/347/16312 (not available for download): Naturalisation Certificate for Livia Maria Huszar, dated 17 November 1950 issued by the Home Office.
24. *Der Spiegel*, 19 January 1955, p.38: http://magazin.spiegel.de/EpubDelivery/spiegel/pdf/31968997
25. Lilian Huszar is listed in *The London Gazette* for 9 January 1951 as Livia Maria Huszar; Hungary; Sales Representative (Plastic Handbags); 40, Queen's Gate Terrace, London SW7, as of 17 November 1950.
26. TNA KV2/15. Unfortunately, the interview with Huszar is not in Vera's file and Huszar's file is not available from the National Archives, Kew.
27. Not available from the National Archives, Kew.
28. TNA KV2/15.
29. TNA KV2/15.
30. TNA KV2/16.
31. Major A.P. Noble was previously with B4b, the detection and prevention of espionage through industry and commerce.
32. TNA KV2/16.
33. TNA KV2/16.
34. TNA KV2/16.

Chapter 20. The Missing Spy

1. Evelyn Amie 'Evie' Pinching (1915–88) was before the war an alpine skier who won the women's 1936 downhill and combined events at Innsbruck and competed in the 1936 Winter Olympics (Garmisch-Partenkirchen).
2. TNA KV2/16.
3. TNA KV2/16.
4. TNA KV2/16, referring to CIB/INT/2428 (194,211,380,408) dated 18 Sep 45 and CIB/INT/2428 (408) dated 1 Oct 45.
5. TNA KV2/16.
6. TNA KV2/16.
7. TNA KV2/16.
8. TNA KV2/16.
9. Searle, op.cit., p.158.
10. Liddell, Guy, *War Diaries*, 30 October 1946, TNA KV4/469, p.44.
11. Nigel West. Personal communication with the author, 22 December 2016.
12. For a discussion of her career, see: O'Connor, Bernard, *Agent FIFI and the Wartime Honeytrap Spies* (Stroud: Amberley, 2016), paperback edition, pp.165–90.
13. Searle, op.cit., p.149.
14. TNA HO45/25408; PCOM9/1497; PCOM9/1497/1.
15. ibid., p.157. This allegation was first made by Matt Wells in *The Scotsman*,

27 January 1999, p.3: 'Tragic Past Turned a Russian Ballerina into a Reluctant Spy'; the *Herald Scotland*, 25 October 2000, p.13: 'Nazi spy's love child linked to reprieve'; *Daily Mail*, 26 October 2000: 'Seductive Theory of How a Nazi Spy with a British Love Child Escaped the Gallows'; Kate Watson-Smyth, *The Independent*, 'Secret baby may have saved Nazi spy from gallows', 25 October 2000, p.167.

17. http://portgordon.weebly.com/vera-erikson.html

18. Quoted in: Ramsey, Winston G. *After the Battle* magazine, no.11, 1976, pp.22–23.

19. TNA KV2/173. See also: TNA WO208/4347.

20. Sir John Anderson. *Hansard*, HC Deb 22 May 1940 vol. 361 cc185–95; Order for Second Reading.

21. TNA KV2/15.

22. TNA KV2/15.

23. The Security Intelligence Centre was set up on 10 June 1940 as a larger staff of the Security Executive, whose task it was to supervise those departments investigating Fifth Column activities. CAB 93/2, HD(S) E and, Hinsley, F.H. & Anthony Simkins. *British Intelligence in the Second World War* (London: HMSO, 1990), Volume 4. *Security and Counterintelligence*, p.65.

24. Philip Cunliffe-Lister (1884–1972), Viscount Swinton (1935–55); 1st Earl of Swinton (1955–72).

25. Hinsley & Simkins, op.cit., p.96.

26. ibid. p.97.

27. ibid. pp.97–8.

28. MacGregor Sadolin, http://noblecircles.com/genealogy/getperson. php?personID=I77642&tree=tree1

29. http://www.mortenclausen.dk/GEDHT/fam090xx/fam09043.htm

30. Thanks to Giselle Jakobs for making this available: http://www.josefjakobs. info/2016/06/tales-of-spies-mysterious-and-beautiful.html

31. Andersen, Kirstine Kloster, *Spurven: Den dramatiske historie om spionen Vera Schalburg* (Copenhagen: Lindhardt & Ringhof, 2018); (translated as *The Sparrow: The dramatic story of the spy Vera Schalburg*)

32. Knowles, Chris, 'Germany 1945–1949: a case study in post-conflict reconstruction', in *History & Policy* (King's College, London & University of Cambridge), 29 January 2014.

33. Kesternich, Iris, et al, 'The Effects of World War II on Economic and Health Outcomes Across Europe', in: *Review of Economics and Statistics* (Cambridge, MA: MIT Press Journals), Volume 96, issue 1, March 2014, pp.103–18.

34. In fact it has been confirmed by Danish journalist Kirstine Kloster Andersen that Vera did die in 1946 as stated on the death certificate: 'Ernst Bodo von Zitzewitz paid for her funeral and her grave, which actually existed in Hamburg until 1971. He also stayed at the Pension Klopstock at the time of her death. (8 February 1946). She was buried the 13 February at 8.30 in the morning. He paid in total 82,50 Reichsmark for her funeral including flowers, music, the grave.' Andersen, Kirstine Kloster, *Spurven: Den dramatiske historie om spionen Vera Schalburg* (Copenhagen: Lindhardt & Ringhof, 2018 (translated as *The Sparrow: The Dramatic Story of the Spy Vera Schalburg*).

BIBLIOGRAPHY

Primary Sources

TNA = The National Archives

TNA: KV2/14-16; KV2/535-539; KV2/1307; KV2/357-8; KV2/18-19;
KV2/1701-06; KV2/17; KV2/916; KV2/1959; FO800-17; FO800-19;
KV2/887-88; KV2/85-88; KV2/81-82; KV2/3306; KV2/173; KV2/22-27;
KV2/534; HO45/23787; KV2/802-05; KV2/1008-09; KV2/1241-42; KV2/3456;
KV2/2389; KV2/267; KV2/534; KV2/977.

Secondary Sources

Allason, Rupert, *The Branch* (London: Secker & Warburg, 1983).

Andrew, Christopher & Vasili Mitrokin, *The Sword and the Shield: The Mitrokin Archive and the Secret History of the KGB* (New York: Basic Books, 1999).

Barnes, James J. & Patience Barnes, *Nazis in Pre-War London, 1930–1939: The Fate and Role of German Party Members and British Sympathizers* (Brighton; Portland: Sussex Academic Press, 2010).

Barnes, James J. & Patience P. Barnes, *Nazi Refugee Turned Gestapo Spy: The Life of Hans Wesemann, 1895–1971* (Westport, CT; London: Praeger, 2001)

Beeby, Dean, *Cargo of Lies: The True Story of a Nazi Double Agent in Canada* (Toronto: University of Toronto Press, 1996).

Benson, Robert Louis & Michael Warner (eds), *VENONA. Soviet Espionage and the American Response 1939–1957* (Washington DC: National Security Agency & Central Intelligence Agency, 1996).

Bierman, John, *The Secret Life of Laszlo Almasy: The Real English Patient* (London: Penguin, 2005).

Boghardt, T., *Spies of the Kaiser: German Covert Operation in Great Britain during the First World War Era* (Basingstoke: Palgrave Macmillan, 2004).

Booth, Nicolas, *Zigzag* (New York: Arcade Publishing, 2007), trade paperback.

Bower, Tom, *Klaus Barbie: The Butcher of Lyons* (New York: Pantheon Books, 1984).

Bunyan, Tony, *The History and Practice of the Political Police in Britain* (London: Quartet, 1977), paperback edition.

Burke, David, *The Spy Who Came in from the Co-op* (Woodbridge: Boydell Press, 2008).

Burke, David, *The Lawn Road Flats* (Woodbridge: Boydell Press, 2014).

Calder, Angus, *The People's War: Britain 1939–1945* (London: Pimlico, 1969).

Clough, Bryan, *State Secrets: The Kent-Wolkoff Affair* (Hove: Hideaway Publications Ltd, 2005).

Clutton-Brock, Oliver, *RAF Evaders* (London: Bounty Books, 2009).

Cook, Andrew, *M: MI5's First Spymaster* (Stroud: The History Press, 2006; eBook 2011).

Costello, John & Oleg Tsarev, *Deadly Illusions* (London: Century, 1993).

Crowdy, Terry, *Deceiving Hitler* (Oxford: Osprey, 2008).

Curry, John, *The Security Service 1908–1945: The Official History* (London: Public Record Office, 1999).

Day, Peter, *Klop: Britain's Most Ingenious Spy* (London: Biteback, 2014).

Dear, Ian, *Spy and Counterspy: Secret Agents and Double Agents from the Second World War and the Cold War* (Stroud: Spellmount/History Press, 2013), paperback edition.

Duff, William E., *A Time for Spies: Theodore Stephanovich Maly and the Era of the Great Illegals* (Nashville & London: Vanderbilt University Press, 1999).

Duffy, Peter, *Double Agent* (New York: Scribner, 2014), paperback edition.

Eppler, John, *Rommel's Spy. Operation Condor and the Desert War* (Barnsley: Frontline Books/ Pen & Sword, 2013), paperback edition.

Farago, Ladislas, *The Game of Foxes* (New York: David McKay Company Inc., 1971), 1st US edition.

Foot, M.R.D., *Six Faces of Courage* (Barnsley: Leo Cooper, 2003).

Foot, M.R.D., *S.O.E. in the Low Countries* (London: St Ermin's Press, 2001).

Gisevius, Hans Bernd, *Valkyrie. An Insider's Account of the Plot to Kill Hitler* (Boston: Da Capo Press, 2009), paperback edition.

Hayward, James, *Hitler's Spy. The True Story of Arthur Owens, Double Agent Snow* (London: Simon & Schuster, 2012), paperback edition.

Hemming, Henry, *M: Maxwell Knight, MI5's Greatest Spymaster* (London: Preface Publishing, 2017).

Hennessey, Thomas & Clair Thomas, *Spooks. The Unofficial History of MI5, From M to Miss X 1909–1939* (Stroud: Amberley, 2010), paperback edition.

Hinsley, F.H. & Anthony Simkins. *British Intelligence in the Second World War* (London: HMSO, 1990), Volume 4. Security and Counterintelligence.

Hollingsworth, Mark & Nick Fielding, *Defending the Realm. MI5 and the Shayler Affair* (London: André Deutsch, 1999).

Holt, Thaddeus, *The Deceivers* (London: Weidenfeld & Nicolson, 2004).

Jago, Michael, *The Man Who Was George Smiley: The Life of John Bingham* (London: Biteback, 2013).

James, Clive, *Cultural Amnesia. Necessary Memories from History and the Arts* (London: Macmillan; New York: W.W. Norton & Sons, 2007).

Johns, Philip, *Within Two Cloaks: Missions with Secret Intelligence Service and Special Operations Executive* (London: William Kimber, 1979).

Jonason, Tommy & Simon Olsson, *Agent Tate. The Wartime Story of Harry Williamson* (Stroud: Amberley, 2011).

Kahn, David, *Hitler's Spies: German Military Intelligence in World War II* (London: Hodder & Stoughton, 1978).

Kavanagh, Julie, *Nureyev. The Life* (New York: Pantheon Books, 2007).

Kern, Gary, *A Death in Washington: Walter G. Krivitsky and the Stalin Terror* (New York: Enigma Books, 2004).

Krivitsky, W.G., *In Stalin's Secret Service* (New York: Harper & Brothers, 1939), 3rd edition.

Macintyre, Ben, *For Your Eyes Only. Ian Fleming & James Bond* (London: Bloomsbury, 2009), paperback edition.

Macintyre, Ben, *Agent Zigzag* (London: Bloomsbury, 2007).

Macintyre, Ben, *A Spy Among Friends* (London: Bloomsbury, 2014).

MacKay, C.G. & Bengt Beckman, *Swedish Signals Intelligence, 1900–1945* (London; Portland, OR: Frank Cass, 2003).

Mackenzie, William, *The Secret History of SOE: The Special Operations Executive 1940–1945* (London: St Ermin's Press, 2000).

MacPherson, Nelson, *American Intelligence in Wartime London: The Story of the OSS* (London: Frank Cass, 2003).

Masterman, J.C., *The Double-Cross System* (London: Vintage Books, 2013), paperback edition.

Masters, Anthony, *The Man Who Was M: The Life of Charles Henry Maxwell Knight* (Oxford: Blackwell, 1984).

McMahon, Paul, *British Spies and Irish Rebels: British Intelligence and Ireland 1916–1945* (Woodbridge, Suffolk: Boydell Press, 2008).

Milton, Giles, *Russian Roulette. How British Spies Defeated Lenin* (London: Sceptre, 2014), paperback edition.

Moon, Tom, *Loyal and Lethal Ladies of Espionage* (San José: iUniverse.com, Inc, 2000).

Morton, James, *Spies of the First World War* (Kew: The National Archives, 2010).

Neave, Airey, *Little Cyclone* (London: Coronet/Hodder & Stoughton, 1985), 4th impression, paperback edition.

Northcott, Chris, *MI5 at War 1909–1918* (Ticehurst: Tattered Flag, 2015).

Ogden, Alan, *Through Hitler's Back Door* (Barnsley: Pen & Sword Military, 2010).

O'Connor, Bernard, *Agent FIFI and the Wartime Honeytrap Spies* (Stroud: Amberley, 2016), paperback edition.

O'Halpin, Eunan, *Spying on Ireland: British Intelligence and Irish Neutrality During the Second World War* (Oxford: Oxford University Press, 2008).

Petersen, Neal H. (ed), *From Hitler's Doorstep: The Wartime Intelligence Reports of Allen Dulles 1942-45* (Pennsylvania: Pennsylvania State University Press, 1996).

Quinlan, Kevin, *The Secret War Between the Wars: MI5 in the 1920s and 1930s* (Woodbridge: Boydell Press, 2014).

Richelson, Jeffery T., *A Century of Spies: Intelligence in the Twentieth Century* (New York: Oxford University Press, 1995).

Robinson, Curtis B., *Caught Red Starred: The Woolwich Spy-Ring and Stalin's Naval Rearmament on the Eve of War* (Bloomington, IN: Xlibris Corporation, 2011).

Seaman, Mark (ed), *Special Operations Executive: A New Instrument of War* (London; NY: Routledge, 2006).

Searle, Adrian, *The Spy Beside the Sea* (Stroud: The History Press, 2012).

Sellers, Leonard, *Shot in the Tower* (Barnsley: Pen & Sword Military, 2015), paperback edition.

Simpson, A.W. Brian, *In the Highest Degree Odious: Detention without Trial in Wartime Britain* (Oxford: Oxford University Press, 1984), paperback edition.

Smith, Douglas, *Rasputin* (London: Pan, 2017), paperback edition.

Stephens, Robin; Oliver Hoare (ed), *Camp 020. MI5 and the Nazi Spies* (London: Public Record Office, 2000).

Stourton, Edward, *Cruel Crossing. Escaping Hitler Across the Pyrenees* (London: Transworld/ Random House, 2014), paperback edition.

Sudoplatov, Pavel & Anatoli Sudoplatov, with Jerrold L. & Leona P. Schecter, *Special Tasks* (London: Little, Brown & Company, 1994)

Taylor, Stephen, 'A Spy Called Vera. The Mystery of Hitler's Mata Hari', in: *Eye Spy* magazine, No.94, 2014/15.

Tremain, David, *Rough Justice* (Stroud: Amberley, 2016).

Trenear-Harvey, Glenmore S., *Historical Dictionary of Atomic Espionage* (Lanham, MD: Scarecrow Press, 2011).

Veress, Laura Louise; Dalma Takacs (eds), *Clear The Line. Hungary's Struggle to leave the Axis During the Second World War* (Cleveland: Propspero Publications, 1995), online version.

Verhoyen, Etienne, *Spionnen aan der achterdeur; der Duitse Abwehr in België 1936–1945* (Antwerp; Appeldoorn: Maklu, 2011).

Volodarsky, Boris, *Stalin's Agent: The Life and Death of Alexander Orlov* (Oxford: OUP, 2015).

Walton, Calder, *Empire of Secrets* (New York: Overlook Press, 2013).

Weissman, Susan, *Victor Serge. A Biography* (New York: Verso, 2013), paperback edition.

West, Nigel & Oleg Tsarev, *The Crown Jewels: The British Secrets at the Heart of the KGB Archives* (London: Harper Collins, 1999), paperback edition.

West, Nigel, *Mortal Crimes* (New York: Enigma Books, 2004).

West, Nigel, *Mask: MI5's Penetration of the Communist Party of Great Britain* (Abingdon: Routledge, 2005)

West, Nigel, *MI6: British Secret Intelligence Service Operations 1909-45* (London: Weidenfeld & Nicolson, 1983).

West, Nigel (ed), *The Guy Liddell Diaries, Vol.1, 1939–1942* (London; NY: Routledge, 2005).

West, Nigel (ed), *The Guy Liddell Diaries, Vol.II: 1942–1945* (London; NY: Routledge, 2005).

West, Nigel & Madoc Roberts, *SNOW: The Double Life of a World War II Spy* (London: Biteback, 2011).

West, Nigel (ed), *MI5 in the Great War* (London: Biteback, 2014).

West, Nigel, *Historical Dictionary of Sexpionage* (Lanham, MD: Scarecrow Press, 2009).

West, Nigel, *Historical Dictionary of World War II Intelligence* (Lanham, MD: Scarecrow Press, 2008).

West, Nigel, *Secret War: The Story of SOE Britain's Wartime Sabotage Organization* (London: Hodder & Stoughton, 1992).

West, Nigel, *Seven Spies Who Changed the World* (London: Secker & Warburg, 1991).

West, Nigel, *A to Z of British Intelligence* (Lanham, MD: Scarecrow Press, 2005).

West, Nigel, *Historical Dictionary of British Intelligence* (Lanham: Rowan & Littlefield, 2014), 2nd edition.

Willetts, Paul, *Rendezvous at the Russian Tea Rooms* (London: Constable, 2016), paperback edition.

Wylie, Neville (ed), *The Politics and Strategy of Clandestine War: Special Operations Executive 1940–1946* (London; NY: Routledge, 2007).

INDEX